Computers and the Cybernetic Society

MICHAEL A. ARBIB

University of Massachusetts
Amherst

WITH MANY EXERCISES SUPPLIED BY

JONATHAN V. POST

Computers and the Cybernetic Society

ACADEMIC PRESS

New York   San Francisco   London

A Subsidiary of Harcourt Brace Jovanovich, Publishers

ACADEMIC PRESS, INC.
111 Fifth Avenue, New York, New York 10003

United Kingdom Edition published by
ACADEMIC PRESS, INC. (LONDON) LTD.
24/28 Oval Road, London NW1

Library of Congress Cataloging in Publication Data

Arbib, Michael A
      Computers and the cybernetic society.

      1.   Computers.   2.   Electronic data processing.
3.   Computers and civilization.   I.   Title.
QA76.A6S6   301.24'3   76-27430
ISBN 0−12−059040−9

For Prue
. . . so much to do,
but may much of it
be ours to do together.

To the Instructor

There seem to be two extremes in books on computers and society. At one extreme is the book that loads the readers down with so many details about how computers work that they have no time or energy left for the social implications. At the other extreme is the book that tells readers so many different effects that computers are having on their lives that they can see no pattern in the details. This book tries to strike a balance. The first two chapters provide a basic understanding of computers. The next five chapters give a comprehensive overview of the impact of computers on the cybernetic society. A final chapter is intended for just a few readers—those who want a step-by-step view of how computer circuitry can follow the instructions we give the computer—and is not used anywhere else in the book.

One of the toughest questions in setting up a course on computers and society is "How much programming?" My feeling is that Sections 1.1 and 1.2 provide the absolute minimum of programming concepts; while Sections 2.1–2.3 provide key concepts—time-sharing, graphics, networks, microcomputers—essential for any serious discussion of what computers can do. Some instructors will find this enough. Others will adopt my compromise—getting students to use Section 1.3 to learn how to program in LOGO. Yet others will want to teach a "real" programming language, like BASIC. Since the choice of language, and the details of implementation, differ from instructor to instructor and from school to school, I thought it best to let each instructor offer his or her own material for supplementary programming rather than burden the text with an extra chapter.

This book has 26 sections. Some sections—such as the introduction to programming in Sections 1.1 and 1.3—require at least two lectures; others—like 1.4 and 2.4—should only require one lecture. For the most part, the material in a section can be covered in one lecture or extended to two.

The order of presentation is very flexible. The first lecture should give an overview of the course and be followed by Sections 1.1 and 1.2. After that, the instructor may wish to leave the basic material on computers for awhile—I often like to go through Chapter 3 before returning to Chapters 1 and 2.

It is also possible to omit sections to bring in guest speakers, add supplementary material, or devote more time to programming. The outline at the beginning of each chapter spells out the prerequisites of each section, and will allow the instructor to decide his or her schedule.

This flexibility of scheduling, and the various features— Suggestions for Further Reading, Summary, Glossary, and Exercises—described below should make the book an easy one to teach from.

The first page or so of each chapter provides an outline for each section of the chapter, stressing the theme or concepts it seeks to establish. Then, for each section, the background required from earlier sections is listed.

Ending each section are a number of features designed to help consolidate the information presented in the section. The first feature is Suggestions for Further Reading, which lists several books or articles containing additional information.

A Summary of the section appears next, followed by a Glossary which lists the definitions of all the important new words introduced in the section. It also repeats some key words from earlier sections that are germane to the discussion at hand. Whenever a word is printed in **boldface,** its definition is given in the Glossary at the end of the section. The words are not listed in alphabetical order as in a dictionary. Instead, they are placed in an order which makes it easiest to see how the different concepts tie together.

The last part of each section is the Exercises. These will help test understanding of the material in the section, and introduce some new ideas as well.

Two supplementary volumes have been prepared to further help the instructor—an *Instructor's Manual* and a volume of *Transparency Masters for Use with an Overhead Projector*. The Instructor's Manual is divided into sections, one for each section of the text. Each section is divided into three parts. The first part, "Classroom Comments," provides some observations on classroom use of the section. The second part provides solutions to a selection of the exercises from the text itself. The third part provides additional questions—some with answers—suitable for use in tests or examinations. The second and third parts also contain further suggestions for classroom discussion.

For those sections for which the instructor wishes to follow the text fairly closely, Transparency Masters for Use with an Overhead Projector are available. The instructor will find it rather simple to prepare a lecture as follows:

(i)   Make a set of transparencies (instructions are provided in the volume of Transparency Masters).

(ii)   Make a paper copy of the slides on which to jot notes.

(iii)   Read through the section, jotting notes on the appropriate page prepared in step (ii).

These standard slides may then be supplemented or replaced for those sections for which the instructor has special expertise.

In a changing field like this, it is a continuing challenge to keep the material in a textbook lively and up to date—so that breathtaking glimpses of the future do not degenerate into tired repetitions of the past. Hopefully the choice of topics provides a solid foundation of material that will not date rapidly—a foundation on which you can build, with material culled from current publications and from your colleagues, to bring students right up to the minute. So that future editions may reflect our cumulative successes, and avoid our cumulative mistakes, any feedback you can give me will be greatly appreciated, with the hope that our students gain a sound perspective of both computer technology and its implications for the cybernetic society.

To the Student

What the Book Is About

Increasingly, computers affect our lives. They communicate, store and retrieve information, and carry out the complex procedures of problem-solving in an impressive array of fields and endeavors. Our bills, checking accounts, and income tax returns are all processed by computers. The data banks in which government agencies and credit-card companies store information about citizens are computer-based. Computer-assisted instruction affects the way we learn and automation affects the way we work. Governments use computers in economic planning. Environmentalists use them to study ecological systems. Miniaturized computers are increasingly being used for special purposes—from driving the display of a digital wristwatch to controlling the ignition of a car.

This book was written to explain the impact the computer has on you today, and to provide the knowledge you need to help decide how computers will be used in the future. For this, you need to know what computers are and how they are programmed—how they can be given instructions to make them perform the jobs described above. Once you have this basic understanding, you can get involved in the many applications of computers, and form your own opinion of where we need greater use of computers, or where their use needs to be restricted or controlled.

The book can be used for self-study and in a variety of classroom situations as well. It is most suited to a junior college or college course on computers and society. But before I describe how you and your instructors can use the book, we shall dwell briefly on the word *cybernetic* in the title "Computers and the Cybernetic Society."

The word cybernetics in its current meaning was introduced in 1948 by Norbert Wiener of the Massachusetts Institute of Technology. He had been struck by similarities between the way some machines work and the way a body works. For example, a steam engine has a device called a governor which keeps the engine from running too fast or too slow. Scientists had compared this to the way in which the brain of an animal controls the heart and lungs to keep the proper amount of oxygen in the blood. Wiener felt that such comparisons between animals and machines deserved systematic study. He gave the name **cybernetics** to *the study of control and communication that compares functions in the animal and the machine.* The word cybernetics comes from the Greek word *kybernetes,* which means *helmsman:* the man who controls the direction of a ship. The word governor is taken from the Latin form of kybernetes; so the political aspects of control are contained in the history of the word. Since 1948, many scientists have applied cybernetic principles to the study of communication and control, not just inside an animal or a machine, but in *groups* of people, animals, and machines.

The **cybernetic society,** then, is one in which people and computers interact in processing large amounts of information. This book will help you understand this interaction and how it can be used to improve the quality of life. To achieve this goal we must continually study both computer questions—How do we make a computer do a particular job?—and social and political questions—What job should we make the computer do? For example, a government needs a great deal of information about its citizens if it is to check the accuracy of their tax returns, call up the right people for military service, and so on. This information can be stored in the computer in a large "electronic file system" called a **data bank.** The existence of these data banks raises many political and social questions: What information should the government be allowed to store in a data bank? What rights do citizens have in correcting or removing information about themselves? Who should be allowed to get information from the data banks? Who should decide such matters? We cannot discuss these questions without knowing at least the basic answers to questions such as: How does a data bank work? How can you make sure that only the "right people" have access to the information stored in it?

The most important fact to remember as you read this book is that modern computers are barely 30 years old. The next 30 years will see such dramatic changes that most of what we describe in this book will come to seem quaint and old fashioned. This means that what you should learn from this book is not just the state of the cybernetic society today, but more importantly, to understand how computers will dramatically change our lifestyles in the future.

How This Book Is Organized

The book has been written so that many sections can be read with little background from earlier chapters. In fact, once you have read the introduction to computers and programs given in Sections 1.1, 1.2, 2.1, 2.2, and 2.3, you will be able to turn to any other chapter and read it with little difficulty.

The first page or two of each chapter will help you decide which sections you want to read. An outline is provided for each section of the chapter, stressing the theme or concepts it explores. Then, for each section, the background required from earlier sections is listed. As already mentioned, this background is kept to a minimum.

At the end of each section, there are a number of features designed to help you consolidate what you have learned from reading the section. First, Suggestions for Further Reading lists several books or articles you can turn to for more information. Of course, you can also go to the library to find books and magazines on your own.

Next comes a Summary of the section, followed by a Glossary which lists the definitions of all the important new words introduced in the section. It also repeats some key words from earlier sections that you should have firmly in mind. The words are not listed in alphabetical order as in a dictionary. Instead, they are placed in an order which makes it easiest to see how the different concepts tie together. Here, for example, is a glossary (which, by coincidence, is in alphabetical order this time!) for the concepts introduced in this section.

Cybernetics: The study of control and communication in the animal and the machine, and in social groups. The *cybernetic society* is thus one in which people and computers interact in processing large amounts of information.

Data: Pieces of information. A single piece of information is called a datum, but many people use data for the singular as well.

Data Bank: An "electronic file system" which stores large quantities of information in a form that allows a computer to retrieve any desired data automatically.

Whenever a word is printed in **boldface,** its definition is given in the glossary at the end of the section. If you come upon a word that is new to you and is *not* in boldface, that means one of two things. If the word was defined in an earlier section, you will find its glossary definition by looking up the word in the index, looking for a page number with a G in front of it, and turning to that page. For example, you will find the entry "Cybernetics, 173, G177, . . ." in the index at the back of the book—and this means that the glossary definition of "Cybernetics" is on page 177, as indeed it is. However, there are a lot of words in this book that are not defined. If you find one that is not in the glossary of any section, make your own glossary. Look the word up in your dictionary, and write the definition on the glossary page of the section in which the word appeared.

The last part of each section is the Exercises. These will help you test your understanding of the material in the section, and introduce some new ideas as well. It is a good idea to read through all the exercises, and try to solve a few of them—whether or not you have to do them for a class assignment. This can help you remember what you have read and can tell you if you have grasped the material fully.

I hope that the above features make it easy for you to find the sections that interest you, and to tie together what you learn from each section. I hope, too, that the material in the body of the section proves stimulating and helpful. It was often hard to write the book, but overall it was fun and worthwhile. May reading the book be an easier task, and just as much fun and equally worthwhile!

Acknowledgments

Much of the merit of this book comes from the generosity of friends and colleagues who offered the expertise I needed to cover the broad range of topics treated here. My heartfelt thanks to Daniel Fishman, Caxton Foster, Harvey Friedman, Robert Graham, Hiram Haydn, Arthur Karshmer, William Kilmer, Henry Ledgard, Jack Lochhead, Robert Mallary, Michael Marcotty, Howard Peelle, Richard Reiss, Edward Riseman, Stanley Rothman, John Roy, Kenan Sahin, Nico Spinelli, David Stemple, and Robert Taylor.

I would also like to express my gratitude to the reviewers, Nell B. Dale (University of Texas, Austin), Diana Fischer (Prince George's Community College), Stephen Gale (University of Pennsylvania), and James Hightower (California State University System), whose careful reading and thoughtful comments were instrumental in shaping the final draft of the manuscript.

The photographs in this book were generously provided by Arthur Karshmer (A Walk through the Computer Center), Kevin Deame (The Squiral Nebula), the Digital Equipment Corporation (The Shrinking Machine), Aaron Marcus and the West Coast Poetry Review (Cybernetic Landscape), Paul Tenczar (PLATO Computer Assisted Instruction), and Thomas Dwyer (Project SOLOWORKS). Special thanks are also due to Paul Bennett and the Technical Information Division of NASA's Ames Research Center for their aid in locating and obtaining

many other photographs used in this text. We are also indebted to
James Meindl for the integrated circuit photograph used on the
cover; René Magritte's painting, "Castle of the Pyrenees," appears on
the cover through the courtesy of the Harry Torczyner Collection, New
York.

The major task of preparing the exercises fell upon Jonathan
Post, with my role there reduced to that of providing some supplementary material and doing the final editing. I thank Jon for his in-
valuable help with this task.

Gwyn Mitchell, Joyce Rodriguez, and Janet Turnbull did a fine
job typing not only the text of this book, but also many rough drafts
and numerous supplementary materials.

Finally, I want to thank the personnel of Academic Press for their
exceptionally constructive role in the development of this textbook.

Contents

1

About Computers

SECTION 1.1. THE IDEA OF A PROGRAM

Before it can do any job for us, a computer must be given a **program.**
This program is a set of instructions that tell the computer how the job is
to be done. **Bugs** are errors in the program which stop it from doing the
job correctly. Once a human has written a program, he can feed it into
the computer which automatically follows the instructions with electronic speed. In this section, we look at some examples of programs. In
particular, we see how to write programs that contain **loops.** A loop is a
sequence of instructions that the computer must follow again and again
in completing its job. We study the difference between **special-purpose**
and **general-purpose** computers. The section requires no background.

SECTION 1.2. MOVING AND STORING INFORMATION

The computer needs **input devices** to read in data and programs and
output devices to send out results. We discuss these devices and how
they are used in **interactive** computing via a **terminal,** and in **batch**
processing. We learn about the difference between **primary** and **secondary** memory. We learn how information is **coded** for use by computer,
the key idea being **binary coding** of information by a string of 0s and 1s
like 0110101110. Finally, we study the use of batch processing to handle
a payroll job, and see how one program can become a **subroutine** in
another larger program. Section 1.1 provides the background required.

SECTION 1.3. TEACHING TURTLE TO NAVIGATE

This is the one section that provides experience in programming in a **high-level language.** The language is called LOGO, and is used to program the drawing of elaborate figures by a simple **robot** called TURTLE. The requisite background is provided by Section 1.1 and the discussion of interactive computing at the start of Section 1.2.

SECTION 1.4. TEXT PROCESSING

We discuss the use of computers to process texts. We find that computers do a poor job of **indexing,** but can be very helpful to a human indexer using the computer in the interactive mode described in Section 1.2. We see how to get a text into a form a computer can ''read,'' and look at some simplified indexing jobs that a computer can perform. The requisite background is provided by Section 1.1 and the discussion of interactive computing and magnetic tape units at the start of Section 1.2.

1.1. THE IDEA OF A PROGRAM

Programming a Simple Robot

A **computer** can do many jobs—printing payroll checks, guiding a robot around a room, or bringing a spaceship back from the moon. For each different job, it must be given the right **program,** which tells it exactly how the job is to be done. Once it is written, the whole program is fed into the computer. The machine executes the instructions with electronic speed without having to wait for a human to feed in each command one by one. Instead, the computer has a **memory** in which the whole program can be stored. Each time it completes an instruction it automatically gets the next one from memory.

We use computers because they are incredibly fast—carrying out millions, or even billions, of operations every second. But the computer only does a job when it is following a program telling it every operation it must carry out to get the job done. This seems to raise a terrible problem. How can we keep up with the machine? How can we give it the millions of instructions that it needs to keep busy? The key idea is summed up in the old saying: ''If at first you don't succeed, try, try again.''

Most programs are written with **loops**—sequences of instructions that the computer must follow *again and again* until some part of its job is done. A program with loops may have only a few hundred instructions, and yet—once it is fed into the machine—it may be able to control the behavior of the computer for a long time indeed.

We now write a string of instructions that will tell a very simple **robot** how to get to a door. This will give us some feel for the way in which a short program with loops in it can control a lot of behavior.

Imagine a robot (Fig. 1) standing in a room at some distance from, but directly facing, a wall. Somewhere along that wall, to the right of the robot, there is a doorway. The doorway is just a gap in the wall. The robot can move forward one "step" at a time by rotating its wheels enough to roll it forward one millimeter. It can turn through any angle by locking the drive wheel on one side, while rotating the other. This robot does not have eyes—it cannot see where the door-way is, and move to it directly. Instead, it can tell if it is touching a wall, and thus can distinguish the wall from a doorway.

We want to write a program—a sequence of instructions—that we can store in the computer's memory. Then, automatically follow-ing the program's instructions, the robot is to move from its present position to the doorway. If we knew that the robot was 3.5 meters from the wall, and that the door was 3.4 meters along the wall from the "impact point," we could write a very simple (and *very* tedious!) pro-gram to make it do the job. We put the sequence of instructions on the left, and give **comments**—which tell us what the instructions make the robot do—to the right of the program.

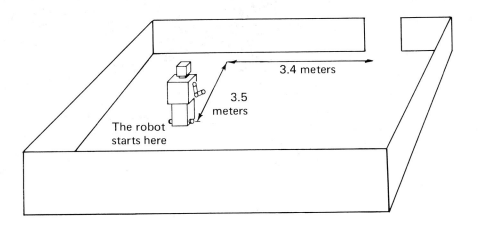

3.4 meters

3.5 meters

The robot starts here

Fig. 1 A robot is facing a wall in which there is a doorway to the robot's right.

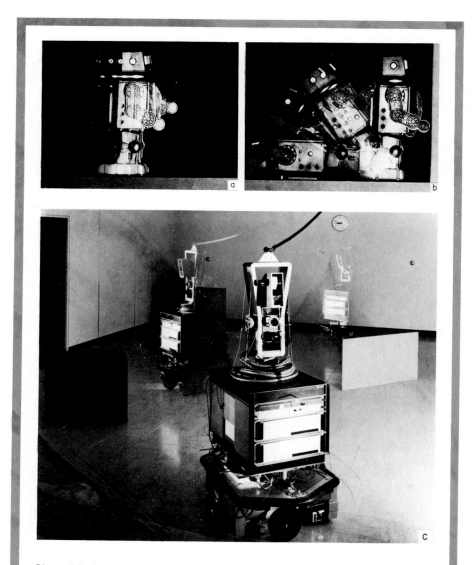

Photo (a) shows a toy robot walking toward a wall. Lacking any sensors or control program, the robot crashes blindly into the wall and falls over (Photo b). By contrast, the robot described in this section takes a small step and then tests to see whether it has made contact with the wall before it takes another step. In this way, it avoids the risk of falling over. In Section 5.2, we shall study more sophisticated robots, like "Shakey" from the Stanford Research Institute, shown in (c). This multiple-exposure shows Shakey avoiding several obstacles. Shakey has a television camera which can relay pictures of the world around it to the control computer. The computer can analyze these pictures and plan appropriate courses of action.

Program	Comments

Advance one step ⎱
Advance one step
.
       .   This instruction is repeated 3500 times (there
       .   are 3500 millimeters in 3.5 meters) to instruct
                   the robot to move to the wall.
Advance one step
Advance one step ⎰

Turn right 90°   Once it has reached the wall, the robot must
                       turn 90° to the right, ready to move parallel to
                       the wall.

Advance one step ⎱
Advance one step
.
       .   This instruction is repeated 3400 times to in-
       .   struct the robot to move along the wall to
       .   the door.
Advance one step ⎰

This has 6901 instructions, and would take ages to type into a computer. It seems easier to *push* the robot to the door than to write a program!

There is another catch with this program. What if we do not know where the robot starts from? Or what if we want it to start from different places on different occasions? It would be very boring to have to write a new program every time, so instead we write a different kind of program. We really want the robot to do three things:

Stage 1.   Go forward to the wall.
Stage 2.   Turn right 90°.
Stage 3.   Go forward to the doorway.

Each stage specifies a **subgoal** for the robot—a goal the robot should achieve on its way to its final goal of reaching the doorway.

Let us see how to write a program that will make the robot carry out this task no matter where it starts from in the room. Remember, though, that we still assume that it is facing the wall, and that there is a doorway in the wall somewhere to the right of the robot. We start by breaking down the first stage as follows:

Advance one step
Test: Are you touching the wall?
           If the answer is NO: Advance another step.
           If the answer is YES: Jump to Stage 2.

For the test to work, the robot must have a device, such as a pushbutton, that sends a signal to the computer whenever the robot bumps into something in front of it.

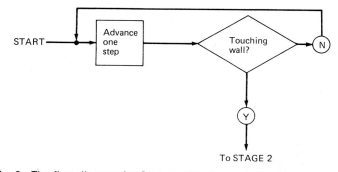

Fig. 2 The flow diagram for Stage 1: "Go forward till hitting the wall."

This can also be shown by the **flow diagram** of Fig. 2. The diagram has one box for each operation and for each test that is to be carried out. The diamond box is a **test** so it has two *exit* lines—the one labeled Y shows where to go for the next instruction if the outcome of the test is a YES, while the N line shows where to go if the answer is NO. The rectangular box shows an **operation,** and so only has one output line—sending the computer on to the test instruction. There are no tests in Stage 2, and its flow diagram takes just one rectangular box (Fig. 3).

The flow diagram for Stage 3 (Fig. 4) is almost the same as Fig. 2 for Stage 1. To carry out this part of the program, the computer must get signals from a device on the side of the robot that tells whether or not it is touching the wall at its side. Here failure of the test "Touching wall?" shows that the robot has achieved its goal of reaching the doorway, and so is no longer touching the wall. At this stage, the computer is instructed to exit from the program—awaiting further instructions, or going on to obey the instructions of the next program already stored in its "memory."

Putting this all together, we can draw a flow diagram for the whole "go to the door program" (Fig. 5). It has two loops—one for Stage 1 and one for Stage 3. Instead of having to give the robot 3500

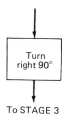

To STAGE 3

Fig. 3 The flow diagram for Stage 2: "Turn right 90°."

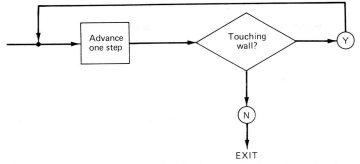

Fig. 4 The flow diagram for Stage 3: "Go forward until reaching the doorway."

instructions to make it advance 3.5 meters, we need only give it two for Stage 1: a test and a step command. In all, the original 6901 instructions of the original program have been replaced by a five-instruction program! The original program was useless unless the robot was 3.5 meters from the wall with the door 3.4 meters along it to the right. The five-instruction program will work for *any* distances, as

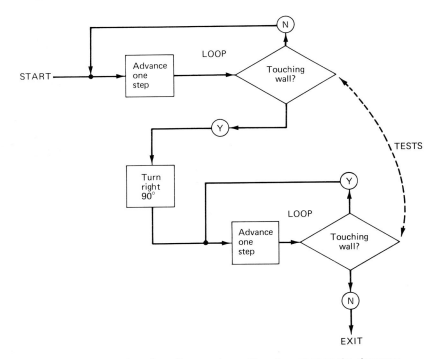

Fig. 5 The complete flow diagram for getting the robot to the doorway.

long as the door is somewhere to the right of the robot along the wall it is facing!

The flow diagram is useful in letting us chart out the flow of instructions in working out the program. However, it is not in a form convenient for putting into the computer. To get the program into the computer, we type it out with one instruction per line (no lower-case letters). As we shall explain shortly, we label some of the instructions by writing a number to the left of them.

Labels	Instructions
1	ADVANCE ONE STEP
	IF NOT TOUCHING WALL GO TO 1
	TURN RIGHT 90°
2	ADVANCE ONE STEP
	IF TOUCHING WALL GO TO 2

The idea is this: after completing an instruction, the computer automatically goes to the instruction on the next line unless a test result tells it to **jump** somewhere else. So it knows where to jump, we **label** those instructions which are the targets of jumps. When it has completed the last instruction, it stops—its job is done. In this example, there are only two targets—the two "ADVANCE ONE STEP" instructions. We give these targets distinct labels—the 1 and the 2 in the left-hand column—to distinguish them.

With this we have seen the crucial ideas of computer programming: We use two types of instructions: (i) *operations*—which say to do something; and (ii) *tests*—which are instructions that tell the computer to test whether it has reached some *subgoal* yet. In this way the computer can repeat a set of operations many, many times until some subgoal is achieved.

In complex programs, what the computer repeats need not be a single operation but a whole sequence of operations, and there may be various tests for subgoals along the way within the "main loop." In any case, our simple example of a 5-instruction program to instruct the computer to get the robot to the door gives us a fair idea of how to write down just a few instructions and yet control the behavior of the system for a long, long time.

The beauty of programming is that we can put the whole program into the machine before it starts. With the program in its memory, the computer automatically will keep going on to the next instruction, carrying out tests to determine which instruction it should do next, etc., until it has completed its job. This is true whether the program is designed for controlling a robot, working out the answer to some complicated mathematical problem, or figuring out a payroll.

One ingredient common to all these computer applications is the **data** we must feed into the computer—the numbers and information that the program operates on to give answers to the human user. We shall see how data are handled in Section 1.2. In the robot example, the only data the program uses are the signals that tell it whether or not it is touching the wall.

Programs in Perspective

We have now seen an example of a program: a sequence of instructions that tells a computer how to do some job. In our example, the job was to control the movements of a robot so that it would get to the doorway. Before we go on to other examples of programs, some important points should be made.

Most computers are **general-purpose.** This means that they can be used for many different jobs, simply by changing the program. A general-purpose machine can be used as a robot controller if it is given a robot-control program; it can be used as an accounting machine if it is given a payroll program such as that described in Section 2.2; and it can be used as a teacher if it is given programs for computer-assisted instruction like those discussed in Section 6.1.

Some computers are **special-purpose,** however. This means that they have special circuitry that makes them best suited for some specific job. Instead of having different programs given to it at different times, a special-purpose computer will usually have a single program wired into it at the factory where it is built. Examples of special-purpose computers are digital wristwatches, and the new electronic devices that control a car's ignition.

We see here the distinction between the **hardware** of a computer—the actual circuitry with which it comes from the factory—and the **software**—the programs written for a computer. This raises the interesting question: "When can software written for one computer be used on the hardware of another computer?" Suppose you are telling a friend how to fix a car. Suppose, just as in writing a good program, you are very careful to spell out step-by-step what must be done. If you speak in English, your instructions will be useless unless your friend *understands* English. Even if you both speak English, your friend will fail if he cannot tell a carburetor from a distributor. We can only run a program on a computer if it is in a "language" the computer "understands."

In discussing our robot example, we said that the computer could not understand flow diagrams, but could understand the five-line program. In particular, it "understands" how to control the robot when it **executes** (carries out) an instruction of the form "ADVANCE ONE STEP" or "TURN RIGHT 90°." It also "understands" where to go for the next instruction when it has carried out the test in an instruction like "IF NOT TOUCHING WALL GO TO 1." Some computers "understand" these instructions; some do not.

English and Chinese are examples of **natural languages**—languages that humans use to talk to each other. We use **programming languages** to talk to machines. Chinese and English have different words, and different rules for putting words together into sentences. In the same way, there are different programming languages. Each programming language has its own format for instructions, and its own rules for how to string instructions together to make different programs.

A general-purpose computer is built with hardware that lets the machine "understand" programs written in one special programming language, called the **machine language.** If you carefully spell out in machine language how a job is to be done step-by-step, then the computer will obey those instructions perfectly. Computers from different manufacturers—and even different "lines" of computers from the same manufacturer—are built with different machine languages.

People usually find it very hard to spell out in machine language how a job is to be done. Because of this, computer scientists have developed what are called **high-level** languages. These are still programming languages—not natural languages—but are designed to make it much easier for people to spell out step-by-step how a job is to be done. Since the computer hardware can only handle machine language directly, it needs to be given a special *program* called a **translator.** Then, when it is given a high-level program, the computer can use the translator to construct a machine language program that describes how the job is to be done. Translators are part of the computer's software, and will be explained in Section 2.1.

You do not really need to know how to program to get a feel for the impact of computers on society. You *especially* do not need to know how to program in machine language. In fact, most computer experts do not use machine language. They find that for most jobs it is more efficient to write in a high-level programming language, and then let the computer use translator software to "understand" the program. Because programs written in high-level language are easier for *people* to understand, they can be written more quickly and with fewer mistakes.

Since most students of this book need not study machine language, it is only developed in Section 8.1, in the last chapter of the book. This material is not used in any of the earlier chapters. It is included only for those students who are eager to understand in some detail how computer hardware is able automatically to follow the step-by-step instructions in a program. We will study a simple *high-level* language in Section 1.3—but again, understanding the remainder of the book will not rest on any of the details of this language.

An important point needs mentioning—the computer needs a machine language if it is to execute your high-level programs, but *you* do *not* have to know machine language to write useful high-level programs!

Should the reader of this book learn a high-level language? Many readers will go on to further study of computers. There they will meet languages like COBOL for business applications, FORTRAN for engineering work, LISP or PLANNER for studies in artificial intelligence, or even ALGOL, APL, PASCAL, PL/1, or. . . . The list goes on and on! I have picked one high-level language which it may benefit readers to study; it is called LOGO.

In Section 1.3 we study how LOGO programs can be used to control a simple robot called TURTLE, making it follow paths of great geometrical beauty. You do not have to read Section 1.3, or do any of the programming exercises—later sections do *not* call on any knowledge of LOGO programming—yet it is probably a good idea to do some of the exercises. Time and again in the book we shall ask "Is this the sort of problem that can be solved by a computer?" In other words, "Does it make sense to write a program that will get a computer to do this job?" If you have never written a program, it will be difficult for you to form your own opinion, and that would be sad—since the aim of this book is to help the reader to become a responsible citizen who can make decisions in an increasingly technological society.

With this perspective, we can now turn to another example of a program. This time, it is a program for a special-purpose computer—a digital wristwatch.

A Digital Wristwatch

Most watches have minute, hour, and second hands (Fig. 6a) that move round and round the watch face to show the time. The hands move gradually around the watch face, rather than jumping from one position to another. Instead, however, new electronic watches have a display (Fig. 6b) that shows the time in numerical

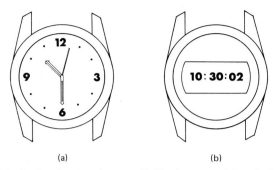

(a)   (b)

Fig. 6 At just after 2 seconds past 10:30, the second hand of a conventional wristwatch (a) has moved beyond the 2-second position en route to the 3-second position; while the digital wristwatch (b) still shows 10:30:02, and will do so until 3 seconds past 10:30, when it will change to 10:30:03.

form. The numbers change in a jump fashion as each second passes. The display on the watch face does not show the gradual passage of time represented by the smooth movement of the second hand of the "old-fashioned" watch.

We call the usual type of watch (Fig. 6a) an **analog** device because the smooth movement of the hands is *analogous to* (that is: shares important properties with) the smooth passing of time. The electronic watch (Fig. 6b) is called a **digital** device because the way it tells time is like counting on our fingers (the *digits* of the hands).

All the computers we study in this book—whether special-purpose or general-purpose—are **digital computers** that store data and programs as strings of symbols. Analog computers—in which numbers are represented by continuously varying quantities such as electrical voltages—do exist. They are usually special-purpose computers, and might form part of the automatic pilot of an airplane, or of the system that controls the thickness of steel in the rolling plant of a steel mill. However, we will not study these devices in this book. The main implications of computers for society can be seen by studying digital computers. In particular, only digital computers can be used in data banks, or to automate libraries, or to provide computer-assisted instruction.

A digital wristwatch is a special-purpose digital computer. It has a program wired into it, rather than being given different programs to do different jobs at different times. In the rest of this section, we see what a time-telling program looks like.

We will look at the design of a 24-hour watch—which shows 00:00:00 at midnight, 12:00:00 at noon, and 23:59:59 one second before midnight. The display has three parts—the *hour,* which can run from 00 to 23, and the *minute* and the *second,* each of which runs from 00 to 59. The circuitry inside the watch includes three **registers**— electronic devices that store the electronic representation of these numbers. Let us call .the registers HOUR, MINUTE, and SECOND, respectively. We use the notation $\langle HOUR \rangle = 13$ to indicate that the number currently stored in the HOUR register is 13. We call this piece of data the **contents** of the register. For example, when the watch-face display shows 07:30:16, we have $\langle HOUR \rangle = 07$, $\langle MINUTE \rangle = 30$, and $\langle SECOND \rangle = 16$.

The electronic circuitry includes a very accurate timing device which emits a control signal every second, with each signal coming precisely one second after the previous control signal. This signal activates the program which updates the display. Here are some examples of updating.

After one second	07:30:16	is updated to	07:30:17
After one second	07:30:59	is updated to	07:31:00
After one second	07:59:59	is updated to	08:00:00
After one second	23:59:59	is updated to	00:00:00

Here then is the updating rule:

Unless $\langle SECOND \rangle = 59$, just add 1 to $\langle SECOND \rangle$.
However, if $\langle SECOND \rangle = 59$, reset $\langle SECOND \rangle$ to 00, and update $\langle MINUTE \rangle$.

Here is the rule for updating $\langle MINUTE \rangle$:

Unless $\langle MINUTE \rangle = 59$, just add 1 to $\langle MINUTE \rangle$.
However, if $\langle MINUTE \rangle = 59$, reset $\langle MINUTE \rangle$ to 00, and update $\langle HOUR \rangle$.

Finally, we must give the rule for updating $\langle HOUR \rangle$:

Unless $\langle HOUR \rangle = 23$, just add 1 to $\langle HOUR \rangle$.
However, if $\langle HOUR \rangle = 23$, reset $\langle HOUR \rangle$ to 00.

Before reading on, the reader should check that these rules really do give the four examples of updating we saw above.

Now we write out a flow diagram for the whole program. We use a special sign :=. At first sight, $\langle HOUR \rangle := \langle HOUR \rangle + 1$ looks like a crazy equation. How can $\langle HOUR \rangle$ equal $\langle HOUR \rangle + 1$?! The answer, of course, is that it cannot. The sign := is not an equals sign. It means "is to be replaced by." Thus

$$\langle HOUR \rangle := \langle HOUR \rangle + 1$$

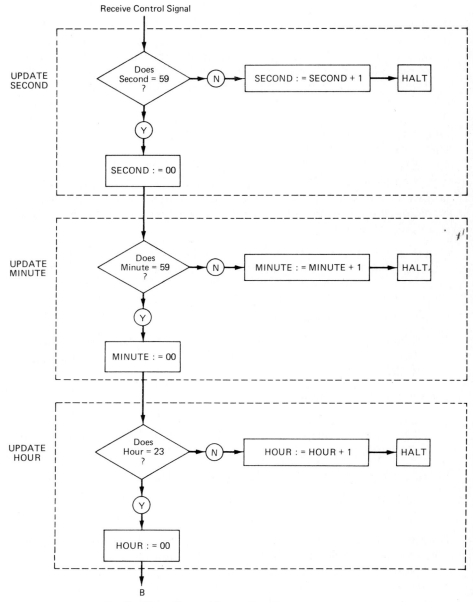

Fig. 7 Flow diagram for the "update time" program.

is an *instruction* (not an equation) which says the new value stored in the HOUR register is obtained by adding 1 to the old value stored there. If ⟨HOUR⟩ equals 13 before executing the instruction, then we will have ⟨HOUR⟩ = 14 after the instruction is executed. In the same way,

$$⟨HOUR⟩ := 00$$

is another way of writing the instruction that ⟨HOUR⟩ is to reset to 00. With this notation, we can write out the full flow diagram of Fig. 7. We use the sloppy form "Does SECOND = 59?" as a shorthand for the more precise "Does ⟨SECOND⟩ = 59?", and so on.

The special exit marked B in the figure is only taken at the end of the day, when the time changes from 23:59:59 to 00:00:00. This is the time at which a calendar watch should update the date. Let us see one way to fill in the "Update Date" box in the high-level flow diagram of Fig. 8.

Suppose that the calendar display is in the form of a 3-letter abbreviation for the month followed by the day—such as

JAN 17

for January 17th. We need a MONTH-register and a DAY-register. ⟨MONTH⟩ can take any value from 1 (for January) to 12 (for December). ⟨DAY⟩ can take any value from 1 to 31. What makes the "Update Date" program interesting is that different months have different lengths. Recall the rhyme

> 30 days hath September,
> April, June, and November.
> All the rest have 31,
> Excepting February alone.

The rhyme goes on to tell us that February has 28 days, except in leap

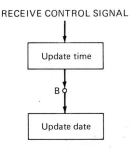

Fig. 8   High-level flow diagram for the updating program for a calendar watch.

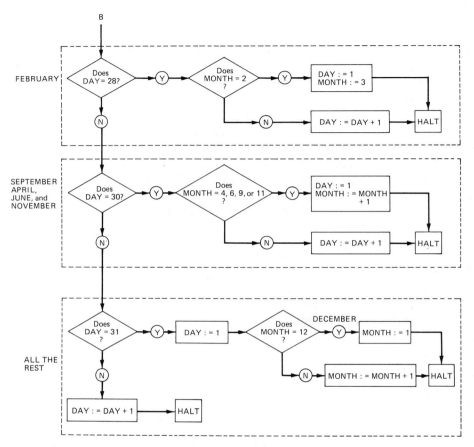

Fig. 9 An "update date" program that works except in leap years.

years—but we shall leave the handling of leap years to the exercises. The rhyme tells us, then, that we normally reset ⟨DAY⟩ back to 1 after the 31st of the month. However, if ⟨MONTH⟩ = 4, 6, 9, or 11 we reset after day 30; and if ⟨MONTH⟩ = 2, we reset after day 28. This yields the flow diagram of Fig. 9. The reader should check carefully, and verify that this does indeed work on a few examples.

Bugs and Learning

It has often been said that "computers can only do what they are programmed to do." We close this section by studying two ways in which this statement is misleading: because programs can have errors in them; and because computers can be programmed to "learn."

The first observation is perhaps more important for most programmers. If you write a complicated program, then you will make mistakes, no matter how careful you are. We call such a mistake in programming a **bug.** Often a programmer will spend more time **debugging** a program (removing the mistakes) than in writing the original, buggy, program. Because of this, much effort is going into the development of ways to write programs that have as few bugs as possible in them, and for which the remaining bugs are fairly simple to remove. (We shall study these techniques in Section 2.4, "Writing and Rewriting Large Programs.") There are programs today with hundreds of thousands of instructions, and usually there is something wrong with them. If something as simple as an automobile can have bugs in it—cars certainly have to be taken in for repairs quite frequently—then it is not too surprising that a very complex computer program will also have some things wrong with it. In simple programs, such as payroll applications, computers certainly do what we believe they are told to do. However, as we try to write programs to enable computers to solve more and more complex problems, we find that it is almost inevitable that they do not do quite what we *thought* we told them to do. The presence of bugs in complex programs is something we must take into account when we consider the use of computers in society.

Even if we provide a program without bugs, the computer may accumulate information which lets it behave in ways that cannot be predicted by the programmer. In some sense, a computer can be programmed to *learn* in the sense that it can change part of its program. A computer need not simply be given instructions on how to do some job, but it can also be instructed on how to learn how to do it even better.

The classic example of a learning program is the checker-playing program that Arthur Samuel wrote in the late 1950s when he was working for IBM. He programmed the computer not only to make use of a great deal of available information about games by master players, but he also programmed the computer to evaluate the board—so that it could plan ahead several moves, estimating for each move what possible replies the opponent might make, and how it might respond to those replies. It would examine a number of alternative moves, chopping out those that were obviously silly, and then—given the ones that remained—trying to see which was most likely to help the computer rather than its opponent. To do this it had to evaluate how valuable were the board positions that it might end up with after a few moves. But how should it evaluate? Certainly, the more pieces it has, the better off, in general, is it likely to be. But what about the number of kings? Should a king count twice as much as ordinary pieces, 1.7 times as much, or 2.3 times as much? Samuel did not know, so what he did was program the computer to keep changing the way it evaluated the board. After each reply by the opponent, the computer would compare how well it was doing with how it had predicted it would do. It would then adjust the relative merits it gave to different aspects of the board to bring its predictions more in line with what actually happened. After the computer had been playing for a while in this fashion, it could beat not only Samuel, but also all but the very best checkers players.

As we build more and more complex computer systems, we will program them to update automatically the information they have available for us, and in this sense they will be learning. As time goes by, the computer will be behaving less and less according to what we gave it originally, and more and more according to what it has learned, just as experience modifies the genetic determination of a human's behavior. We shall see computer systems which grow and learn over time. One of the interesting questions we will ask, as many anxious parents ask about their children, is "How do we communicate?"

Suggestions for Further Reading

T.H. Nelson: "Computer Lib/Dream Machines." Hugo's Book Service, Box 2622, Chicago, Illinois, 60690, 1974.

> This is a "Whole Earth Catalog" of computers, with many fascinating essays. It is strongly recommended to supplement this textbook. There are numerous strong opinions, many of them correct. Pages 11–35 give a good introduction to programming, including a feel for several different programming languages.

P. T. White: Behold the Computer Revolution, *National Geographic*, November 1970, pp. 597–633.

> This article is a reasonable overview of the impact of computers by 1970 with many good photographs.

R. L. Didday and R. L. Page: "FORTRAN for Humans." West Publishing, St. Louis, Missouri, 1974.

> This is perhaps the most enjoyable introductory programming text. It is dedicated to a frog!

T. M. Walker: "Fundamentals of BASIC Programming." Allyn and Bacon, Rockleigh, New Jersey, 1975.

> Walker's is one of the hundreds of introductory programming books. The same author has variants of this book on FORTRAN, COBOL, and PL/1.

Readers will find further information on computers and society in a number of books, three of which are:

S. Rothman and C. Mosmann, "Computers and Society." Science Research Associates, Chicago, Illinois, 1972.
C. C. Gotlieb and A. Borodin, "Social Issues in Computing." Academic Press, New York, 1973.
J. Martin and A. R. D. Norman, "The Computerized Society." Prentice-Hall, Englewood Cliffs, New Jersey, 1970.

Summary

This section introduced many new concepts, and their definitions are given in the glossary below. We saw that a general-purpose computer could handle many different jobs, as long as it is given a program—written in a programming language which it can "understand"—which tells it step-by-step how the job is to be done. An example of programming a simple robot showed that loops allow relatively short programs to control a great deal of computation. Both this example, and the example of a program for a digital wristwatch, showed how the use of tests can enable a single program to handle many different situations. Finally, we noted the problems we may have with bugs in a program, and saw how we might program a computer to "learn from experience."

Glossary

Program: A *program* is a sequence of instructions that spells out step-by-step how a job is to be done.

Data (the plural of datum):   *Data* are the pieces of information that are worked with in solving a problem.

Computer: A *computer* is a machine that can store a program and data, and then automatically execute the instructions with electronic speed. In *analog computers,* numbers are represented by continuously varying quantities such as electrical voltages. However, in this book, we study *digital computers,* which store data and programs as strings of symbols.

Bug: An error in a program which causes a computer under its control to behave differently from what was intended is a *bug*.

Debugging: *Debugging* is the process of revising a program to remove the bugs.

Memory: The region in a computer where data and programs are stored for automatic use by the machine is the *memory*.

Register: A *register* is a device in a computer for storing a single instruction or piece of information. We use the notation $\langle A \rangle$ for the *contents* of register A. An instruction A := B means "replace $\langle A \rangle$ by the value of the expression B."

Execution: A computer *executes* an instruction when it carries it out. We say a computer executes a program when it operates according to the instructions of that program.

Comments: When we write a program, we often write notes to remind us of what different parts of the program make the computer do. These notes are called *comments*. The complete package of comments together with the program in human-readable form is called *documentation*.

Loop: A sequence of instructions that the computer must follow again and again in doing its job is a *loop*.

Subgoal: A *subgoal* is a goal specified as a stepping-stone toward completing some overall job.

Operation: An instruction is an *operation* if it tells the computer how to change some information.

Test: An instruction is a *test* if it tells the computer to test whether or not some specified condition is met—such as whether or not some number equals zero. The outcome of the test determines which instruction the computer will go to next.

Jump: The instructions of a program are usually written one after another in a list. After it has executed an instruction, the computer usually goes to the next instruction in the list. If this is not the case, we say that a *jump* occurs.

Label: A *label* is a number or other name we can give to an instruction to tell us where it occurs in a program. We label those instructions of a program which are the targets of jumps.

Flow diagram: This is a diagram that has one box for each operation or test in a program, or in a description of the program. A line goes from an operation box to the next step in the program. Two lines go from a test box—one to the step to be taken next if the answer to the test is YES, the other to the step to be taken next if the answer is NO.

Robot: A *robot* is a machine, often computer controlled, that can sense things around it as it carries out human commands. It may have touch sensors to tell when it has bumped into things, or a TV camera for visual input; it may have hands to pick up objects, or wheels on which to move around.

General-purpose computer: A computer that can be used for many different jobs, simply by changing the program, is *general-purpose*.

Special-purpose computer: A computer with circuitry that makes it best suited for a specific job is a *special-purpose computer*.

Hardware: The actual circuitry of a computer is its *hardware*.

Software: The programs written for a computer are its *software*.

Language: A *language* is a systematic way of arranging symbols into strings to express meaning. It may be a *natural language* like English, Chinese, or Swahili that humans use to communicate with one another; or a *programming language* in which to write programs for a computer.

Machine language: The instructions which the hardware of the computer is wired to execute directly comprise the *machine language.*

High-level language: A programming language that a human finds easier to use than *machine language* is a *high-level language*. A *translator* is a special program that a computer needs to enable it to execute a program written in high-level language.

Exercises

1. Here are three program applications. Which of these might use a program that is designed to remain in a loop forever (or until shut down manually)? Why?

    (a) An automatic system to monitor the heartbeats of hospital patients in critical condition?

    (b) A robot with an arm to pick up rocks on Mars?

    (c) A computer to play chess against Bobby Fischer?

2. Indicate whether the following statements are true or false.

    (a) The first computer program was written before 1865.

    (b) "Bug" is a nickname for a small robot.

    (c) "Bug" is a nickname for a transistorized circuit.

    (d) A label can refer to an instruction in a program.

    (e) A data base might be stored on a collection of magnetic tapes.

3. Modify the flow diagram of Fig. 5 to handle the case where the robot is facing a wall, but not necessarily the one with the door. *Note:* Use "touching wall" to mean with sensors in front of the robot, while "brushing wall" means with sensors on side. [*Hint:* Assume that the room is rectangular.]

4. Write a program for the robot of the previous (flowchart) problem. Use the types of statement (informal programming language) seen in the text, plus an EXIT statement. The EXIT statement may occur in the middle of the sequence of instructions—it means "if you have just completed executing the *previous* instruction, ignore all following instructions and stop." Also, if necessary, you may use an UNCONDITIONAL GOTO, such as "GO TO 3" which means "whatever is going on when you reach this statement, never mind making any test, just jump to label 3."

5. *Bugs:* What is wrong with each of these variants of the robot program? What would each do?

```
          a                              c
1  ADVANCE ONE STEP          1  ADVANCE ONE STEP
   IF NOT TOUCHING WALL          IF NOT TOUCHING WALL
      GO TO 1                        GO TO 2
   TURN RIGHT 90°                TURN RIGHT 90°
   ADVANCE ONE STEP          2  ADVANCE ONE STEP
2  IF TOUCHING WALL GO TO 2      IF NOT TOUCHING WALL
          b                           GO TO 1
1  ADVANCE ONE STEP              ADVANCE ONE STEP
   TURN RIGHT 90°                IF TOUCHING WALL GO TO 2
   IF NOT TOUCHING WALL
      GO TO 1
2  ADVANCE ONE STEP
   IF TOUCHING WALL GO TO 2
```

6. Modify the February portion of the "update date" program of Fig. 9 so that it works whether or not the year is a leap year. Use a YEAR register which can store the values 1, 2, 3, or 4—with 4 corresponding to a leap year. Do *not* modify anything except the February portion of Fig. 9. [*Hint:* Do you have to update the YEAR register at the end of December?]

7. Give a flow diagram for an "update day of the week" program for a wristwatch that has a register WEEKDAY which can hold any number from 1 to 7; and a display which shows SUN when $\langle$WEEKDAY$\rangle$ = 1, MON when $\langle$WEEKDAY$\rangle$ = 2, etc.

8. *Modular arithmetic:* We said that a high-level language was one which made it easier to write programs. The reader will notice that in our wristwatch programs we kept on using the idea of counting up to a certain number, after which we reset to 0. Mathematicians find this happens so often that they use the expression, for any number A with $0 \le A < B$,

$$A + 1 \text{ MODULO } B$$

as shorthand for the number which is $A + 1$ *unless* $A + 1$ equals B, in which case the number is 0. For example, we count seconds MODULO 60. The "update second" portion of Fig. 7 can be replaced by the single instruction SECOND := SECOND + 1 MODULO 60. However, we still need a test to decide whether to go on to the "update minute" portion. We might write out the "update second" portion in the form

SECOND := SECOND + 1 MODULO 60
IF SECOND = 0 GO ON ELSE HALT.

   (a) Write out the complete "update time" program of Fig. 7 in this language.
   (b) Write out the "update date" program of Fig. 9 in this language. [*Hint:* Make the MONTH register run from 0 to 11.]

9. In what ways are (1) a complete score (sheet music) for a symphony and (2) a color-by-number painting, like a computer program? Can you imagine a computer program being considered as a work of art? As part of a work of art? Explain.

10. What is wrong with the following instructions on a container of shampoo?
   "1. Wet hair.
    2. Apply shampoo.
    3. Lather.
    4. Rinse.
    5. Repeat."
If possible, answer in terms of the concepts of loop, test, label, and bug.

11. What do each of these have in common with a program, as defined in this section, and how do they differ?
   (1) Cookbook recipe?
   (2) Table of contents?
   (3) Sergeant shouting "Hup, two, three, four, ..." to a private?
   (4) Rules of a solitaire game?

12. Set a book in front of you. Follow these two "programs," starting with a book in the same position each time.

    (1)   Start; A; B; C; Stop

    (2)   Start; C; A; B; Stop

where A means rotate the book 90° clockwise, B means keeping what is now the left-hand edge of the book in place, flip the book over to the other side, C means keeping what is now the top edge of the book in place, flip the book over to the other side—as shown in the accompanying figure. What is the final

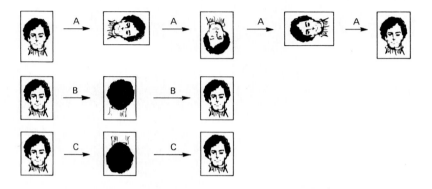

position for each program? Give another example of two three-step programs like the above that differ in instruction order and result. Give an example of two three-step programs that differ in instruction order but give the same result.

13. When we wrote the robot program we broke the problem down into subproblems each of which ended with the attainment of a subgoal. Is it reasonable to assume that practice in programming in this way will improve a person's ability to solve personal problems, or problems of the community? Can you name some types of problems which are not solvable by this sort of analytic attitude?

A Walk through the Computer Center

Before studying computer operation in more detail, let us take a quick walk around the computing center at the University of Massachusetts at Amherst, with the help of photographs taken by Arthur Karshmer. We find ourselves in a large room, crammed with equipment. If we ask "Where is the computer?" we find it is all over the place. We see the console of the machine

with cabinets of electronics stretching back to the "mainframe," a six-foot

high collection of circuitry, opened up here to show one of the panels of seemingly endless "spaghetti"—the wiring that links the many different elements of the computer's hardware.

One of the striking things about the computer room is that only 3 or 4 people—the computer operators—are working there. Yet perhaps hundreds of different jobs are being run on the computer. How is this possible? The answer is that users—the people who actually write programs that process data to get results—never enter the computer room. Instead, they can get their program onto the machine in one of two ways.

In interactive processing, the user sits down at a terminal—a typewriter-like device—and dials the computer on the telephone! When the computer answers—with a new dial tone—the user places the handset in a coupler, which relays signals back and forth between the terminal and the computer. The user can be in the same building as the computer, or miles away in his own home.

For batch processing, the user types at a keypunch to make up a deck of punched cards which contains the entire program and data. The computer operator then takes the deck and places it—along with the decks from many other users—into a card reader which scans each card and sends the instructions and data on to the computer in electronic form.

If a batch user wants to use a program again and again, or wants to build up a data base for use on different occasions, he does not have to keep huge boxes of punched cards. Instead he can program the computer to transfer the program and data onto magnetic tape or magnetic disks. Here are three of the magnetic tape units which can transfer information back and forth between a reel of magnetic tape and the computer's primary memory.

Here are seven of the magnetic disk units—looking a lot like a laundromat.

The round plastic container on top of each unit is used to store the disks. The actual "stack of magnetic platters" is inside the unit, whirling round at immense speed, sending information to the computer, and recording the signals it gets back in return.

Thus the batch user can either submit a large deck of punched cards to a computer operator; or else just a few "job control cards" to tell the computer where to find the program and data already stored on magnetic tape or disk. At any one time, the computer may be handling several batch jobs and as many as a hundred interactive terminals. One of the computer operators sits at the console, watching a display on which the computer reports the status of all the jobs it is doing, ready to clear up any problems that may arise.

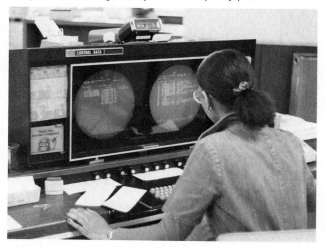

For the batch user, results can be stored on magnetic tape or disk, printed at immense speed by a line printer:

or punched out on a deck of cards:

The results may even take the form of attractive pictures taken from an x–y plotter whose pen moves back and forth under the computer's control.

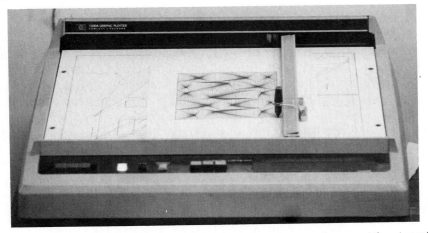

For the interactive user, results from the computer keep getting typed out at the terminal as he types in new instructions and data.

Finally, it should be noted that not all computer users work with the large computer at the computer center. Many people use smaller computers—costing perhaps ten thousand dollars instead of the millions of dollars that the central computer costs—which can be used for work in their own laboratory or small business without having to be shared with other users. However, for many people it is still cheaper to rent a little computer time than to buy a little computer. Other people have jobs so large that only a huge computer can handle them.

1.2. MOVING AND STORING INFORMATION

The Shape of a Computer System

In Section 1.1 we learned that a computer is a machine that can store a program and data, and then automatically execute the instructions with electronic speed. Thus, if the computer is to be of any use to us, there must be a way for us to feed programs and data into the computer, and a way for the computer to give us the results of its computation. We thus have the general situation shown in Fig. 1. The **input device** takes the user's data and instructions and transfers them to the memory of the computer. Whenever the computer has generated results, the **output device** transforms them into a form the user can understand or use in some other way.

At each stage, the information is carried in a different form. To get a feel for this, let us briefly examine a system more familiar to most readers: a tape recorder. A tape recorder is a system that can record sound on a magnetic tape, and can later play back whatever was recorded.

Consider the use of a tape recorder to record and play back a spoken message (Fig. 2). The input device of a tape recorder is a microphone that converts the speech coming out of the person's mouth (which reaches the microphone as pressure waves in the air) into electrical signals. The output device is a loudspeaker that converts electrical signals into pressure waves in the air which will enable the user to hear the original sound, or at least a slightly distorted reproduction of it.

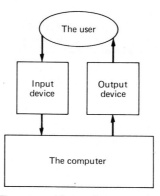

Fig. 1 The general form of a computer system.

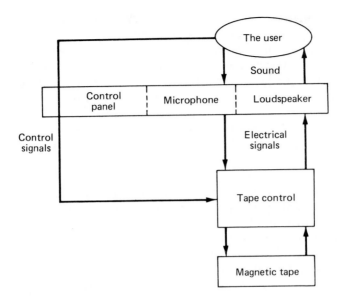

Fig. 2   The flow of information in the use of a tape recorder.

The transforming of information from one form to another is called **coding**. Each form of the information is called a **code.** Thus the microphone converts speech from the air-pressure code to the electrical signal code; and the loudspeaker works the other way. There is another code in Fig. 2: speech can be stored on magnetic tape as a pattern of magnetization. (The details of this are not important. What is important is your own experience that speech—or other sounds, for that matter—can be recorded on magnetic tape, and that the code of the sound on the tape is neither pressure nor electrical current.) During recording, the job of the tape control is to see that the electrical signals are converted into the appropriate pattern of magnetization on the magnetic tape. During playback, the job of the tape control is to convert the magnetization on the tape into the correct pattern of electrical signals which will make the loudspeaker recreate the recorded sound.

Sound is the medium of the main input to, and output from, a tape recorder. To complete our tour of Fig. 2, though, we have to note another kind of input: control signals like PLAY, RECORD, REWIND, FAST FORWARD, and STOP. These control signals enable the user to decide just what the machine will record, and what and when it will play back.

With the example of the tape recorder for comparison, we can now see how a computer is used in **interactive mode** in which the user gets results as soon as the computer generates them, and can type in new data and new instructions at any time. (Later on we shall look at **batch mode,** in which the user gives the complete program and data to a computer operator, who returns the results to the user when the computer has completed its job.)

The user interacts with the computer through a device called a **terminal** (Fig. 3). The most common type of terminal (we shall talk about graphics terminals in Section 2.1) looks much like an electric typewriter except for two differences: it has cables connecting it to the computer; and it is fed by a roll of paper instead of sheets of paper (so that you do not lose valuable computer output while you are trying to put in a fresh sheet of paper!).

When the user types away, he not only obtains the information typed on the paper, but he also has the typed symbols converted into electrical signals which are sent along the cable to the computer. When the terminal receives electrical signals from the computer, it will type out the corresponding symbols on the paper in the terminal. Thus, these functions of the terminal are like the microphone and loudspeaker of the tape recorder.

What corresponds to the magnetic tape of the tape recorder? It is the **memory,** which (as we saw in Section 1.1) is the region in the computer where data and programs are stored for automatic use by

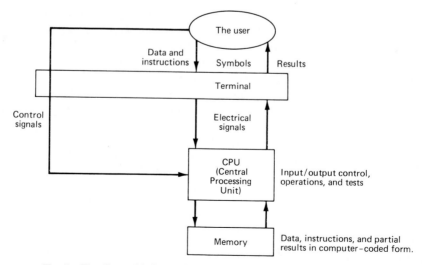

Fig. 3 The flow of information in the interactive use of a computer.

the machine. In the next subsection, we shall discuss the way in which symbols may be coded in the computer memory. For now, it is enough to note that such a code exists. As data and instructions come into the computer as electrical signals, the **central processing unit** (**CPU,** for short) must make sure that the information is stored in properly coded form in the right place in the memory. As results are generated, the CPU must make sure that the proper electrical signals are sent to the terminal to make it type out the results for the user.

To this extent, the CPU is like the tape control of the tape recorder, but it does more. A computer does not simply store and retrieve information. It also follows the instructions of a program to process the information. It is the job of the CPU to take one instruction at a time out of memory. If it is an input instruction, the CPU will read information into the memory. If it is an output instruction, the CPU will send the appropriate information to the terminal. If it is an operation instruction, the CPU will retrieve the necessary data from memory, carry out the operation (adding two numbers together, for example), and—if appropriate—store the results at some designated place in memory. If the instruction calls for a test, the CPU will perform that test, and then go on to the instruction specified by the outcome of the test. [What sort of circuitry does the CPU need to do all this? We do not really need to know if we just want to use computers, rather than work with electronics. However, the circuit enthusiast will find in Section 8.1 an outline of how hardware fetches and executes instructions. This material will not be used elsewhere in the book.]

To complete our tour of Fig. 3, we must see what sort of control signals the user can type in at the terminal. They are messages to the computer that are neither data nor part of a program. Instead, they tell the computer things like: "What I type in next will be data, so store it in such-and-such a part of memory," or "What I type in next will be a program in FORTRAN, so use the proper translator when it is time to execute the program," or "I have finished typing in my program and data; so start executing the program to process the data." Usually, the computer does not understand English, and so these control signals must actually be written in a special programming language called a **job control language.**

Now that we have seen the flow of information in the interactive use of a computer, we turn to a discussion of batch processing. Here, the user's program and data are given to the computer by a computer operator, who later sends the completed computer output back to the user (see the top circle in Fig. 4).

The user has his data and program converted into some suitable

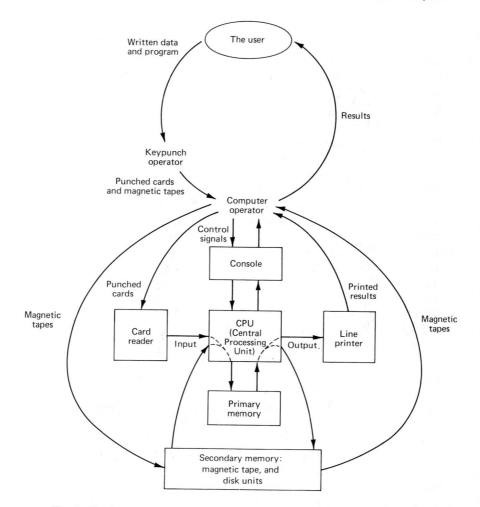

Fig. 4   The flow of information in batch use of a computer with card reader input and printer output.

form. This might be a deck of specially **punched cards.** These cards are prepared by using a **keypunch,** a machine with a typewriterlike keyboard which punches a pattern of holes in special cards to encode the typed-in information. (We shall see what this code looks like in the next subsection.) Another approach is to use a magnetic tape— instead of using a tape recorder with a microphone input to record sound, you can use a special tape recorder with a typewriter input which will store symbols on the tape in a code of magnetization patterns.

The computer operator gets the complete data and instructions from the user. He loads the punched cards into a **card reader,** or mounts the magnetic tape on a **magnetic tape unit,** and then types in the control signals on the keyboard of his terminal, which is called the **console**. Often, the control signals like "This is data," or "This is a FORTRAN program," or "Start executing" are punched on cards in the punched card deck—these special cards are called **job control cards.** The process is similar for magnetic tapes. Then the computer operator has simply to type in at the console instructions like "Read in from the card reader," or "Read the tape on Unit 4." The computer reads in the program and data and starts its work.

Each program tells the computer which results are to be sent out, when, and using what output device. The computer has various output devices. A **line printer** types out line after line of results in much the same way as a typewriter does, but at incredibly high speed. A **card punch** punches the results out on cards—which can be either stored for later use, or fed into a printer which accepts its input from punched cards—or the computer can set the results up on the magnetic tape. Later in this section, we shall look at a payroll program which uses a check printer as its output device.

We close this subsection with some comments on memory. Under control of the program it is executing, the computer can transfer information from the memory to the tape in the magnetic tape unit, as well as reading information from the tape to memory. In short, the CPU can electronically exchange information with the magnetic tapes, and other devices such as **magnetic disks** (more about these later). Thus these devices function as a **secondary memory.** If we want to stress the distinction, we refer to the main memory as **primary memory.** The CPU can get information in and out of primary memory more quickly than it can for secondary memory, but secondary memory is cheaper and can hold more information.

The art of efficient memory management, then, is to transfer into primary memory a large chunk of information which will meet the CPU's data and instruction needs for a reasonable length of time. Bad management is to let the CPU hunt back and forth along the tape for each fresh instruction—so that it can only execute ten instructions in a second instead of the millions of instructions it can execute when all the instructions are in primary memory.

The reason that we cannot afford to put all the data in primary memory is that a large data base may contain *billions* of characters (individual letters or digits) while primary memory will hold only thousands or at most a few *million* characters. For example, computers programmed for weather prediction use data from weather satellites. These satellites provide billions of numbers *each month*—and, month after month, weather just keeps happening. Weather forecasters want to retain all this information in a data bank so that they can detect when current weather patterns resemble, for example, the great blizzard of 1946 and get trend data into the computer quickly. With 1975 computer technology, computers took only 4 hours to make fairly accurate predictions several days ahead—in time to ensure that enough natural gas is piped to the region before the cold snap hits, and that electric utilities reallocate resources. Early disaster warnings may save hundreds of lives and millions of dollars. Much effort is now being devoted to developing accurate predictions months in advance to help oil refineries decide what proportions of fuel oil and gasoline they should produce. The colder the weather, the greater the need for fuel oil. Again, such predictions can help farmers plant crops in a manner best suited to the weather pattern.

The excellence of US telephone service is due in large part to the fact that the main US telephone company, AT&T, has a **data bank** keeping track of all supplies. When a New York telephone exchange burned out in 1975, the use of this data bank saved months of time in getting all the complex replacement parts together from all around the country. This data bank contains several billion symbols. This then is another example of a really large base that must be quickly mobilized. We shall say more about the software associated with data banks in Section 4.1. Here, let us briefly look at the hardware.

The current standard form of secondary memory for a large data base is the *disk storage unit,* which can hold about 800 million characters. Like a magnetic tape unit, the disk storage unit codes information as patterns of magnetization. Instead of using tapes, the unit uses a stack of rapidly spinning disks much like phonograph records, but with rings of patterned magnetization instead of a spiral groove. An arm moves in and out under computer control to read information from and write information on the disk as it whizzes past.

However, since a disk storage unit holds less than a billion characters, the Weather Bureau must add several new disks every month. The US Internal Revenue Service must use hundreds of disks—far too many to fit in a single computer room—at the peak period for income tax returns each April. The US Social Security Administration has 300,000 tapes! Thus finding the tape with needed records on it may be very tough—especially if tapes get mislabeled. Because of this, a major focus of current hardware research is the **terabit memory** for archival storage—a single device which uses modern breakthroughs in electronic circuitry and which can store more than a trillion **bits** (it takes five or six bits to store a character) far more cheaply and in far less space than magnetic tape or disk units—as much information as can be typed on 30 million sheets of paper. Such a memory eliminates the work of purchasing and storing thousands of reels of magnetic tape. Even more important, it also keeps all storage directly accessible by the computer, and thus avoids slow and error-prone handling of magnetic tapes, including the risk of mislabeling and the resultant loss of a tape on the endless shelves of a large tape library.

Coding

The usual numbers we write down, like 123 or 2965, are **decimal numbers:** each one is written as a string of **digits.** There are ten digits—0, 1, 2, 3, 4, 5, 6, 7, 8, and 9—one for each digit (finger or thumb) of our two hands.

In this section we study **binary numbers,** like 101 or 110110111, each of which is written as a string of **bits.** There are two bits—0 and 1. The word "bit" was chosen for two reasons: because bit is short for "*bi*nary di*git*"; and because the choice between a 0 and a 1 is the smallest bit of information you can store.

We all know how to count in decimal:

0, 1, 2, 3, 4, 5, 6, 7, 8, 9, 10, 11, . . . , 98, 99, 100, 101, . . . , 999, 1000, . . . ,

and so on. Here is how to count in binary:

0	1	10	11	100	101	110	111	1000	. . .
zero	one	two	three	four	five	six	seven	eight	

Can you see the rule? To understand it, let us look at the rule for finding the next decimal number; and then modify it to get the rule for finding the next binary number.

Here are four examples of going to the next decimal number:

108	goes to	109
109	goes to	110
199	goes to	200
999	goes to	1000

If the units digit is not 9, we change it to the next higher digit. If the number is all 9s, we change each 9 to a 0 and put a 1 in front of the string of 0s. In every other case, we change the whole block of 9s at the right-hand end of the number to 0s, and then replace the next digit to the left by the next higher digit. For example,

$$2\ 9\ 2\ 3\ \overbrace{9\ 9\ 9}$$

Change 3 to the next ────→ ↓   ↓ ←──── Change right-hand block
higher digit, which is 4.   of 9s to all 0s.

$$2\ 9\ 2\ 4\ 0\ 0\ 0$$

In binary coding, there are only two bits, 0 and 1, where 1 comes after 0, and 0 comes after 1 with a carry 1—just as, in decimal, 0 comes after 9 with a carry 1. So the recipe for finding the next *binary* number is easily obtained.

If the rightmost digit is a 0, we change it to 1. If the number is all 1s, we change each 1 to 0 and put a 1 in front of the string of 0s. In every other case, we change the whole block of 1s at the right hand end to 0s, and replace the 0 to the left of it by 1.

You should check that this rule really does yield the sequence:

0	1	10	11	100	101	110	111	1000	1001	1010	1011	1100
zero	one	two	three	four	five	six	seven	eight	nine	ten	eleven	twelve

We now see how binary coding lets us code information for computers. Suppose you had four switches, each of which could be either up or down. Let us write a 0 if a switch is down, and 1 if a switch

Fig. 5.   Switch positions coding a 4-bit binary number—with UP for 1 and DOWN for 0.

is up. Then the setting of the switches shown in Fig. 5 can be coded in the form 1001. Here is a list of all the different settings of these 4 switches:

0000	0100	1000	1100
0001	0101	1001	1101
0010	0110	1010	1110
0011	0111	1011	1111

There are 2^4 (shorthand for $\overbrace{2 \times 2 \times 2 \times 2}^{4\ twos}$) = 16 different settings. If we only had 2 switches, there would be $2^2 = 2 \times 2 = 4$ settings. With 8 switches we could get $2^8 = 2^4 \times 2^4 = 16 \times 16 = 256$ different settings.

We have seen that a bit is a 2-choice symbol—like 0 versus 1, or up versus down—while a digit is a 10-choice symbol. We saw that with 4 bits we could get 16 different patterns of information. Since 16 is

$0 \rightarrow 0000$	$5 \rightarrow 0101$
$1 \rightarrow 0001$	$6 \rightarrow 0110$
$2 \rightarrow 0010$	$7 \rightarrow 0111$
$3 \rightarrow 0011$	$8 \rightarrow 1000$
$4 \rightarrow 0100$	$9 \rightarrow 1001$

Fig. 6. A standard 4-bit encoding of the 10 decimal digits.

more than 10 we can **code** each digit as a *different* 4-bit pattern. Figure 6 shows the usual code based on the way we learned to count in binary.

We now see the clue to storing information in the computer. The computer's memory has little devices that can be in two different states—called the 0-state and the 1-state. The device could be magnetic (Does the North pole of the magnet point up to represent 0 or down to represent 1?) or electrical (Is the voltage in a circuit low to code 0 or high to code 1?). The details of such devices need not concern us here. All that matters for now is that tens of thousands, or even millions, of these devices can be put together to form the primary memory of the computer.

So that we can find information stored there, the memory is divided into **locations**. A **word** is the amount of information stored in a single location, and will represent either an instruction or data, since the memory must store both. Each location in memory is a device made by wiring up some of the 2-state devices. A computer is called an **n-bit** computer if every location in primary memory is made up of the same number n of 2-state devices. Thus the words in a 32-bit computer are patterns of 32 0s and 1s.

The locations in memory are numbered 0, 1, 2, ... The number of a location—like the number of a house on a street—is called its **address.** There are also locations—called **registers**—in the CPU. For example, the accumulator is a register in the CPU that holds data that are currently being worked on. The machine language of a computer contains instructions like "Add the number at address 17 to the number in the accumulator," or "If the number in the accumulator is 0, get the next instruction from location 235." The reader interested in such things can learn more about machine language instructions in Chapter 8, but we do not need to know about them for the rest of the book.

How would you store 2 digits (in other words, any of the 100 numbers from 00 to 99) as a pattern of 0s and 1s? You could use the code of Fig. 6, coding each digit by 4 bits. For example,

43 → 01000011, since 0100 is the code for 4, 0011 is the code for 3. However, this is rather wasteful, since just 7 bits allow us to code 128 different patterns—so we do not need an 8th bit unless we insist on coding each digit separately. We can instead "count up" to the number in binary, using the counting rule we introduced earlier. Anyway, the details of different codes are not important for this book. The only point to make is that there are different ways to code the same information in **binary form**—as a pattern of 0s and 1s—for the computer. Some are easier for humans to understand; others require fewer bits, and so make more efficient use of the available memory.

To close this subsection, we list three ways of coding characters. Do *not* try to memorize these codes. They are simply for reference purposes, to give you some idea of how differently the same information can be coded as a string of 0s and 1s.

With 6 bits we can form $2^6 = 64$ different patterns. This is more than enough to code all 26 letters of the alphabet and all 10 digits, as in the standard 6-bit **BCD** (the so-called **binary-coded decimal**) code of Fig. 7.

With 8 bits we have $2^8 = 256$ possibilities. This lets us code lower-case letters differently from upper-case letters, and lets us code

Character	6-Bit BCD code	Character	6-Bit BCD code
0	001010	5	000101
1	000001	6	000110
2	000010	7	000111
3	000011	8	001000
4	000100	9	001001
A	110001	N	100101
B	110010	O	100110
C	110011	P	100111
D	110100	Q	101000
E	110101	R	101001
F	110110	S	010010
G	110111	T	010011
H	111000	U	010100
I	111001	V	010101
J	100001	W	010110
K	100010	X	010111
L	100011	Y	011000
M	100100	Z	011001

Fig. 7 BCD (binary-coded decimal) code.

Character	Binary code	Character	Binary code	Character	Binary code
Blank	01000000	d	10000100	H	11001000
¢	01001010	e	10000101	I	11001001
.	01001011	f	10000110	J	11010001
<	01001100	g	10000111	K	11010010
(	01001101	h	10001000	L	11010011
+	01001110	i	10001001	M	11010100
|	01001111	j	10010001	N	11010101
&	01010000	k	10010010	O	11010110
!	01011010	l	10010011	P	11010111
$	01011011	m	10010100	Q	11011000
*	01011100	n	10010101	R	11011001
)	01011101	o	10010110	S	11100010
;	01011110	p	10010111	T	11100011
¬	01011111	q	10011000	U	11100100
−	01100000	r	10011001	V	11100101
/	01100001	s	10100010	W	11100110
,	01101011	t	10100011	X	11100111
%	01101100	u	10100100	Y	11101000
—	01101101	v	10100101	Z	11101001
>	01101110	w	10100110		
?	01101111	x	10100111	0	11110000
:	01111010	y	10101000	1	11110001
#	01111011	z	10101001	2	11110010
@	01111100			3	11110011
'	01111101	A	11000001	4	11110100
=	01111110	B	11000010	5	11110101
"	01111111	C	11000011	6	11110110
		D	11000100	7	11110111
a	10000001	E	11000101	8	11111000
b	10000010	F	11000110	9	11111001
c	10000011	G	11000111		

Fig. 8   EBCDIC (extended binary-coded decimal interchange code).

many other characters as well, as in the **EBCDIC (extended binary-coded decimal interchange code)** of Fig. 8.

   The coding of a number or instruction inside the computer may be different from its code elsewhere. For example, punched cards do not use the BCD or EBCDIC codes. Instead, the card has 80 columns, with one character coded in each column. The most commonly used card code is the Hollerith code of Fig. 9a—we see an example of its use in Fig. 9b. The rows printed with the numbers 0 through 9 on the card also act as rows 0 through 9 in the code. The two rows above the numbered rows are then rows 11 and 12.

Character	Hollerith code	Character	Hollerith code
0	0	W	0-6
1	1	X	0-7
2	2	Y	0-8
3	3	Z	0-9
4	4		
5	5	&	12
6	6	¢	12-2-8
7	7	.	12-3-8
8	8	<	12-4-8
9	9	(	12-5-8
		+	12-6-8
A	12-1	|	12-7-8
B	12-2	−	11
C	12-3	!	11-2-8
D	12-4	$	11-3-8
E	12-5	*	11-4-8
F	12-6	)	11-5-8
G	12-7	;	11-6-8
H	12-8	¬	11-7-8
I	12-9	/	0-1
J	11-1	,	0-3-8
K	11-2	%	0-4-8
L	11-3	—	0-5-8
M	11-4	>	0-6-8
N	11-5	?	0-7-8
O	11-6	:	2-8
P	11-7	#	3-8
Q	11-8	@	4-8
R	11-9	'	5-8
S	0-2	=	6-8
T	0-3	,,	7-8
U	0-4	Blank	
V	0-5		

(a)

Fig. 9 (a) shows the Hollerith code; while (b) shows the pattern of holes in a punched card coding the message "HERE IS 1374 IN HOLLERITH CODE." Note that in English the blank itself is a symbol—and its Hollerith code is blank, too!

A Payroll Job

We next look at the job of printing a payroll as an example of batch processing. Here the job is to control the printing of the weekly paycheck of each of 2000 of a company's employees. The program takes information about each employee from a magnetic tape, which serves as the program's data base; figures out the deductions for

HERE IS 1374 IN HOLLERITH CODE

advanced 508I

(b)

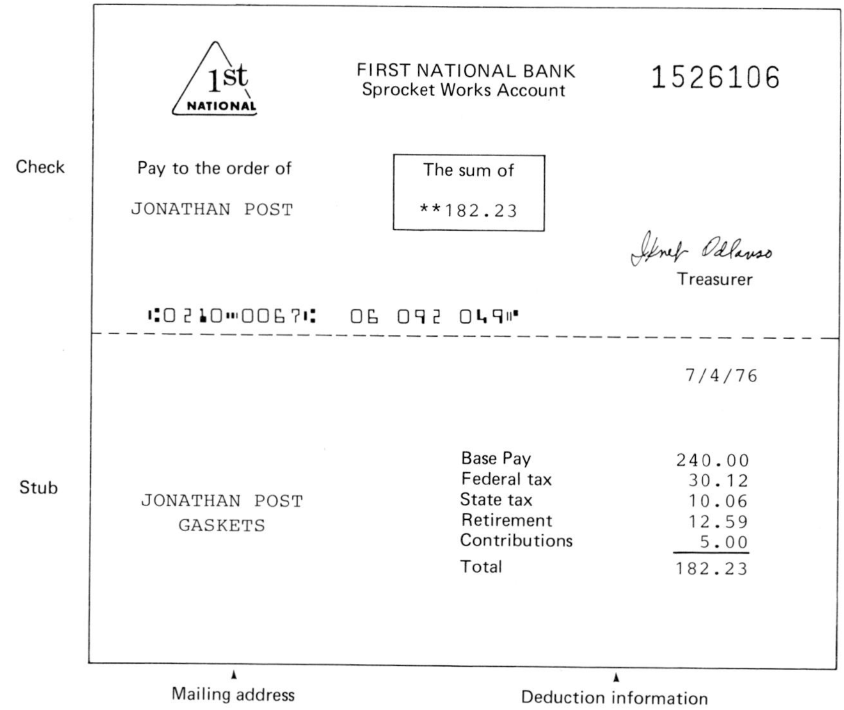

FIRST NATIONAL BANK
Sprocket Works Account

1526106

Check

Pay to the order of

JONATHAN POST

The sum of

**182.23

Treasurer

⑈0 ⒉1 0⣿0 0 6 7⣿   0 6 0 9 2 0 4 9⣿

7/4/76

Stub

JONATHAN POST
GASKETS

Base Pay	240.00
Federal tax	30.12
State tax	10.06
Retirement	12.59
Contributions	5.00
Total	182.23

Mailing address   Deduction information

Fig. 10 The paycheck and stub as computed and printed for each employee by the payroll program.

taxes, and so on; and then prints out both a check and a stub with information about deductions, as shown in Fig. 10.

The **record** on each employee—the information about him stored in the company's data base—would contain entries showing the employee's

Name
Department
Base pay
Contributions
Retirement plan
Dependents

as well as other information the company needs about the employee.

Here is an outline of how the program might process these filed data to compute the deductions and print the paycheck:

(1) Read the file from the data bank into primary memory. [Remember that the computer can perform its instructions far more

quickly on numbers stored in primary memory than on numbers in secondary storage like magnetic tape.] We might program the computer to store the filed information in the following memory locations:

Address of location	Contents	Description
1	JONATHAN POST	The employee's name
2	GASKETS	His department
3	240.00	His weekly pay before deductions
4	5.00	The weekly deduction he has authorized for payment to charity
5	2	He subscribes to the company's second retirement plan
6	1	He has one dependent

(2) Compute the Federal tax for a taxpayer with the pay rate stored in location 3 and the number of dependents stored at address 6. Store the result in location 7. This computation requires a whole sequence of instructions of its own. We will not spell out these instructions. We call such a program—written to be used as just one part of a larger program—a **subroutine** or **subprogram.**

(3) Compute the state tax for a taxpayer with the pay rate stored in location 3, and the number of dependents stored at address 6. Store the result in location 8. This needs another subroutine.

(4) Compute the retirement deduction appropriate to the pay rate stored in location 3 for an employee whose retirement plan has the number stored in location 5. Store the result in location 9.

(5) Add together the contents of location 4, 7, 8, and 9—the total deductions for the week—and subtract the total from the content of location 3—the weekly base pay—to obtain the total pay for the week after deductions. Store the result in location 10.

At this stage the computer's first ten storage locations will be filled as follows:

Address	Contents	Description
1	JONATHAN POST	Name
2	GASKETS	Department
3	240.00	Base pay
4	5.00	Contributions
5	2	Retirement plan
6	1	Dependents
7	30.12	Federal tax
8	10.06	State tax
9	12.59	Retirement
10	182.23	Total pay

(6)   Finally, the computer controls the printing, placing the date (so this must be stored somewhere in the computer, too!), the name (the contents of location 1), and the total pay (contents of location 10) on the check at the appropriate place; and placing the contents of locations 1, 2, 3, 7, 8, 9, 4, and 10 at the appropriate places on the stub. The printing subroutine thus includes instructions to move the typewriter head to the proper place and then type out the contents of the appropriate storage location.

The overall flow diagram for the paycheck program for computing the deductions and printing a *single* check and stub is shown in Fig. 11. The crucial point about this paycheck program is that it will work for *any* employee at *any* time so long as the data base contains up-to-date information on the employee, filed in the proper format.

To process all the checks, we use the *payroll program* whose flow diagram is shown in Fig. 12. It uses the paycheck program as a subroutine. The necessary configuration of input and output devices and of secondary memory is shown in Fig. 13.

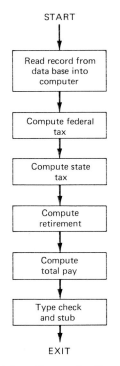

Fig. 11   High-level flow diagram for the paycheck program.

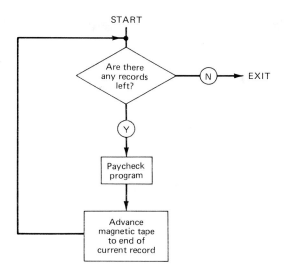

Fig. 12 Flow diagram for the payroll program. The paycheck program is given by the flow diagram of Fig. 11.

If a payroll were done by hand, it would require a great deal of work every week for people to look through the pages in the ledger and work out all the deductions for the week, and then write out each check by hand—as would have been done prior to the widespread use of computers. The payroll job thus shows that a little programming can save a huge amount of repetitive effort. It is worthwhile to write the payroll program and go to all the trouble of putting a record on magnetic tape for each employee because we only have to do it *once*. Then, each week, an operator simply loads the program and the data base into the computer. The computer then *automatically*—without any further human effort—computes the deductions and prints out the checks for all 2000 employees.

Of course, other programs are required to update the record when someone is hired or promoted or fired or retired; and extra work is required each time there is a new union contract. Again, each tax subroutine must be changed each time the government changes its tax tables or withholding schedule. Finally, a "real" payroll program will be more complicated than the one outlined here—for example, it will probably update a record of total withholdings for taxes and retirement made so far in the current year.

Clearly, it is a long way from understanding the overall construction of the program we have sketched to actually writing these programs yourself, formatting them, and loading them into the system so

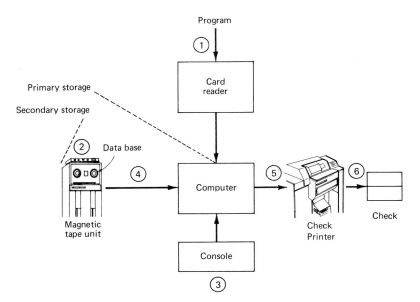

Fig. 13 This figure shows how the payroll program is used.

(1) The operator loads the deck of cards containing the program into the card reader.

(2) The operator places the magnetic tape containing the data base in the magnetic tape unit.

(3) The operator types in the commands at the console which gets the computer to read in the program. The program deck includes job control cards which get the computer to execute the payroll program. It does this by:

(4) Reading one record at a time from the data base, and computing the deductions and total pay.

(5) Sending numbers and positioning information so that

(6) The typewriter types out the check and stub

that they will run correctly. In a book like this, you will not see how to carry out these detailed techniques. Rather, you will see in the next section how to program geometric patterns in the high-level language called LOGO. This will help you appreciate the general idea of writing a program that can use subroutines to solve real-world problems on the computer. This understanding will provide a firm basis for looking at the impact of computers on the cybernetic society.

Suggestions for Further Reading

M. S. Wu: "Introduction to Computer Data Processing." Harcourt, New York, 1975.

Chapter 3 gives a useful account of number systems for computers; while Chapters 4–8 present information on punched-card systems, computer hardware, secondary storage devices, and input and output devices.
T. H. Nelson: "Computer Lib/Dream Machines," Hugo's Book Service, Box 2622, Chicago, Illinois, 60690, 1974.
Pages 36–43 give an overview of different types of computers now in use.

Summary

We studied input and output devices, which transferred information from a form a human user could understand to a form the computer could use. We distinguished interactive processing, in which the user can communicate with the computer while it is running his program, from batch processing. We saw how the central processing unit executed a program, controlling the input and output devices, and using both the high-speed primary memory and the cheaper, larger, but slower, secondary memory of magnetic tape and disk units. We learned what a bit of information is, and studied various types of binary coding, as well as the Hollerith code used for punched cards. Finally, we studied a payroll job. We saw that once a program was punched on a deck of cards, and a data base was set up on magnetic tape, batch processing could handle the job week after week with almost no human effort. We also saw the way in which a paycheck program acted as a subroutine for the overall payroll program.

Glossary

Input device: The *input device* takes the user's data and instructions and transfers them to the memory of the computer.

Output device: The *output device* transforms results generated by the computer into a form the user can understand or use in some other way.

Line printer: A *line printer* is an output device that prints the output line by line.

Central Processing Unit *(CPU)*: The *CPU* is the part of the computer that carries out the instructions in a program: obeying operation instructions, carrying out tests, and controlling input and output devices in response to input and output instructions.

Magnetic tape unit: Just as a tape recorder can store sound on magnetic tape by setting up an appropriate pattern of magnetization, so can a *magnetic tape unit* store information for computer use. It records information from the computer, and can play back stored information to the computer.

Magnetic disk unit: This unit functions like a magnetic tape unit, but using patterns of *magnetization* on a stack of *disks,* instead of a tape, to store information.

Terabit memory: A device that can store a trillion (a million million) bits of information is a *terabit memory*.

Memory: The *memory* of a computer comprises a *primary memory* to and from which the CPU can very quickly move information; and a *secondary memory,* made up of devices like magnetic tape units and magnetic disk units which are larger and cheaper than primary memory, but also much slower.

Peripherals: It is sometimes convenient to distinguish the *mainframe* of the computer—the CPU and primary memory—from *peripherals* which are "added on"—such as input and output devices and secondary memory.

Data base: A *data base* is a collection of *data* on some particular topic—usually stored in secondary memory—which the computer can use again and again on many *different* occasions. It may be divided into *records,* each of which contains information about some specific person, policy, project or other basic unit about which information is collected.

Coding: *Coding* is the process of transforming information from one form to another. Each way of representing information is called a *code*. Besides those discussed in this section, examples of coding include coding a message in some hard-to-read "scrambled" form (a "secret" code) and translating a flow diagram into a program properly written out in some programming language.

Bit: A piece of information representing one of two possible choices, such as 0 or 1, is a *bit*. For example, the pattern of ups and downs of four light switches would be a 4-bit pattern. We say information is in *binary form* when it is coded as a string of *bits* such as the string 0111010110 of 0s and 1s. By contrast, our usual *decimal numbers* are made up of strings of *digits,* each of which represents one of the 10 possible choices 0,1,2,3,4,5,6,7,8,9. An example of coding is transforming a decimal number into *binary code*—a string of 0s and 1s.

Location: The primary memory of a computer is divided into *locations* which can each hold the binary code for an instruction or piece of data. Each location can be referred to by a distinct number, called its *address*. If every location in memory is built with the same number n of two-state devices, it is called an *n-bit machine*. A *word* is the information stored in a single memory location. Thus the words in an n-bit machine are strings of n 0s and 1s.

Register: A *register* is a device within the computer to store an instruction or piece of information. For example, the CPU has registers for holding the current instruction, the data it is operating on, and the address from which the next instruction is to be retrieved from memory.

Interactive mode: The *interactive mode* is the use of a computer through an input–output device called a *terminal* which lets the user monitor the progress of a computation, intervening when something seems to be going wrong, and responding to queries from the computer.

Batch mode: In *batch mode,* the computer executes a complete program without any *interaction* with the user before it has printed out all the results. A *job* comprises a single program together with the data it is to process. A whole stack of jobs—called a *batch*—may be placed in the input devices at any one time. The computer then runs the jobs one after another. The computer operator uses a *console* to initiate the reading in of programs and data for each batch.

Subroutine: A *subroutine* is a program that is to be used again and again, so written that it can be used as part of other larger programs without having to be rewritten in full when we write the other programs; also called a *subprogram* or *subprocedure*.

Job control language: The *programming language* in which we write the instructions (on the *job control cards,* for example) that tell the computer what input is data and what a program, and instructs the computer when to start using a program to process the data.

BCD (Binary-Coded Decimal): *BCD* code is a scheme that uses 6 bits to encode numerals and upper case letters.

EBCDIC (Extended Binary-Coded Decimal Interchange Code): *EBCDIC* is a scheme that uses 8 bits to code digits, upper and lower case letters, and numerous special symbols.

Punched card: One way of communicating with computers is via *punched cards*. Each card has 80 columns, and the punching of holes in each column codes a single character. The usual code is called *Hollerith code*. Typing characters on the keyboard of a *keypunch* causes it to punch the proper code in a card. The *card reader* is the input device which reads the code off a card, and transmits it to the computer in a code suitable for storage; and a *card punch* is the corresponding output device.

Exercises

1. Many computers have speeds measured in MIPS (Millions of Instructions Per Second). An instruction can store or retrieve, typically, 32 bits of information in primary memory. Roughly how many bits can a 3-MIPS computer transfer from primary memory in one minute? If you wrote this information on ordinary lined paper, with 40 zeros or ones to a line, 25 lines to a page, how many pages would you need? (You can use both sides.)

2. Indicate whether the following statements are true or false.
   (a) A "terminal" is a typewriter with a computer inside.
   (b) Magnetic tape devices are considered "peripherals."
   (c) A teletype terminal is a peripheral.
   (d) Core memory and registers are peripherals.
   (e) Secondary storage is faster than primary storage.

3. Suppose that the basic component of a computer was a three-state device, perhaps an electronic circuit with a voltage that was either positive, negative, or neutral. The nonzero digits—those from 1 to 9—could be coded with only two of these devices as indicated below (note that it would take 4 two-state devices to code the same digits):

```
1  - -        4  0-        7  + -
2  -0         5  00        8  +0
3  - +        6  0+        9  + +
```

How many three-state devices do we need to code the alphabet? Upper case, plus lower case, plus the digits, plus any 19 of the special character on the EBCDIC table? How many states does an array of N of these devices have? Why do computers use two-state devices if three-state devices code more compactly?

4. Primary memory is expensive, so computers often use magnetic tape as "secondary storage." This is cheaper, but slower. It is possible to store 1600 BPI (bits per inch) on tape. Unlike audio tape, this comes in 7 or 9 tracks, and can move 100 inches per second. If a tape is 2400 feet long, how many bits can be stored on it? How long would it take to read the entire tape?

5. How can weather satellites produce "billions of numbers each month" and what are these data?

6. (a) Translate the following 6-bit BCD data into ordinary characters (see Fig. 7):

$$111001 \quad 100101 \quad 110110 \quad 111001$$
$$100101 \quad 111001 \quad 010011 \quad 011000$$

   (b) Translate the following EBCDIC data into character data:

$$11110010 \quad 01001110 \quad 11110010 \quad 01111110 \quad 01101111$$

   (c) Write down the binary code for the numbers 20 through 27.

   (d) The binary code for eleven is $1011 = 2^3 + 2^1 + 2^0 = 8 + 2 + 1$. What number has binary code 11010110?

7. Several *small* companies have similar payroll problems, but their retirement plans differ in the percentage to be deducted. Is it worth their while to use a computer for their payroll?

8. Recall the list 0000, 0001, 0010, . . . of 4-bit patterns following Fig. 5. Suppose the numbers are stored in 4 1-bit registers called A, B, C, and D, where A holds the leftmost bit, and D the rightmost bit. Draw a flow diagram for a program that converts a 4-bit number into the next one on the list— where after 1111 we go back to 0000 again. [*Hint:* Start with the program shown in the accompanying figure.]

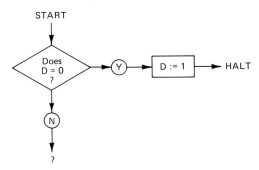

9. Why does the CPU sometimes output to secondary memory (see Fig. 4) instead of always outputting data immediately to the line printer?

10. Why are control signals and data signals kept separate? Consider Fig. 2 and the accompanying discussion of tape-recorder operation. What would happen if the control signals, "PLAY, RECORD, REWIND, . . . ," were input as sound? Could this be more complicated than a mechanical control panel? More expensive? Could a conversation picked up by the microphone accidentally stop or erase the tape? Similarly, consulting Fig. 3, what would happen if control signals and data flowed through the same channels in a computer? What would happen if job control language and data were confused?

11. Why hire a keypunch operator to type data on cards, which a computer operator puts in a card reader, which the card reader passes to the CPU? [Why not have an operator feed information directly to the CPU?] [*Hints:* Consider proofreading, special instruction to people (not in job control language), speed of keypunching, producing data in any order (not necessarily the order to be input).]

12. If a terabit memory can store the number of characters which would fill 30 million sheets of paper, how many 300-page books is this equivalent to? Why not just replace a local book library with a terabit memory? Consider lending, magazines, output devices, copyright laws. Which would you prefer access to? Why?

13. *Library Project:* The Universal Product Code (UPC) uses all those funny-looking parallel bars printed on the wrappers of all supermarket items. UPC uses thin bars, medium bars, thick bars, and spaces. Printed on each label along with the bars are ordinary numerals. Using a few cans, bags, and bottles as clues, can you figure out the code? I was not able to! The entire issue of *IBM Systems Journal,* Vol. 14, No. 1, 1975, is devoted to this, on both technical and lay level. Use it to answer the questions: How is each digit represented? What kind of input device reads UPC? What is its role in the market? How does it affect the consumer?

The Squiral Nebula

Computers can be programmed to draw pictures. In this collection, we see how a single program called SQI can be used to draw different pictures by giving it different numbers. SQI S A W means: take a step of length S, turn through an angle of A degrees, take another step longer by W than the previous one, and keep going—taking longer and longer steps each time, with an angle of A degrees between successive steps.

By choosing different values for S, A, and W we can obtain a surprisingly rich range of pictures, as the following examples made by Kevin Deame show.

SQI 0 350 1 draws a spiral starting from the middle and working out. As the steps get longer, we begin to see the curve breaking up into edges—SQI is short for squiral (square spiral).

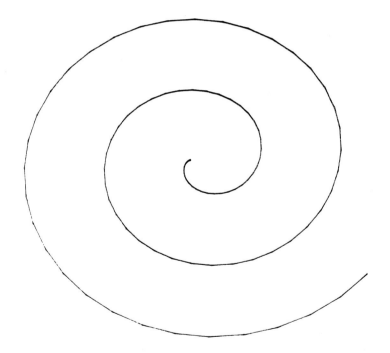

SQI 0 350 1

With SQI 3 50 1, the patterns get more interesting, as the squiral folds back on itself and begins to make new patterns.

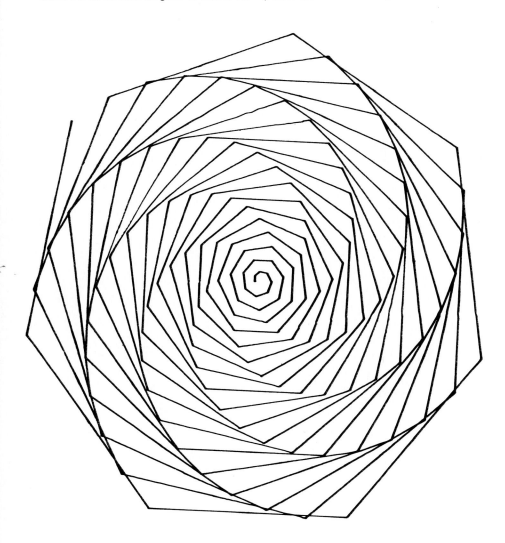

SQI 3 50 1

As the parameters are varied further, we begin to see the emergence of texture :

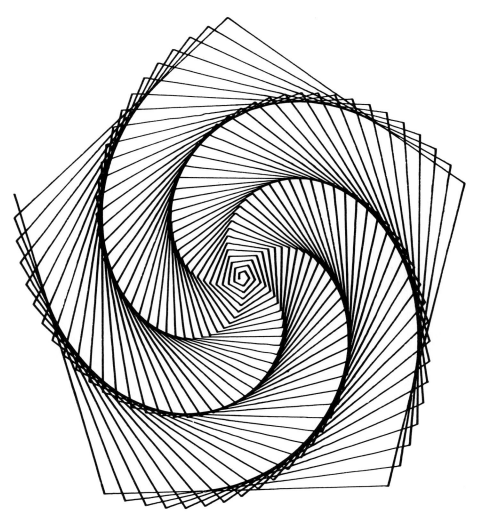

SQI 10 72 3

SQI 0 89 1

and this texture can become very rich indeed :

SQI 10 121 3

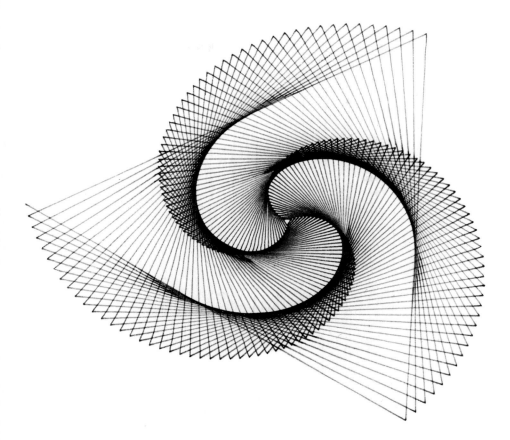

SQI 1 121 1

We close with a surprise. SQI 10 175 3, even though generated by the same program, has a completely different "style."

SQI 10 175 3

The computer made these drawings with a very simple program—and yet already they exhibit a pleasing variety of shape and texture. People argue over whether or not computers can contribute to art. My answer is that they certainly can—so long as we think of the above pictures not as the complete work of art, but rather as single strokes of a wonderful electronic paintbrush.

1.3. TEACHING TURTLE TO NAVIGATE

We mentioned in Section 1.1 that there are many **high-level languages** which help people write programs with much less effort, and far fewer mistakes, than if they were writing in machine language. [If you have forgotten what machine language is, remember that you can look it up in the index at the back of this book, and find the page on which its glossary definition occurs.] These high-level languages include COBOL for business applications, FORTRAN for engineering work, LISP or PLANNER for studies in artificial intelligence, and many, many others besides.

In this section we study the language called LOGO, and use it to write programs that control a simple robot called TURTLE, making it travel intricate and interesting paths. LOGO is not a very useful language "out in the real world." COBOL, FORTRAN, and LISP are all better for their stated applications. However, LOGO has several advantages, and that is why we have chosen it here:

(1)   It is *very* easy to learn. LOGO was developed by Seymour Papert of the Massachusetts Institute of Technology and by the Cambridge, Massachusetts consulting firm of Bolt Beranek and Newman to give young teenagers a feel for programming, but even nine-year-olds can use and enjoy it.

(2)   It shows that computers can be used to make pictures—a very different thing from the **number-crunching** and record retrieving of such programs as the payroll program.

(3)   Even if you do not have a computer, you can still understand the LOGO programs, and follow the LOGO instructions to draw patterns yourself.

Writing in LOGO will give you some idea of what is required to go from a problem to a program that solves it; of how easy it is to make mistakes along the way; and of the fact that it is up to you, not the computer, to correct them. The computer will follow the instructions you give it, not the instructions you thought you gave it!

The Basic Instructions

To program the TURTLE's movements, you will need a computer with a LOGO translator which will let it "understand" your high-level programs. You will need a terminal to let you communicate with the computer, and you will need an output device. This can be a TURTLE with its control box (Fig. 1); or it can be a graphics terminal (more about these in Section 2.1) with a TV screen on which the computer can draw a picture of the path that the TURTLE would have taken; or it can be an x–y plotter (we saw one in our tour of the computer center) in which the computer moves a pen back and forth to draw the picture on a piece of paper.

In the rest of the section, we shall talk as if we were programming an actual TURTLE. If you use an x–y plotter or a graphics terminal, you will find it easy to change a few minor details of our description—the LOGO programming does not change.

To control TURTLE, we type in LOGO programs at the terminal. The computer is equipped with special **translator** software, and so it transforms our programs into a form that the TURTLE control box understands. This control box sends instructions via a connecting cable to make the TURTLE move forward or backward, turn through some angle, turn a light on or off, toot a horn, and raise or lower a pen. When the pen is lowered, the TURTLE will draw its path on a large sheet of paper on which it has been placed.

As our first example of a LOGO instruction, let us see what happens when we type in

FORWARD 100

(note the space after the D) and press the carriage return key after the 100. The carriage return is our signal that the instruction is complete. Without it, the computer just waits—for all it knows, we might be

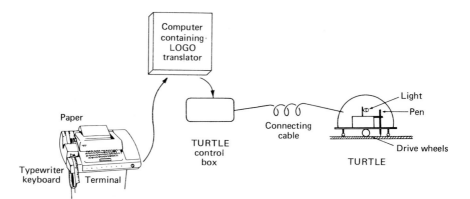

Fig. 1 LOGO programs typed in at the terminal are *translated* by the computer to yield a sequence of commands which the control box can transmit to determine the behavior of the TURTLE.

pausing in the middle of typing FORWARD 1001 or FORWARD 10029. The computer will translate FORWARD 100 into a string of 100 separate "MOVE FORWARD ONE MILLIMETER" commands. On receiving each command, the TURTLE control box will activate TURTLE's motors just enough to cause the drive wheels to advance the TURTLE one millimeter. Thus the overall effect of the command FORWARD 100 is to cause the TURTLE to go forward 100 millimeters. If we then typed in

FORWARD 73

completing the line with a carriage return, the TURTLE would move forward 73 millimeters.

We may type in the command

LAMPON

(always completing the line with a carriage return) which will cause the control box to switch on TURTLE's lamp, and the command

LAMPOFF

which will turn it off.

When typing in a program for a machine, we must always follow the format specifications very carefully. If we typed in LAMP OFF—with a space after the P—the computer would *not* turn the lamp off. Instead, it would make the terminal type out

I DO NOT UNDERSTAND LAMP

Remember that the job of the translator software in the computer is to translate your typed LOGO instructions into commands for the control box. If you type a space after P, the translator takes this to signal that LAMP is a complete word, and so looks in its memory to find what the word means. Since the word LAMP is not stored in memory, it types out the **error message** I DO NOT UNDERSTAND LAMP. When you get an error message, it means that the computer will ignore the last line that was typed in and wait for you to send in the correct message. Then you can type in LAMPOFF and get the lamp off after all. [You can also use a special key to scrub a line if you spot an error before pressing the carriage return.]

Here are some other commands—each with their interpretation described to the right. After typing each command, hit the carriage return button, and the computer will send the proper instructions to the TURTLE control box.

Command	Effect
TOOT	The TURTLE toots its horn.
PENDOWN	Lower the pen (so that TURTLE's movements will now be traced out).
PENUP	Raise the pen (so that TURTLE stops leaving tracks).
FORWARD 20	Go forward 20 millimeters.
BACK 193	Go back 193 millimeters. [Note the space: if you typed in BACK193 then hit the carriage return, the computer would type out I DO NOT UNDERSTAND BACK193.]
LEFT 46	Turn left through an angle of 46° relative to the direction in which TURTLE is facing—the cable is the "tail." This changes the direction TURTLE is facing, but not its position. It does *not* mean "Move 46 mm. to the left of your present position."
RIGHT 32	Turn right through 32°.

To make TURTLE draw a square which is 20 millimeters along each side, we type in the instructions listed in Fig. 2a. If TURTLE starts at point A in Fig. 2b facing in direction →, the result will be the square shown in the figure. Each FORWARD 20 causes TURTLE to draw a side of the square, while RIGHT 90 makes it turn 90° to the *right* on

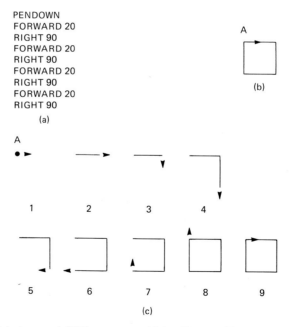

```
PENDOWN
FORWARD 20
RIGHT 90
FORWARD 20
RIGHT 90
FORWARD 20
RIGHT 90
FORWARD 20
RIGHT 90
      (a)
```

Fig. 2 (a) shows a LOGO program which will cause TURTLE to trace a square like that shown in (b), with 20 millimeters to a side. (c) shows the path traced out by TURTLE at the end of each instruction. The arrowhead shows the direction in which TURTLE is facing at each stage.

reaching the end of the side (as shown in Fig. 2c). TURTLE ends up facing in the same direction as that in which it started. [Would the picture *look* different if we had left out the last RIGHT 90 command?]

Naming Programs and Subroutines

Suppose that you wanted TURTLE to draw the square in Fig. 2b several times. It would be pleasant to teach the computer some new words, so that it will "understand" that some word like SQUARE was an abbreviation for the above 9-line program. Fortunately, the people who designed the LOGO translator gave it the ability to "learn" new words. For example, we might like to use FORT (or any other simple word) as an abbreviation for the two instructions

FORWARD 20
RIGHT 90

which we used again and again in the last program. To do this, we type in

TO FORT
FORWARD 20
RIGHT 90
END

Starting the input with TO FORT tells the translator that FORT is going to be your abbreviation of the program or subroutine you type in next. (Remember that a **subroutine** is a program to be used as part of another program.) The END tells the translator you have finished typing in the definition of FORT. When you give it a definition, the computer does not make TURTLE move. Instead it simply stores the definition in memory for later use. Once we have given the translator the definition, it will unpack each FORT it sees as the two instructions it stands for. For example, it can then follow the program

PENDOWN
FORT
FORT
FORT
FORT

just as if it were the original program of Fig. 2a.

It should be stressed that there was nothing special about the choice of FORT as the name of our subroutine. We could just as well have written

```
TO  SCRAMBLE
FORWARD  20
RIGHT  90
END
```

and then written

```
PENDOWN
SCRAMBLE
SCRAMBLE
SCRAMBLE
SCRAMBLE
```

to get TURTLE to draw the square.

Parameters

Having defined FORT, we can repeat the trick again to define
SQUARE:

```
TO  SQUARE
PENDOWN
FORT
FORT
FORT
FORT
END
```

Then every time we type in SQUARE at the terminal, TURTLE will trace
out a square, 20 millimeters on a side, as in Fig. 2b. However, while—
in making geometric designs—we may often want TURTLE to draw a
square, it is unlikely that it will be 20 millimeters on a side. Can we
make the translator understand that

SQUARE 20

means "Draw a 20-millimeter square," that

SQUARE 4197

means "Draw a square 4197 millimeters long," and so on? What we
are saying is that we want our instruction to have a **parameter** in it—a
number that we can fill in each time we use the instruction.

The A in FORWARD A can be filled in with any number. This is an
example, then, of an instruction with a parameter. Each time we
choose a different number to fill in A, we obtain a different instruction,

namely that which makes TURTLE advance the given number of millimeters.

We can carry these parameters into our definitions by using a letter or word in the TO . . . line of the definition, and then using that same letter or word in the program inside the definition. For example,

```
TO F A
FORWARD A
END
```

gives us a handy abbreviation for FORWARD A. It tells the computer to translate F 111 as FORWARD 111, F 294 as FORWARD 294, and so on.

With this use of parameters, it is now easy to build our "general square program" with the name SQUARE SIDE which will get TURTLE to trace out a square whose side length in millimeters is whatever number we type in place of SIDE:

```
TO FORT SIDE
FORWARD SIDE
RIGHT 90
END
TO SQUARE SIDE
PENDOWN
FORT SIDE
FORT SIDE
FORT SIDE
FORT SIDE
END
```

Recursion

Mathematicians have a notation that uses an exclamation mark. When they write 5!, they do not mean "5, by golly," but instead they read it as "5 **factorial**" and understand that it means "the number you obtain by multiplying together all the numbers from 1 up to and including 5." Thus we have

$$1! = 1$$
$$2! = 2 \times 1 = 2$$
$$3! = 3 \times 2 \times 1 = 6$$
$$4! = 4 \times 3 \times 2 \times 1 = 24$$
$$5! = 5 \times 4 \times 3 \times 2 \times 1 = 120$$

If you look carefully, you will see that

$$1! = 1$$
$$2! = 2 \times 1!$$
$$3! = 3 \times 2!$$
$$4! = 4 \times 3!$$
$$5! = 5 \times 4!$$

Thus we can write out the definition of n factorial for any number n in two ways:

$$n! = n \times (n - 1) \times \cdot \cdot \cdot \times 3 \times 2 \times 1$$

or

$$1! = 1 \quad \text{and} \quad n! = n \times (n - 1)!$$

We call this second definition of factorial an example of **recursion**—because the definition of factorial **recurs** again and again in the definition of $n!$ (unless n equals 1).

Let us now see how recursion may be used in LOGO programs. Leaving parameters aside from the moment, let us see how we can use recursion to avoid having to write FORT four times in defining SQUARE. Consider the following definition:

```
TO SQ
FORT
SQ
END
```

(To simplify things, assume that we make sure the pen is down before typing SQ, so that we need not include PENDOWN in the definition.) What happens if we give the computer this definition, then type in the single command SQ? The translator will consult its definition table, and see that SQ is defined by a *recursion,* with FORT followed by SQ. It then goes to execute the first instruction, finds that FORT translates to FORWARD 20 followed by RIGHT 90 and so sends TURTLE forward 20 millimeters and then 90° to the right. It proceeds to the second instruction—and finds that it is back at SQ again! So it proceeds to send TURTLE forward 20 millimeters, and 90° to the right—and goes back to SQ again.

Thus the flow diagram for SQ is that shown in Fig. 3a. The program is just the endless repetition of the FORT subroutine. The program SQ certainly sends TURTLE around a 20-millimeters square (Fig. 3b)—but there is no terminating condition to make it stop after drawing four sides, and TURTLE will keep going round and round the

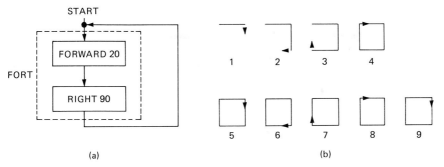

(a)   (b)

Fig. 3   (a) shows the flow diagram for SQ; (b) shows the trace of TURTLE after the first few passages around the loop.

square until we override the computer and tell TURTLE to stop (which is done by simultaneously pressing the "CONTROL" and "C" keys on the terminal keyboard).

Clearly, then, we need some sort of **counter** to count each side as TURTLE draws it. We then want the computer to tell TURTLE to stop when the counter reaches 4. In other words, we start the counter at 0, add 1 to it each time we go round the loop in the flow diagram, and stop when the count hits 4.

Before going on, it may help the reader to recall our discussion of the digital wristwatch. We needed several registers to store the value of the current second, minute, hour, and so on, inside the computer. (Remember: a digital wristwatch is a special-purpose computer.) We then had special instructions to update the numbers to keep the correct time. In the same way, the LOGO translator will need to be able to set aside a location in the computer's memory for each counter. We must now spell out the LOGO instructions used to update the number in the counter.

We have already seen "commands to TURTLE" instructions and "define a new subroutine" instructions. What follows are the LOGO instructions for storing numbers, updating them, and **testing** their values. The first is the MAKE instruction.

$$\text{MAKE} \quad A \quad A+1$$

is the LOGO way to write $A := A+1$. It does not ask the impossible, like "make 2 equal 3." Instead, A is the name of a storage location, like a *counter,* into which the program may place values, and the instruction is short for

Make the *new* contents of A equal to the *old* contents of A plus 1

Thus if A contained the number 2 before executing the instruction, it would contain 3 afterwards.

$$\text{MAKE A } 2*B$$

would be LOGO for "Make the new contents of A equal to 2 times the old contents of B."

LOGO uses instructions starting with IF for its tests. For example, the instruction

$$\text{IF A}=4 \text{ STOP}$$

tells the computer "If the number in counter A is 4, stop computing—otherwise go on to the next instruction."

Now consider the revised program definition (to which we give the name SQR, so the translator will not confuse it with SQ)

```
TO SQR
FORT
MAKE A A+1
IF A=4 STOP
SQR
END
```

(Note that both A+1 and A=4 are typed without any spaces.) The translator is set up so that we may create a counter initialized to the value 0 by typing Make A 0 before we type in SQR. Then when we type in SQR, the counter will be 0, but the counter is not reset—and it will hold the value 4 on exit from SQR. To see this, look at the accompanying tabulation to see what happens as the translator goes through the instructions in SQR.

Instruction	Contents of A	TURTLE movement
FORT	0	FORWARD 20 then RIGHT 90
MAKE A A+1	1	
IF A=4 STOP	1	(Since 1 ≠ 4, the computer goes on to SQR, which it translates as FORT, . . .)
FORT	1	FORWARD 20 then RIGHT 90
MAKE A A+1	2	
IF A=4 STOP	2	
FORT	2	FORWARD 20 then RIGHT 90
MAKE A A+1	3	
IF A=4 STOP	3	
FORT	3	FORWARD 20 then RIGHT 90
MAKE A A+1	4	
IF A=4 STOP	4	(Since 4 = 4, the computer stops—and TURTLE has traced four sides of the square, just as desired)

Thus, any time you want to draw a square, you first type in PENDOWN if the pen is not down; then type in MAKE A 0 to get the counter A *reset* to 0 (since it will be set to 4 if you have previously used SQR); then type in SQR to have TURTLE carry out the square-drawing movements.

To summarize, the moral of the SQ and SQR programs is the same as that of our study of loops in Section 1.1.: "If at first you don't succeed, try, try again—but keep testing to see if you've succeeded yet." What is different about SQ and SQR is the use of *recursion:* defining loops in the program by *letting the program call itself*—so that the use of the program may *recur* again and again during its execution.

We can combine our knowledge of parameters and recursion to modify SQR to obtain a program SQV which draws a square with a side of any desired length—this length being indicated by the parameter SIDE:

```
TO SQV SIDE
FORWARD SIDE
RIGHT 90
MAKE A A+1
IF A=4 STOP
SQV SIDE
END
```

This definition tells the translator that whenever you type in SQV followed by a space and then a number, it is to use the above program with SIDE replaced by that number. For example, if we type in SQV 50, the translator will decode this as

```
FORWARD 50
RIGHT 90
MAKE A A+1
IF A=4 STOP
SQV 50
```

Remember, though, that once it has started obeying your instruction, the computer does *not* reset the counter A to 0 each time it interprets SQV 50—instead it preserves the contents for the next run around the loop.

We can have more than one parameter—and in fact can use a parameter to keep count during our recursion. To show this, we now write a program SQUR SIDE N which draws N sides of a square of length SIDE.

Definition	Comments
TO SQUR SIDE N	
IF N=0 STOP	Stopping condition: stop if no more sides are required.
FORWARD SIDE⎫ RIGHT 90 ⎭	The TURTLE instructions
SQUR SIDE N−1	Recursion line: one less side to go.
END	

Instead of using a counter to count *up,* we use N to count *down* until, when N = 0, the instruction IF N=0 STOP halts the computation. Note that if we type in SQUR 30 0, the IF condition will stop TURTLE before it moves at all—drawing 0 sides as desired. We show the behavior for SQUR 30 3 in Fig. 4.

To close the section, we look at the program Kevin Deame used to draw all the geometric patterns in our collection, "The Squiral Nebula." It is called SQI and is defined as follows:

```
TO SQI S A W M
IF S>M STOP
FORWARD S
RIGHT A
SQI S+W F W M
END
```

TURTLE Track	Value of N	Comment
→	3	N ≠ 0, so go on to
		FORWARD 30
		RIGHT 90
		Then replace N by N − 1, and go to SQUR 30 2
30 mm	2	N ≠ 0, so go on to
		FORWARD 30
		RIGHT 90
		Then replace N by N − 1, and go to SQUR 30 1
	1	N ≠ 0, so go on to
		FORWARD 30
		RIGHT· 90
		Then replace N by N − 1 and go to SQUR 30 0
	0	N = 0, so halt, with 3 sides completed, as desired.

Fig. 4   Execution of SQUR 30 3.

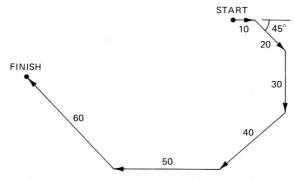

Fig. 5 The path of TURTLE for SQI 10 45 10 60.

By now, you should have little trouble seeing what the program does. Each time around the loop of the program, the computer makes TURTLE move forward a distance S mm, then turn right through an angle A°. The computer then adds W mm to obtain the new value of the side length S, and starts over again. The program keeps on running till the first time the new side length exceeds the stopping value M. Figure 5 shows what TURTLE does for SQI 10 45 10 60. TURTLE goes 10 mm further each time, turning 45° right after completing each side, until the new side length exceeds 60—so that it completes six sides (since it is not true that 60 > 60, but is true that 70 > 60). The figures in "The Squiral Nebula" show the amazing variety that can be achieved with a single simple program.

Suggestions for Further Reading

D. Stemple: "TURTLE Manual." University Computing Center, University of Massachusetts, Amherst, Massachusetts, June 1973.
   This is a useful summary of the basic LOGO commands and how to use them.
R. DuBoulay and T. O'Shea: "How to Work a LOGO Machine: A Primer for ELOGO," DAI Research Report, Department of Artificial Intelligence, University of Edinburgh.
   Perhaps the best primer available for any version of the LOGO language—in this case the E(dinburgh) version.
R. Mallary: Computer Sculpture: Six Levels of Cybernetics, *Artforum,* May 1969, pp. 29–35.
   A look at the impact of computers on art.
N. Lindgren: Art and Technology, *IEEE Spectrum,* Part I, April 1969, pp. 59–68; Part II, May 1969, pp. 46–56.
   Explores the possibilities for collaboration between artists and technologists.

Summary

We have seen how to program in LOGO. In particular, we have seen how to define programs using parameters and recursion. Our last example showed that even a simple program can generate many different patterns with differing choice of the input parameters.

Glossary

High-level language: A programming language which a human finds easier to use than *machine language* is a high-level language. A *translator* is a special program that a computer needs to enable it to execute a program written in high-level language.

Error message: A message typed out by a computer when the user has made a mistake that the computer can detect is an *error message*. The computer can easily be programmed to detect when the user types in an instruction that does not belong to the programming language. It is unlikely that a computer could be programmed to tell the user "YOU TYPED IN FORWARD 100. DIDNT YOU MEAN FORWARD 200?"

Number-crunching: What a program does if it just works with numbers is number-crunching. A payroll program does both number-crunching and record retrieval. There are many programs, however, that draw pictures, or process texts, and so on, which are not number-crunchers.

Subroutine: A *subroutine* is a program that is to be used again and again, so written that it can be used as part of other larger programs without having to be rewritten in full when we write the other programs; also called a *subprogram* or *subprocedure*.

Parameter: A given command or subroutine may have several *parameters*—entries that must be replaced with numbers before the computer knows what to do. For example, the instruction FORWARD X has one parameter, namely X. When we replace X by a number we obtain a command that the computer can execute—FORWARD 100, for example, will get the computer to send 100 "one step forward" commands to a robot.

Counter: A *counter* is a place in which a computer stores a number which keeps track of the number of times some process has been repeated, e.g., keeping a count of how many times a loop has been traversed, or how many numbers in a list have been added together, or . . . .

Test: An instruction is a *test* if it tells the computer to test whether or not some specified condition is met—such as whether or not some number equals zero. The outcome of the test determines which instruction the computer will go to next.

Factorial: For each whole positive number n, we write $n!$ (pronounced "n factorial") to stand for the product of all the numbers from 1 up to and including n. Thus, $4! = 1 \times 2 \times 3 \times 4 = 24$.

Recursion: Defining loops in a program by letting the program call itself—so that the use of the program may recur again and again during its execution—is a *recursion*.

Exercises

1. Write a program TRI SIDE that makes TURTLE draw a triangle with all three sides of the same length SIDE.

2. If TURTLE can only move forward, backward, and turn through some angle, is it possible for TURTLE to draw a perfect circle? Approximate a circle?

3. Suppose you have available subroutines that, for each letter of the alphabet, can draw that letter—starting at one end, and finishing at the other. If you want to use them to spell your name, can you just tell TURTLE to make one letter after another? If not, what must you add to the program?

4. If a computer can detect a mistake by a user and print out an appropriate error message, why can it not just correct the mistake and continue with program execution? Give two examples.

5. Suppose you wanted to have TURTLE run a box maze made out of boards and discover its way out of the maze. What extra gadgets would TURTLE need? What instruction(s) would you have to add to TURTLE's repertoire?

6. Suppose you have a program that will draw one tree. How can you use this program to draw a forest of trees?

7. Given a function with the recursive definition

$$1@ = 5, \qquad n@ = 1 + 3 \times [(n - 1)@]$$

calculate $3@$.

8. Here is a recursive program for TURTLE:

```
TO SPRINT N
IF N = 0 STOP
FORWARD N
SPRINT N − 1
END
```

What will the program

```
PENDOWN
SPRINT 2
END
```

cause the TURTLE to do?

9. Why does TURTLE have the instructions PENUP and PENDOWN? Why not just leave the pen in writing position?

10. Why not put the computer into the TURTLE itself, instead of using a connecting cable, translator program, and control box? After all, there are only a couple of dozen instructions needed.

11. Suppose TURTLE could follow some kind of signal (like a radio wave or light beam). Can you think of any new problems or new behavior that TURTLE could demonstrate? What could you do with two TURTLE's that you cannot do with one?

12. A *real* squiral (the word was made up by a child in elementary school!) is a square spiral like that shown in the accompanying figure:

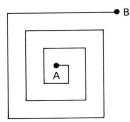

(a) Write a program that starts TURTLE at A, and draws a squiral with the first side 8 mm long, and with each successive side 3 mm longer than the one before it—without ever stopping.

(b) Use recursion to write a program that draws the squiral of the same dimensions as in (a) but starting at B and *stopping* at A.

1.4. TEXT PROCESSING

The payroll job of Section 1.2 is an example of what "everybody" knows a computer can do. It involves retrieving records from a data base and then doing number-crunching—taking piles of numbers, carrying out arithmetic on them, and printing out the results. However, a computer can be used for many symbol-manipulating jobs that have nothing to do with arithmetic. In Section 1.3, we used the computer to draw pictures—programming the movements of TURTLE, a simple robot. [We shall have a lot more to say about robots—especially about how they can "see," "plan," and "talk"—in Chapter 5.] In this section, we study how a computer can be used to help prepare an index for a book, and see how computers can process the typed or printed text of a book or a magazine.

Interactive Preparation of an Index

We first see how a human might use a computer in an interactive mode to simplify the task of indexing a book.

An **index** for a book is an alphabetically arranged list of words and phrases, with one or more page numbers following each entry—pointing the reader to pages on which information about that entry may be found. In making the index, then, the indexer of a book must try to guess the words that might come to the mind of a reader when looking for something in the book. What makes index preparation difficult is that very often the word in the index does not appear on the pages to which the index refers. For example, the phrase "preparing apple pie" on page 37 of a book might yield the following entries in the index:

> apple pie, 37
> cooking, 37
> dessert, 37
> food, 37
> pie, 37

A good indexer is one who can think of just the right words to put in the index. If the book is a cookbook, he would not put "food" or "cooking" in the index, since they are mentioned on almost every page. Further, a cookbook might be designed so that all the desserts are listed in Chapter 5, say—and then the index would have

> dessert, *see* Chapter 5

instead of a list of all the pages on which a dessert was mentioned.

Here, then, is the "program" that a good indexer will follow in reading the book.

1. Set N = 1.
2. Read page N.
3. For every word or phrase W that describes something on page N that is interesting or important, take a fresh file card and write on it the word or phrase W followed by the number N.
4. Is page N the last page of the book? If the answer is YES, go on to 5. If NO, increase N by 1, N := N + 1, and then go to 2. [In more human terms: turn the page and repeat the process until you have read the whole book.]
5. Arrange the cards in alphabetical order of the Ws. Then merge all the cards with the same W, listing all the Ns in increasing numerical order on the one card that remains for W. Type out the contents of the cards in that order, and you have your index.

What is important and interesting about this "program" or procedure that the human indexer follows is that *almost* every step can be done by a computer. Unfortunately, it is the most interesting part that the computer *cannot* do: telling what words or phrases describe something interesting or important on a page. We shall discuss this in the third subsection, and in the last subsection we shall discuss cases in which we might let the computer prepare an index anyway.

What we want to stress here is that the author of a book has no trouble finding the Ws that are interesting or important; but that he has a lot of trouble keeping track of hundreds of file cards. However, doing the electronic equivalent of keeping track of file cards is one of the things that a computer does very well. This suggests that we *share* the work between the human and the computer. Let us write down the instructions we might give a human for such an **interactive** preparation of an index, and then outline a program that will get a computer to do its part of the job.

Here are the instructions to the human indexer:

0. Set the book up so that you can read it comfortably and at the same time type words on the terminal keyboard.
1. Turn to the next page you want to index. Say it is page M. Type Page=M on the keyboard, followed by a carriage return.
2. For each word or phrase W that describes something on page M that is interesting or important, type in W followed by a carriage return.
3. Repeat 1 and 2 for every page you want indexed. When you have finished, simply type in PRINTOUT, and the computer will type out the index for you.

With facilities like this at his disposal, a human indexer will find his job relatively pleasant, and will be able to do the job far more quickly, and with far less strain, than if he had to juggle all those file cards.

To handle its share of the task, the computer has two main problems: adding entries to the list it is storing for the index; and rearranging the entries to get them in alphabetical order. The first uses an INSERT subroutine, which we now describe, while the second requires a sorting routine, which we shall briefly describe later.

We will describe the problem of adding entries to the list in rather high-level terms, but in such a way that we can see that the job can be spelled out in sufficient detail for a computer to handle it. Briefly, we assume that the computer has in memory a list of entries of the form of a word W followed by one or more numbers, with each number preceded by a comma. For example,

APPLE, 7, 29

means that information about apples can be found on page 7 and page 29. We want to write a program called

INSERT W N

with two **parameters** W and N, where W is a word and N is a number. If W already has an entry, then the program will add N to the end of that entry; but if W has no entry, then the program will add a new entry to the list. For example, if we type in

INSERT APPLE 7

before an entry for APPLE is on the list, the computer will add a new entry—APPLE, 7—to the list. If, however, we next type in INSERT APPLE 29 the computer will *not* create a new entry APPLE, 29 but will instead replace APPLE, 7 by the entry APPLE, 7, 29.

We may thus draw the flow diagram for INSERT W N shown in Fig. 1. This looks simple enough, but it conceals two problems: The first is that, in setting aside part of the computer memory to store the list, we must specify how much space is reserved for each entry; but if a term is frequently discussed in the book we are indexing, it may *overflow* the allotted space. Suppose we allowed 20 characters to an entry. Then (count the blank spaces too!)

FOOD, 19, 37, 64, 91

will fit in the reserved space (exactly 20 spaces), but there is not room

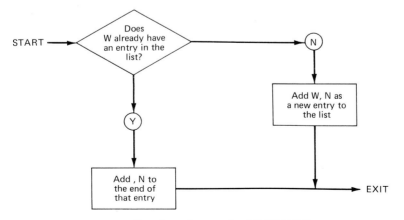

Fig. 1 First flow diagram for INSERT W N.

for more. One solution is to start a *new* entry for food. This yields the revised flow diagram for INSERT W N shown in Fig. 2, where we say that an entry is full if the number of characters in it plus the number of characters in N is greater than 16 (for adding a space followed by the comma and N would then take more than 20 spaces).

The second problem, briefly, is: "Where do the new entries go?" Ideally, we would like each entry in alphabetical order. However, we do not know in advance which entries will occur in the index and so we may not have enough space to insert, say, APOPLEXY between APE and APPLE. It is often too expensive to relocate all the other entries each time we need space for a new one. One solution is simply to add each new entry at the end of the index. Then, *when the entries are completed,* we can have the computer use a **sorting program** which will arrange all the entries in alphabetical order. The human indexer calls the sorting program when he types PRINTOUT. Writing an efficient sorting program is a real challenge, which we will not take up here. Instead, let us simply look at a program that sorts numbers.

To make it very simple, we consider the case where the user gives the computer only three numbers, and the computer sorts them in increasing order. For example, (2, 9, 7) would be sorted as (2, 7, 9); (3, 9, 11) is left as (3, 9, 11); and (4, 3, 4) is sorted as (3, 4, 4). The basic idea is to look at the first two numbers A and B. If $A \leq B$, we leave them in that order. If A is larger than B, however, we change the order:

Starting with (2, 9, 7), we leave (2, 9) as is.
Starting with (3, 9, 11), we leave (3, 9) as is.
Starting with (4, 3, 4), we change (4, 3) to (3, 4).

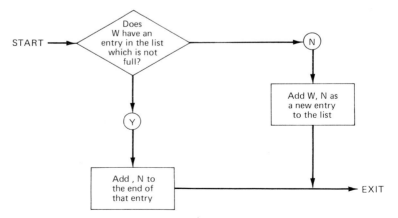

Fig. 2 Flow diagram for INSERT W N to take care of overflows.

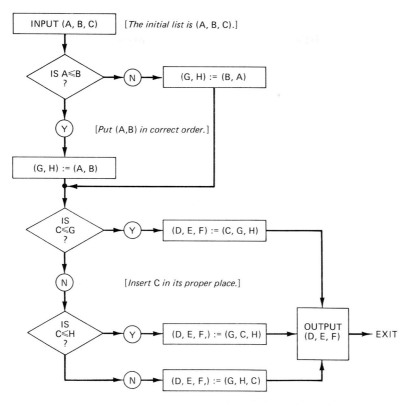

Fig. 3 Flow diagram for sorting three numbers in increasing order.

Then we take the third number C, and compare it to the numbers in the earlier list to determine where to put it:

> Inserting 7 in the right place in (2, 9) gives (2, 7, 9).
> Inserting 11 in the right place in (3, 9) gives (3, 9, 11).
> Inserting 4 in the right place in (3, 4) gives (3, 4, 4).

Figure 3 shows the flow diagram for going from the input list (A, B, C) to the output list (D, E, F). We use (G, H) for the sorted order of the two-element list (A, B). You can check that the program does the right thing for our three examples.

Clearly, a sorting program that would arrange index entries in alphabetical order would be much more complicated, but it is also clear that such a program can indeed be written to get a computer to do the job. Suppose, then, that we have a program called INDEX that will sort the list in the computer's memory and then print it out. With this we can illustrate the action of the computer in interactive index-

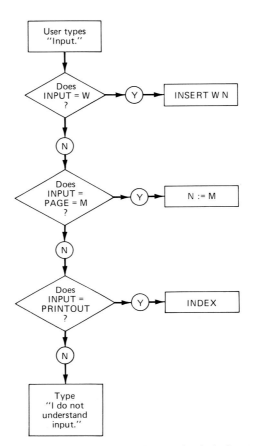

Fig. 4 Flow diagram for interactive indexing.

ing by the flow diagram of Fig. 4. When the user types in PAGE=M, the computer simply updates the number in its "page-number register" N; when the user types in W the program inserts W, N in the list it is preparing, using its page-number register to obtain the current value of N; when the user types in PRINTOUT, the computer uses INDEX as a subroutine to sort and print out the index. If the user types in anything else, the computer returns an **error message.**

Getting a Text into the Machine

In the interactive indexing job, it was the human who read the book, not the computer. For other jobs—we shall describe some later in the section—it is the task of the computer to "read" the book. We must then have the book in a form to which the computer can have electronic access without further human intervention. There are two main approaches:

(a) Retype the book at a terminal that will produce a coded version on magnetic tape in a form that the computer can access via a magnetic tape unit.

(b) Take typed or printed pages and put them into an **optical character recognition (OCR)** system that will scan the letters line-by-line, recognizing the letters and coding them onto magnetic tape for the computer.

We shall say more about OCR systems below. First, we should note that a magnetic tape may be available for a book simply because of the way it was made. In many cases, the people who print books use magnetic tape in setting up the type from which a book is printed. The compositor, the person who types up the book for printing, does so at a special keyboard which has keys for both the letter and the type of printing. An ordinary typewriter lets you specify whether a letter will be UPPER or lower case; but a compositor's keyboard also lets him specify the typeface—whether the letter will be *italic* or **boldface,** large, or small, etc. In older systems, hitting the key would cause the proper piece of lead type to fall into place. In the new computer typesetting systems, hitting the key causes the code for the letter and typeface to be stored on magnetic tape. At the same time, a picture of what the printed page would look like can be displayed on a TV-like screen (we say more about computer graphics in Section 2.1), so that the compositor can see any mistakes and correct them then and there. The completed, edited, magnetic tape is then fed into a machine that reads the code, selects a picture of the coded letter, and projects it into the correct place on a photographic film—to produce a master copy of the printed page. Clearly, the magnetic tape can be saved to be used for purposes other than typesetting. In particular, it can be fed to a computer for further analysis.

Suppose, however, that you have a copy of a printed book—or perhaps just a typescript—and that no magnetic tape is available. You could have a typist retype the whole document at a computer terminal to make a magnetic tape, but this is a huge and expensive job. It would be far more pleasant if a computer system could "read" the page itself, converting each character into computer code. In fact, there do exist optical character recognition (OCR) systems that will scan a page of type line-by-line and letter-by-letter, recognizing whether each letter in turn is "a," or "b," or "c," or . . . and placing the computer code for the letter on magnetic tape. Unfortunately, OCR systems do not work very well—and to get acceptable performance, it is often necessary to use a special typeface. Thus we seem to be back where we started—it is unlikely that the book will be printed in the right typeface for the OCR system to read. However, the situation is not so bad. It is cheaper, quicker, and easier to type at a typewriter equipped with the OCR-readable typeface, and then to have an OCR system code this for the machine, than to type into the computer directly. This is because a typewriter is much cheaper than a system for coding onto magnetic tape. It is better to have the slow operation—the human typing—done on a cheap machine, and then have the computer get through its job rather quickly—and thus less expensively.

Banks use OCR systems to scan checks to automatically update accounts. The characters used on checks are especially easy for an OCR system to read. A code like

$$\text{⑈06092049⑈}$$

printed on the check indicates the bank that issued it, and a similar code indicates the acount number. A human operator reads the amount of the check—OCR systems to recognize human script are still inefficient and prohibitively expensive—and types a code like

$$\text{⑆0000002500⑆}$$

in the bottom right-hand corner—in this case to indicate that the check was for $25.00. Note that the code leaves space for amounts just one cent short of a hundred million dollars! The check is then fed to the computer which automatically ensures that the right account is debited the right amount. Such systems do make mistakes, although very rarely.

Computers Cannot Do Everything

We said that the heart of indexing was to find words or phrases that *described* something interesting on a page, even if the word itself *did not occur* on the page. In this subsection, we spell out why it is almost impossible at the present time to write a computer program to prepare a really good index for books on a wide variety of topics.

In trying to write such a program, we would want the computer to recognize what words to include in an index besides the words on the page. For example, we might want to include an entry for FOOD

for every food-word we add to the index; and then add an entry for
SOUP if the food is a soup, and so on. Thus we might program the
computer to carry out the operation of Fig. 5 for every food word.

This is a very unsatisfactory program. For one thing, it will make
entries for APPLE and PIE, when you really want a single entry for
APPLE PIE. More importantly, it begs the question of how to specify a
subroutine that will let the computer conduct the test "Is W a food
word?" A subroutine for this would have to include a list of every food
word. If the book includes unusual food names like ZABAGLIONE (an
Italian dessert), which might not occur in a standard food-word list,

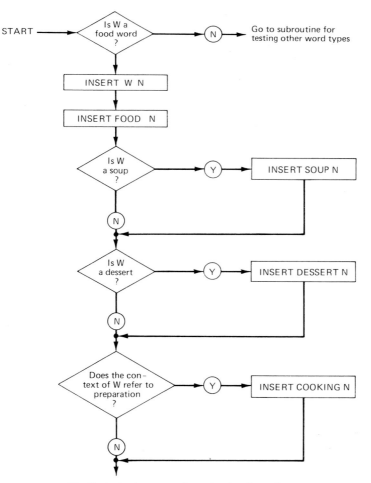

Fig. 5   Indexing operations for food words.

then the computer would fail to index it as a food word. A human indexer solves the problem by reading what the page says about zabaglione, and figuring out from the **context** that it is a dessert. Again, it is easy for a human to decide whether or not a word is important enough to include in the index, or to find a single word that summarizes a whole paragraph. In short, it is far more work to *program* a computer to do a good job of indexing than it is to make the index itself—especially when the human indexer has an interactive computer available.

Thus our study makes the point that there are jobs for which computers are unsuitable. This may seem obvious to you. However, most of the book is devoted to showing that computers can do many things you might not have expected them to be able to do, and so it seemed a good idea to set some limits. We must not only learn *how* to use a computer, we must learn *when* to use it. During the 1960s, many companies installed million-dollar computers as a prestige item, without first checking to see whether their data-processing jobs could be handled more efficiently by the computer than by their staff. Often the best solution proved to be a group working with a smaller computer or a time-sharing system (see Section 2.1) or even, in some cases, more efficient organization to eliminate the computer entirely.

In approaching any problem we must proceed as follows:

1. Specify the problem.
2. Make sure you know what you are talking about!
3. Examine alternative methods of solution.
4. Specify the method of solution.
5. Choose the proper tools for implementing the solution.

The mistake made by many businessmen in the 1960s was to assume that whatever the data-processing problem, a million-dollar computer must be the tool to solve it.

Keywords and Concordances

We saw that a computer could not now be programmed to do a good job of making a really "rich" index for a book. However, once a book is coded on magnetic tape, so that the computer can process word after word, many other tasks are possible. For example, if the book is in a specific subject like chemistry, there are a lot of keywords like "acid," "base," "benzene," "methane," and "molecule" that should occur in the index. A **keyword index** is one that only lists the

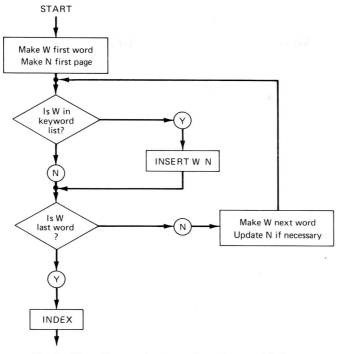

Fig. 6 Flow diagram for preparing a keyword index.

keywords that actually occur in the book and the pages on which they occur. Clearly, if the computer has a list of keywords, and the text of the book is on a magnetic tape or readable via an OCR system, it can automatically prepare a keyword index with a program structured as in Fig. 6.

Another type of index well suited to computer preparation is a **concordance.** This is an index that includes *every* word in a book (except, perhaps, some very common words like "a," "and," "but," "the," and "to"). It will often include the sentence in which the word occurs. A concordance is an aid to scholars who are interested in the specific pattern of word usage in such major documents as the Bible, or the works of Shakespeare. For example, a Biblical scholar might use a concordance to determine the frequency with which words are used as a clue to whether or not different books of the Bible had the same author. In the United States, this type of computer research was used to study the authorship of *The Federalist Papers.*

Suggestions for Further Reading

S. Y. Sedelow, Language Analysis in the Humanities, *Communications of the ACM,* **15,** pp. 644–647, 1972.
  The author argues that the computer's use for language analysis is not limited to the preparation of indexes and concordances, but can also help with the analysis of literature, or with teaching a student to write a composition.
I. Shenker: Computers Hum As the Saints Go Marching In, *The New York Times,* Thursday, February 5, 1976, p. 33.
  Shenker tells how two Rutgers historians, Donald Weinstein and Rudolph M. Bell, are conducting a computerized study of 1500 saints to analyze the role of religion in society.

Summary

This section showed the limited usefulness of computers for text-processing. We saw how the computer could be used in an interactive mode in the preparation of an index. We saw how to get a text on magnetic tape for automatic computer access. The computer could not be programmed to choose words to describe important and interesting aspects of a page. However, the computer could be used to prepare restricted types of index in batch mode, such as keyword indexes and concordances.

Glossary

Index: A list, in alphabetical order, of words and phrases that describe interesting or important items in a text is an *index*. Each entry includes a list of the numbers of the pages on which information about the item can be found.

Keyword index: An index that lists only the occurrence of certain preselected words—called *keywords*—in the indexed text is a *keyword index*.

Concordance: A *concordance* an index that includes almost all the words that occur in the text, but no words that do not occur in the text. It will often include the sentence in which the word occurs.

Interactive mode: The *interactive mode* is the use of a computer through an input–output device called a *terminal* which lets the user monitor the progress of a computation, intervening when something seems to be going wrong, and responding to queries from the computer.

Error message: A message typed out by a computer when the user has made a mistake that the computer can detect is an *error message*. The computer can easily be programmed to detect when the user types in an instruction that does not belong to the programming language. It is unlikely that a computer could be programmed to tell the user "YOU TYPED IN FORWARD 100. DIDNT YOU MEAN FORWARD 200?"

Parameter: A given command or subroutine may have several *parameters*—entries that must be replaced with numbers before the computer knows what to do. For example, the instruction FORWARD X has one parameter, namely X. When we replace X by a number we obtain a command that the computer can execute—FORWARD 100, for example, will get the computer to send 100 "one step forward" commands to a robot.

Sorting program: A program that accepts a list of items as input and arranges them in some specified order is a *sorting program*. One sorting program would arrange numbers in increasing order, another would arrange words in alphabetical order, and so on.

Optical character recognition (OCR) system: A system that can accept typed or printed pages as input, and provide computer code of the symbols on the page as output is an *OCR system*.

Context: The *context* of an item is the material surrounding the item that helps define its meaning. For example, "pen" has different meanings in the two contexts "The pig is in the pen" and "The ink is in the pen."

Exercises

1. A numeric program inputs and outputs a sequence of numbers. Why do computers deal with *nonnumeric* information? Give two examples from this section. Most programs are, before execution, input to translator programs (like that used for LOGO in Section 1.3) which transform them into programs which the computer is equipped to handle directly. How does this involve nonnumeric processing? (*Hint:* What characters are in a program? In all of these examples, what is the input and what is the output of a nonnumeric computer program?)

2. Referring to the flow diagram of the 3-number sorting routine (Fig. 3), fill in the table below. The table gives the current value of each variable during each step of the execution of the program. "?" means the value is undefined. "Decision" is the branch taken on each successive question, for instance "Is $A \leq B$?"

Example

A	B	C	D	E	F	G	H	Decision
6	4	2	?	?	?	?	?	N
6	4	2	?	?	?	4	6	Y
6	4	2	2	4	6	4	6	?

Problem

A	B	C	D	E	F	G	H	Decision
1	5	3	?	?	?	?	?	
.	.	.	.	.	.	.	.	.
.	.	.	.	.	.	.	.	.

3. *Reading Between the Lines:*   Look at a sheet of printed music. What difficulties can you see in getting this information into the computer? What could you do with it then? How might the computer be used as a musical instrument itself? What parallels do you see between text-processing for printing books and printing music?

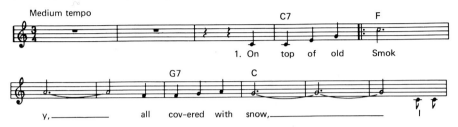

4. *Symbol Manipulation:*   You are to flowchart a program that takes as input a character string that represents an algebraic expression and determines whether the parentheses are balanced. A balanced expression is one in which the total number of open parentheses "(" equals the total number of close parentheses ")", and such that on scanning from left to right, at no time does the number of close parentheses exceed the number of open parentheses. (Why?) For example,

$$\text{``(DISTANCE} = ((1/2)*\text{ACCELERATION}*(\text{TIME}*\text{TIME})))\text{''}$$

is balanced, while

$$\text{``X} = (A + (B/(C - D) + E) - F)*G) + (H*I)\text{''}$$

is not. Assume you have available a subroutine NEXTCHAR that looks at the next unexamined character (starting with the first), a subroutine OPEN that tests the current character for equality to "(", a subroutine CLOSE that tests current character for equality to "(", a subroutine QUOTE which tests the character for equality to the quote mark (which will occur only as the first and last character of the expression), GOOD that outputs that the string is balanced, and BAD that outputs that it is nonbalanced.

5.   Look at the flow diagram in Fig. 4 for interactive indexing.
   (a)   Why is the test for W in front of the test for PAGE=M?
   (b)   Can you think of a reason for putting the test for PAGE=M *before* the test for W, instead of after it?
   (c)   Why is the error message in this flow diagram a bit "fishy"? (*Hint:*   What is a W?)

6.   Suppose you have successfully gotten the text of a book into the computer's memory. What difficulties would you expect in getting it to read out loud to you?

7.   Can you think of any really practical uses for a computer that inputs text and outputs acoustical signals which approximate spoken words and sentences? Three examples to get you started: automatic stock-market reports over the phone; an actual minicomputer in a fire engine in Glasgow, Scotland, for sound-alike street names; automatic danger signals in a jet plane.

8. Suppose you had a factory manufacturing a large number of complex widgets. Each type of widget is made of a large number of assemblies, and each assembly is built of a big bunch of thing-a-ma-jiggers. How could automatic indexing help in improving the efficiency of the factory? Give several, specific examples.

9. Word processing in the office is a multibillion-dollar field now being invaded by the computer industry. Devices such as IBM's MTST (Magnetic Tape Selectric Typewriter) are available on a sale or rental basis—several hundred dollars per month. An MTST, while the user types on an extended typewriter-like keyboard, simultaneously outputs onto ordinary paper *and* stores the characters on a magnetic tape cassette. Along with the text characters (letters, numbers, punctuation) are control characters (skip a line, indent, left-justify, set margin, . . .). The user can rewind the cassette automatically to any point—perhaps the first place the phrase "Dear Sir" occurs. He can then replace the text in that location with an update, correction, revision, or expansion. The MTST can now retype, from the cassette, the new text onto new paper. (1) What is this good for? (2) How does it change the operation of a typical office? (3) How does this differ from computers described in this chapter? (4) In what sense is a secretary, with an MTST, a programmer? (5) What applications could this kind of device have if it were much less expensive—say $25? (6) When is a pen or pencil better?

2

More about
Computers

SECTION 2.1. TRANSLATORS, OPERATING SYSTEMS, AND TIME-SHARING

We start by contrasting two kinds of system for translating programs from one programming language to another: **interpreters,** which translate one instruction at a time, and **compilers,** which translate the program as a whole. We then see how **operating systems** were built as supervisory programs to control the use of a high-level program and its translator; and then see how this led to operating systems that could handle several jobs at once. In particular, we discuss **time-sharing,** which lets many users interact with the computer at one time. Sections 1.1 and 1.2 are required as background. We refer to the LOGO high-level language of Section 1.3, but we make no use of the details of that section here.

SECTION 2.2. GRAPHICS AND NETWORKS

Computer graphics let users interact with a TV-like screen on which the computer can display messages and pictures; and on which the user can ''draw'' with a device called a light pen. For example, an architect could ''draw'' a rough sketch of a house, and have the computer straighten the lines, change some of the lengths, and then display on the screen how the house would look from different angles.
Computer networks can link terminals and computers together into networks that span a whole country or even tie together several continents. These networks can link terminals to a single central

computer—as in an airline reservations network—or they can be decentralized networks giving users access to many different computers. We shall look at airline traffic control and at **computer conferencing** as interesting uses of computer networks. The section is almost self-contained, and can be read with little background. It helps to recall the distinction between interactive and batch processing from Section 1.2 and the use of compilers to translate high-level languages from Section 2.1.

SECTION 2.3. THE SHRINKING MACHINE

The technique of electronics called **integrated circuitry** allows complex circuits to be produced in very small "**chips.**" This allows the production of ultra-small computers called **microcomputers,** which are surprisingly cheap. As a result, computer power can be used in many places where it could not be used before. This section requires Section 1.1 for background, and the notions of central processing unit and memory from Section 1.2.

SECTION 2.4. WRITING AND REWRITING LARGE PROGRAMS

A large program may contain hundreds of thousands of instructions, and require hundreds or even thousands of man-years to write. We discuss **structured programming** and **chief programmer teams** as ways to organize the writing of a large program so that it can be handled efficiently by a team of programmers. We look at the problem of **program validation:** making sure that a program does what it is claimed to do. We relate this to social problems such as ensuring that a data bank obeys legal restrictions on its use. Finally, we look at the problem of rewriting large programs to meet changing needs. This section can be read with little background beyond "The Idea of a Program" (Section 1.1).

2.1. TRANSLATORS, OPERATING SYSTEMS, AND TIME-SHARING

Translators

We discussed two quite different styles of programming in Chapter 1. Although we did not go into the details (which are discussed in Chapter 8) we saw that in **machine language** programming, we have to keep track of the way in which the computer's circuitry was wired up to process information. In fact, when we write a machine language program, we must specify a location for every stored item and instruction, giving it its own address in memory. Each operation in machine language must spell out from where in memory the data are to be retrieved, how the accumulator and other circuits in the **CPU (Central Processing Unit)** are to be used in working on the data, and exactly where in memory the result is to be stored.

On the other hand, LOGO—which we used in Section 1.3 to teach TURTLE to navigate—was an example of a **high-level programming language,** where the user does not have to worry about the location of numbers and instructions in memory. We still have to be careful about the format in which we write programs—we cannot let the computer "figure out what we meant" the way we count on a listener to fill in the details when we speak in natural language. However, a high-level language does free us from keeping track of all those details required for machine language programming.

The problem with a program written in a high-level language is that it cannot run on a "naked" computer which can only accept programs written in machine language. As we have seen in Chapter 1, the computer needs a program called a **translator,** which—as shown in Fig. 1—can take the high-level program and translate it into a machine-language program that the computer can follow to do the job for which the high-level program was written. The translator produces a program as its output that the computer can execute to do the job—either for the complete program or for a single high-level instruction at a time.

Each time a new high-level language is designed—to make programming in some particular application area easier for users—a hard-working team of professional programmers must write a translator for it. The translator is usually a very complicated program whose input will be a program written in the new high-level language, and whose output will enable the computer to execute this high-level program. There are two types of translators which such a team can provide: an interpreter and a compiler.

An **interpreter** is provided with both the high-level program and the data on which the program is to operate. The interpreter then translates one instruction in the high-level language at a time, and then operates on the data with it. When it has finished executing that

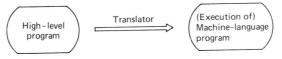

Fig. 1 A translator lets a computer "understand" a program written in a high-level programming language.

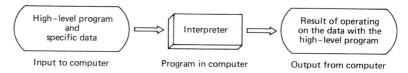

Fig. 2 Translating with an interpreter. One high-level instruction at a time is translated into a machine language subroutine, which is executed before translation of the next high-level instruction.

high-level instruction, it then goes on to translate the next instruction. So it goes, until the complete high-level program has been executed on the given data. The structure of an interpreter is shown in Fig. 2. This is the style of operation that we described in discussing TURTLE in Section 1.3. In that case, the computer had to contain an interpreter which would take LOGO instructions, as well as instructions we defined by giving names to subroutines, and translate them into the appropriate string of commands to the TURTLE control box, as well as commands for updating and testing counters.

Let us look at translation of a more familiar kind. Imagine that you are visiting France, and that a friend has given you instructions on how to get to his house in the countryside outside Paris. Unfortunately, the directions are in French and your knowledge of the language is still rather poor. Although you can translate a sentence from French to English with a little effort, you cannot "think" in French. Thus you have to translate each instruction from French to English. Using an interpeter in a computer is like having one instruction at a time translated as you drive from Paris to your friend's country home. As you come to a line you translate it into English, and then follow the directions contained in that instruction—and it is only when you have completed that part of the route that you go on to translate the next instruction.

Of course, if your French is very bad, you will want to have someone translate the complete text from French to English for you before you start on the journey, or, even if your French is not so bad but you prefer to go over the complete instructions before you set out, you will want to turn all the instructions from French to English before you follow them (Fig. 3). The corresponding computer translator is called a "compiler."

A **compiler** is a program that enables a computer to take a high-level program as input and produce a corresponding program in another programming language (called the **object language**). This is shown in the top half of Fig. 4. In the process of *compilation,* then, we supply the computer with a special program called the "compiler,"

*OK, I have the next line translated now;
it says "When you reach the river, turn left."*

Fig. 3 Translating from French to English.

and then provide it with some program written in the high-level language as its input. The compiler treats the high-level program as *data*.
It does *not* treat it as a series of instructions it is to follow—any more
than the person who translated our road directions from French into
English had to set off along the indicated roads. After the compiler
has processed the high-level input, the output is a compiled program.
If the object language is machine language, this compiled program is
a machine language program which will do the job specified by the
original high-level program. Now, if we want to operate on any
specific data with the original program, we can feed the compiled
program into the computer. Since, in this case, the compiled program
is a machine-language program, the computer can now accept any

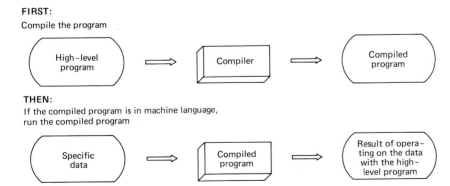

Fig. 4 A compiler requires two passes—*compilation* to prepare a compiled
program, and then—if the object language is machine language—a *run* to process
the data with the compiled program.

specific data as input, and act on them to produce answers in just the way specified by that high-level program. We show this in the run in the bottom half of Fig. 4.

To summarize: An interpreter (Fig. 2) takes a high-level program and some data, translates one instruction at a time into a machine-language subroutine, and then executes that subroutine on the data. A compiler (Fig. 4), on the other hand, translates the high-level program into a complete object-language program. If the object language is machine language, this compiled program can then be run directly on the computer with any set of data.

The translator—a compiler or an interpreter—must be designed to handle a specific high-level language and a specific object language. For a given high-level language, different translators must be designed for different machines. (Remember that different types of computers can have different instructions wired into their circuitry—and, thus, different machine languages.) However, the translator for a given high-level language and a given object language need only be written once. Then, no matter how many hundreds or thousands or even millions of programs are written in the given high-level language, the translator can operate on them to enable their execution on a machine using the given low-level language. In the same way, once you really know French and English, you can translate *any* French sentence into English.

In the case of an interpreter (Fig. 2) in which one instruction is translated at a time and then executed, it is clear that the computer which is doing the translating is the same as the computer which is following the instructions. However, as we see in Fig. 4, the process of compilation and the process of running a compiled program on particular data are quite separate. Because of this, compilation could be carried out on a different computer from the one on which the compiled program is run. In other words, the language in which the compiler is written need not be the object language into which the compiled program is translated.

In many applications, the interpreter is the more efficient form of translator, since it only requires the computer to store one high-level instruction at a time in its much more lengthy machine language form. However, if a program is to be used hundreds or even thousands of times on a whole range of different input data, it wastes a great deal of computer time to translate every instruction each time it is executed. In this case, it is better to compile the high-level program once and for all, and then keep a copy of the compiled program—the machine-language version—available in the library, ready to be fed into the computer every time we need to carry out the computation specified by the original high-level program. Even if a program is only used once, compilation is economical if repeated execution of loops gets instructions executed millions of times in a single run of the program. However, interpreters make a lot of sense when the computer is used in an interactive mode, since the user can then monitor the effect on the computer of individual instructions as he types them in.

We must now see that a compiler may translate programs from one high-level language into another. In other words, a compiler does *not* have to translate programs into machine language. Moreover, the compiler need not itself be in machine language. Let us see how this works.

Suppose that we have available a *compiler* that translates the high-level language FORTRAN into the machine language of our computer. Suppose that we want to work with programs written in COBOL for business applications. Then we need a COBOL compiler. However, because FORTRAN is a high-level language, we know it would be easier to write a COBOL → FORTRAN compiler than to write a COBOL → MACHINE LANGUAGE compiler. We also know that it would be much easier to write the compiler in FORTRAN than in MACHINE LANGUAGE. Figure 5 shows that we can get away with it! We proceed in four steps:

Step 1. We build a COBOL → FORTRAN compiler written in MACHINE LANGUAGE by first writing a COBOL → FORTRAN compiler written in FORTRAN, and then processing it with the FORTRAN → MACHINE LANGUAGE compiler that we had at the start.

Steps 2 and 3. We use this machine-language COBOL → FORTRAN compiler to translate a COBOL program into MACHINE LANGUAGE by first using our new compiler to translate the COBOL program into FORTRAN, and then translating the result into MACHINE LANGUAGE using the original compiler.

Step 4. Then at last we can process our data.

We will not provide flow diagrams for translators in this section—the reader who is keen on details may consult Section 8.2. However, it should be clear that program translation is the sort of thing that a computer can be programmed to do. Taking a single instruction in a programming language and providing an equivalent subroutine in another programming language is an easy task to program. Keeping track of all the details of a whole program is much harder than handling single instructions, but it can be done—and the

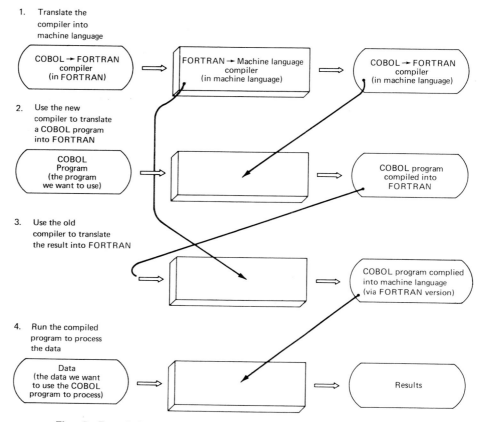

1. Translate the compiler into machine language

2. Use the new compiler to translate a COBOL program into FORTRAN

3. Use the old compiler to translate the result into FORTRAN

4. Run the compiled program to process the data

Fig. 5 Translating from COBOL to machine language with a COBOL → FORTRAN compiler written in FORTRAN.

writing of compilers and interpreters has become a routine task for expert programmers.

Operating Systems

Consider the job of the computer operator in using a compiler in the fashion shown in Fig. 4. He has to run two jobs. The first is the *compilation job*. He must load the data (in this case the high-level program) and the program (in this case the compiler) into the machine. When the job is completed, he has a card-deck as output, which contains the compiled version of the high-level program. The second job is the actual *run:* the operator loads the data on which the high-level program was written to operate and the deck containing the compiled program. When the job is completed, he can collect the results and send them to the user. Note the two types of data here.

Data are what a program must be given to operate on. The compiler must be given a program to translate—so its data are the parts of the program that are to be translated. But then the translated program needs new data of its own that it has to process.

An **operating system** is a program designed to take over a number of these tasks from the human computer operator. (In the rest of this section we shall see a number of functions that an operating system can perform.)

Before operating systems were programmed, the compiler would be a program on a deck of cards. (Do not read further until the discussion of batch processing at the start of Section 1.2 is clear in your mind.) The computer operator would load the deck of cards into the card reader every time the compiler was needed. Since a compiler could have thousands of instructions, reading in this deck wasted a great deal of time. To save time, then, we instead store the compiler in **secondary memory:** on a magnetic tape or a magnetic disk.

Here is another way that much of the computer operator's time was wasted. He had to wait around while the compiled program was punched out on a deck of cards, one instruction per card. He then had to take the whole deck, and load it into the card reader, together with a deck of cards for the data (the bottom half of Fig. 4). Only then could he *run* the program to process the data.

Cards are, however, punched out far more slowly than a computer can figure out what should be punched out. The silly thing is that all the instructions of the compiled program had to be in the computer before they could be punched on cards, so why not just leave them in the computer? In the early days of compilers, the answer was simple. The primary memory was too small. One had to clear the compiler out of memory to leave enough room to run the compiled program. However, this is no longer a problem, for two reasons. First, primary memory is larger. Second—and this is more important—modern operating systems can move blocks of information back and forth between primary and secondary memory at appropriate times.

Figure 6 shows how an operating system handles a batch processing job. The operating system sits permanently in primary memory. The compilers that the operating system needs are in secondary memory—on disks, say. The important point is that the operating system has a table that tells it where the compiler for each high-level language is stored. When a **job**—the high-level program and data—comes in, the operating system reads in the program. A job control card tells the operating system what high-level language the program is in. Thus the operating system can copy the correct compiler into

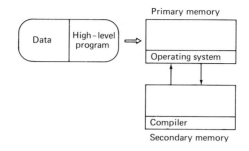

The operating system reads in the high-level program and makes a copy of the compiler in primary memory.

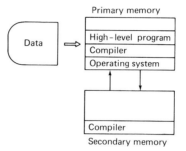

Fig. 6 Batch processing under control of an operating system.

primary memory. The copying still leaves the original copy of the compiler available on the disk for later jobs. Note that there are many different high-level languages—and so the operating system will probably have many compilers available in secondary memory, not just the one shown in Fig. 6.

For example, the payroll program we discussed in Section 1.2 could be in COBOL. The computer would then have to translate the program into machine language. After the translation, the computer would follow the compiled instructions to read in records from the data base (stored on one of the magnetic tapes) and print the results out on the paychecks and stubs.

Once the high-level program and compiler are inside primary memory, the operating system sets the compiler to work. When the compiler has finished, the operating system keeps the machine language program that was compiled, but erases from primary memory the compiler and the original high-level program.

The operating system turns control over to the compiler which translates the high-level program into a compiled program in machine language. Then the operating system erases the high-level program and compiler from primary memory.

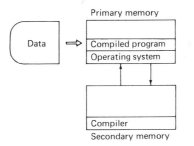

The operating system then turns control over to the compiled program, which reads in data, computes, and puts out the results of processing the data. When this is finished, the operating system erases all trace of the compiled program from primary memory, and is then ready for the next job.

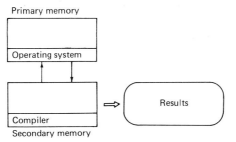

Fig. 6 continued.

At this stage, just the compiled program and the operating system are in primary memory. The operating system then sets the compiled program to work. It reads in data, computes, puts out some results, reads in more data, and so on, until it has finally put out its last results, which were obtained by using the program to process the data. The job is done. Then the operating system resumes control, erasing all trace of the compiled program and its computation. After this erasure, everything but the operating system is cleaned out of primary memory and the operating system is ready to process the next job.

With this use of a batch operating system, we have saved the human operator from having to load the compiler into the computer at the beginning of each job. We have also saved him from having to wait for the compiled program to be punched out, and then having to reload it. In fact, the human operator can simply load up the card reader with a whole stack of jobs. Each job will have job control cards telling the operating system what high-level language the program is in, where the program ends, and where the data end. The computer operator can get on with other tasks—like setting up results in a form the user can pick up—while the operating system automatically works through one job after another. This stack of jobs is called a **batch**— and is the basis for the name **batch processing.**

We have seen, then, that a **batch operating system** saves a great deal of human time. But it still wastes a great deal of CPU (central processing unit) time. In the time that one word can be transferred from a disk to primary memory, the CPU can execute a hundred instructions. In the time that a human takes to type in an instruction at a terminal, the CPU can execute between a million and ten million instructions! Is there any way to avoid "throwing away" the chance to do all those millions of operations? The answer is "yes." It was achieved by coupling new computer hardware with advances in operating system design.

The basic novelty in hardware was to redesign the CPU so that the circuits which handled the fast operating and test instructions could work at the same time as the circuitry controlling the input and output devices. It also became possible to build computers with larger primary memories. This allowed the design of operating systems that could handle several users' programs *at the same time*. This was called a **multiprogramming operating system** because it could handle *multiple* programs at any one time.

We illustrate the use of a multiprogramming operating system in Fig. 7. In this case, the operating system is already working with two jobs J1 and J2 in primary memory, and is reading in the program for a third job J3. It starts reading a card of J3, and then turns control over to one of J1 or J2. By the time the input control circuitry has read in that one card of J3, the operation/test circuitry may have executed 10,000 instructions for one of the other jobs. And so it goes. The operating system must keep track of what jobs it is working on, and

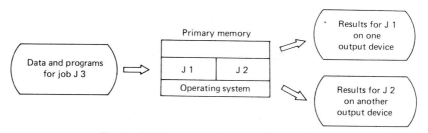

Fig. 7   Multiprogramming operating system.

how far along it is in each job. Then, when it sets one job aside, it will know which instruction to execute next when it returns to the job later.

With multiprogramming, a computer can handle from 2 to 10 times as many jobs as it could using one-job-at-a-time batch processing.

Time-Sharing

One of the most important developments in operating systems is that of **time-sharing** systems, which enable a central computer to work in **interactive mode** with hundreds of users at the same time. The users may be at terminals close to the central computer, or may be hundreds or even thousands of miles away. Each user sits at his terminal typing in data or instructions, or manipulating information on a graphics screen (more of this in the next section). Some form of communication, such as telephone lines, carries messages back and forth between the terminal and the computer. If the input is in a high-level language, the computer will automatically interpret the instructions, and respond to them appropriately.

First let us see the advantages of the interactive mode. It enables the user to monitor the progress of the computation, having the computer print out partial results. He thus has a reasonable chance of seeing any **bug** in the program as it comes out in the computation. By the same token, if the computer, during its compilation, discovers mistakes in format in the high-level program, it can immediately send an **error message** to the user, and ask him to correct the mistake. By contrast, the user of batch processing may wait for hours or even days before he sees his results. If there was a bug in the original program, it may be several days before the user can do anything about it. Similarly, if the run of the program suggests some new ideas on how to improve the program, or explore different alternatives, it will again be days before the user can do anything about it.

The disadvantage of the interactive mode is that *without a time-sharing system* valuable CPU time is tied up—time to execute millions of test/operation instructions while the user types in a single instruction or line of data.

But how do time-sharing systems enable a computer to process hundreds of programs at the same time? Time-sharing systems are a natural development of the multiprogramming systems described above, but with special features to handle a large number of *interactive* users.

The problem with the original multiprogramming operating system was that once a job J1 took over the test/operation portion of the CPU, the operating system would let J1 run until it came to an input or output instruction. Only then would the operating system let any other job execute its test and operation instructions. Unfortunately, there are jobs so large that many minutes will go by between any input or output activity. This causes no problems for multiprogramming in batch mode; but it is intolerable in interactive mode. Suppose you were running TURTLE in the interactive mode, typed in a simple command like FORWARD 100, and found that TURTLE had still not moved after 5 minutes! You would think that the computer was broken. In a badly designed time-sharing system, annoying delays in computer response are all too common even if a delay is more like 20 seconds than 5 minutes. The art of designing a good time-sharing system is not only to let you know that the computer is working, but also to give you the feeling that the computer is *always* at *your* command—and to give hundreds of other users the same feeling at the same time!

To avoid long waits by users typing in instructions which demand an immediate response, the time-sharing operating system gives each user an equal share of every second. Thus if there were a hundred active terminals, each user would receive 1/100 second of CPU time each second.

There is another difference from multiprogramming. When there are 100 jobs being processed at the same time, there is no way of fitting all the necessary programs, data, and partial results in primary memory. At any time, then, 3 or 4 jobs may be running in multiprogramming mode in primary memory. Each 1/100 second, the operating system **swaps** jobs—storing the programs, data, and partial results for one job in secondary memory, while bringing another job into primary memory, and setting it going at the instruction it had reached when it was last swapped.

In conclusion, let us just mention one bug called **thrashing** that can creep into a time-sharing operating system. Thrashing can occur when too many users are working on the system. Each time a user's job gets swapped in for its short fraction of a second, the computer must retrieve the files from secondary memory and place them in the primary memory. In this way, the user once more has access to his current program, the current data, and the information that has already been computed from that data. Later, before the next user's job can be swapped in for its fraction of a second, the previous user's files must all be stored away in secondary memory. The operating system must keep a record in primary memory of where in secondary memory each user's files are stored, so that no information will be lost. This transfer thus involves use of CPU time by the operating system software—time that cannot be spent on user jobs. If the number of users gets large, then the time allowed to a user in each second gets small. If the size of the user's program gets large, then the time required to transfer the information in and out of secondary storage gets large. Thus, with more users and larger jobs, the swapping time may come dangerously close to the user's complete "time slice." In the end, all the time may go into swapping, with no time left for computing! For this reason, a time-sharing operating system must be written to take account of careful estimates of the pattern of usage that is expected.

As can be imagined, a really good time-sharing system is a far more complex structure than a compiler. In fact, a number of compilers will be subsystems of a good operating system. An operating system may require years of effort by tens or even hundreds of programmers, but this effort is worthwhile because the resulting system will save tens of thousands of users many many months of frustration each. In such a system, the huge storage and immense speed of truly large computers are made available to many users.

As we shall see in Section 2.3, small but powerful computers are becoming available for only thousands, or even hundreds, of dollars. For many applications, people will increasingly choose to buy their own small machine which can be dedicated to a specific task, rather than being configured to respond to diverse needs of many different users. However, a small businessman needs only a few minutes of CPU time each week to handle his accounts, and a student may use only a few seconds of CPU time for help with his lessons (see Section 6.1 on Computer-Assisted Instruction). For such a user, time-sharing will be cheaper and just as convenient—and will have the advantage of placing at his disposal a wide variety of compilers and other software available through the operating system.

Suggestions for Further Reading

R. M. Fano and F. J. Corbató: Time-Sharing on Computers, in "Computers and Computation: Readings from Scientific American." pp. 79–87. Freeman, San Francisco, California, 1971.
An excellent 1966 account of the early development of time-sharing systems.

Waiting for the Great Computer Rip-off, Fortune, July 1974, pp. 143–50.
An excellent account of computer crime, with special attention paid to the problems and opportunities posed by time-sharing systems.

Summary

We studied **interpreters** and **compilers.** In particular, we saw how a compiler written in one language can itself be compiled into another language; and how a program could be compiled from one language to another in stages. We saw how **batch processing** could be handled by an **operating system** which kept a variety of compilers available in **secondary memory.** We saw how **multiprogramming** could run multiple jobs to make efficient use of CPU time when the input or output devices were in use. Finally, we saw how **time-sharing** systems could enable many users to interact simultaneously with a single computer.

Glossary

Machine language: The instructions that the hardware of the computer is wired to execute directly comprise the *machine language*.

High-level language: A programming language which a human finds easier to use than machine language, is a *high-level* language. A *translator* is a special program that a computer needs to enable it to execute a program written in high-level language.

Bug: A *bug* is any error in a program that causes a computer under its control to behave differently from what was intended. *Debugging* is the process of tracking down and correcting such errors.

Error message: An *error message* is one typed out by a computer when the user has made a mistake that the computer can detect. The computer can easily be programmed to detect when the user types in an instruction that does not belong to the programming language. It is unlikely that a computer could be programmed to tell the user "YOU TYPED IN FORWARD 100. DIDNT YOU MEAN FORWARD 200?"

Interpreter: An *interpreter* is a translator which takes a program written in a high-level language and some data, and translates one instruction at a time into a machine-language subroutine, and then runs that subroutine on the data before going on to the next instruction of the high-level program.

Compiler: A *compiler* is a computer program that enables a computer to take a program written in a high-level language and translate it into a complete program—designed to process data to obtain the same results—in another language, called the *object language.* If the object language is a machine language, this compiled program can then be run on the computer with any set of data.

Central processing unit(CPU):   The *CPU* is the part of the computer that retrieves and carries out the instructions in a program: obeying operation instructions, carrying out tests, and controlling input and output devices in response to input and output instructions.

Memory: The *memory* of a computer comprises a *primary memory* to and from which the CPU can very quickly move information; and a *secondary memory,* made up of devices like magnetic tape units and magnetic disk units, which are larger and cheaper than primary memory, but also much slower.

Interactive mode: The *interactive mode* is the use of a computer through an input–output device called a *terminal* that lets the user monitor the progress of a computation, intervening when something seems to be going wrong or some change is required, and responding to queries from the computer.

Batch mode: Using the computer to execute a complete program without any *interaction* with the user before it has printed out all the results is the *batch mode.* Each program, together with the data it must process, is called a *job.* A whole stack of jobs—called a *batch*—may be placed in the input devices at any one time. The computer then runs the jobs one after another. The computer operator uses a *console* to initiate the reading in of programs and data for each batch.

Operating system: The *operating system* is a set of programs, permanently resident in the computer, which make the computer easier to use. For example, an operating system can schedule jobs, transfer compilers from secondary memory to primary memory, and balance out the use of input/output devices and actual computing.

Batch operating system: An operating system for batch processing is a *batch operating system.* The operating system reads in one program at a time, compiles it, then runs the compiled program on the data. It then automatically moves on to the next job in the batch.

Multiprogramming operating system: A *multiprogramming operating system* is one that has several jobs in primary memory at any time, using the fast test/operate circuitry of the CPU on one job while other jobs use input/output devices or await their turn.

Time-sharing system: A system that enables many human users to interact with a single computer at the same time is a *time-sharing system.* The operating system gives a fraction of each second of CPU time to the needs of each user, *swapping* the user's file back and forth between secondary and primary memory. *Thrashing* occurs when swapping uses up all the available CPU time, and no jobs get done for the users.

Exercises

1. At the United Nations, whenever a speech is given in one of the five official languages (English, Russian, French, Spanish, or Chinese) highly skilled human translators provide "simultaneous translations" in each of the other languages. These are available to any listener hooked into the system of earphones and switches, with only a few seconds lag behind the original speech. Is this most like interpretation or compilation? Why? Why is this done?

2. When you read an English translation of a book written originally in another language, the book was probably translated by a single person. That person probably worked for years on it, and did not publish the translation until it was complete. Is this more like interpretation or compilation? Why? Why is this done?

3. What are the main advantages and disadvantages of interactive mode, compared to batch processing?

4. Suppose we have a high-level language program LOOPY (see accompanying figure) to be translated. We can use either a compiler or interpreter.

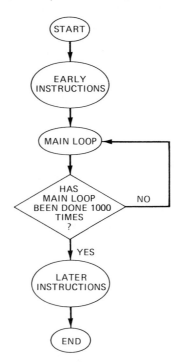

Suppose the "early" and "later" instructions to be only a small part of LOOPY—which depends on the main loop being repeated 1000 times. Assume it takes either translator 0.001 seconds to translate the "main loop" into machine language and 0.0001 seconds to execute the machine language translation of main loop. How long will it take to run LOOPY with the compiler? With the interpreter? Which is better to use, if speed is the objective? Explain.

5. The simplest time-sharing systems allocate a fixed "time slice" to each user in a cycle—1st user, 2nd user, . . . , last user, 1st user, . . . , etc. If each time slice is 1/100 second and there are 50 users, how long a delay will each user observe in any interaction with the computer?

6. Go to a fast-food restaurant and study how customer orders are "translated" into delivered meals. Is the process more like a compiler or an interpreter—that is, are items processed one at a time, or the whole order at once? Is it more like batch processing or time-sharing—that is, is there a stack of orders run through one at a time, or are several customers' orders prepared in an interlaced, mixed-together way? Why are orders placed with a cashier instead of directly to the cooks? How is money processed, in the above terms? Explain and discuss other analogies with operating systems.

7. A multiprogramming operating system can work on several jobs at one time by executing instructions of one while waiting for I/O processing of another to finish. Can you see why multiprogramming becomes less effective when all jobs require very little I/O (or all require mostly I/O and little CPU time)? Explain.

8. Consider the industrial technique of the assembly line for producing, say, cars. Contrast this with building the cars one at a time. Why could each of these methods be preferred? Compare by analogy with computer, interpreter, batch mode, time-sharing where each car is likened to a job (program to translate and run).

9. When you have a large number of things to do in a short time, do you ever experience anything like "thrashing" (where the computer spends all its time switching from one job to another, never getting any done)? What does it feel like? What do you do when this happens? How can it be avoided?

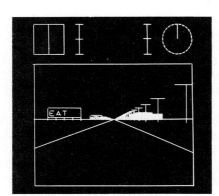

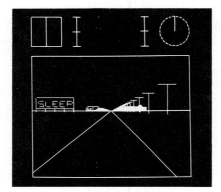

Cybernetic Landscape

At the Computer Graphics Laboratory at Princeton University, Aaron Marcus has developed a series of cybernetic landscapes utilizing programs in FORTRAN for a PDP-10 digital computer and an Evans and Sutherland LDS-1 interactive computer graphics display system. The cathode ray tube device permits images in stereo and color as well as two-dimensional pictures that can be altered smoothly and instantaneously. These simulated landscapes combine abstract visual forms with conventional verbal and typographic elements. By using the interactive equipment (a "joystick" and knobs to control the display), the viewer may look at and wander through this symbolic space at will. The illustrations show various views of *Cybernetic Landscape I*. The small diagrams at the top indicate the location of the viewer on the groundplane (dot in the square) and direction of view along the groundplane (line in the circle).

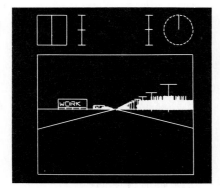

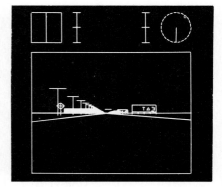

Bars indicate height above the groundplane and a vertical viewing angle. As Marcus describes it, "the space is organized with slogans of the 'consumptive good life' distributed along a central axis. At certain locations, other visual elements are to be found in the space away from the main path, and the viewer may explore these as desired. In one quadrant of the space is a whirlwind of letterforms rotating silently with a pulsating rhythm, independent of the viewer's position or movement. The space is cyclically infinite—each side wraps around electronically to the opposite side so the viewer moving off one edge would emerge instantly into the space again at the opposite edge. To signal the beginning or end of the journey, a canopy of points, stars, and periods hovers in space at one terminus of the path."

Adapted, with permission, from "Soft Where, Inc., The Work of Aaron Marcus." West Coast Poetry Review, Reno, Nevada, 1975.

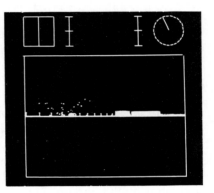

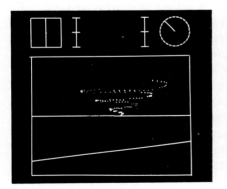

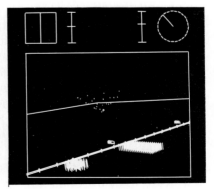

2.2. GRAPHICS AND NETWORKS

One of the main trends in computer science is to make computers easier to use so that people without special training in the writing of computer programs can make use of the computer in their own work. For example, an airline reservations clerk needs only a few hours of training before being able to use a simple terminal connected to a large central computer to obtain information about the availability of space on different flights, and to make reservations for a customer. In this case, the clerk sends queries and commands to the computer via a typewriter input, and gets the answers back displayed on a TV-like screen.

This example introduces the two topics we study in this section. The first is **computer graphics**—the use of computers coupled to TV-like screens so that people may interact with the computer in terms of pictures as well as symbols. The second is **computer networks**—which can connect terminals and computers to give users access to a great variety of computer resources.

Computer Graphics

The picture on a normal black-and-white TV set is "painted" by an electron beam passing back and forth across the screen of a **cathode ray tube,** with the line moving down the screen—much as your eyes scan the page in reading a book. The intensity of the electron beam determines the brightness at the point where it hits the phosphor on the screen. The signal from the TV broadcasting station varies the intensity of the electron beam in such a way as to recreate a picture on the screen. This picture is either that scanned by a TV camera in the studio, or one that was earlier stored on videotape (magnetic tape that records pictures as well as sounds). In computer graphics, the picture on the TV screen is generated by a computer, instead of by signals broadcast by the TV station.

In the type of graphic display used by the reservations clerk, the job of the screen is not to display a picture as TV does, but rather to print up the lines of letters which have been read out from the computer memory. Special circuitry can "beam up" each letter, rather than building it up line by line. The circuitry has a **template,** which describes each letter, and can place the letter in any position it is instructed to by the computer. In this way letters can be printed up on the screen very quickly by changing the template selection each time that the positioning is changed to put the next letter up on the screen. Of course, the phosphor on the screen must be chosen to let a letter persist long enough for a complete printing job to be done, by which time the electron beam can be used to either reprint the letter, or to replace it.

Everything we have said so far assumes that the information required to generate the picture is already inside the computer. One way to get a picture into the machine is simply to have a TV picture fed into the computer so that the computer stores the intensity for each point of the image. Then, by various processes, it can determine where straight lines and other features occur in the picture, to come up with a compact representation of it. However, a more useful procedure is often one which allows the user to "draw" on the screen. One way of doing this is with a **light pen** (Fig. 1). The light pen does not really draw on the screen. Instead, it can detect light on the screen. The computer follows the movement of the light pen by displaying a dot on the screen and moving it to keep up with the light pen—which sends a signal to the computer whenever it "sees" the dot. Thus if you want to draw a line on the screen, you point the light pen at the place where you want the line to start, then you tap a button saying "Draw a line"—or some message to that effect—and move the pen along the screen until you get to the place where you want the line to stop, and then tap another button. The computer can then automatically draw a straight line on the screen between the two end points. At the tap of another button, you can use the light pen to rotate the line about one end point, or to lengthen the line, or to move the

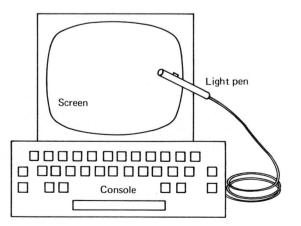

Fig. 1   A graphics console with both typewriter and light pen input.

whole line about. As you put together more and more complex draw-ings, you can use the light pen to move one part of the drawing relative to another. Then, once the drawing is coded inside the com-puter memory, you can type in instructions on the console to have the computer manipulate the picture in any of the many ways we now describe.

A circuit designer might want to use computer graphics to lay out a circuit on the screen, and then have the computer execute programs to tell him the electrical properties of the circuit as he makes alterations of it then and there. An architect might sketch the outline of a building on the screen, and then have the computer rotate the "building" and show it to him from a different perspective. A biologist may take many photographs of a brain cell as seen through the microscope as he slices through different levels of tissue. He can then feed these pictures into a computer that is programmed to make

An airplane designer uses a light pen to move a wing simulation about on the screen of a computer graphics system.

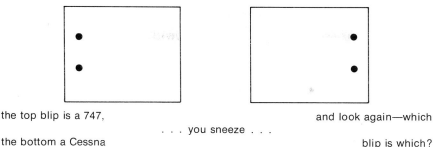

the top blip is a 747,   and look again—which

. . . you sneeze . . .

the bottom a Cessna   blip is which?

Fig. 2   The problem of blip identification.

a three-dimensional reconstruction of the cell and display on the screen how it looks from a number of different angles. In each of these cases, the input to the computer and the output from the computer are primarily pictorial in form—the user wants to make a rough sketch on the screen, and have the computer work with him in refining the sketch and coming up with precise information about it. Again, a spaceflight control engineer at Mission Control might want to find out the effects of different strategies of rocket firing on the motion of a spaceship. He will find it much easier to make sense of the computer output if it is displayed as a motion picture on the graphics screen than if it is given to him in page after page after page of numbers showing the position of the moving spaceship at different times.

For a more detailed look at computer graphics, consider *air traffic control*. Each traffic control center has its own air space in which it is responsible for the routing of traffic. Traffic control is using more computers these days but is still human dominated, with traffic controllers watching the progress of blips on a radar screen, with each blip signaling the location of a plane in their air space. This can lead to problems. Suppose you were looking at a radar screen, showing two blips, one for a Boeing 747 and one for a light plane, say a Cessna. If your attention is diverted, as in Fig. 2, how do you tell whether the way the planes flew when you were not looking was

To avoid the tragedy that might result from making the wrong identification, systems designers have developed a computer graphics system that lets the user attach a label to a blip which the computer will automatically move along with the radar blip.

In addition to the position of the planes under his control, a flight controller may need to know:

The flight number
The destination
The priority number
The time of arrival
The fuel reserve
Plane type

A typical list for one flight might read

AA 44
Kennedy
42
0615
3
707

which means that the flight is American Airlines flight 44 bound for New York's Kennedy Airport; of all the planes currently heading for Kennedy it is scheduled to be the 42nd to land; its current planned time of arrival is 6:15 a.m.; it has enough fuel left for three hours flying; and the plane is a Boeing 707.

To display this information for each of the 100 planes on the screen would be overwhelming and unreadable; so instead the system designer gives the user a **menu,** listing in a column at one side of the screen each of the items about which the user might ask. The "menu" is an important idea in graphics, and is used in any application where the user can choose which of a small number of facilities he wants from the computer. This use of the menu is a simple example of the data base management we study in Section 4.1.

In the display shown in Fig. 3, the controller has pointed the light pen at the word DESTINATION on the menu and has just tapped a key on his console telling the system to respond to the choice indicated by the light pen. In response to this, the computer has attached the airport code to each blip—three are flying in to JFK (John F. Kennedy Airport in New York), while three are going elsewhere, one to ORD (Chicago's O'Hare Field), one to BDL (Hartford's Bradley Field), and one to SFO (San Francisco International Airport).

In this case, the position of the dots is taken off a radar system by the computer—and the job of the computer is to keep track continually of which dot is which, so that it can always display the correct information along with the dot. In a system like that shown in Fig. 3, the controller could, by typing in the appropriate message on the console, have a different menu displayed, and could then use the light

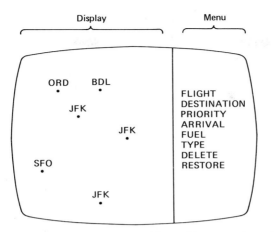

Fig. 3 Graphics display of airplane position, with menu of user's options.

pen only to keep—for example—track of those planes that are converging upon the airport at that time. The computer keeps track of which plane is which, and stores all the information the controller requires about the planes. It could also be computing to continually correct the estimate of fuel reserves that it has—to make it easy for the controller to detect an emergency condition in any of the planes. In the 1940s, air traffic into one airport might be measured in hours per plane; today a large airport lands several planes per minute. It is this change in *quantity* that gives a change in the *quality* of air traffic control—moving from written lists of flights and voice communication by radio to the increasingly sophisticated use of computers.

Computer Networks

A **computer network** is a net made up of **nodes,** with each node being joined to one or more other nodes by **links.** Each node contains either a computer or terminal, and the links pass programs and data back and forth.

In a **centralized computer network** (also called a **star** network, for reasons that can be seen from Fig. 4), there is a single central computer, with all the other nodes just being terminals. The time-sharing systems of Section 2.1 are examples of star networks.

The airline reservations network (Fig. 5) is an increasingly famil-iar example of a centralized computer network. The airline reserva-tion net has one large computer with the huge **data base** that stores up-to-date information on all flights for some extended period of time,

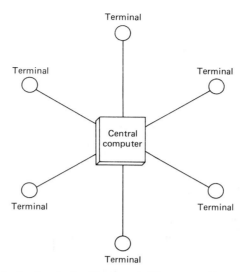

Fig. 4 A star (centralized) network. There are seven *nodes*—one node for the central computer, and six nodes for the terminals by which the users communicate with the central computer. There are six *links*—each terminal has its own link over which signals are sent back and forth to the central computer.

including the names, seat assignments, and special needs (including flight connections) of all passengers, as well as flight schedules and fare schedules for all flights. Users at terminals throughout the country—and, possibly, in other countries as well—can type in a flight number and date, and get seating information on the screen. They can then type in a person's name and the type of seat they want, and have the system update its file, adding the person's name and their seat assignment, or dietary preferences, and decreasing the list of

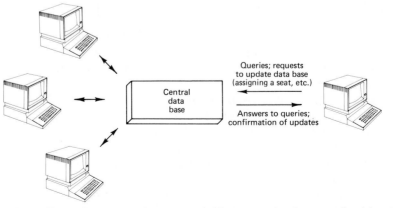

Fig. 5 The airline reservations network is an example of a centralized (or star) computer network.

vacant seats. In this case, the terminals have little computing power of their own, but provide the keyboard and graphics display that let the reservations clerk interact with the data base in a natural fashion. All the "intelligence" of the network is in the central computer.

In the previous subsection, we saw how computer graphics could aid an airline traffic controller working with planes in his own air space. Let us now see how networking can help controllers in different regions work together. Air space is divided into somewhat overlapping regions, each with its own control center (Fig. 6). When a plane in the air space of control center A enters the air space of controller B, a communication link between the centers can pass from the A computer to the B computer all the necessary information about the flight. Especially important information would be about emergencies that require rerouting the flight, or getting it to land quickly (perhaps because a passenger has had a heart attack). Again, during a fuel shortage at one airport, flights leaving that airport might have to make extra stops for refuelling in addition to the scheduled stops— and this must be communicated to all control centers along the way.

Air traffic control provides our first example of a **decentralized computer network** in which each node has its own large computing power, but where the computers are linked so that information may be shared between them. In other decentralized networks, users at one node may even run programs on computers at other nodes, rather than just using the links to send data.

A user at node A may have developed a program P that solves some problem X— say a problem in planning traffic flow. Now a user in another town, B, may also have a traffic flow problem, yet not have

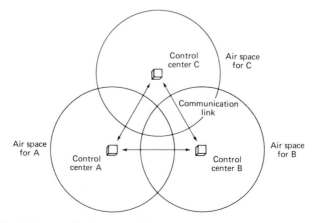

Fig. 6 A decentralized network for letting air traffic controllers in different regions share data and transfer control.

any program on his computer that can solve such problems (Fig. 7). One solution is "simply" to make a copy of the program P and run it on B's machine. This is *not* as simple as it seems, however. The two computers at A and B might have different **machine languages**—and so a program designed for the computer at A might not run on the computer at B. Recalling our discussion of high-level languages in Section 2.1, you might reply that while there are differences in machine language, it is quite likely that the program P is written in a high-level language like FORTRAN. If this is so, why not send the FORTRAN program to B, where it will run on the B machine with a FORTRAN compiler. There is still a catch! FORTRAN has "dialects." When the programmers at a computer center write a FORTRAN compiler for their machine, they often change FORTRAN a little. They might add a new kind of instruction they think will make it easier to write FORTRAN programs. They might also change FORTRAN by asking the program writer to include some extra statements that are not really part of a FORTRAN program, but that will speed up the work of the compiler in translating the user's program into a form the machine can execute. This is fine when the users all know the center's "dialect." However, if the FORTRAN program is written elsewhere, a programmer must then sit down and carefully rework the program into the local "dialect." He may well introduce some **bugs** in the process, which may require a great deal of work to remove.

Rewriting (Fig. 7, Solution 1) may thus be a major problem—and a computer is only worth using if the programming effort is not out of proportion to the problem at hand. In other words, it may be cheaper to leave the problem unsolved than to get into the major task of rewriting

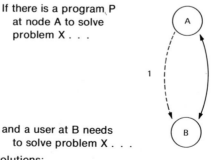

If there is a program P
at node A to solve
problem X . . .

and a user at B needs
to solve problem X . . .

there are two solutions:

1. Rewrite program P so it will run on the computer at B.
2. Use the network to let the user at B run program P on the computer at node A.

Fig. 7   Strategies for letting a user at B use programs developed at A.

program P and debugging it on the system at B. Even were the program rewritten to take the "dialect" into account, there may still be problems because the program was written to use special equipment available at computer center A, and no such equipment has been installed at computer center B.

The second solution then is for the user at node B to get a manual on how to use program P, send his data to the computer center at node A, have them **batch process** the data for him, and then mail back the results. In many cases, this is the simplest and cheapest solution. However, we can carry this one step further—replacing the mails by electronic communication, so that the computer at each center serves not only as a computer in its own right, but also as a terminal for every other computer to which it is linked. The advantage of using the B computer as a terminal is that the user at B need not use only batch processing. He can also have the advantage of all the *interactive* facilities available at computer center A, including **HELP programs.**

HELP programs are designed to help the interactive user clear up confusion about how program P works—much better than wading through a 100-page manual!—or help him pinpoint the source of any errors he might make in providing data to the computer. A user having trouble with the system can type "HELP," and have the computer type out a description of the options available to the user.

We again see the *human engineering* aspect of much of today's computer work. Programmers do not simply write a program that, if provided data in an *exactly* specified format, will grind out the answer. Rather, they design an *interactive* program that makes it easy for a human to solve his problem with the aid of the computer. Once again, time and effort must be considered. It is only worth writing this extra "HELP" material if the program is going to be used so often that it really pays to help people avoid the costly mistakes that often come with failure to read complex instructions with sufficient care.

There now exist many large networks. TYMNET is a large commercial computer network. It tends to be more in the centralized mode of operation, in that the majority of nodes are terminals for customers who want to buy time on one of the relatively few major computers on the network. The ARPA network is far more a "community of equals," linking research computer centers throughout the United States as well as some in Europe. It was designed to help researchers keep track of, and make use of, the latest developments at other centers on the network. [There are ARPA nodes at both MIT and Stanford—two of the leading centers for the research on artificial

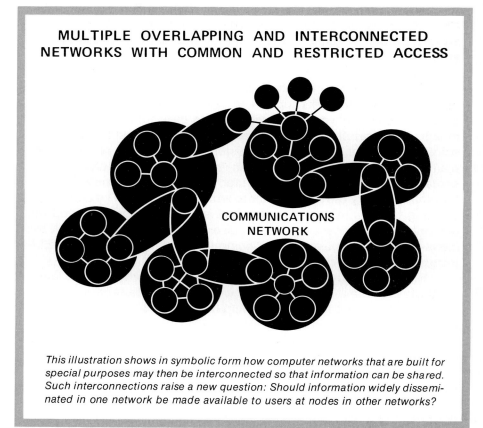

MULTIPLE OVERLAPPING AND INTERCONNECTED
NETWORKS WITH COMMON AND RESTRICTED ACCESS

COMMUNICATIONS
NETWORK

This illustration shows in symbolic form how computer networks that are built for special purposes may then be interconnected so that information can be shared. Such interconnections raise a new question: Should information widely disseminated in one network be made available to users at nodes in other networks?

intelligence which we shall study in Chapter 5. The workers at Stanford valued the work of one MIT researcher so highly that they directed their computer to detect whenever this man used the MIT machine, and to print out everything he did! As a result, the Stanford scientists knew more about his work than his colleagues at MIT. This anecdote both shows the power of computer networking, and also raises serious questions about privacy—questions to which we return in Chapter 4.]

ARPA is the Advanced Research Projects Agency of the United States Department of Defense. It provides research funds for many groups, including the computer centers of the ARPA network, some of which receive more than a million dollars in annual support. In Section 5.4 we shall discuss The Automated Battlefield—and see how ARPA-funded research is changing the nature of war. This ARPA research on artificial intelligence, computerized decision-making, computer-networking, and so on, also promises to offer some of the technology that will prove most important in facing up to the global problems of hunger, overpopulation and pollution that we shall discuss in Chapter 3. We shall develop this theme in Chapter 7. In the same way, the military may fund air-traffic control to improve their capacity for making war—and yet the spin-off increases the safety of civilian air traffic. However, direct funding of civilian projects seems to many citizens to be preferable.

Computer Conferencing

Computer networks can also be used to enable people to communicate in new ways, which combine the advantages of mail and of the telephone. To see this, let us compare these two forms of communications:

Mail: A letter can be reread before it is sent, to ensure that it says what you mean it to. Both the sender and receiver can have copies of the letter which can be easily referred to in later communication. You can write a letter when you want to. You can read a letter when you want to. However, a letter may take days to be delivered.

Telephone: Communication is fast and interactive. Each party can respond to unexpected viewpoints expressed by the other party. However, it is often difficult to schedule a call at a mutually convenient time, and the caller may interrupt important work—or important relaxation!—of the person he is calling.

If both parties have terminals on a computer network, they can communicate in a fashion that has most of the advantages of mail and telephones, and few of the disadvantages. Each person has a reserved area of secondary memory in a computer on the network which is called his **mailbox.** This mailbox has an *address*—perhaps the name of the person, plus a codeword that helps route messages to the right memory area, and avoids mix-ups with someone else with the same name. Then anyone else can sit down at his terminal on the network and type in the receiver's address followed by his own address for identification, followed by a message. The **operating system** of the network will use the receiver's address to open a path from the sender's terminal to the receiver's mailbox; check that the sender's address is a legal one for the terminal he is using (so that he can be sent a bill for the message!); and then deposit a copy of the message in the receiver's mailbox, together with the sender's "signature."

Just as a person can read his mail anytime after it is delivered, so can the user read any messages in his *computer* "mailbox" as soon as they are delivered. The difference, of course, is that—thanks to the electronic speed of the network—messages arrive at almost the moment they are sent, instead of days later. To read what is in his computer mailbox, the user simply sits down at his terminal and types in a command like "PRINT MAIL." The computer then types out—or displays on a graphics screen—all the messages that have arrived since the user last read his mail. The user can either have the computer erase a message from memory after it is typed out, or he can have the computer store some or all of the messages for future references. Then, by typing in appropriate commands at the terminal, a user can refer to any messages he has kept on file in the computer—as well as copies of messages he has sent out.

This system of computer communication has all the advantages of the mail. It avoids the telephone's inconvenient interruptions. The only disadvantage arises when the receiver goes days without checking his mailbox. In that case, a phone call may be worthwhile to get the interchange started up again!

This method has been extended to **computer conferencing** in

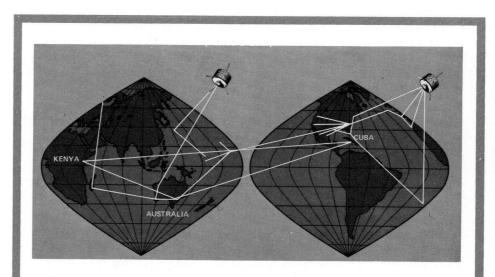

Worldwide computer networks have become a possibility thanks to the establishment of worldwide communications networks that use satellites to cover the globe.

which 10, 20, or even more people communicate via a computer network. Here is how it works. A group of experts is needed to discuss some important problem—such as how a country should respond to increasing petroleum prices. These people might include high government officials, oil company executives, representatives of consumer groups, executives of electricity utilities, university experts on economics and energy policy, experts on foreign affairs, and so on. Most of these people have such busy schedules that it might be over a year before a block of 3 days comes up at which a majority of them are free to get together. Yet the problem is so important that policy decisions must be made within the month. How can one proceed? One way is to have the policy-making done by a small group of government officials in the nation's capital. These officials would phone up experts when the officials had particular questions they wanted to ask. However, this would lose the give-and-take of a conference, in which someone suddenly sees an unexpected connection between his work and that of another participant—and gets a new idea which makes an important contribution. Conference telephone calls are of little help. Three or four people can keep up a fairly good conversation over the phone, but with more people the conversation is "taken over" by just a few people, and the valuable opinions of the less aggressive participants tend to get lost.

One solution to this problem is called the **Delphi method** which is a sort of conference by mail. The coordinators running the conference make up a list of questions and mail it to every participant. When a participant receives the questionnaire, he answers all the questions about which he has expert knowledge or strong opinions, and then mails his reply back to the coordinators. The coordinators try to put all the replies together. Some questions seem completely answered, and so they write up a clear statement of the solution. In other cases, the replies seem to generate more questions than answers, and so the coordinators try to summarize the situation, and ask a new set of questions to try and clear the matter up. They then send this packet of information out with the new questionnaire. Given the speed of the mails, it may take several weeks for one round of questions-and-answers to be completed. It may then take several rounds, and two or three months, before the coordinators have gathered enough information to write up the final report which sets policy.

For many problems, a response time of three months is fine. For other problems—and setting energy policy is one of them—a clear policy must be established in a few weeks. This is where computer conferencing comes in. The method is much like the Delphi method, except that computer networks replace the mail as the path of communication. One of the important points about computer conferencing is that the user can have access to a number of different mailboxes. One mailbox may be used for information that everyone is meant to have, and for questions that everyone is expected to answer. Then there may be mailboxes for each of a number of "task forces"—one mailbox for a group of engineers and economists concerned with purely technical questions of the effects on prices of different levels of use of petroleum, coal and solar energy; another mailbox for a group concerned with the impact of energy decisions on relations with other countries; and so on. These would be public mailboxes—anyone could read them and add their comments, although only members of the task force would have to keep track of everything in that mailbox. Finally, there would be *private* mailboxes. For example, a group in one region of the country might want a private mailbox to share ideas on what policy would be best for them before they typed their messages into the public mailboxes.

A system of this kind—with a few phone calls to chase people who are slow in responding—can reduce the time for policy making to a few days. Yet computer conferencing gives each participant a chance to carefully read and reread any material that seems important to him, and then take his time to spell out a really thoughtful reply. Important ideas do not get lost because someone "could not get a word in edgewise" at the conference table or in a telephone call; and important ideas do not get garbled over the telephone. Finally, these very busy people can work on the conference problems every day—even though there is never an hour at which they would all be free to get together by telephone. Thus a group of people, some even thousands of miles apart, can be knit into an effective policy-making team by computer conferencing. We shall return to this idea in Section 7.1, Networks for Planning, when we see ways to combine computer conferencing with the computer's power for simulation which we shall discuss in Chapter 3.

Suggestions for Further Reading

T. H. Nelson: "Computer Lib/Dream Machines." Hugo's Book Service, Box 2622, Chicago, Illinois, 60690, 1974.
For a lively account of computer graphics, see "Dream Machine," pp. 6–7, for how cathode ray tubes work, and pp. 20–41 for people interacting and making movies, pictures for shading as well as lines, educational uses, and much more.

I. Sutherland: Computer Displays, *in* "Computers and Computation: Read-
    ings from *Scientific American,*" pp. 53–69. Freeman, San Francisco,
    California, 1971.
    Details of color graphics are included.
M. Turoff: Unique Communication Forms, *Proceedings of 2nd International
    Conference on Computers and Communication,* 1974, pp. 135–142.
    This is a good introduction to the Delphi technique, and to computer
    conferencing.
D. C. Engelbart: Design Considerations for Knowledge Workshop Terminals,
    Proceedings of the National Computer Conference, 1973, pp. 221–227.
    Suggestions are made as to how human intellect might be augmented
    through access to a computer network in which participants in a work-
    shop can share data and problem-solving tools.
B. Combs: TYMNET, A distributed network, *Datamation,* July 1973, pp. 40–43.
    The workings of one of the largest commercial computer networks are
    described.
Computer Networks, *Computer,* August 1973.
    A special issue with useful articles on computer networking technology,
    nontechnical issues in network design, and so on.

Summary

We saw that information could be displayed on a **computer graphics**
screen line-by-line as on a TV screen; or using **templates** to display symbols;
or with lines drawn on the screen under computer control. A **light pen** can be
used to guide a spot of light across the screen under computer control. This
lets the user "draw" sketches on the screen, which can then be processed by
the computer. The light pen can also be used to make choices from a **menu**
displayed on the side of the screen, to tell the computer what information to
display or what program to run.

A **computer network** links terminals and computers. **Centralized**
networks—like time-sharing systems or an airline reservations system—give
users access to a central computer. In a **decentralized** network there are
many computers. Links between computers may be used simply for
communication—as in air traffic control and **computer conferencing**—or may
be used to let a user at one node run programs on a computer at another
node.

Glossary

Cathode ray tube: A *cathode ray tube* has an *electron gun* at one end and a
phosphoresent screen at the other end. The tube is completely empty, and
the electron gun fires a stream of *electrons* (small negatively charged parti-

cles which form the cloudlike shell around the nucleus of an atom) through the vacuum. The inside of the screen is coated with a *phosphor* that glows whenever it is hit by electrons. The higher the *persistence* of a phosphor, the longer it is before the glow fades. The beam can be used to "paint" pictures on the screen by suitably adjusting the electric current applied to *deflection plates*—magnetic plates arranged around the tube close to where the beam leaves the electron gun.

Graphics terminal: A *graphics terminal* has a TV-like screen, possibly equipped with a teletype and a light pen.

Computer graphics: *Computer graphics* is the use of a TV-like graphics terminal as an input/output device for a computer, enabling a person to communicate with a computer in terms of pictures as well as symbols.

Light pen: A *light pen* is a photoelectric device for sensing the location of patterns on the screen of a graphics console—with the help of a computer. It can let a human operator "write" on the screen, move patterns around, select items from a menu, etc.

Mask: A *mask* is a plate from which *templates*—patterns representing standard symbols—have been cut out. The patterns may then be projected on a screen by a beam of light or *electrons*.

Menu: A *menu* is a list of items displayed on a graphics screen from which one may be selected by a light pen.

Computer network: A *computer network* is made up of *nodes,* with each node being joined to one or more other nodes by *links*—where each node contains either a computer or a terminal, and the links pass programs and data back and forth. A *centralized* (or *star*) *network* links many terminals to a single central computer with large data base and great computing power; a *decentralized network* links many computers, so that a user at any one computer can run programs on, or share information with, another computer on the network.

Data base: A *data base* is a collection of data on some particular topic to which the computer can refer on many occasions. It may be divided into *records,* each of which contains information about some specific person, policy, project, or other basic unit about which information is collected.

Batch mode: Using the computer to execute a complete program without any *interaction* with the user before it has printed out all the results is the *batch mode*. A whole stack of jobs—called a *batch*—may be placed in the input devices at any one time. The computer then runs the jobs one after another. The computer operator uses a *console* to initiate the reading in of programs and data for each batch.

Interactive mode: The *interactive mode* is the use of a computer through an input–output device called a *terminal* that lets the user monitor the progress of a computation, intervening when something seems to be going wrong or some change is required, and responding to queries from the computer.

Bug: An error in a program which causes a computer under its control to behave differently from what was intended is a *bug*. *Debugging* is the process of tracking down and correcting such errors.

Operating system: The *operating system* is a set of programs, permanently resident in the computer, that make the computer easier to use. For example, an operating system can schedule jobs, transfer compilers from secondary memory to primary memory, and balance out the use of input/output devices and actual computing.

HELP program: An important feature of the latest operating systems is the use of *HELP programs*. A user having trouble with the system can type in HELP, and have the system type out a description of the options available to the user.

Machine language: The instructions that the hardware of the computer is wired to execute directly comprise the *machine language*.

High-level language: A programming language that a human finds easier to use than machine language is a *high-level-language*. A *translator* is a special program that a computer needs to enable it to execute a program written in high-level language.

Compiler: A *compiler* is a computer program which enables a computer to take a program written in a high-level language and translate it into a complete program—designed to process data to get the same results—in another language.

Computer conferencing: *Computer conferencing* lets humans conduct a conference even though widely scattered geographically, by communicating through a computer network. Each user has a *mailbox*—a reserved section of memory in one of the computers on the net—in which other users can leave messages by typing in the right instructions at their terminal.

Delphi method: The *Delphi method* is a technique for obtaining information on a subject by sending out a questionnaire; combining the answers to this questionnaire with new questions; sending these out, and so on. After several rounds, enough information has been collected to put out a report on the subject.

Exercises

1. State two advantages and two disadvantages of a CRT terminal compared to a typewriter terminal.
2. How could an ordinary TV display a CRT picture?
3. State three ways a CRT differs from a TV.
4. Choose the word or phrase that best completes each of the following sentences.
    (a) A centralized computer network is also called a _____ network.
        (1) link, (2) node, (3) star, (4) time, (5) ARPA.

(b) The airline reservation network has one _____ and many _____.
    (1) terminal/nodes, (2) terminal/computers, (3) computer/data
    bases, (4) data base/computers, (5) data base/terminals.

(c) All the "intelligence" in a star network is in the _____. (1) central
    computer, (2) communication links, (3) schedules, (4) termi-
    nals, (5) conferencing.

(d) A decentralized network has _____ at each node. (1) different lan-
    gauges, (2) its own computing power, (3) several terminals,
    (4) to debug, (5) human engineering.

(e) Computer conferencing requires a special _____. (1) telephone,
    (2) terminal, (3) operating system, (4) address, (5) TYMNET.

5. What types of safeguards need to be built into a remote access data
processing system to maintain security and privacy?

6. Martin Greenberger coined the term "computer utility" [*Atlantic Monthly,*
May 1964] for the distribution of computational power in a way analogous to
the distribution of water or electricity by public utility companies—
government-regulated, privately owned, public interest, competitive corporations for computer-based information services. How valid do you think this
analogy is? Why?

7. Explain, in a paragraph, how a "menu" might be used in an air traffic
control.

8. The FCC now regulates approximately 3000 communications common
carriers, of which the largest is the American Telephone & Telegraph Company. What new regulations might be required for computer conferencing?

9. Draw a diagram of a centralized network, and one of a decentralized
network. Indicate: terminals, computers, data links.

The Shrinking Machine

This sequence of pictures—supplied by DEC (The Digital Equipment Corporation)—gives dramatic evidence of how computers have shrunk with the introduction of integrated circuitry.

The first picture shows an assembly of vacuum tubes from a 1952 IBM computer—it took 375 of these modules to make the computer's central circuitry.

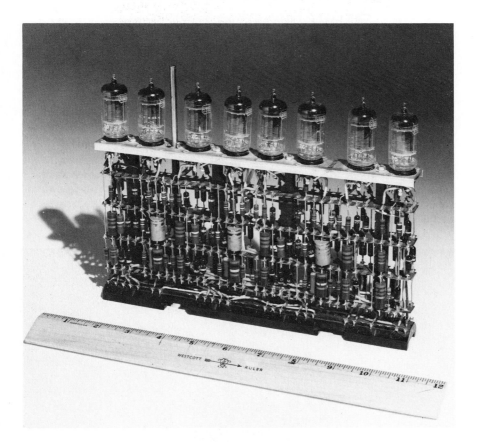

When the first minicomputers were built—such as DEC's PDP-5, which was introduced in 1963—over 300 modules were still needed for the central circuitry, but the modules were smaller, and the hot power-consuming vacuum tubes had been replaced by transistors. However, the transistors were still made separately, and had to be wired together with other components to make a module, as shown atop the next page.

By the time DEC built its PDP-8/1 in 1968, integrated circuitry techniques could produce 5 to 10 transistors on a single chip. Below we see four of these integrated-circuitry packages wired together to form a single module. It required 100 such modules—each with from 4 to 9 packages on them—to make up the computer's central circuitry.

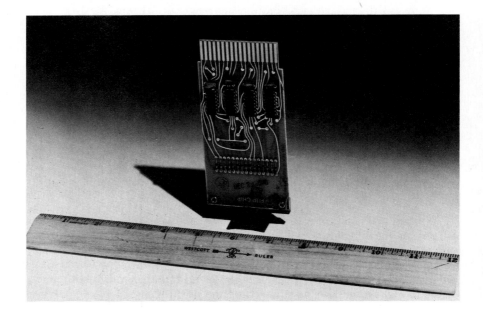

In 1974, integrated-circuitry packages could be made with 25 to 50 transistors. DEC's PDP-8/A was made with just 3 of the modules shown below, each containing over a hundred packages.

In 1975, DEC was able to put the complete circuitry of its LSI-11 computer, with more than 100,000 transistors, on a single board the size of a sheet of exercise paper (next page). The machine has 65,000 bits of memory. The complete circuitry of the LSI-11 occupies perhaps 4 times as much space as a single module of the PDP-5—and the PDP-5 required over 300 modules. Yet the LSI-11 is more powerful than the PDP-5. Perhaps even more impressive is the fact that the LSI-11 sells for under 1,000 1975 dollars, while the PDP-5 sold for 27,000 1963 dollars.

When we see this dramatic reduction in price and size—and energy requirements—of computers, and the increase in computing power, we see why we can expect computers to become more and more part of our everyday life in the future. The personal computer is not science fiction, but is instead well on the way to becoming reality.

2.3. THE SHRINKING MACHINE

When Howard Aiken and his colleagues built the first American* digital computer in 1944—the Mark IV computer at Harvard—it was built with thousands of vacuum tubes, like those in the first picture of the preceding photo essay. It required a device occupying 90 cubic inches and dissipating 10 watts to store a single bit of information. If you think of the heat emitted by hundreds of 100-watt light bulbs, you can see that keeping the machine cool was a very real problem. Yet this was a machine with *very* little computing power by today's standards.

As a result, science forecasters of the early 1950s told of a future in which, to solve mankind's problems, we would use giant computers the size of the Empire State Building, which would require a flow of water equal to Niagara Falls to keep them cool. This prediction about the size of computers was wrong. Today's computers are indeed far more powerful than their ancestors, but they are much smaller and easier to cool. The reason for this is the shift from vacuum tubes to transistors to integrated circuitry. In this section, we study integrated circuitry and see why it makes the 1950s predictions about computers seem quaint and old-fashioned.

Hardware Trends and Microcomputers

The small transistor radio, powered by a single battery and cool to the touch, replaced the large radio which used vacuum tubes, had to be plugged into the mains for power, and was hot to the touch. In the same way, transistors came to replace vacuum tubes in computer design. By the early 1960s the 90-cubic-inch 10-watt vacuum tube device for storing a bit of information had been replaced by a small transistorized flip–flop which could do the job while consuming only half a watt.

Not only are transistors smaller and more efficient in their use of energy than vacuum tubes, they are also cheaper and easier to mass produce. They are made by making "sandwiches" of very thin layers of silicon (obtained by melting and purifying sand) and smaller amounts of other more expensive materials. These "sandwiches" are then etched to yield the right electrical properties for the circuits, and

---

* Code-breaking machines constructed in Britain at that time under military secrecy also had many of the qualities of a digital computer.

then sliced up to make one transistor from each small piece of the "sandwich."

A second dramatic advance came with the transition to **integrated circuitry.** Instead of using individually made transistors and wiring them together into a circuit, it became possible to etch all the components and all the connections required for the circuit on a single "sandwich" of silicon, by using photographic techniques. Suddenly, the circuitry required to store one bit of information shrank to something like a hundredth of a cubic inch. An integrated circuit—or **chip,** as it is often called—of the early 1960s could be printed with about 20 components. The last ten years or so have seen dramatic increases in the refinement of this integrated circuitry. By 1974, there were chips containing over 20,000 components in a space less than a quarter of an inch on a side! By the time you read this, the number will probably have passed the 100,000 mark, and still be rising.

Instead of filling an entire room, as did the Mark IV, the entire **central processing unit** of a moderately powerful computer can be placed on a few chips. Instead of requiring the power consumption of a town of several thousand people, the processing unit can now run on the power of a single battery. This is a billion-to-one improvement in power consumption!

The transistor made possible the **minicomputer,** which is a computer the size of a desk or smaller. The latest integrated circuitry gives us the **microcomputer,** one whose circuitry can be fitted on a few chips. One of the first minicomputers was the PDP8, introduced by the Digital Equipment Corporation in 1965. It was the size of a filing cabinet, and was more powerful than the larger PDP5 which had been introduced two years earlier and sold for $27,000. Yet the PDP8 was sold for only $18,000. With the new integrated circuitry this trend of falling size and prices has continued even more dramatically. In 1975, the same firm was able to offer the LSI-11, a complete computer with 65,000 bits of memory and more than 110,000 transistors for less than $1000. The circuitry covers an area the size of a piece of writing paper.

One of the smallest of the new generation of general-purpose computers is the TDY52 made by the Teledyne Systems Company. Its circuitry fits on a ceramic wafer two inches on a side and one fifth of an inch thick. In quantities between 50 and 500 the Teledyne microcomputer, designed chiefly for military systems, sold for $1295 in 1975. The TDY52 is a programmable **16-bit** microcomputer. (In other terms, the computer's word is a string of 16 0s and 1s.) Conventional minicomputers, which occupy several cubic feet, typically process words of from 12 to 32 bits and are up to ten times faster. Otherwise, the microcomputer is as powerful as the minicomputers. The largest elements of the TDY52 are two chips containing some 6000 transistors each. These two main chips control four slightly smaller chips for doing arithmetic and testing. In all, the system contains more than 100,000 transistors. It "communicates with the outside world" through 120 leads, 30 on a side.

The dramatic reduction in cost of the computing circuitry does not, unfortunately, mean that a complete computing system will become very cheap, although it does mean that it will be reasonable to add computing power to machines (like traffic lights or automobile ignition systems or alarm clocks) that did not have it before—as we shall see in the next subsection. If a computing system is to be used in the way we described in Section 1.2, then it needs all the peripheral devices we discussed in that section: a typewriter or punched card or magnetic tape input devices, as well as suitable output devices. These peripherals cost the same whether or not the CPU uses integrated circuitry. They are not microminiaturized as integrated circuits are—we cannot miniaturize our fingers to type on microminiature keys!

When you buy a computer system, the actual cost of building the system accounts for only about a quarter of the sales price, with marketing, software development, research, and profits taking up the remaining three quarters. Within this quarter of the total cost, the processor usually costs about one third, with the remainder going to memory and input and output devices. Finally, the actual electronics of the processor may account for less than a third of its total cost. In other words, in current computer systems, the processor electronics cost one third of one third of one quarter—that is, only about 3%—of the total costs. Even if CPU circuitry becomes as cheap as a dollar, as has been predicted, the cost of a computer will only drop to 97% of its current price! It is thus clear that the dramatic impact of microcomputers will not be so much in bringing down the cost of computers of the kind we have today as it will be in opening up new uses for computer power.

Of course, this prospect of new uses is very much the story that followed the original introduction of the computer. In the early days, computers were expected to take over large tasks of computation that had required a team of people using adding machines to work for weeks on end. An example would be preparing actuarial tables telling an insurance company how to set its rates. When IBM introduced its first commercial computers in 1952, a careful market analysis suggested that 25 such machines could fill the demand for years to come, since very few businesses or government offices made use of large teams of adding machine operators. Today, the number of general purpose digital computers approaches 200,000 around the world. In looking ahead, we may project the use of millions of such computers—perhaps even reaching hundreds of millions, with every relatively well-off family boasting a computer of its own. The number of special-purpose computers (just think of digital wristwatches!) will reach into the billions.

Let us look at one reason for this huge increase in computer use. The rest of the book provides a wide range of other reasons. Once computers were available, the mere fact that a company did not have to hire a roomful of people using adding machines meant that a lot of information-processing tasks suddenly became "do-able." The payroll job of Section 1.2 is just one example of this. In addition, as we saw in Section 1.4, people soon found that there were many jobs for computers of a kind completely different from the original "number crunching" of the adding machine teams. With cheaper and cheaper minicomputers and microcomputers, there are more and more such applications. We discuss some of them in the next subsection.

New Uses for Microcomputers

In the remainder of this section, we look at some of the places where computers are being used for the first time as a result of the economics of size, cost, and energy brought about by integrated circuitry.

Until recently, it has been the practice to build the control systems for traffic lights using integrated circuits which will automatically put the lights through their cycle. However, it is clear that a traffic control device would work better if it is in fact programmable, with the custom-wired circuitry being replaced by a microcomputer. Then the control system can be tailored for state and city regulations, the particular pattern of traffic at a given intersection, and even for the time of day. Such controllers are in fact now being installed.

Integrated circuitry is already being built for driving digital wristwatches with amazing accuracy. As Section 1.1 makes clear, we can program a calendar watch to take care automatically of the different lengths of the months, even taking care of leap years by remembering when it is necessary to add a 29th day to February. This program is wired in. With some extra microcomputer circuitry, we can let the owner "program" his watch. With some suitable way of tapping knobs on the side of the watch and checking the result on a digital readout displayed on the face of the watch, one could set the watch to ring an alarm at programmed intervals, even displaying the nature of the appointment on the face of the dial when it rings.

Many readers have already bought pocket calculators, which use integrated circuitry. We can expect the increasing sophistication of microcomputers to make such systems even easier to use while getting greatly increased program ability into them.

Communications systems will also make increasing use of microcomputers. In current transmission of a TV picture, every dot of the screen must be "repainted" many times each second. However, if you look carefully at a TV picture, you will see that at any moment great regions are not changing. They provide the background for attention-getting movement. With an appropriate computer system, it will be possible to transmit information only about the changes, and have the system at the other end decode the message to update its current representation of the picture on the screen—rather than requiring the TV set to receive the complete picture over and over again. This might increase by a factor of 100 the capacity of the various channels, thus making them available for many other uses. We shall discuss some of these in Section 6.2 (Computers and the Media) and in Chapter 7.

In Section 5.1, we shall look at attempts to build artificial limbs that could decode nerve signals in the limb stump of an amputee. We shall discuss attempts to convey visual information directly to the brain of someone who had lost their sight through damage to the eyes. In such applications, we can expect microcomputers to play an important role in letting the necessary coding and decoding be carried out in a highly portable system with minimal energy requirements.

Microcomputers will also play a role in building portable teaching machines as we shall see in our discussion of DYNABOOK in Section 6.3; and within ten years will certainly be commonplace in the home in appliances, security devices, and innumerable gadgets and toys—including chips that will convert the TV set into an electronic games room.

Cars are already equipped with integrated circuitry for monitoring brakes, for seatbelt interlocks, for skid control, etc. We can expect these uses to be increasingly taken over by microcomputers, which can be easily reprogrammed for individual conditions.

Microcomputers can also be used to verify customers' credit.

Instead of a sales clerk having to phone an office to have a clerk there check the printout to see whether the customer's credit is still good, one can simply place the customer's credit card in a special device. The microcomputer within the device can then recognize, from the magnetization on the card, the credit card company and the credit card number of the customer. It can then automatically dial the connection to the credit card company's computer, automatically request information about the customer—and then automatically display on a screen whether or not the customer's credit is good. All this within a fraction of a second.

The list of microprocessor applications could go on and on. Let us close briefly, though, with the suggestion that microprocessor technology puts the home computer within easy reach. With a TV set and an electric typewriter, you have already acquired the expensive peripherals. Just add a few more chips, and you have an elegant computer. Set up communication lines, and you have a system with dramatic implications for the way you retrieve information (Section 6.2, Computers and the Media) and the way you influence local and national decision-making (Section 7.2, Democracy in the Computer Age). A price of a hundred dollars or so for the computing equipment seems completely feasible once a sufficiently large company or government agency decides to gear up for the distribution of millions of these household units, making the transition from expensive toy to mass-produced household standby.

Suggestions for Further Reading

J. W. Mauchly: On the Trials of Building ENIAC, *IEEE Spectrum,* 1975, pp. 70–76.

An account is given of the problems of building a computer in the early 1940s—when people could not see that a machine with 18,000 vacuum tubes and costing $500,000 could ever become practical.

B. Randall: Colossus, *Proceedings of the Los Alamos Conference on the History of Computers,* 1976.

This essay presents the first detailed look at British work on computer-like devices during World War II—made possible by the gradual release of classified material on code-breaking.

W. C. Hittinger: Metal-Oxide Semiconductor Technology, *Scientific American,* August 1973, pp. 48–57.

A view of some of the advances in integrated circuitry that are making microcomputers possible.

A. G. Vacroux: Microcomputers, *Scientific American,* May 1975, pp. 32–40.

This is a useful account of "computers on a chip or two."

C. C. Foster: A View of Computer Architecture, *Communications of the ACM,* **15,** 1972, pp. 557–565.
> Takes a look at the possible impact of microprocessors that can be placed on a single, inexpensive, chip of integrated circuitry. [The article was originally titled "When the chips are down," but this was changed by the journal's editors.]

J. Lewis: The Calculator Threat to Numeracy, *New Scientist,* November 13 1975, Calculator Supplement, pp. xv–xvi.
> Will pocket calculators stop us from learning to think with numbers?

S. E. Madnick: The Future of Computers, *Technology Review,* July/August 1973, pp. 35–45.
> Surveys the trend of computers to become more powerful, cheaper, and easier to use.

Summary

We saw that transistors allowed the building of **minicomputers,** and that **integrated circuitry** allows the building of **microcomputers.** As a result, modern computers are far more powerful than the machines of the 1960s, yet use less power, take up less space, and are far cheaper. Because integrated circuitry can pack thousands of components into a fraction of a cubic inch, microcomputers can be tiny in size yet large in computer power.

Computing circuitry accounts for about 3% of the cost of a conventional computing system and its peripherals. Thus even a dramatic drop in the cost of the central circuitry will not greatly reduce the cost of conventional computers. Instead, we can expect many new computer applications, with "dots of intelligence" placed in machines both in industry and in the home.

Glossary

Integrated circuitry: *Integrated circuitry* is a complete circuit of many transistors produced by photographic techniques on a single piece of silicon, called a *chip*. This replaces circuits in which transistors are made separately, then wired together.

Minicomputer: A computer the size of a desk or smaller is a *minicomputer*.

Microcomputer: A computer whose central circuitry can fit into a volume the size of a book or smaller is a *microcomputer*. Such a computer need only be small in size, not in computing power.

Central processing unit (CPU): The part of the computer that retrieves and carries out the instructions in a program—obeying operation instructions, carrying out tests, and controlling input and output devices in response to input and output instructions—is the *CPU*.

n-bit machine: The primary memory of a computer is divided into *locations* that can each hold an instruction or piece of data. Each location can be referred to by a distinct number, called its *address*. If every location in memory is built with the same number *n* of two-state devices, it is called an *n-bit machine.* Thus the words stored in a single memory location of an *n*-bit machine are strings of *n* 0s and 1s.

Exercises

1. Why can the cost of manufacturing computer circuitry be reduced to nearly the cost of printing photographs?

2. (a) An electron carries one unit of negative charge. Neutral matter has one proton (with a unit positive charge) for each electron. A proton–electron pair weighs 1.67×10^{-24} grams. With respect to a magnetic field, a single electron can be aligned (each electron is a little magnet) either "up" or "down." Supposing we could store one bit of information per electron in a device, how many bits could we store per gram?

   (b) How does the one-bit-per-electron memory compare in bit density (bits per gram) with the tube hardware flip-flop mentioned in the text (90 cubic inches, 10 watts dissipation)?

3. Think of some applications for a microcomputer in a television.

4. What use might be made of microcomputers in your refrigerator? your shoe? in a swimming pool? your door? your telephone?

5. A watt is a measure of electrical power. A current of 1 ampere at 1 volt requires 1 watt of power. House current in the U.S. is about 120 volts, so a 100 milliamp (10^{-2} amp) vacuum tube flip-flop (1944 technology) uses $120 \times 10^{-2} = 12$ watts. Modern computers use 5 volt power, typically, and draw less than 10^{-3} watts per bit of memory. Why does the wattage of an electronic device affect its cost?

6. Draw the components of the valid-credit system described briefly in the text. Include customer, credit clerk, sales clerks, telephone, credit card, and print-out. Use stick figures and labeled boxes with lines for links.

7. IBM's analysis that at most 25 computers could be sold in America (1952) was heavily price dependent. Suppose the automobile was just invented this year, with the initial model costing $1 million. How many people or organizations might buy one? Who? Note that roads were built as cars were sold, making cars more desirable by positive feedback.

8. Early industrial activities in England were dependent on water power. By tradition then, factories had one large turning shaft powered at first by water wheels, then by coal-burning steam engines. Individual power tools, such as drills and lathes, were connected mechanically to the shaft by belts. When the electric motor was invented, factories copied the old pattern by purchasing one large motor and running all tools from a single motorized shaft. It was decades before a simple idea caught on: put a small electric motor in each power tool, making them independent. Compare this to the situation with a large central CPU versus many distributed microcomputers.

9. Why can't perhipherals be miniaturized? Would you use a hand held console with a keyboard of tiny keys to be pushed with a pencil point? Is line-printer output on paper preferable to, say, a compact microfilm printer which requires a microfilm to read? Could these be cheaper than conventional peripherals? Explain.

2.4. WRITING AND REWRITING LARGE PROGRAMS

The development of high-level languages that make programming easier for us is one of the central research problems in computer science. This trend in computation is well described as "human engineering": matching the style of a computer's operation to the style of human problem solving. In addition to designing input/output devices and high-level languages which are easier to use, computer scientists are also looking at techniques that will help people write programs that are relatively free from error. In this section we shall see ways in which a team of programmers can keep track of what they are doing even on a complex problem that requires hundreds of thousands of instructions.

Large Programs

We have discussed the idea of a program, and learned how to program the behavior of TURTLE. However, the programs there were all short ones—perhaps requiring at most a few hours to write. This is a very far cry indeed from an **operating system** or a **data base management system** (see Section 4.1 for further details) which may require tens or even hundreds of thousands of instructions.

One dramatic example of a large program is associated with Skylab, the first orbiting American space station in which astronauts could live for weeks on end. Before Skylab was launched, elaborate mission **simulations**—computer tests of how the system would work—were carried out on earth to make sure that every aspect of the life support system would function properly, and that the astronauts would know how to use the facilities in space. The programs required for the simulation totaled about 400,000 instructions. It has been found that on programming projects of this size, a programmer can complete something like 5 to 10 high-level instructions per day. It would thus have taken one man at least 120 years to complete the Skylab program! Of course, no single programmer could live that long, nor could the project management afford to wait so long to receive the completed program. Thus it becomes necessary to put a whole team of programmers to work on any large program.

One of the main ideas we shall explore in this section, then, is how we can take a large programming task and break it down in such a way that the work can be shared by many programmers. Before we do this, however, we should return to the statement that a programmer only completes 5 to 10 instructions per day on a large project. This seems very strange indeed. If you did any of the TURTLE assignments in Section 1.3, you may have found that 5 statements could be written in an hour or two. You would thus expect that an experienced programmer might complete the task in a mere 15 minutes. Why then should the output of experts be only 5 or 10 instructions per day?

There are a number of reasons for this low productivity. One is that the time required is not only the time to write out the instructions. In advance, one has to work out the job those instructions are to do. After the instructions are written, time is required to test them, debug, and rewrite them until a program that does the job is obtained. In writing a large program, a programmer may lose track of how his piece of the program relates to other pieces of the program. This is one of the things that makes debugging of part of a very large program far harder than debugging a 10- or 20-line program.

Another problem a programmer on a large program may have is that in correcting an error he has found in his part of the program, he may change the way in which his program is used by somebody else. Suddenly that other person will find that their part of the program, which had been working perfectly, is now defective. As you can imagine, the task of tracking down the effect of changes other people have made in their part of the program, and figuring out whether this messes up your part of the program, can take a great deal of time indeed. One might say that the errors made by the programmer are not so much errors in writing out a few instructions of a program as much as they are errors in thinking through what job his part of the program has to do.

It is because of the problems of coordinating the many programmers on large projects that we need management practices that put a great deal of care into assigning parts of the job to the different programmers on the team. The team leaders must make sure that each programmer can go about his task without causing problems for any of the other programmers. At the same time, this structuring of the programming process can make clear what each piece of the program is doing, and thus make it much easier to understand what the overall design is all about. Finally, once one has clearly specified the job of each part of the program, it becomes much easier to test that the program really does what it is intended to do. This is because testing can proceed piece by piece, rather than trying to test the entire program at one time.

Structured Programming

The general approach of breaking the job of writing a program into meaningful pieces which can be fairly well tackled one at a time is called **structured programming.** There are many different ideas among programmers today about how best to structure a program, including various rules about how to use test instructions to jump from one part of the program to another. What seems to be really important, however, is the idea that the overall task must be broken down into meaningful pieces, and that these pieces must be broken down into yet finer pieces, and so on, until one finally reaches a stage at which the detailed writing of line after line of a program is appropriate. This contrasts strongly with the approach, taken by many programmers, of starting to write down instructions in their favorite programming language as soon as they begin to understand the problem. They then add new instructions and remove old instructions as they go to shape up their program until it fits the specifications better and better. In other words, they do not have any real understanding of the problem except to the extent that they can write it down as a sequence of instructions. By contrast, in structured programming, the programmer starts by trying to get a clear statement of the overall job of the program, and then breaks it down into meaningful pieces. We can see an example of this (Fig. 1) in the way in which we approached the task of programming the robot to get to the doorway in Section 1.1. We first clearly specified the situation: the robot had to go to the wall in front of it and then along the wall until it reached the door. We then saw that we could break the task of the robot down into 3 pieces:

(1)   program the robot to go forward until it hits the wall,
(2)   program the robot to turn right through 90°,
(3)   program the robot to go forward until it finds the door.

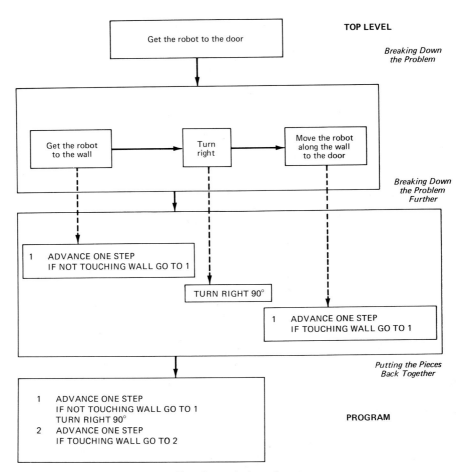

Fig. 1 Top-down design of a program.

We specified that the first step should take place with the robot facing directly toward the wall. We specified that the third stage should take place with the robot moving along and touching a wall to the left of it, with the doorway somewhere ahead.

In a simple task like that shown in Fig. 1 we would not have to assign the programming of different pieces to different people. However, in a much more complicated situation, one might imagine that each of the pieces would be a challenging job for literally months of work by a skilled programmer. If this were the case, it would clearly improve the programmer's efficiency immensely if he could work on his task without continuously having to dash off and see how the work of other programmers was coming. However, Fig. 1 shows that some care must be taken in putting the pieces together again. In this example, we see that the programmers working on the first and third stages both used the **label** "1" in their subroutines. This is the sort of thing to be expected if the subroutines are written separately. Thus the person who puts the subroutines together must carefully check that labels and names used in one part of the program are not used in another part to refer to something else.

In summary, then, the key idea of structured programming seems to be involved in the idea of **top-down design:** one gets an overall specification of what the system is to do, then breaks this down into pieces each of which can be tackled separately. These pieces may be broken down in turn, until one finally reaches the stage at which the pieces are small enough to be programmed in a reasonable length of time. These basic pieces are usually required to be simple enough to be covered in a page of program. The idea here is that each piece should be sufficiently small that the programmer can carry in his head a full understanding of what all the instructions in that piece are meant to be doing. This not only reduces the chance of his making mistakes, but also makes it much easier for him to locate those mistakes that do occur.

However, it must be confessed that top-down design of a large system will not always proceed smoothly "from top to bottom." One reason for this would be that the specified design from the top down calls for a piece to do a job that, it turns out, cannot be met by any program. It may even be logically impossible. For example, one designer working on the specifications for a large network of power stations found that the specification he had designed for one part of the network required it simultaneously to decrease fuel consumption and increase energy output. The way he had specified this part of the network had not made this contradiction clear. It was only when working out the detailed specifications that this was discovered. As a result, many other parts of the system had to be redesigned so that the demands on this part became realistic. Of course, the top-down approach is still a good one, because when the inconsistency in specification of one part is discovered, it is relatively easy to check what impact the redesign of that part will have on the parts that are mentioned elsewhere. If, however, the mistake had been found in an unstructured program, it would be almost impossible to track down what portions of the thousands or even hundreds of thousands of lines or program had to be corrected.

We often use the word **hierarchy** for a system that is divided into a relatively small number of subsystems, each of which may be further subdivided. We may thus paraphrase the above discussion by saying that structured programming involves the breaking down of a large programming task in a hierarchical manner. The important point about each subsystem within the hierarchy is that it must be a clearly defined programming task which can be further broken down without reference to any of the details of the internal programming of any of the other subsystems. For example, returning to our robot example, when a programmer works on stage 3, all he knows is that he must get the robot to the doorway when it is guaranteed that the doorway lies ahead along the wall which the robot is touching to its left. In carrying out this task, any further information about what is being done in the other parts of the program is irrelevant to the programmer.

A story about two watchmakers suggests the greater reliability of a hierarchically designed system. The two watchmakers, named Hora and Tempus, both manufactured watches made of 1000 parts each. The difference between them was the way in which they built their watches. Tempus worked in such a way that if he ever put down a partially assembled watch it immediately fell to pieces and he had to start all over again. On the other hand, Hora designed his watches in terms of subassemblies of 10 elements each. He would thus start off by making a hundred subassemblies of ten parts at a time. He would then put these together 10 at a time to make a total of ten larger assemblies, and would finally put all 10 of these together to make the whole watch. Whenever he was interrupted, the watch would only disassemble back to the subassemblies. As you can imagine, Tempus hardly ever completed a watch except on the calmest of days, whereas Hora could complete many watches despite constant interruptions, so long as those interruptions gave him time to put at least 10 pieces together.

We can see how this story relates to structured programming. A programmer who at any time has only got to keep straight in his head the interaction between 20 or 30 instructions and a clear specification of the job they must do is going to make relatively few mistakes, and have little trouble debugging the program. A programmer who is wrestling with 1000 instructions, without having made any attempt to really partition the job into manageable pieces, will very likely get confused. He may forget why he wrote an instruction some time ago, and so is more likely to make mistakes, and less likely to track down bugs when they occur.

We may call the subsystem in a structured program a **module.** The important thing about a module is not only how it is built—in other words how it is broken down into submodules—but also the fact that its behavior is clearly specified before we start to break it down into smaller pieces. We might say that the module is specified by a **contract** between it and the other modules. This contract is a binding agreement with two parts. The THEN parts spells out the job the module must do. The IF part spells out what assumptions the module must make about the behavior of other modules before it can do its job properly. For example (Fig. 2), in our getting-the-robot-to-the-door program, we may say that the contract for stage 3 consists of a guarantee that "IF I start operation when the robot is facing along the wall, the robot touching the wall to its left, and the doorway lying somewhere ahead of the robot along that wall, THEN I will get the robot to that doorway."

A well-written program, then, should contain not only the instructions written in the programming language, but should also include a clear statement of the contract that a given block of instructions satisfies. We usually refer to anything written with the program to help people understand what the program is about as **documentation.** In most cases, the documentation on programs consists of a few

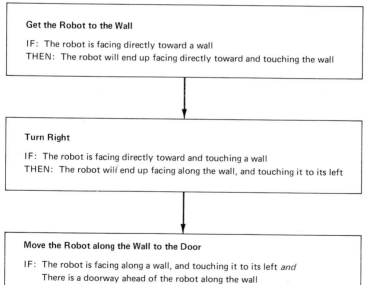

Fig. 2 Contracts for the second-level modules of the top-down design of Fig. 1.

comments which the programmer puts down to indicate the general idea he had in mind when he wrote a large block of instructions. All too often, these comments are not detailed enough to let the programmer himself—let alone anyone else—really find out what is going on at some later date when changes in the program are to be made. These changes may be necessary to correct errors, or to take account of new demands on the system. Requiring, as part of structured programming, that the documentation includes the full contracts for each module in the program will make it far less likely that the programmer will make errors in the first place. It will also make it much easier for the programmer and for other users to understand what a large program is all about, and will make it far easier to debug and to update the program.

Programming Teams

The above description of structured programming makes it fairly clear how a group of programmers should proceed in writing a large program. First, there must be an initial design phase, in which the overall problem is broken down into high-level modules. Then, these modules in turn must be further broken down. Finally, modules can be turned over to programmers who will implement them in an appropriate programming language, and then test those modules to make sure they work. Meanwhile, however, the high-level design must be tested, by running programs which use program "stubs" to simulate the presence of those modules which are yet to be implemented, to ensure that if those modules satisfy their contracts, then the overall system can run correctly.

One apparently successful approach to dividing these responsibilities among the members of a team has been taken by IBM with what they call their "chief programmer team." Here, the overall top-down design is the sole responsibility of the chief programmer, and of a deputy-chief who shares with him the task of top-down design. The chief programmer can then farm out the different modules to individual programmers, who may take part in further top-down design to break their modules down into yet smaller modules, and then do the actual programming. In addition to the chief programmer and his deputy, there is also a program librarian, whose job it is to ensure that as each module is developed, it is carefully documented in a standardized and readable form. The librarian also makes sure that a complete record is kept of all the test runs which have been made with a module—including runs that have ended in failure, because information on how the program went wrong is crucial in getting it to run right. The record of all these modules and their performance is kept in what is called the "DSL" (Development Support Library). In this library, the chief programmer and his deputy can find the information they need to find out which modules have been programmed, and whether or not they have successfully met their contracts. The individual programmer can quickly get access to information on any of the modules he has designed, and check whether they are performing correctly. Now, there are other programmers working on other modules, from which his module will receive various partial results and control signals. He can check to see whether these other modules have yet been shown to satisfy the performance criteria which enter into the contract of his own modules. In a group working on a really large project, the programmers may well be assisted by typists who can write up their documentation, as well as by computer operators who can carry out the actual tests of different parts of the program.

In all this, the chief programmer is the focus of responsibility. He has many resources at his disposal, but it is his job to use these resources to ensure not only that each module meets its contract, but also that these contracts enable the modules to work together in accordance with the overall design of the system.

One of the first achievements of an IBM group using the chief programmer team approach was to design an information bank for the New York Times which required 83,000 instructions in a high-level language. A six-man team completed the task in 22 months—almost 30 lines per man-day, several times the normal rate of programming for a large project. Even more impressively, the program appeared to have an exceptionally small number of bugs in it. The moral seems to be that, by breaking a program down into manageable pieces and keeping careful track of both what each piece is supposed to do and what it actually does, one can produce a working program in a fraction of the time that would be required if one had not carefully planned the whole task in advance.

Program Validation

Clearly, it is not enough to design a large program and simply hope that it works. One must check it out carefully. As the above discussion suggests, it is much easier to check it out if one has broken it down into meaningful pieces, and ensured that each piece does what it is supposed to. Nonetheless, no matter how carefully one checks out the individual pieces, there is always the chance that when the program is up and running "out in the field," some errors will be found. Perhaps a user is typing in messages of a kind that the programmer had not anticipated, and so the system must be revised to handle these messages in some proper way. Once again, structured programming seems to help with this problem of **maintenance.** With a structured program it is much easier to check which module has the responsibility of handling this new situation. You can then update this module using the contracts to ensure that when you change the module, you will not damage the performance of any other module.

Our concern in this book with the social implications of large systems such as data banks (Chapter 4) suggests that there is quite a different type of program validation from that which checks if the program does what it was originally designed to do. We must check whether the corporation that built the system *designed* it to do what they *claim* they designed it to do!

Imagine that a court has just ruled that a data bank must include certain safeguards to protect the privacy of people about whom information is stored. (We shall see more on this in Section 4.3, the Privacy Act of 1974.) Suppose that the company or government agency that owns the data bank replies that it has indeed adhered to the guidelines set down by the court, and offers as proof 300,000 instructions in some programming language! This makes it difficult for anyone to check the data bank owner's claims. Investigators must dream up all manner of fancy ways of asking questions to the data bank, to see whether they can find some way of getting information that the owners say should not be accessible. By contrast, if the program has been properly structured, and if each module is fully documented with all its comments, then the owner can be required to set forth a careful account showing that if the modules all meet their contracts, then the system *must* protect the privacy of individuals. Then, instead of blindly having to attempt to trip up the 300,000 instruction monster, the court-appointed computer specialists have the huge—but now relatively manageable—task of

> (1)   checking that the claim of the owners is true if each module satisfies its contract; and then
> (2)   checking through the instructions in each module to verify that it does indeed meet its contract.

It should be made clear that the state of the art in program validation is still rather poor. A programming team will often believe that it has shown that its program will perform without fault, and yet will find bugs in the program when it is in operation. By the same token, even if experts were to certify that a complex data bank program would respect the privacy of individuals, it might still be possible for some ingenious programmer to find some way of interacting with the system in an unanticipated way to retrieve information to which he should have no access. Thus, checking that a data bank performs as specified, and is not being abused, will not only require advances in the methodology of structured programming and program validation, but will also require a great deal of good old-fashioned detective work. If an individual believes that someone else is damaging him by misuse of information that is found in some data bank, then it will probably be detective work, rather than a programming exercise, that will track the culprit down, and bring him to court. We shall discuss some related issues when we look at corporate crime in Section 4.2.

Rewriting

We saw that writing a program in modules would make it easier to debug a program—tracking down errors and making appropriate changes. However, a large system may also require changes because different demands are placed on the system. For example, a credit card company may have set up a system for use only in France, and then want to extend its operations internationally. Presumably, the basic procedures for reporting expenditures and payments by individual customers remain the same. However, there is now a need to add modules that can convert expenses in one currency to the currency in which the customer will pay—taking into account the rate of exchange (how many French francs to the United States dollar, and so on) on the day of purchase. In a case like this, then, structured programming makes the task of updating the system relatively easy, for it is straightforward to specify exactly what addtional tasks the system must have, to design modules for these systems, and to ensure that the old modules will meet the contracts required to ensure that the new modules perform satisfactorily.

However, the problem of top-down design becomes very complicated when the system we are designing has social implications. For example, suppose that one were designing a computer system that would be used by the state for welfare—for distributing money to the needy. The program would take information about the size of a person's family, how long it is since a member of the family last held a job, the income of the family members when they held the job, the state of health of various family members, and so on, to determine whether or not they were eligible for welfare, and, if so, to determine the size of the check, and print it out ready for mailing. Once we know the proper formula, there is no problem in designing such a program—it is just like the payroll program of Section 1.2. The *real* problem is that we do not know what the formula is. The legislature may pass a bill designed to help the needy, only to find that when implemented it encourages many people who were otherwise productive members of the work force to stop work because they can receive more money under the new welfare legislation. The usual response to such a discovery is to "patch" the system. One might add a module to test for the conditions under which a person left their last job before deciding whether they are indeed eligible for welfare. One might check to make sure that they have really tried hard to get a job before they are eligible for welfare. One might try juggling the size of the welfare check relative to the minimum wage, to try to make it more desirable for people to keep a low-paying job rather than to go on welfare.

In this way, the laws get more and more complex, and the formula for determining the size of welfare checks gets more and more complex. As a result, the staff of case workers whose job it is to check out the data required by the welfare system gets so large that the costs of making sure that only eligible people get welfare threaten to become as large as the costs of providing welfare to those people who really need it. The constant checking on them may distress the people on welfare. At such a stage it becomes silly to try to "correct" the program without changing its overall top-down design. It is time to start all over again. For example, some legislators have suggested that rather than a welfare system, one should try a guaranteed minimum wage, a sort of negative income tax, which ensures that every citizen will receive the minimum amount required to obtain food, clothing, and lodging. Whether or not such an approach would work, it is clear that it would do away with a great deal of the welfare bureaucracy, and would require a complete redesign of the welfare system, rather than a simple patching of it. In the same way, we can expect that many large programs will require constant inspection to determine when patching must give way to complete redesign.

Suggestions for Further Reading

H. Mills: Top-Down Programming in Large Systems, in *Debugging Techniques in Large Systems* R. Rustin (ed.), pp. 41–55. Prentice-Hall, Englewood Cliffs, New Jersey, 1971.

N. Wirth: Program Development by Stepwise Refinement, *Communications of the ACM* **14** (1971), pp. 221–227.
  These are two basic papers on some of the notions presented in this section.
F. P. Brooks, Jr.: "The Mythical Man-Month, Essays on Software Engineering." Addison-Wesley, Reading, Massachusetts, 1975.
  This is a readable discussion of the management problems involved in putting together very large programs.
H. A. Simon: "The Sciences of the Artificial." MIT Press, Cambridge, Massachusetts, 1969.
  Chapter 4. "The Architecture of Complexity," contains an excellent discussion of hierarchies, including the story of the two watchmakers.
F. T. Baker and H. D. Mills: Chief Programmer Teams, *Datamation,* December (1973), pp. 58–61.
  The notion of chief programmer teams is discussed and IBM's success with this approach is enthused over.

Summary

Large programs may contain tens of thousands of instructions. To ease the writing of such programs, and to make it easier to track down and correct errors, we used **structured programming.** This uses **top-down design** to break the problem into **modules**—each well-**documented** with its own **contract**—which may be turned over to different programmers. This top-down approach may be very important when it is necessary to demonstrate that a controversial program does what is *claimed* to do. We look at the problem of rewriting programs to meet changing needs, and see that while top-down design can help when only small patches are required, there may eventually come a time when a new overall design is required.

Glossary

Operating system: The operating system is a set of programs, permanently resident in the computer, that make the computer easier to use.

Data base management system: This is an operating system designed to handle *data bases* on the computer.

Simulation: A *model* of an object or process is another object or process that shares crucial properties with the original, but is easier to manipulate or understand. A *scale model* has the same appearance as the original save for size and detail. However, increasing use is being made of *computer simulation:* the model is a computer program that lets a machine compute how key properties of the original will change over time. It is easier to change a program than to rebuild a scale model if we want to explore the effect of changes in policy or design.

Structured programming: Structured programming is a body of techniques for writing programs with fewer errors, which are also easier to correct. A key technique is *top-down design* which specifies the overall problem, then breaks this into pieces called *modules,* breaking this down again into smaller and smaller modules, eventually producing modules easily programmed by a single programmer. Each module has a *contract* which lets the programmer handle that module without knowing the fine details of other modules. The contract says that IF other modules have done certain jobs, THEN this module in its turn will do its own job.

Comments: When we write a program, we often write notes to remind us of what different parts of the program make the computer do. These notes are called *comments*. In a top-down design, these comments could include the contracts of all the modules in the program. The complete package of comments together with the program in human-readable form is called *documentation*.

Hierarchy: An organization whose components are arranged in levels from a top level on down to the bottom level is a *hierarchy*.

Program validation: Checking out a program to make sure that it does the job it is designed to do is *validating* the program.

Maintenance: In a very large program, bugs may not be discovered until the program has been in use for months or even years. *Maintenance* is the process of tracking down errors and correcting them after the program has gone into service.

Label: We place *labels* on those steps of a program that are targets for jump commands—so that the computer knows which instruction it must switch to when the jump is required.

Exercises

1.   Provide a top-down design—like that shown in Fig. 1—for the program for updating both time and date that we discussed in Section 1.1. Use at least three levels before the bottom level. Some second-level modules should break down through a different number of levels from others.

2.   When a program is broken down into modules, with at most one person writing each module, how do we decide how large a module is, and how many people are needed? Let us consider, for example, that we need to write a program called BIGBUCKS, which we expect to sell for a million dollars. BIGBUCKS will need to be roughly 100,000 lines long to do its job. The programmers available for a standard pay of $50 per day can all write an average of 10 lines per day. Discuss the advantages and disadvantages of each of these strategies.

   (a)   Divide BIGBUCKS into 10,000 modules of 10 lines each, and hire 10,000 programmers.

(b) Divide BIGBUCKS into 10 modules of 10,000 lines each, and hire 10 programmers.

(c) Divide BIGBUCKS into 200 modules of 500 lines each, and hire 50 programmers.

3. Name three of the major problems involved in writing a program 1,000,000,000 (one billion) instructions long. (*Hints:* Cost, number of people, documentation, machine.)

4. Name three problems (*not* computer problems) that no one person could do alone, but which are routinely solved by teams of roughly 1,000 people working together.

5. Suppose you had to program a hand-eye robot to play a game of table tennis and you wanted to break the program into four modules. What are some natural modules? (*Hint:* What separate functions does a person perform?)

6. Write contracts for each of the three modules in the "Update Date" program for a digital calendar watch shown in Fig. 9 of Section 1.1.

7. Suppose a team of 100 people were going to play as a single side in a game of chess against an expert player. How might the ideas of structured programming, top-down design, contracts, and documentation suggest an organizational plan? Consider the number of different pieces to move in a typical position (at most 32), the need to plan at least five moves ahead, the books of standard openings avilable, the individual variation among the 100 players, the possibility of collectively picking a few possible moves and having each person work out one in detail, a hierarchy headed by one player who listens to the others' advice before actually making the move.

8. You have a three-month vacation to do anything you want, and $5,000 to spend. Discuss the advantages and disadvantages of dividing your time into 12 one-week subvacations, with a different plan for each week.

3

Simulating
Complex Systems

SECTION 3.1. THE IDEA OF SIMULATION

When we think we understand something, we can often build a **model** of it that will behave in much the same way. More and more, we use computer models—programs that will enable a computer to make predictions about how the original system will behave. This process of using computer models is called **computer simulation.** We study a number of models, and look at control problems, especially those involving negative **feedback.** This section is self-contained, except for the use of a flow diagram (Section 1.1) in one example.

SECTION 3.2. PREY AND PREDATORS

To get a feel for what is involved in **ecological modeling,** we analyze the interaction between a population of prey (rabbits) and a population of predators (wolves). We stress the idea of **model validation**—of using field study to make sure that the model's predictions can be trusted. We write down a few equations—but the reader whose eyes glaze over at the sight of mathematics can still understand the main points of the section. The section is basically self-contained.

SECTION 3.3. WORLD SIMULATION

We look at attempts to model the impact of ecological and economic changes on the world's entire human population. We shall see that the use of computer simulation here can be misleading unless the models and the data are more reliable than is yet the case. We shall discuss ways in which models may be made more realistic; and ways in which we might get better data. This section requires Sections 3.1 and 3.2 as background.

3.1. THE IDEA OF SIMULATION

No sane aircraft company, wishing to introduce a new plane, would go directly from a drawing of an attractive shape to the building of an actual plane. It is all too likely that the plane would have bad aerodynamic qualities and would either not take off—in which case the company would be laughed at—or would crash soon after takeoff—with a disastrous loss of human life. In either case, the result is an extremely expensive failure. Instead, the company builds a *scale model* of the new design which can be tested in a wind tunnel to find out whether the plane will take off, whether there is any danger of its stalling at various speeds and angles of climb, and so forth. If the model fails in any way, it is relatively inexpensive to modify it, and remodify it, until a shape with satisfactory properties is found. Then, and only then, is it worth the cost of building a full-size plane. Of course, the decision to build the plane requires not only this modeling of its flight properties, but also a market survey to make sure that the company can cover its development costs and return a profit.

Again and again, we want to make predictions about the likely behavior of some system—be it an airplane, a spacecraft, national economic trends, or the weather. The central theme of this chapter, however, is that rather than build a scale model of a system to make predictions, *we can often "build" a* **model** *inside the computer*. We do not, of course, twist the wires inside the computer to make them look like an airplane or a hurricane! Instead, we write down a careful description of the *structure* of the system. We then use this to define a program that will let the computer calculate answers to our questions about how the system will *behave*. For example, we use a careful description of the shape of the wings and fuselage to compute how the plane will respond to the pilot's controls under different conditions.

For a classic example of mathematical model-making, we may go back to **Newton's laws of motion,** developed 300 years ago to describe the falling of an apple or the motion of the planets around the sun, or of the moon around the earth, in terms of the gravitational attraction between them. We all know that it would be extravagant to send a spaceship to an apple, and the height of folly to eat the moon. Yet when it comes to describing the way they *move,* the same mathematical equations describe them. What Newton discovered was a way of setting down equations that show how bodies interact—whether they be the earth and the moon, the sun and the planets, or an apple and the earth. He showed that the spatial relationships of the objects and the masses of the objects determined the gravitational forces between them, and gave laws of motion that let him deduce from these forces how the bodies would move over time.

In Section 1.3, we looked at parameters in programs and instructions. In an instruction like FORWARD A, the symbol A is a parameter which can be replaced by a number to get a specific command like FORWARD 17—move TURTLE forward 17 millimeters—or FORWARD 293—move TURTLE forward 293 millimeters.

In the same way, a good model has **parameters**—places we can substitute numbers to get the model to apply to a specific situation. For example, Newton's basic model showed how two bodies would interact under the gravitational attraction that each exerted on the other. The model had just two parameters: the mass of each body (roughly speaking, how heavy it was). Once you substituted actual numbers for these two parameters, you had a set of equations that would let you predict where the two bodies would be, and how fast they were moving at any time—provided you specified their initial positions and velocities. If you substituted the mass of the moon and the mass of the earth, the model predicted the moon's motion traveling around the earth. If you substituted the mass of an apple and the mass of the earth, the model predicted the speed at which an apple falls to the ground.

Again, a mathematical model of an airplane would have parameters corresponding to the shape of the wings, the outline of the fuselage, the mass of the plane, and so on. It is the parameters that make the model useful. For if we choose one set of numbers, and find that the predicted behavior is not satisfactory, then we can simply change parameters, rather than having to think of a completely different model.

In **computer simulation** of a system, we take the equations in the mathematical model, and write a computer program that can com-

For many years, engineers have used scale models to test the properties of full-scale systems. This photograph shows a large model of a new airplane in a wind tunnel.

pute for us how the system will behave for each choice of parameters, and each choice of initial condition. It is easier to change a program than to rebuild a scale model if we want to explore the effect of changes in policy or design.

In the rest of this section, we shall develop some further concepts of system theory, and discuss ways in which we can use computer simulation to help make decisions. In Section 3.2, we shall see how to write equations that describe a simple ecosystem—in which we study the population levels of a rabbit population and a wolf population. With this background, we can turn in Section 3.3 to a study of the simulation of ecological and economic systems on a worldwide scale.

The State of a System

When we decide to study some system, we are breaking off a piece of the world from its environment (Fig. 1). If we study a space-

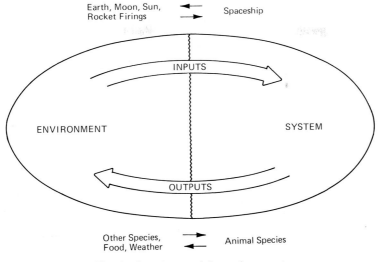

Fig. 1 A system and its environment.

ship, the relevant environment includes the gravitational attraction of the earth, the sun, and the moon, and the way in which we can fire the rockets. If we study an animal species, the relevant environment contains other species with which it interacts, its food supply, and the weather. If we have a vending machine, the only relevant impact of the environment may be the way in which money is fed into the slot and levers are pulled.

What must we include in the description of a system—whether or not we plan to study it by computer simulation? We can get an idea by looking at the vending machine of Fig. 2. We see that we must specify the **input** to the system—what the environment can do to the system—and the **output** of the system—what the system can do to its environment. In this example, the input to the system is made up of the coins we put in the slot and the lever we pull. The output is made up of a candy bar and change. The relationship between the input and output is not a direct one, however. We will only get what we want if the machine has enough change or we put in the right money and if there are still candy bars left in the hopper for which we pulled the lever. Thus, to describe the machine, we must not only specify the inputs and outputs, but also the internal **state.** In the case of our vending machine, the internal state is made up of the position of the candy bars in the hoppers and the contents of the change hopper (Fig. 3).

OUTSIDE

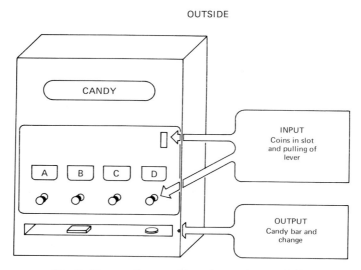

Fig. 2   The vending machine as seen from outside.

Whenever we apply an input to the system, it changes state and emits an output. If we wanted to simulate the system on a computer, we would have to write a program that would get the computer to keep track of the inputs, states, and outputs.

Let us do this for the situation of Fig. 3. We shall assume that every candy bar costs 15¢, and that the computer will make change for 25¢ or two 10¢ pieces, as well as accepting 15¢ as a 10¢ plus 5¢ or as three 5¢ pieces.

To specify the input, we must specify the money put in, and the lever pulled. We thus represent the input by a pair (x_1, x_2), where x_1 is a list of numbers specifying the money: it could be (5, 5, 5) or (25) or any other list of 5s followed by 10s followed by 25s. We will design the machine to return the money if too many coins were put in. x_2 is just a symbol A, B, C, or D corresponding to the lever choice.

The output is just an x_1 if money is returned, but no candy bar; a pair (x_1, x_2) if both change x_1 and a candy bar x_2 (in the output, A, B, C, and D are the names of candy bars, not levers) are vended; and just an x_2 if a candy bar is vended but no change.

To specify the state, what is in each hopper must be specified (we shall assume that each hopper is stacked with only the right candy bars). Thus to hold the coding of the internal state, the computer needs 7 registers. The registers named A, B, C, and D hold

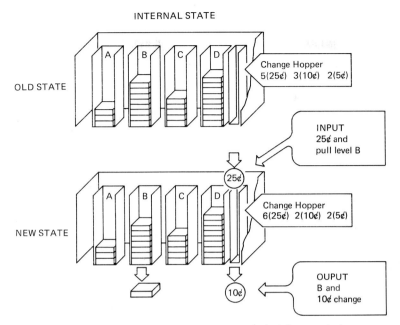

Fig. 3 The vending machine with internal state revealed.

the number of candy bars left in the A, B, C, and D hoppers of the vending machine. The registers E, F, G hold the number of 25¢, 10¢, and 5¢ pieces left in the change hopper.

Figure 4 includes a box labeled $W_{(25)}$—that part of the flow diagram for our simulation if the input (x_1, x_2) has $x_1 = (25)$. It first checks to see if there are any of the desired candy bars left—is $x_2 > 0$? If $x_2 = A$, the A-register will be nonzero if there are any A-bars left. In this case, the computer next checks to see if it can make change. If $F \geq 1$, it can return a 10¢ piece. If $G \geq 2$, it can return two 5¢ pieces.

In addition to determining what the proper output is, the computer must also update the state. For example, if the vending machine takes in a 25¢ piece, and puts out an A-bar plus a 10¢ piece, then the number of 25¢ pieces in the change hopper increases by 1—represented by $E := E + 1$ in the computer—while the number of A-bars and the number of 10¢ pieces inside the computer decreases by 1—$A := A - 1$ and $F := F - 1$. In other words, the complete specification of a system includes not only the inputs, outputs, and states, but also the **state-transition function,** which describes how the

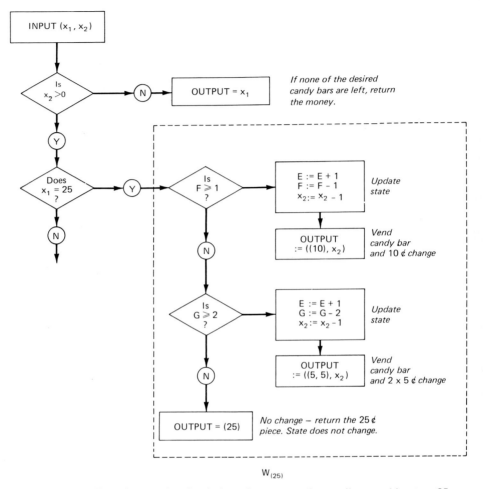

Fig. 4   Flow diagram for simulation of response of a vending machine to a 25¢ input and the pulling of a lever.

state changes, and the **output function,** which specifies what the next output will be (Fig. 5).

Figure 6 shows that part of the flow diagram that tests for the money input—with the money being returned if the money input is not acceptable. You should be able to fill in the boxes $W_{(10,10)}$, $W_{(5,10)}$, $W_{(5,5,5)}$ along the lines of $W_{(25)}$ in Fig. 4.

Before leaving this example, we should stress that what we include in our model of a system and its environment depends on what

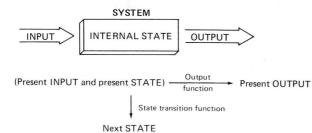

(Present INPUT and present STATE) $\xrightarrow{\text{Output function}}$ Present OUTPUT

State transition function

Next STATE

Fig. 5 The elements of the description of a system.

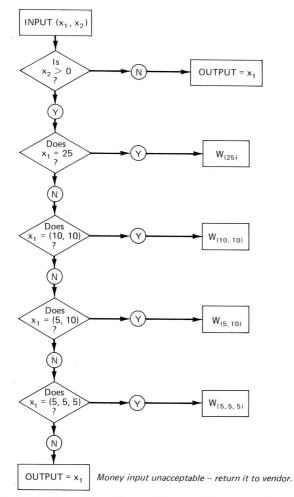

Fig. 6 Outline of flow diagram for simulation of vending machine.

we want to know about the system. The simulation of Figs. 4 and 6 would be a fine subroutine to keep track of how the vending machine would respond to well-behaved customers. However, if we were machine builders trying to make sure that people could not get candy just by kicking the machine, the model would be quite different, and would have to take account of the effect of sudden impacts on the gears and levers inside the machine.

In Newton's original study of the orbits of the moon and the planets, the state of a heavenly body was given by its velocity and position. The inputs were the forces acting on the moon and the planets due to the gravitational pulls of the moon, the earth, the other planets, and the sun. Today, however, spaceships and man-made satellites have joined the other heavenly bodies, and to the natural forces of gravitation we add the humanly controlled forces: the thrust provided by the rocket motors. Thus where Newton asked how a system would behave:

"Given the gravitational pull, how will the planets move?"

today's engineer or astronaut turns the question around to ask how to choose the inputs to **control** the system, making the system behave in some desired way:

"Given an orbit I want the spacecraft to go into, what are the necessary forces to apply?"
"How can I do this with the least fuel?"
"How can I do this as quickly as possible?"

Newton invented the mathematical method called **calculus** (a German, named Leibnitz, made this discovery, too) which enabled him to write equations that described the gravitational forces acting on any system of bodies. The equations he wrote were called **differential equations.** He also invented a technique called **integration** to go from the equations to the description of how the positions and velocities of the bodies would change with time. Few readers will know any calculus—although we hope that many will learn it, since it is so important in helping us understand science and engineering, and ecosystems, too. In any case, the specification of the Newtonian method and the modern development of control theory in Fig. 7 should be clear. From this has grown a whole array of applied mathematics which allow us to write down equations that accurately de-

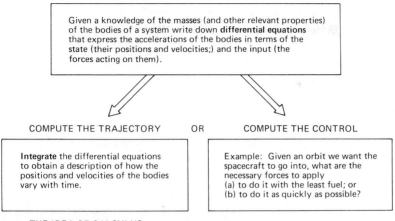

THE IDEA OF CALCULUS

Fig. 7   The Newtonian method and control theory.

scribe a whole variety of mechanical and aerodynamic and hydrodynamic systems.

Negative Feedback

We closed the last subsection by mentioning the **control** problem of choosing inputs to make a system behave in some desired way. In particular, there is the problem of *hitting a moving target*—whether it be a person hitting a ball, a spaceship hitting the moon, or a missile hitting a plane. Consider how you grab a moving ball. You could look, estimate where the ball is heading, shut your eyes, and just "shoot" your hand out in that direction; but you would probably miss. So, you normally keep looking. You shoot your arm in the general direction of the ball. Then as the arm gets close, you use visual control to adjust the movements to get it there. You track the discrepancy between where you are and where you want to be, with the error between actual and desired performance controlling the behavior. We can show this in Fig. 8.

We have what is called a **negative feedback system** because the actual performance is *fed back* to determine a compensation which acts to *negate,* or at least reduce, the error. The observation of the moving ball gives the *desired* performance—where you want your hand to be. The observation of the hand—the controlled system— gives the *actual* performance, where the hand actually is. The differ-

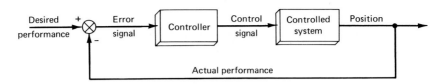

Fig. 8 Negative feedback.

ence between actual and desired performance is the **error signal** which the controller—in this case your brain—can use to compute the proper control signal to change the muscle tension to move your hand in the right direction to get the ball.

What might go wrong in a feedback system? Suppose the error is that the hand is to the right of the ball, so the controller, in this case your brain, sends out a command, "Go to the right," and you move your hand to the right. If, however, you give too strong a movement, what will happen? Instead of ending up on the ball, you just go whiz-zing past—you have overcompensated. Then the brain discovers that the error is the other way, and sends a command to move your hand to the left and the process simply repeats itself. In other words, if the **gain**—which determines the size of the control signal in terms of the size of the error signal—is too large, then, instead of smoothly catch-ing the target, you will wildly swing your hand back and forth without ever catching the ball.

Perhaps the best known example of a negative feedback system is a thermostat. In this case, the setting of the thermostat gives the desired temperature, while the actual temperature is read by the thermometer. The system to be controlled is the heating system for the room, and the controller is the device that decides whether it is time to turn on the heat or not. A really fancy system could have both a heater and an air conditioner and switch from one to the other, but the job of most heating systems is only to raise the temperature above an uncomfortably low outside temperature. If the actual temperature is below the desired temperature, the controller will turn the heater on and bring the heat up. Once the room gets hot enough, the controller will turn the heater off. If the gain is right, the room should stay comfortable. If the gain is too high, the controller will turn the heat on too long for the desired correction, and the temperature will swing up too high, and it will be a long time before it decays down again—only to swing up too high once more. So the room, instead of staying around 20°C, will be oscillating between 18°C and 25°C.

Consider the thermostats of a double electric blanket, with switched controls. Now what happens in the feedback situation? You are a little too hot, so you turn down what you believe to be your control, but all this does is lower the temperature on your friend's side. Your friend reaches over and turns up "his" setting. This makes you even hotter, so you turn "your" setting way down. Your friend is then really freezing, so he turns "his" setting way up, ... This is an example of a **positive feedback system**—the feedback system sends out control signals which increase the error, instead of reducing it. Be careful—this is the *engineering* definition of positive feedback. Do not confuse it with the popular *psychological* use of the term to mean the same thing as positive reinforcement—praising people when they do something well.

We have already met the overall aims of **cybernetics** in the introduction. The man whose 1948 book started much of the activity in this field was Norbert Wiener. He was led to develop cybernetics because he had studied feedback systems in his work on World War II artillery, and had become very interested in the analogy with the movement of the arm. Thus he asked his clinician friends at Harvard Medical School and Massachusetts General Hospital whether they had seen illnesses that corresponded to the wild swings of a negative feedback system where gain is too high. They told him there is a disease called *ataxia* which affects a part of the brain called the *cerebellum*. Human patients with ataxia have exactly this high-gain problem. When they reach for a glass of water, their hand shoots out too far; then they pull back, going into uncontrolled oscillations, until they just decide to stop. A horrible disease, but one easily understood in terms of the simple principle of feedback design: you must adjust the gain so that the system does not overreact to the error signal. Note that it would also be bad if the gain were too low. In this case, the compensation for an error would be too small—for example, a low-gain system might never catch up with a moving target. Thus it is a delicate problem to make sure that the gain is adjusted properly, so that the way in which the system goes from the error signal to the correction signal is appropriate. This is true whether in evolving the biological circuitry that we have for tracking moving objects in our world, in designing a missile or a spaceship, or in determining how nations should respond to environmental changes.

As we noted in the introduction, cybernetics grew from the insight that the study of biological systems and the study of engineered systems—which use the applied mathematics that has grown from the work of Newton—have important concepts in common. Cybernetics was originally a science that compared control and communication in the animal and the machine. As we also noted in the introduction, cybernetics is now used to study other systems as well. In the remaining sections of this chapter, we will emphasize the study of ecological and economic systems. Section 3.3 will briefly examine "The Limits to Growth," a book commissioned by the Club of Rome, a select group whose members are concerned that the world is set on a dangerous course in which pollution, starvation, and overpopulation will lead to a global disaster. The model of the world offered in "The Limits to Growth" supports the notion of global catastrophe occurring in the 21st century. However, the model is too simple, and cannot let us explore strategies for avoiding disaster. Later in Section 3.3, then, we look at a more flexible approach to world simulation. We shall also see other faults of the "Limits" model. We shall return to this theme in Section 7.3, when we suggest that a worldwide computer network might offer a practical tool for real economic and ecological decision-making in the future.

The discipline of **computer simulation** is twofold:

1.   You must know enough about the subject to describe a model that is sufficiently accurate to answer the questions of importance to you. Newtonian mechanics gives a method for answering questions about how an apple will move when thrown; but we must turn to the medical sciences to describe the fate of the apple when eaten. In the next section, we shall see what to do when you *cannot* find an accurate model.

2.   Use the formal description to write a computer program to compute the answer to your question. Feed in data or possible inputs to the system, and possible parameters in the system description and the program to a computer; read out the results.

The second item reminds us that, for even a moderately complex system, it is one thing to write down a model of the system, and quite another thing to compute with the model to come up with the answers to your questions. Once you know Newtonian mechanics, you can easily write down equations that describe the earth with its gravitational field, the moon with its gravitational field, and a spaceship, with its rockets, and show what force will act on the spaceship for any given position between the earth and the moon and for each amount of thrust of the rockets. However, it requires a great deal more work to go from the equations to a specification of a program of rocket firing which will get the craft to land at a specific place on the moon without taking too much time or fuel. This is a huge task of grinding away with the equations and "crunching" numbers. There are billions of arithmetic operations required, and only a computer can handle them. As we stressed in Chapter 1, the "secret" of the computer is that you can give it a program telling it how to "crunch" away that is much shorter than the amount of "crunching" it has to do.

It may take weeks of programming to give the computer all the information it requires about what the equations are that govern the system, what the masses are of the various objects, what effect the fuel distribution has on the dynamics of the spaceship. The resulting program with perhaps a few thousand instructions will include tests of the kind, "Is this a good enough answer? If not, go back and try again, try again, try again," or loops of the kind "Ok, now you have worked out what will happen during one hundredth of a second of the spaceship's flight. Now use that information to work out what will happen in the next hundredth of a second." We tell the computer both to try, try, try again to find out what will happen in every small interval of time, and then to extend the computation for longer and longer periods of time. In this way, thousands of instructions can be used to control billions of operations of the computer.

Suggestions for Further Reading

C. C. Gotlieb and A. Borodin: "Social Issues in Computing." Academic Press, New York, 1973.
    Chapter 7 discusses systems, models, and simulation.
M. A. Arbib: "The Metaphorical Brain." Wiley (Interscience), New York, 1972.
    Chapter 3 provides an introduction to system theory, discussing the concepts of states, algorithms, feedback, and adaptation.
A. Anderson, Jr.: Forecast for Forecasting: Cloudy, *The New York Times Magazine,* December 29, 1974, pp. 10–31.
    Takes a look at the current status of weather forecasting by computer.

Summary

We saw that a model of a real **system** need not be a look-alike scale model, but could instead be a computer program, often based on mathematical equations, which could be used to make predictions about the behavior of the system. The same model could be used to describe many different situations by suitable choice of **parameters. Newton's** model of gravitational attraction could predict the fall of an apple or the orbit of a planet around the sun. **Computer simulation** runs these program models to give us information about how the system might respond in different conditions.

The choice of model depends on the questions we want answered about the system—a model of the normal operation of a vending machine is very different from a model of how the machine will react to being kicked by vandals or frustrated customers.

The model of a system includes the specification of its **inputs** and **outputs,** as well as its **internal states.** It must also include rules for specifying how the state and output change over time as new inputs keep coming in. In a **control** problem—like getting a satellite into orbit—we must choose the inputs to make the states or outputs behave in some desired way. Control usually involves **feedback**—using information about the output to help figure out the best input to apply next.

Computer simulation is only helpful if the model and data used in the simulation are accurate enough.

Glossary

Model: A *model* of an object or process is another object or process that shares crucial properties with the original, but is easier to manipulate or understand. A *scale model* has the same appearance as the original save for size and detail. However, increasing use is being made of *computer simulation:* the model is a computer program that lets a machine compute how key properties of the original will change over time. It is easier to change a program than to rebuild a scale model if we want to explore the effect of changes in policy or design.

Model validation: Checking the predictions of the model against the actual changes of the original over time is called *validating* the *model*. An analysis of differences can be used to modify the model to obtain one that more accurately predicts important activities of the original.

System: A *system* is an object or process—or collection of objects or processes—that we choose to study. The *environment* comprises those processes that we expect to have an effect on the system. The *inputs* to the system are the effects of the environment on the system. The *outputs* of the system are the measurable responses of the system. The *states* of the system relate the inputs and outputs. The *state-transition function* describes how the states change over time in response to inputs. The *output function* describes how the state determines the output.

Parameter: In simulation studies, we use *parameters* to distinguish between systems that are described by similar sets of equations. The parameters in a model are the places where we can substitute numbers to get the model to apply to a specific situation.

Newton's laws of motion: These are basic laws describing how objects will change position and velocity in response to forces. Newton invented the mathematical method called the *calculus* to study the motion of objects. The equations describing the forces acting on a number of objects are called *differential equations*—calculus uses *integration* to solve these equations to find how the objects move over time. For example, the simulation programs used to describe space shots are based on these equations.

Control: *Control* is choosing the inputs to a system to make the state or output change in some desired way, or at least close to it.

Feedback: The process whereby output signals are fed back to the input of a system, so that the system can respond to information about its own performance, is *feedback*. A *negative feedback* system uses this information to negate (or at least reduce) the *error signal*—which is the difference between the actual output and some desired output. For example, in a thermostat the actual temperature is compared to the temperature setting. In a feedback system, the *gain* measures how big a compensation will be made in response to an error signal. In a *positive feedback system,* the change in input *increases* the error, rather than reduces it.

Cybernetics: *Cybernetics* is the study of computation, communication, and control in the animal and the machine. It has been extended to the study of information processing in social systems too, in which humans may interact with machines.

Exercises

1.   Why all this complicated use of the computer in modeling? To understand a system, why not just change it slightly in one way—change one variable— then see what happens, change another variable, and so on, until you know how each variable affects the system?

2.   The rocket was invented in China in the 11th century. Legend has it that a prince, fascinated by the application of gunpowder to flight, had a large number of rockets strapped to a chair. He sat in the chair, had his servants light the fuses, and amid a cloud of smoke vanished into explosive oblivion. How did the prince's idea of testing differ from the method explained in this section for new aircraft?

3.   Carefully examine the vending machine's internal state in the second part of Fig. 3. Draw a picture of the internal state and output after the following input: 10¢ 10¢ pull lever B. Explain.

4.   Draw the $W_{(10,10)}$ box from Fig. 6 in detail, as the $W_{(25)}$ box has been drawn in Fig. 4.

5.

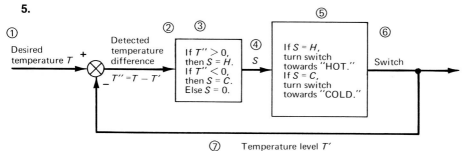

In the accompanying diagram of the control system of person and electric blanket, identify (by number) the following components: desired performance, error signal, controller, controlled system, and actual performance. What happens if $T'' = 0$?

6. Feedback can occur whenever two variables can affect each other, or when a cycle occurs, such as when X changes Y, Y changes Z, and Z changes X. For complex, richly connected systems, the multiplicity of feedbacks can produce extremely complex behavior—in patterns impossible to explain in terms of the separate feedback loops, let alone the separate variables. We will see some examples of this later in this chapter. How many feedback loops are in each of the accompanying diagrams?

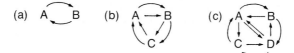

7. Match the appropriate pairs of concepts.

1.	location of earth, moon, sun	a. system
2.	rocket thrust	b. environment
3.	laws of motion	c. input
4.	location of rocket	d. output
5.	motion of rocket	e. state-transition function

8. Isaac Newton was probably never bonked by an apple. But he did consider the following theoretical problem: A cannonball is shot horizontally from the top of a very tall mountain. As the cannon charge is increased, the ball will land further and further from the mountain. After a still larger charge, the ball will go more than halfway around the world, and land closer to the mountain. What would happen with a charge much larger than that? You may, for this problem, disregard the drag on the ball produced by air friction by imagining the mountain to be 100 miles high. What did this model suggest to Sir Isaac?

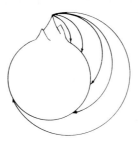

9. The accompanying graphs show the temperature in our house for a day with two different air-conditioning systems we are considering buying. Each has a thermostat. Which unit should we buy, and why? (Explain in terms of feedback.)

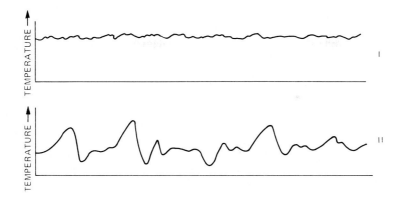

10. The following is a demonstration from mathematical sociology that knowing how every pair of objects in a system affect each other does not tell us everything about the total system interaction. Six people are at a party. Each of the 15 possible pairs of people is either two people who love each other or two people who hate each other. Draw several diagrams as below on some paper or a blackboard (draw the mutual love connection in one color, the mutual hate in another) to illustrate the following surprising result: there is always at least one group of three people, all of whom love each other, or all of whom hate each other. How could you prove this fact? Do you think this is a useful model of social interactions at a party?

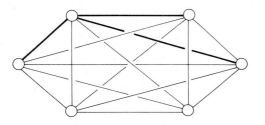

3.2. PREY AND PREDATORS

In Section 3.3, we shall look at ambitious simulation projects which try to predict the effect on the world's human population of industrial development, food resources, pollution, economic investment, and so on. Before we turn to these grand projects, it will help us to look at a relatively simple ecological system.

Imagine that we live in an area where the two main wild animals are wolves and rabbits. The wolves are **predators**—they eat the rab-

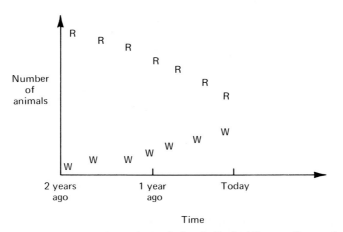

Fig. 1 A graph that shows for each time in the last 2 years, the number of wolves (the height of the W above the time line), and the number of rabbits (the height of the R above the time line).

bits, who are thus their **prey.** Suppose that we like rabbits, using them as a source of meat; but dislike wolves, because they steal our chickens. We are thus alarmed at a town meeting, when one of our friends reports that, over the last two years, the rabbit population has been dropping steadily, while the number of wolves has greatly increased. The situation is shown in Fig. 1, where the number of wolves and rabbits has been plotted for the last 2 years.

At this rate, it appears that soon all the rabbits will be gone, and that with so many wolves, the chickens will not be safe either—and soon we shall have neither rabbits nor poultry to eat. The obvious thing to do is to kill off a large number of wolves, and this is the action for which the townspeople clamor. We shall see, however, that intuition can be wrong, and that a more careful analysis may suggest a different course of action. It is to that analysis that we now turn.

Isolated Species

Our job is to understand the relationship between the rabbit population and the wolf population. To start with, though, let us imagine what would happen if the rabbits were on one island, and the wolves were on another. The rabbits would happily eat grass, and breed (like rabbits!) and as time passed there would be more and more rabbits. That is why we drew the line labeled + (plus) on the rabbit circle in Fig. 2. The poor wolves, however, find little nourishment on their island, and they begin to die off, schematized by the −

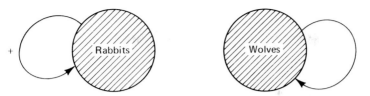

Fig. 2 Schematic representation of the isolated wolf and rabbit populations.

(minus) on the wolf circle of Fig. 2. Before we put the wolves and rabbits together, we can write some equations. [The reader who finds equations disturbing should relax: it will all be explained in English, too. However, if you get to be really serious about solving ecological problems, you will have to learn how to write equations to describe the ecosystem you care about, and you will need a computer to solve these equations.]

We write R_t to denote the number of rabbits alive on day t. Then we said that if the rabbits are left to themselves, their number will increase. This yields the equation

FOR RABBITS WITHOUT WOLVES: $\boxed{R_{t+1} = R_t + aR_t}$

where the number a is bigger than zero, and represents the amount by which a given rabbit is more likely to reproduce than to die in any given day. For example, if R_6 were 100 and $a = 0.03 = 3/100$, we would have on the seventh day of our study $R_7 = R_6 + aR_6 = 100 + 3/100 \times 100 = 103$ rabbits. This type of population increase is called *exponential growth*. To see why this is so, we look at some formulas that use the notion of an exponent from high-school algebra:

Suppose we know that there are R_0 rabbits at day 0, the day we started keeping track of the rabbits on the wolfless island. Now recall that in Section 1.2, we used the notation $2^4 = \underbrace{2 \times 2 \times 2 \times 2}_{4 \text{ times}}$. In general we can write m^n as shorthand for $\underbrace{m \times m \times \cdots \times m}_{n \text{ times}}$. We read this as "$m$ to the power n," or just as "m to the nth," and we call n the **exponent.** Then the above formula tells us that

$$R_1 = (1 + a)R_0 = (1 + a)^1 R_0$$
$$R_2 = (1 + a)R_1 = (1 + a)(1 + a)R_0 = (1 + a)^2 R_0$$
$$R_3 = (1 + a)R_2 = (1 + a)(1 + a)(1 + a)R_0 = (1 + a)^3 R_0$$

Continuing in this way we clearly have the formula

$$R_t = (1 + a)^t R_0$$

If we start with $R_0 = 100$ rabbits, and each day R_t increases to $R_{t+1} = 1.03 \times R_t$ (looking at the example $a = 0.03$), how long will it take for R_t to reach 200? In other words, what is the doubling time? We are trying to find the k for which R_k is closest to 200. However, the formula for R_k is $1.03^k \times 100$, and if $1.03^k \times 100 = 2 \times 100$, then $1.03^k = 2$. So we want the k for which 1.03^k is closest to 2—and the answer is that k is 24: 1.03^{24} is approximately 2.

After another 24 days, we have

$$R_{48} = 1.03^{48} \times 100$$
$$= \underbrace{1.03 \times 1.03 \times \cdots \times 1.03}_{48 \text{ times}} \times 100$$
$$= \underbrace{1.03 \times \cdots \times 1.03}_{24 \text{ times}} \times \underbrace{1.03 \times \cdots \times 1.03}_{24 \text{ times}} \times 100$$

which is approximately $2 \times 2 \times 100 = 400$. Thus it goes—every 24 days, the population doubles.

Returning to the general situation, as long as the number a is greater than 0, we can pick a number k for which $(1 + a)^k$ is approximately 2. We can then plot R_t in the graph of Fig. 3 where k is this number of days it takes the population to double. We call k days the **doubling time.** This pattern of rapid increase is called **exponential growth.** Remember that we said that n was the exponent in the expression m^n?

Now we see that in the formula

EXPONENTIAL GROWTH: $\boxed{R_t = (1 + a)^t R_0}$

the time t appears as the *exponent* which tells us how many copies of $(1 + a)$ must be multiplied together to go from the population R_0 on day 0, to the number of rabbits R_t there will be t days later.

It is important to stress that exponential growth cannot go on forever. Even if there were no predators on their island, the growth of the rabbit population would be checked by the **carrying capacity** of the island. This is the highest level—perhaps a million rabbits—that could be fed by the amount of grass growing on the island even if they did not trample it. Now the fact is that

$$2^{20} = 1,048,576$$

and so if we start with just $32 = 2^5$ rabbits, it would only take 15 doubling times before the population would theoretically reach

$$R_{15k} = 2^{15} \cdot R_0 = 2^{15} \cdot 2^5 = 1,048,576$$

If, however, only a million rabbits can live on the island, the population could not keep growing exponentially.

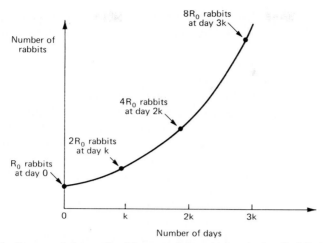

Fig. 3 Exponential growth of the population. k days is the doubling time.

The message of this is that *any model—no matter how compli-cated it may be—has a limited range of applicability.* We cannot trust the exponential growth model if the number of rabbits overloads the food resources. (When we put the wolves and rabbits together, the wolves will see to that!) But what model should we use when we must take into account the limited food resources? We see three pos-sibilities in Figs 4–6.

In Fig. 4, the population never reaches carrying capacity. As the population increases, it becomes harder for a rabbit to find all the food it needs. Weak rabbits will die more rapidly. Female rabbits will

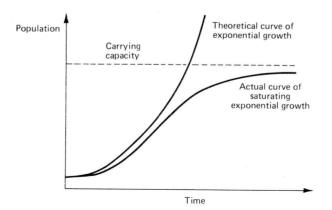

Fig. 4 Exponential growth saturating as it approaches carrying capacity.

reproduce less often. As a result *a* gets smaller, until finally it gets very close to zero—in other words, births and deaths balance. Then

$$R_{t+1} = (1 + 0)R_t = R_t$$

and the total number of rabbits stays much the same.

In Fig. 5, the population swings up above the carrying capacity. Young rabbits do not eat as much as older rabbits, but once these rabbits grow up, there is no longer enough food for everybody, and so many rabbits starve to death. It is not until the population has dropped well below carrying capacity that there is enough food around so that the births can once again exceed the deaths.

In Fig. 6, we show the worst possible case. As the number of rabbits goes beyond carrying capacity, the animals become desperate for food. They are so hungry that they do not just nibble the grass—they dig at it, and eat it, roots and all. As the roots are eaten, less and less grass can grow. Soon there is nothing left to eat. All the rabbits die.

Which of these three situations is the one that would really describe the fate of the rabbits on their little island? No amount of discussion will tell. **Field work** is required—actually studying how rabbits behave. Does a desperately hungry rabbit eat the roots of the grass? Do baby rabbits require less food than adult rabbits? How does lack of food affect the birth rate and the death rate? Without careful study of what really happens, we do not know. However, if we

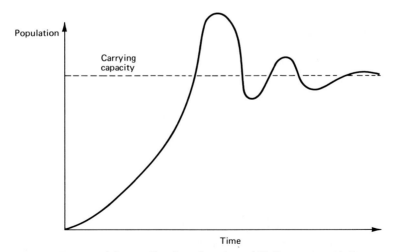

Fig. 5 Exponential growth changing to oscillations around the carrying capacity.

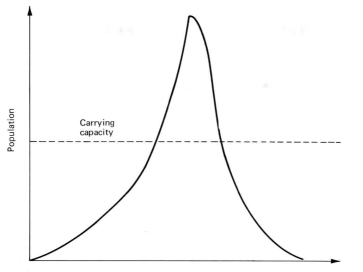

Fig. 6   Extinction of a population that has passed carrying capacity.

do field study on one island, then we can be much more confident of our predictions about another island. This is the process of **model validation.** We start with a model—or a choice of models—of how something in the real world behaves. We compare the predictions of the model with what actually happens. We may change the model so that it fits better with reality. After doing this again and again

Predict → Compare with reality → Change model

we may obtain a model that time and again makes predictions that turn out to be close enough to what really happens. At that stage we can probably afford to do less field work, and base our behavior on the predictions of the model.

Engineers can confidently control a spaceship using the predictions of Newton's laws of motion about how firing the rockets will alter the spaceship's trajectory. Newton's model is well validated for that sort of problem. However, when we turn to ecology and economics, the models are often very poorly validated. It is as if one bet a great deal of money that Fig. 5 was better than Fig. 4 or Fig. 6 because "I have a hunch that those waves—well, they just *feel* right," instead of having careful studies to back you up. Because of this lack of model validation, many of the predictions that we shall discuss in Section 3.3 are highly controversial. We need to think about them, but we do not know if they are right.

It is now time to model the wolves on their island. Because they are carnivorous, they decline in numbers when isolated from the rabbits, and so—if there are W_t wolves alive on day t—we obtain the equation

FOR WOLVES WITHOUT RABBITS: $\boxed{W_{t+1} = W_t - bW_t}$

where the minus sign in front of the positive number b is the mathematical sign of the *decline* in wolf population. Without rabbits to eat, the wolves are more likely to die than to reproduce. Just as for the rabbit equation, we can write the equation

EXPONENTIAL DECAY: $\boxed{W_t = (1 - b)^t W_0}$

which has a graph like that shown in Fig. 7, where m is the number such that $(1 - b)^m = \frac{1}{2}$, so that every m days the number of wolves is *halved.* We call m days the **halving time.** Clearly, **exponential decay** ceases to be a good model well before the predicted level of $(1 - b)^t W_0$ drops below 1!

Putting the Species Together

The problem that worried us at the town meeting was a decline in the number of rabbits, and an increase in the number of wolves; yet our model shows that, left to themselves, the rabbit population grows exponentially while the wolf population decays exponentially. As we can see from Fig. 8, there *seems* to be a contradiction. Of course, this is *not* a contradiction. We know that the problem is caused by wolves eating rabbits.

It is time to stop pretending that wolves and rabbits are on separate islands. We must put them together. This means we must add

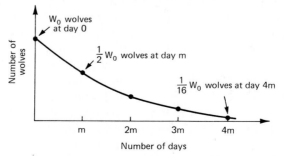

Fig. 7 Exponential decay of the population. m days is the halving time.

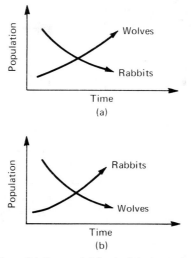

Fig. 8 (a) The problem; (b) the model for isolated species. A contradiction?

interaction terms to our model. Thus, in Fig. 9, we not only have the "side-loops" for the "natural" birth and death processes, but we also have two additional arrows.

The 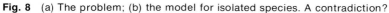 indicates that rabbits help wolves grow; the indicates that wolves eat the rabbits, and so decrease their numbers. The more wolves there are, the less the rabbits grow; the more rabbits there are, the more the wolves grow. How do we write an equation to describe this? The more often a wolf meets a rabbit, the more often will a rabbit be eaten—leading to a decline in the rabbit population by 1, and an increase in the likelihood that the wolf will have another offspring. However, the chance that a wolf meets a rabbit increases with the *product* $R_t \cdot W_t$ of the number of wolves and rabbits; for if we *double* the number of wolves and *double* the number of rabbits, there is *four times* the chance of a rabbit–wolf encounter. Each wolf is now twice as likely to meet a rabbit, and there are now twice as many

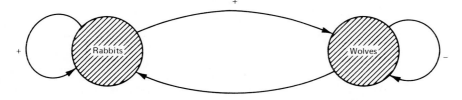

Fig. 9 Putting the wolves and rabbits together.

wolves to do the meeting (and eating). Now we obtain our fancy **prey–predator equations**

Expected number of rabbits
eaten by wolves in one day

RABBITS
INTERACTING WITH
WOLVES

$$R_{t+1} = (1 + a)R_t - \overbrace{cR_t \cdot W_t}$$

$$W_{t+1} = (1 - b)W_t + \underbrace{dR_t \cdot W_t}$$

Expected increase in wolf
births as a result of rabbit
food supply

To summarize:

a = rate at which rabbit population increases in isolation,
b = rate at which wolf population decreases in isolation,
c = rate at which rabbit–wolf encounters decrease the rabbit population,
d = rate at which rabbit–wolf encounters increase the wolf population.

Equations like this were first developed (but using calculus, instead of the day-by-day census) by the Italian mathematician Volterra in his book "La Lutte pour la Vie"—"The Struggle for Life." He showed that his equations had cyclical solutions as shown in the graph of Fig. 10. This is a new kind of graph called a **phase plane**

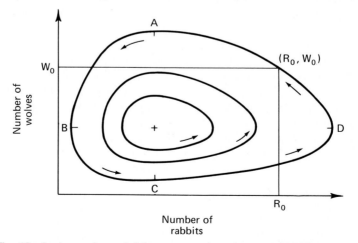

Fig. 10 A phase plane plot for prey–predator interactions. Each closed curve shows one possible way in which the wolf and rabbit populations could change together over time.

plot; and each curve is called a **trajectory.** Suppose at some time—
call it day 0—we find there are R_0 rabbits and W_0 wolves. If we pick the
trajectory on which the point (R_0, W_0) lies, and then follow it in the
direction of the arrow, we shall see how the two populations change
with time. We have only shown three trajectories, but they are enough
to show the general pattern. Let us follow the population around the
outer trajectory.

From D to A: The number of rabbits decreases, the number of
wolves increases.

From A to B: The number of both wolves and rabbits decreases.

From B to C: The wolves continue to decrease, but the rabbits
now increase.

From C to D: The number of both wolves and rabbits increases.

The figure shows two other trajectories—corresponding to different
starting populations.

In fact, Volterra deduced this shape of the trajectories by logic
alone. Straight mathematical reasoning shows that the populations
change in this cyclical fashion. [To be more accurate, the smooth
trajectories solving Volterra's calculus equations join up perfectly
after each cycle. In the real world—and in our "day-at-a-time"
equations—the populations come back to *almost* their original values, but not exactly their original values. However, that is close
enough for our purposes.] Without getting too far into the mathematics, let us see if we can understand what is going on.

(1)   From B to C
At first, there are so few wolves and so few rabbits, that the terms
$cR_t \cdot W_t$ and $dR_t \cdot W_t$ are both very small. As a result, the wolves continue
to die out, and the rabbit population growth is hardly slowed at all by
the attacks of the wolves.

(2)   From C to D
Look again at the equation describing the wolf population:

$$W_{t+1} = (1 - b)W_t + dR_t \cdot W_t$$
$$= W_t - b \cdot W_t + dR_t \cdot W_t$$
$$= W_t + dR_t \cdot W_t - b \cdot W_t$$
$$= W_t + [dR_t - b] \cdot W_t$$

W_{t+1} is bigger than W_t as soon as $dR_t - b$ gets larger than 0, because
the add-on term $[dR_t - b] \cdot W_t$ is then positive. Now C is the place

where W_t stops getting smaller, and starts to increase again, so C must be the place where $dR_t - b$ goes from negative to positive. However, we can solve $dR_t - b = 0$ to obtain $R_t = b/d$. Thus we deduce that at C the rabbit population is b/d.

As we move from C to D, the rabbit population still increases, but now there are plenty of rabbits for the wolves to eat, and so their population increases, too.

(3)   From D to A
Eventually, there are so many wolves that they start to eat rabbits faster than the rabbits can reproduce. Eventually, the wolves have eaten so many rabbits that they bring the rabbit population down to b/d again—which is why A lines up with C in Fig. 10.

(4)   From A to C
Thus A is the place where $dR_t - b$ gets less than zero again and—as a result—the wolf population begins to drop. So, in this last phase of the cycle, there are still enough wolves to eat the rabbits more quickly than they can reproduce, but there are no longer enough rabbits to prevent the wolves from declining. Eventually, we get back to (a population level near to that of) C, and the whole process starts all over again.

Solving the Problem

After this long excursion into setting up equations to describe the interactions between wolves and rabbits, and seeing how the populations change over time, we at last know what we are talking about. Our approach to solving the problem of wolf increases and rabbit decline can now be based on a firm knowledge of the situation, rather than on a scare reaction to the population statistics.

The closed curve of the last figure—obtained by pure logic, without using computers—tells us that populations go in cycles. Without any human intervention we shall finally reach (at point B) a stage at which we have the desired combination of falling wolf population and rising rabbit population. A little thought reveals, however, that this information is not enough. How far ahead is B—three years, ten years, a century? and, meanwhile, how high is the wolf population at A? Can we put up with that many wolves for that long a time?

The only way to answer these questions is with numbers. The numbers we need are of two kinds:

1.   *Data.*   We need to know the actual values of the **parameters** *a, b, c,* and *d* in our model. To find these values we must go out and do

field work, learning enough about reproduction patterns and diseases in the rabbit and wolf populations, as well as observing the hunting behavior of the wolves and the defensive mechanisms of the rabbits.

2. *Computer trajectories.* Once we have (R_0, W_0) and the system parameters from our field work, we can then go to the computer and program it to compute the trajectory, plotting its estimate of each day's population levels, and printing out the population levels at A, B, C, and D and the day numbers on which these stages will be reached.

It may be that the number of wolves may never get so high as to be a danger, and that the rabbit supply may not get unduly low. What happens, however, if the wolf population *will* become dangerously high if no action is taken? In this case it may be necessary to kill some wolves. We can use our model to examine the effect of killing off wolves.

Suppose the operation is to start when the population level is G, in Fig. 11. If we kill wolves—but leave the rabbit population alone—we move down the line through G. Where we stop depends on the number of wolves that are killed. At each place we stop—such as G_3 or G_0 or G_5—the wolf and rabbit populations will continue to interact, as shown by the trajectory through that point. Naively, one might think that the best strategy is to kill as many wolves as possible, perhaps reducing the population to G_5. What a terrible mistake! With so few wolves around, the rabbit population explodes, providing so much food for the few remaining wolves that their population grows

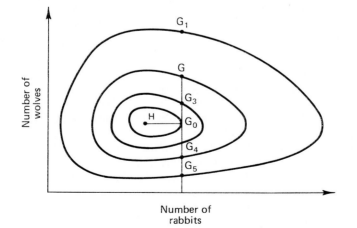

Fig. 11 Starting at G, we see the different trajectories that we would see after killing of different numbers of wolves.

and grows till we finally reach G_1, with a wolf problem larger than that with which we started. It is clear that by killing wolves alone, the best trajectory we can get is that through G_0. If we also kill rabbits, however, to go from G_0 to H, we can make the peak wolf population as small as possible!

Here is a *paradoxical,* **counterintuitive** discovery: *To reduce the predator population, it may prove most effective to reduce the prey population.*

This seems to fly in the face of common sense. Of course, someone wise in the ways of the countryside knows about this particular case. However, as we go from situations with two variables to situations with hundreds of variables, even the best intuition fails, and careful systems analysis becomes necessary. Even in the present case, where we have used the Volterra equations to develop our intuition to the point that it masters the "contradiction" of Fig. 8, we may still need the field data and the computer runs to determine how large the harvesting of wolves and rabbits should be.

Incidentally, H may *not* be the best point after all. It may well be that another trajectory will yield a far better harvest of rabbits for human consumption, so we may tolerate a larger wolf population in return for a better food supply. Many of our decisions require the balancing of many goals, rather than a straightforward push toward any one of them. To make the matter really complicated, if we wish to evaluate these questions very carefully, we may have to expand the model to include the raids of wolves on chicken yards, and the usual pattern of human hunting, so that we can obtain the best estimate of the total food supply of chicken and rabbit together. This four-species model need not detain us further here, however, except to note that the great art of model-building and decision-making is *learning what can be safely ignored.*

Suggestions for Further Reading

J. M. Smith: "Mathematical Ideas in Biology" Cambridge University Press, London and New York, 1971.
E. O. Wilson and W. H. Bossert: "A Primer of Population Biology." Sinauer Associates, Sunderland, Massachusetts, 1971.
    These are two useful introductions to the type of modeling discussed in this section.
A. Pasquino and H. A. Peelle: Teaching Biology with A Programming Language, *The American Biology Teacher,* 1975.
    Some simple programming examples based on the concepts of this section are presented.

Summary

To understand complex ecosystems, we need mathematics (especially calculus) to set up equations that describe the system and determine its general properties; we need **field-work** to estimate the parameters that enter into the equations and to **validate** the model; and we need computers to determine the effects of different strategies on the system behavior. Moreover, the behavior revealed by this systems analysis will often be **counterintuitive.**

In particular, we analyzed the **exponential growth** of an isolated rabbit population and the effects of **carrying capacity;** we saw the **exponential decay** of an isolated wolf population; and we looked at the cyclical behavior of the two populations when interaction (wolves eating rabbits) took place.

Glossary

Predator: If there are two species with one feeding on the other, we say that the *predator* feeds on the *prey*.

Prey–predator equations: Equations describing the population growth of two interacting species, with one prey and one predator, are called *prey—predator equations. Interaction terms* describe how the size of one population affects the changes in size of the other population.

Exponent: When we write m^n for $\underbrace{m \times m \times \cdots \times m,}_{n \text{ times}}$ we call n the *exponent*. For example, 5 is the exponent of "two to the fifth" $2^5 = 32$.

Exponential growth: Consider something increasing over time—like the size of a population or the level of pollution. We say that the *growth* is *exponential* if there is some time interval, call it the *doubling time,* such that in a time period of this length, the size always doubles. Usually any process of growth (whether exponential or not) reaches *saturation*—levels off—when some *carrying capacity* is reached at which the available resources cannot support any further increase in size.

Exponential decay: Consider something decreasing over time—like the area of open countryside. We say that the *decay* in size is *exponential* if there is some time interval, call it the *halving time,* such that in a time period of this length, the size is always cut in half.

Field work: *Field work* consists of careful studies of, say, an ecological system to gather data for *model validation*—for finding out whether or not the predictions of a model can be trusted.

Phase plane: If a process can be described by two key variables, we can plot the change of those variables in two dimensions—the *phase plane.*

Trajectory: The path followed by the variables of a system as they change over time is the *trajectory.*

Parameters: In simulation studies, we use *parameters* to distinguish between systems that are described by similar sets of equations.

Counterintuitive behavior: When we first work with a new class of systems, we may find that their behavior is quite different from what we expected.

Exercises

1.   If the rabbits eat grass, why don't we have to model the amount of grass in the sample ecosystem?

2.   10% annual interest gives a doubling time of approximately 7 years. $1000 in the bank will become $2000 in 7 years, $4000 in 14 years. How long will it take the $1000 to become more than a million dollars? How much is that worth if inflation averages 10%?

3.   Plants take in carbon dioxide and excrete oxygen. Animals breath in oxygen and exhale carbon dioxide. Which phase plane graphs show a possible trajectory for the total mass of plants and animals in this system? Why?

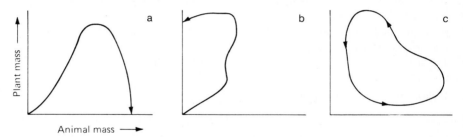

4.   Exponents are a short-hand way of indicating multiplication. For instance:

$$5^7 = \underbrace{5 \times 5 \times 5 \times 5 \times 5 \times 5 \times 5}_{7 \text{ times}}, \qquad 3^1 = \underbrace{3}_{1 \text{ time}}, \qquad x'' = \underbrace{x \cdot x \cdot x \cdot \cdot \cdot \cdot \cdot x}_{y \text{ times}}$$

As Oresme noticed in the 14th century, we may write (for any number $A = 0$)

$$A^0 = 1$$

by considering the series

$$A^3 = A \times A \times A, \qquad A^2 = A \times A, \qquad A^1 = A$$

and seeing that each time the exponent decreases by 1, we divide by A. In the 17th century, John Wallis and Isaac Newton (again!) described several other formulas. Can you explain, by common-sense reasoning as above: (1) $A^{-1} = 1/A$; (2) $A^{-B} = 1/(A^B)$; (3) $A^{B+C} = A^B \times A^C$; (4) $A^{B-C} = A^B/A^C$.

5.   Inflation is a rising level of prices. When the inflation rate is measured at 10%, it means that, say, a book that cost $10 today will, if prices continue their pattern of increase, cost $11 next year. Let $P_0 =$ the average price of some standard set of goods today, and P_t = the price some t years from now. Then

$$P_{t+1} = 100\% \text{ of } P_t \text{ plus } 10\% \text{ of } P_t$$
$$= 110\% \text{ of } P_t$$
$$= (1.1)P_t$$

Hence

$$P_t = (1.1)^t P_0$$

As prices rise, workers demand (and eventually get) higher wages. As wages rise, the cost of producing goods rises, so prices go up. Can you explain inflation as a feedback behavior?

6. What fieldwork could we do on wolves to find the coefficients b and W_0 in the equation $W_t = (1 + b)^t W_0$? (See the accompanying graphs.)

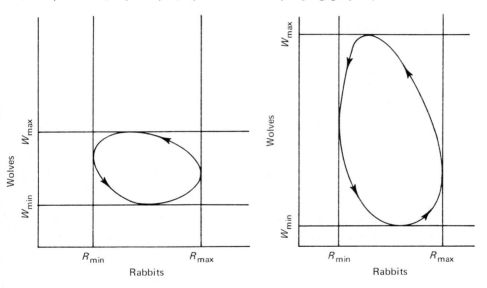

7. Insects damage crops, lowering harvest yield. Insecticides kill the pest insects, increasing harvest yield. But insecticides also kill animals which eat the pest insects. If we consider pest insects as prey, and the insect-eaters as predators, the Volterra equations suggest that the numbers of pest insects, and their predators, both oscillate. Hence crop yields will vary up and down in a cycle. What might happen if farmers try to eliminate the cycle (and its occasional bad years) by using massive doses of insecticide chemicals. Consider both the effect of the chemical on the pests and the predators. Why is it risky to "upset the balance of nature"?

8. You are the mayor of a town that has a large rabbit and wolf population. How can you convince the (human) citizens to limit wolves by killing rabbits? Include the word "compromise" in your answer. (*Hint:* The purpose of the question is to make you think of the political problems in using technical results.)

9.   If a TV station runs more commercials in each hour of broadcast, they will make more money. But if they have too many commercials, viewers will switch channels in disgust, lowering the Nielsen ratings of the shows on that station, making the advertisers less willing to buy commercial time on that station. Explain this in terms of feedback and carrying capacity.

10.   Total world population was about 5 million in prehistoric times, 250 million at the birth of Christ, 500 million in 1650, 1 billion in 1820, 2 billion in 1920, 3 billion in 1960, 4 billion in 1976, and predicted to be about 6 billion in 2000. Estimate the doubling time at various dates. Why does it change?

11.   Explain why B lines up with D in Fig. 10.

3.3 WORLD SIMULATION

We have looked at models that capture important aspects of the interactions of the parts in a complex system. With computer simulation we can handle even very complex systems, computing the effects that different courses of action will have on the system. In particular, we can use these predictions to help us choose a course of action that will prove of greatest benefit. In this section, we look at world models—attempts to predict on the computer ecological and economic changes affecting the population of the entire world. It should be stressed that there are many models of complex systems far better developed than world modeling—weather prediction, for example. However, we develop world simulation in some detail because some of the studies have captured headlines in newspapers and magazines. They have thus had an impact on the way many citizens view the world's social problems, and the way they view the computer's role in society.

Why do people build world models? It is because many people feel that with mounting population, decreasing reserves of oil and metals, and more and more starvation, we are heading toward a worldwide crisis for the human race. Something must be done to avoid this crisis. What? Some people feel that we should use computer simulation to explore different courses of action, to try to find options for the human race that will make the world a better place for our grandchildren and for their grandchildren in turn. We will examine two models commissioned by the Club of Rome—a group we met briefly in Section 3.1. We shall learn quite a bit from studying them, but we shall see that the models are rough and the data are unreliable. Their predictions of the state of the world 50 years from now are to be trusted *much less* than the weather forecast for a week from today. We are still at the stage where we must put most of our effort into model validation, and little of our trust in the predictions that today's primitive models yield.

Garbage In/Garbage Out

"Garbage in/garbage out" is an old saying in the computer business. It does not matter how fancy a computer you have—if the data you feed in are garbage, then the results your program prints out will be garbage. This message also applies to **computer simulation:** you cannot get good predictions unless you have a good **model** of the **system** and good data on its **inputs** and its **parameters.**

In spacecraft control, the models and the data are both excellent. For hundreds of years, scientists have been studying laws of motion—they really know how to write down the effect of forces on the movement of an object. When engineers build a spacecraft, they know exactly what each piece weighs, and where one piece joins another, and how big a force you get by turning on Number 2 engine for one-tenth of a second.

In traffic control, the models are reasonably satisfactory. One can write down equations that show how many cars will get across each intersection in the time a traffic light is green. The data are probably not as reliable—the town planner may have information on the number of cars using a city street each hour, but not be able to tell how many of these people would take a detour if available, and how many people must use this street to get to their destination. Nonetheless, the data and the models are accurate enough to let planners change around the one-way streets and reschedule the traffic lights, and be pretty sure that the traffic will move better as a result.

When we come to weather prediction, the situation becomes more interesting. Weather prediction is still not a "sure thing," but it is far better than it has ever been before. This is because of two breakthroughs in technology. The first breakthrough is in space technology. We now have satellites that can provide a continual photographic record of cloud patterns over the entire planet. The other breakthrough is in computer technology. The millions of photographs would be of little use if they had to be searched through by hand; but put them all on magnetic disks, and it becomes possible to set the computer searching for patterns that no human would have the time or patience to find. The problem is: there is too much data. What cloud patterns really matter in predicting the weather? How likely is rain if a cold front meets a hot front over a lake? Over a desert?

Meteorologists—the people who study the weather—are continually devising new models to predict the way that weather changes from day to day. Using computers, they can handle more realistic models, because they can process far more information than they could with hand computation. Because of the huge data base they have on their magnetic disks, they can test their models more completely—seeing how well the model could predict weather in a certain region on a certain day from information on the weather on earlier days; then repeating the test for many different days and different regions. One model may work better in winter than another, another may work best for desert regions. By trying to preserve the best features in each model, the meteorologists can build more realistic models.

As we mentioned briefly in Section 1.2, the cost of making weather predictions is worthwhile, because *if the predictions are accurate enough,* the economic impact can be immense. Day-by-day predictions are now fairly reliable. More challenging—and far more important economically—are long-term predictions, a year or more in advance. Such predictions do *not* have to be precise. It really does not matter whether the temperature will be 22 or 35°C at 1:00 p.m. on the third Thursday of next summer, but it is very important to know if the total rainfall that summer will be normal, or whether it will deviate on the high or low side. If a farmer can be sure of very high rainfall, he can start planning for flood control, and hold back on crops that die if water-logged. If a drought is likely then the farmer must invest in an irrigation system, and avoid "thirsty" crops. Decisions like this can be worth billions of dollars to a nation's economy—and have a dramatic effect on how well the nation's people are fed. That is why space technology and computer technology are not playthings—they are vital tools to help humans live as best they can on this planet.

Many people talk of **ecology** as a movement to restore the world to "a state of nature," but does this mean nature at the time of the dinosaurs; or nature as it was before the agrarian revolution; or nature 1000 years ago before the rise of modern industrialism? None of these seem satisfactory. It seems that one of our aims in studying ecology—the interrelations between different species of plants and animals and the environment—must be to ensure that this planet will be a fit home for humanity. We now realize that fresh water, clean air, and decent food are not inexhaustible. We realize that some animals are needed to help maintain an environment that supports us—while others should be preserved because they make the world a richer place. It would be sad if our grandchildren could see neither giraffes nor elephants—as I already regret that I shall never see a dodo. This does not mean, however, that the ecological movement should turn away from technology. Rather it should make wise use of technology—and the technology of weather prediction is an important example—to help us learn how to balance what we consume with what we can work with nature to provide, while preserving a diversity of animal life and natural scenery to cater to our spiritual needs.

In setting up world models, we must not only take into account ecological factors—studying the interactions between populations of organisms with each other and with their environment. We must also look at the impact of human industry, taking **economics** into account—the study of the development and regulation of the material resources and means of production of a community, nation, or group of nations.

Attempts to model the world extend the methods we saw in Section 3.2 for the study of prey–predator relations, but include many economic, as well as ecological, factors that affect the human population. Some of the numbers in the model are just what the model is meant to predict—like the wolf and rabbit populations. Other numbers are **parameters**—like the breeding rates of rabbits and wolves—and must be found out before we can run the model. When we come to the study of the world system in its impact on the human population, we find that some parameters must be found by careful study—such as the death rate caused by different concentrations of pollutants in the atmosphere. Other parameters—such as the birth rate—may well depend on government policy, such as birth control and abortion.

Thus only some of the important variables can be described in a moderately satisfactory way by the methods of the previous section. For example, no network of population interactions can explain why the political system in India has not been able to bring about a really effective birth control program in the Indian villages. Again, these models cannot explain why the approach taken by Chairman Mao in China has led to a cultural restructuring that has successfully brought about a dramatic lowering of the birth rate. (Of course, political scientists do try to develop models to explain these things—but they are pencil-and-paper models of the way people's attitudes change, not computer models of population interactions.)

Since they do not have particularly accurate predictions about many of the key parameters, systems planners have developed the concept of a scenario. In computer simulation a **scenario** is an imagined sequence of events, such as social and political choices, that determine key system inputs and parameters. For each scenario, one can then run the model of the interactions of system variables, to see how they will change over time.

As our discussion of weather prediction makes clear, we use these test runs in two ways. We use scenarios that describe situations that have already occurred to see how valid the model is. In this process of **model validation,** we keep adjusting the model so that it gives better and better approximations to what has already happened. Then, when the time comes to make predictions about the future, we can run our best model using scenarios that correspond to different plausible situations or policy decisions. On this basis, one can suggest that certain choices will lead to beneficial effects, while others will lead to disastrous effects. The results would suggest the wisdom of mounting a dramatic campaign to change people's values to avoid policies that lead to disaster. If certain outcomes occur in all scenarios, this suggests that no matter what choices are made, these outcomes will indeed come about. However, the outcome of a simulation is more likely to be to suggest a warning of the kind "Only if you do thus-and-so, can disaster be averted."

It is worth noting that the scenario need not be specified in its entirety prior to the run. In other words, the simulation can be used in **interactive mode** instead of **batch mode**. For example, the user in Fig. 1 might specify the scenario for a year or so, and then let the simulation run to see what the response would be to that particular policy. If he finds that certain variables are getting out of line, then he may make certain changes in overall strategy. The user can see which of several scenarios for the coming year yields the best effects; and then find the scenario for the next year that yields the best follow-up.

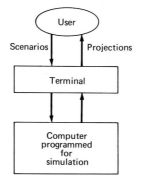

Fig. 1 Computer simulation in interactive mode.

If the outcome continues to be good, he is building up a good *long-term* scenario. If not, he may switch to another scenario for the first year—some sacrifices in the short run may pay off in long-term gains.

In this way, we obtain some of the effects that the military does in their war games and situation rooms—experience in responding to somewhat unexpected changes in the overall situation. In any case, the interactive mode lets the system become a *computer-based planning and decision-aiding tool,* which enables the user to assess the effects of different strategies by studying their impact on the numerous submodels of the overall model.

Before going on, we should note that the interactive use of scenarios is just one of many tools for decision-making. When a space engineer looks at the **control** problem of finding a pattern of rocket firing that will get a spacecraft into a specified orbit, he does *not* use the scenario method. Instead he uses computer programs that work backwards from specified outputs to find sequences of inputs which will make the system's outputs change in the required way. In economic and social systems, the available computer programs for control do not work as well as they do for spacecraft because the interactions are less clear. However, the best strategy for detailed economic planning will use a mixture of scenario analysis to set general courses of action, and control programs to help specify the numbers—investment rates, food production, etc.—within that general plan.

The Limits to Growth

With this general perspective, we can turn to specific world simulations. A graph of the world's total population looks something like the curve of Fig. 2, with the population doubling in the last 75 years to a figure around 4000 million (4 billion).

Recalling the notion of **exponential growth** from Section 3.2, you might suggest that this growth is exponential, with a doubling time of 75 years, but if you look closely, you will see that the growth is *faster* than exponential, with the doubling time getting shorter and shorter. One of my friends, Heinz von Foerster of the University of Illinois, plotted the curve more carefully, and found that if it continued this way, the world population would go to infinity on April 23, 2024! Of course, there are many reasons why the population of the world cannot reach infinity on April 23, 2024, or any other date—including the limited **carrying capacity** we discussed in Section 3.2.

The first report to the Club of Rome, "The Limits to Growth," presents an alternative approach, in line with the model-building of

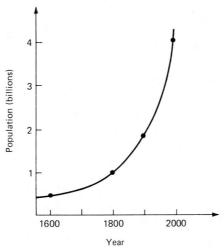

Fig. 2 Growth of human population worldwide from 1600 to 2000.

Section 3.2. Taking a curve and extrapolating it gives no idea of the mechanisms involved. They sought to understand the key variables and their interrelationships. A *small* extract from these relationships is shown in Fig. 3. At the top of the figure we see a *positive* feedback loop—the higher the population, the more births per year, serving to *further* increase the population. We also see a *negative* feedback loop—the higher the population, the more deaths per year, which goes *against* increased population.

    Fertility is the rate at which people reproduce—it can be measured by the average number of children per year for each thousand people. **Mortality** is the rate at which people die—it can be measured by the average number of deaths per year for each thousand people. The population will increase as long as fertility exceeds mortality, just as we saw in our discussion of the isolated rabbit population in Section 3.2.

    Figure 3 suggests two ways in which fertility and mortality can be brought more into line to prevent the population explosion sketched in Fig. 2. At the left we see that increased birth control can reduce fertility—lowering the number of children each woman gives birth to—and thus slow down population growth. At the right, we see a more sinister check to population growth. As population increases, so does pollution. People weakened by pollution can die more easily of many different diseases. Thus increasing pollution increases mortality, and this too counteracts population growth.

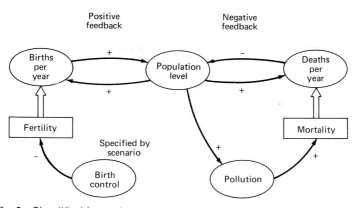

Fig. 3 Simplified form of the population–pollution interactions in "The Limits of Growth" world model.

The full "Limits" model not only modeled the interaction of population and pollution. It also modeled interactions with natural resources, food production, and industrialization. The model was run with many different scenarios.

In one run, natural resources would be depleted, yielding a slowdown in investment rates as more money was tied up in buying scarce and expensive resources. Eventually, the available investment money would be too little to replace worn-out equipment, let alone buy new equipment. As a result, industrial output would collapse, and agricultural collapse would follow as needed fertilizers and equipment became unavailable. Finally, as food resources dwindled, mortality would rise as starvation set in. The human population would drop catastrophically in the middle of the 21st century.

In another run, the scenario assumed that new technology would maintain a supply of resources. As a result, industrial output would be maintained. In this run, both population and pollution increase at an alarming rate. Then, in 2050, the pollution climbs to such a high level that the negative feedback loop of Fig. 3 takes over. Pollution deaths become so widespread that world population drops catastrophically.

The "Limits" team emphasize that their model cannot predict the *exact* date of catastrophe, but they do suggest that without policy changes of a drastic kind, their projection of population collapse somewhere in the middle of the next century is inevitable.

Because they are convinced of the reality of this predicted collapse, the team argues for strong measures to avoid it. They advocate *an end to growth:* population must be held at present levels, they say; the **per capita** industrial output (that is, the average amount of indus-

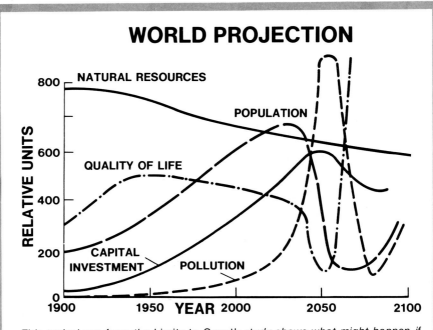

WORLD PROJECTION

This typical run from the Limits to Growth *study shows what might happen if pollution is allowed to increase unchecked. By 2020, pollution would begin to increase the death rate drastically. The population and the quality of life would plunge as pollution skyrockets until sometime after 2050. By then, the world population will have been so catastrophically reduced, and the industrial base so damaged, that pollution will begin to abate, and the population can once more begin to rise.*

trial products produced by each person) must be held at the 1975 level; goods must be recycled and pollution controlled; soil restored; and consumer goods made more durable.

Is it really true that our present growth is dangerous—a cancer—or is the model too simple, or its data too unreliable? Perhaps a more careful analysis will allow us different courses of action. We may all argue that recycling goods and controlling pollution and restoring the soil are fine things to do; but must everything we use from now on be a patched-up hand-me-down? Can we grow without inviting disaster in the next 100 years?

The answer to these questions is not clear. In the next subsection, we shall see another world model that lets us explore courses of action that could not be included in the "Limits" scenarios. Then, in the final subsection, we shall look at data that suggest that we have far more room for growth than the "Limits" team suggests. However, we shall see that there are many inequalities between different nations, and between different groups of nations, so that dramatic changes in policy are still required. Inequalities must be reduced even if we reject the call to stop growth as being based on too simple a model of the world. We shall explore the challenge of such changes both to computer technology and to political institutions in Chapter 7.

A Regional Approach to Global Planning

The "Limits" study modeled the world as a lumped system, so that variables such as population, land resources, etc., all referred to totals for the entire world. As we have just seen, the "Limits" team predicted that present trends would lead to a worldwide collapse in the middle of the 21st century. Their runs showed that even if steps were made to restrict one variable at a time—such as depletion of natural resources—other variables would reach catastrophic levels. They recommend an immediate slow-down of economic growth as the only solution to the problem. However, the *second* report to the Club of Rome, "Mankind at the Turning Point," stressed that one cannot take any single position on growth. While they agree that population growth should be halted, they still wish to see medical services improved—even though this decreases the mortality rate. While the current rate of depletion of resources by the developed world suggests that their rate of materials consumption should decline, a strong case can nonetheless be made for an increase in materials consumption in the developing nations. The key to the "Turning Point" approach is to model the world as a system of ten distinct regions; including the four regions of the "market economy-oriented, developed, world," namely,

> North America
> Western Europe
> Japan
> The rest of the market economy oriented world, including Australia, South Africa, and Israel.

The next two regions

> Eastern Europe and the USSR
> China

are the two regions with a primarily socialist economy. The next region

> North Africa and the Middle East

has emerged as a region of striking global significance in its own right, because of its enormous share of the oil reserves. The other three regions

> Latin America
> Tropical Africa
> South and Southeast Asia

are the regions that we think of as the least developed nations—although here the contrast between Brazil and some of the other Latin American nations is striking.

A quick glance at these ten regions immediately convinces us that the "Limits" model was far too simple, for it is clear that we cannot hope to make meaningful predictions without distinguishing the fate of these different regions. It should be observed, however, that further refinements are indeed possible. For example, lumping Australia and South Africa together in one region immediately rules out an analysis of the impact of African nationalism. Another problem is that the regions are based on existing political entities. A useful development would find out what states could work together in their planning to form more realistic regions.

Even though the choice of these ten regions is thus somewhat unsatisfactory, this ten-region model did allow the "Turning Point" team to make a number of important projections. We look at two of them, one concerning *population control* and another concerning *international transfer of development funds.*

We all know that world population is rising drastically. Some might hope, however, that a *gradual* solution to the problem would be sufficient. They might hope that 50 years is a reasonable period in which to achieve an **equilibrium fertility rate**—one in which the birth rate equals the death rate. However, "Turning Point" computer runs show that—if there was no massive starvation meanwhile—North America would have an additional 4 people per square kilometer by 2024, while South Asia would have 160 more people per square kilometer. This *increase* for South Asia is greater than the *current total* for already densely populated Western Europe—which now supports 85 people per square kilometer. The message is clear: while North American birth rates are already at a manageable level, the birth rate of South Asia is at a crisis level, which must be *speedily* reduced.

To pinpoint the dangers of delay in implementing a population control policy, the "Turning Point" team studied scenarios that project the *population level of the whole underdeveloped world.*

Scenario 1:   In the first scenario, no population policy is implemented. The simulation shows that if current trends continue unchecked, the population will reach 12 billion by 2010. This number is already so high as to be unsupportable. This means that famine on a hitherto unimaginable scale will strike the underdeveloped world long before 2010 unless current birth rates are drastically reduced. (We shall see in the next subsection, however, that not all food experts agree: some believe that the Earth *can* feed many more people.)

Scenario 2:   In the second scenario, a massive birth control program is initiated immediately, which succeeds in providing an equilibrium birth rate by 2010. In this case, the computer projects an equilibrium level of 6.27 billion in the underdeveloped nations by 2050.

Scenario 3:   For a 10-year delay in implementing the birth control program, the population projection for 2050 rises to 7.97 billion.

Scenario 4:   For a 20-year delay, the population projection for 2050 rises to 10.17 billion.

Thus a simple 20-year delay in implementing a birth control program can mean an increase in *projected* population of the underdeveloped world from 6.27 billion to 10.17 billion. The "Turning Point" team believes that it is unlikely that food could be found for all these extra mouths, and that this 20-year delay would result in 500 million additional child deaths. Equally terrifying would be the abject stupor in which many of the survivors would live, due to gross malnutrition.

While it is clear that prompt action must be taken, it is also clear that—no matter how quickly the birth rate starts to level off—huge population increases will occur during the rest of this century. Such increases do not simply require more food. Jobs and housing must be found, children must be educated, the sick must be cared for. Tarzie Vittachi, Executive Secretary of the United Nations World Population Year, has estimated that to cope with its population increase, India alone must build 10,000 houses *every day* for the next 20 years. It seems unlikely that such a massive effort can succeed without development aid from the richer nations. Thus we now turn to scenarios that explore the impact of different schedules for delivering that aid. Let us make the *very optimistic* assumption that people and governments respond to population warnings like those we have just seen, and that each region implements policies that help them achieve an equilibrium fertility rate by the year 2000. On this assumption, current development projections show the per capita income in the developed world increasing from $3500 to $14,000 by 2025. The current 5 to 1 ratio of income in the developed world to the average in Latin America would go to 8 to 1; while the ratio for South Asia would remain at a staggering 20 to 1. The next three "Turning Point" scenarios examine the cost of international aid from the developed countries if all underdeveloped regions are to have at least one-fifth of the developed nations' per capita income by 2025.

Scenario 1:   Continuous aid is to be supplied from now until 2025 to maintain the growth rate of each underdeveloped nation at a level required to achieve the target ratio of 5 to 1 in 2025. The projected total cost is $7200 billion, with a peak of $500 billion in any one year of the aid project. The cost to individuals in the developed world is a fall in per capita income from the projected $14,000 in 2025 to $11,000 in 2025—which is still a dramatic increase from $3500.

Scenario 2:   In this scenario, we again measure the cost of delay. If we let the gap between rich and poor nations widen until 2000, and then try to apply "Operation Catch-up" in only 25 years, the projected cost jumps to $10,700 billion. This is a dramatic increase of 50 percent over the cost projected in Scenario 1; and all the more painful because it must be paid out in only half the time.

Scenario 3:   Once again, we have seen the high cost of delay—quite apart from the suffering that this delay brings to those who must endure reduced living standards for the extra 25 years. Could it be that the humanitarian impulse to provide the aid even more quickly could also prove economically attractive to the developed nations? In Scenario 3, early action is taken to ensure that the 5 to 1 ratio is reached by 2000 rather than by 2025. Surprisingly, the total cost is $2500 billion, only a third of that projected for Scenario 1 (and less than a quarter of the Scenario 2 cost), and the peak annual cost is $250 billion per year. Not only is the total cost far less, but the early action strategy yields economic self-sufficiency for the developing regions by the year 2000.

Some readers may still be disturbed by the 5 to 1 gap between the income levels in rich and poor nations—although the political challenges of implementing any of the above three scenarios are large enough as it is. However, it must be stressed that per capita income is not a true measure of the quality of life. For example, it can well be argued that a villager who is within walking distance of his fields is better off than a family that must have at least 2 cars because they live far from jobs and shops and have no public transportation. There is then no reason for the villager to envy that family the extra $8000 of "property" that those cars represent. Many thoughtful people have argued that underdeveloped nations would not profit by trying to imitate the inefficient and costly "American way of life," and that they *can* and *should* develop new patterns of housing, employment, transportation, and technology which can yield a highly satisfying life style on a relatively low per capita income.

The Danger of Despair

The reports to the Club of Rome have been widely publicized. Many people are convinced that population growth must be halted at once. We certainly feel that attempts to raise living standards must go hand-in-hand with a reduction in population growth, so that our grandchildren will not only have enough to eat, but will still be able to explore a countryside free of high-density human dwellings. If the shock of a possible catastrophe in 2050 can help people cut back the size of their families, and use the available resources to enrich their lives and their children's lives, we are all for it.

Unfortunately, though, the vision of catastrophe has also stirred ugly talk. Some people argue that if resources are so scarce, then we should not waste them on nations like Bangladesh (a country of 70 million people to the northeast of India) which have soaring populations and poor food resources. These people ask us to cut off all aid to such nations, letting them starve to death. Better that some of us get all we need to lead healthy lives, these people say, than that we all lead miserable undernourished lives.

However, it appears that the time for such cruel decisions is not yet upon us. Here are some observations from an article called "Myths of the Food Crisis" by Nick Eberstadt, *The New York Review of Books,* February 19, 1976, pp. 32–37. They show how careful we must be before we carry out such drastic actions based on poor models and inadequate data:

> How little we know about the world food problem is frightening. There are really no accurate figures on food production for any poor country; the margin of error in the estimate for India alone could feed or starve twelve million people. Nutritionists' estimates of the "average" daily adult protein requirement have ranged from 20 grams a day to over 120. Perhaps most astonishing, we do not

know the world's population within 400 million people. In short, we do not know how much food there is, how much food people need, or even how many people there are. (p. 32)

Turning from the general ignorance of worldwide figures, we have the following eye-opening figures on Bangladesh.

We think Bangladesh a basket case because it uses every inch of its land, sends 85 percent of its work force to the fields, and still seems to grow too little food to get by. But how many of us know that rice yields per hectare in Bangladesh are only 53 percent as great as the world average, 24 percent as great as America's, and only 15 percent as great as can be obtained on experimental stations *in Bangladesh?* Were Bangladesh merely to raise its rice yields to the world average, its per capita production would be over 530 pounds, higher than Japan's at the beginning of the 1960s. There is no technical reason why this should not be done. (p. 35)

In other words, the help Bangladesh needs is help to tap its own resources, so that it may realize its full potential as a food producing nation. This may require land reform, farmer education, and the building of industry for fertilizers and agricultural equipment. International aid toward these ends is realistic, and can help reduce tragic inequalities in nutrition levels. The fact that none of these may come without major changes in politics and people's attitudes reminds us of how much is still to be done before the models we have discussed can become reliable planning tools.

In terms of evaluating our simulations, we see that useful actions must be based on hard data on each individual region, not on general predictions made on very rough models. In the case of weather prediction, we saw the value of building up a massive data base of very accurate information, and then using this as in a process of model validation to obtain better and better computer simulations; but the best weather predictions only extend a short way into the future, and require accurate data on the region involved as well as the regions which surround it. In the same way, we can expect the best projections of ecological and economic trends to run at most a few years into the future, and to be anchored in solid data on the regions involved.

Having seen the need for better data, let us say something about the need for better models. When—as in Section 3.1—we have to make decisions about the control of a spaceship, we know exactly how to set up a model. Newton's laws of motion provide the tools. Here, there is no controversy. When we turn to world models, however, the tools are still controversial. During the worldwide recession and inflation of the early 1970s, there was no agreed-upon theory to direct the search for economic recovery. Some capitalist economists put all their faith in giving more power to big industry; radical economists would take all power from private industry and put the means of production under government control. There is no single framework in which these differences can now be resolved.

People with different views can use their models to spell out the assumptions that lead to their predictions; and because they spell them out, and because we can determine more of the implications by computer simulation, it should be possible to debate carefully the best features of each model. In this way, political dialog might contribute to model validation. However, the problem of communicating the findings of such models to the general public may be a formidable one, which we will discuss in Section 6.2.

Even if we agree on which simulation model to use to try out the effects of different policies to see how well they will achieve different goals, we must still agree on the goals. Here is a very concrete example: In a time of energy crisis, a country's real goal may be to ensure that it has as much energy as possible so that it can maintain its current level of energy usage. This is a very different goal from the "Turning Point" goal of trying to ensure a relatively fair distribution of energy resources throughout the world. Presumably, this will remain a political process—the sort of thing by which that political parties will win or lose elections.

Even if we agree on both economic theory and goals, we still cannot sensibly make plans for the next 50 years that are to be followed without revision over the full half century. This is because of both technological and political "surprises," and because the models are less and less reliable the longer the range of the prediction.

A breakthrough in technology such as the atom bomb can greatly change the balance of power, or the importance of different types of resources. A political "aberration" such as the rise of Hitler in Germany will change considerations so drastically that any long-range policy must be sacrificed for awhile to return political stability of some kind. Thus certain scenarios which seemed plausible at the start of a planning period may have to be abandoned simply because they did not foresee these events. While a science fiction writer in 1900 could have "foreseen" the development of an explosive able to wipe out huge cities in a single explosion, or while a writer of historical romances could imagine the impact of a modern Atilla-the-Hun upon Europe and the world, it is quite another thing to include these factors in planning. At the turn of the century, the limits of the available technology ruled out plans for warfare that included explosives of that size. In fact, it was hard to convince the military to take the possibilities of airplanes seriously as late as World War I. If one considers too many "wild" scenarios, one ends up with a prediction that "anything can happen," which is no more help than having no prediction at all. At the other extreme, if one considers scenarios that take no account of possible "surprises," then they cannot help us prepare for a time of rapid change.

We must also continually revise our plans because the models that one uses will always be too crude. How strongly is the rate of production of copper in Zaire coupled with the growth of the telephone network in Western Europe? Even if a model included an explicit term for such a relationship, it would be very approximate. It would have to be made more accurate numerically, and would also have to be expanded to depend on a great many other factors if it were accurately to represent the situation. Thus, while we can expect a model to hold fairly steady for a few years, the odds are that its predictions will become less and less accurate over a period of time. Thus we must constantly compare the predictions made a few years ago with the performance of the real world today. We can then use the result of this comparison to go back and analyze the model to find out where it went wrong. In some cases, we will realize that certain relationships that we had ignored are very important, and add them to the model—so that, hopefully, over the next few years the predictions made by the model will turn out to come closer to the unfolding reality. Model validation is a never-ending process, as model-builders continually receive feedback (Fig. 4) from these comparisons of prediction and reality.

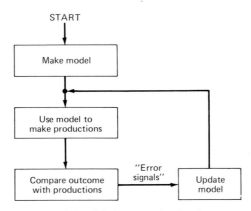

Fig. 4 Model validation as a feedback process.

Suggestions for Further Reading

D. H. Meadows, D. L. Meadows, J. Randers, and W. W. Behrens III: "The Limits to Growth" Universe Books, New York, 1972.
   This is the first report to the Club of Rome's Project on the Predicament of Mankind. It is written for the general public.
H. S. D. Cole, C. Freeman, M. Jahoda, and K. L. R. Pavitt (eds.): "Models of Doom" Universe Books, New York, 1973.
   Computer runs that show that forecasts of the world's future are very sensitive to key assumptions are presented. They suggest that the "Limits" model and data are faulty. They take up questions of politics, social structure, and human needs missing in the "Limits" study.
W. D. Nordhaus: World Dynamics: Measurement without Data, *The Economic Journal,* December 1973, pp. 1156–1183.
   A critique is given of the book "World Dynamics" by Jay Forrester, which provided the starting point for "The Limits to Growth." It suggests that the model is based on too little hard data, and does not use sophisticated techniques already used by the economists.
W. L. Oltmans (ed.): "On Growth." Capricorn Books, New York 1974.
   A series of chatty interviews were conducted by Oltmans with 70 scientists, authors, and politicians on their reactions to "The Limits to Growth."
M. Mesarovic and E. Pestel: "Mankind at the Turning Point." Dutton, New York, 1974.
   This is the second report to the Club of Rome, stressing an analysis of the world in terms of 10 regions.
E. Eberstadt: Myths of the Food Crisis, *The New York Review of Books,* February 19, 1976, pp. 32–37.
   Eberstadt gives a useful survey of our misunderstandings about food resources.
P. H. Abelson (ed.): "Food: Politics, Economics, Nutrition and Research." American Association for the Advancement of Science, Washington, D.C., 1975.
   This was a key source of material for Eberstadt's article.
A. Anderson, Jr.: Forecast for Forecasting: Cloudy, *The New York Times Magazine,* December 29, 1974, pp. 10–31.
   A look is taken at the current status of weather forecasting by computer.

Summary

We stressed that accurate predictions about a system require both a good model of the system and good data on its inputs and parameters. For complex systems, the best predictions will tend to be those which are short range and firmly based on accurate data. **Model validation** is an on-going process—comparing what actually happens with what the model predicts, and using this to improve the model. We saw that **interactive** use of a computer to explore different **scenarios** can provide a valuable computer-based planning and decision-aiding tool—especially if aided by control programs of the kind used by space engineers.

We studied two world models, presented as reports to the Club of Rome. The "Limits to Growth" model predicted a worldwide catastrophe in the mid-21st century unless all growth were halted immediately. The "Turning Point" model advocated a leveling off of population, but suggested that international aid programs could promote healthy growth in underdeveloped nations. We closed by stressing the huge improvements in both data-gathering and modeling techniques required before it is wise to base drastic action on long-range predictions of world models.

Glossary

Model: A *model* of an object or process is another object or process that shares crucial properties with the original, but is easier to manipulate or understand. A *scale model* has the same appearance as the original save for size and detail. However, increasing use is being made of *computer simulation:* the model is a computer program which lets a machine compute how key properties of the original will change over time. It is easier to change a program than to rebuild a scale model if we want to explore the effect of changes in policy or design.

Model validation: Checking the predictions of the model against the actual changes of the original over time is called *model validation.* An analysis of differences can be used to modify the model to obtain one that more accurately predicts important activities of the original.

System: A system is an object or process—or collection of objects or processes—that we choose to study. The *environment* comprises those processes which we expect to have an effect on the system. The *inputs* to the system are the effects of the environment on the system. The *outputs* of the system are the measurable responses of the system. The *states* of the system relate the inputs and outputs. The *state-transition function* describes how the states change over time in response to inputs. The *output function* describes how the state determines the output.

Parameter: In simulation studies, we use *parameters* to distinguish between systems that are described by similar sets of equations.

Scenario: A *scenario* is a sequence of possible events to be studied in the simulation of a system of interest.

Control: Choosing the inputs to a system to make the state or output change in some desired way, or at least close to it, is *control.*

Feedback: The process whereby output signals are fed back to the input of a system, so that the system can respond to information about its own performance, is *feedback.* A *negative feedback* system uses this information to negate (or at least reduce) the *error signal*—which is the difference between the actual output and some desired output. For example, in a thermostat, the actual temperature is compared to the temperature setting. In a feedback system, the *gain* measures how big a compensation will be made in response to an error signal. In a *positive feedback* system, the change in input *increases* the error, rather than reduces it.

Exponential growth: Consider something increasing over time—like the size of a population or the level of pollution. We say that the *growth* is *exponential* if there is some time interval, call it the *doubling time,* such that in a time period of this length, the size always doubles. Usually any process of growth (whether exponential or not) reaches *saturation*—levels off—when some *carrying capacity* is reached at which the available resources cannot support any further increase in size.

Ecology: *Ecology* is the study of the interaction of populations of organisms with each other and with their environment.

Economics: *Economics* is the study of the development and regulation of the material resources and means of production of a community, nation, or group of nations.

Fertility rate: The rate at which a population reproduces is the *fertility rate.* It can be measured in terms of the average number of births per year in each 1000 members of the population.

Mortality rate: The rate at which a population dies is the *mortality rate.* It can be measured in terms of the average number of deaths per year in each 1000 members of the population.

Equilibrium: A value for some variable that does not change unless disturbed by some external factor is *equilibrium.*

Equilibrium fertility rate: This is the rate that, for a given mortality rate, will lead to an equilibrium in the population after a transition period.

Per capita: *Per capita* is Latin for "per head." For example, if we talk of "per capita income" we mean the average income for each person—how much per head—in a population.

Batch mode: Using the computer to execute a complete program without any *interaction* with the user before it has printed out all the results is the *batch mode.*

Interactive mode: The *interactive mode* is the use of a computer through an input–output device called a *terminal* that lets the user monitor the progress of a computation, intervening when something seems to be going wrong, or some change is required and responding to queries from the computer.

Exercises

1. Refer to the world model extract of Figure 3 to determine whether the following statements about the dynamics of the model are true or false (avoid making common-sense inferences).

   (a)   Increased birth control decreases fertility.
   (b)   Birth control influences pollution level *directly*.
   (c)   Population level and deaths per year affect each other.
   (d)   When births per year increase, deaths per year do too.
   (e)   Mortality decrease comes from pollution level increase.
   (f)   Population level change varies birth control.
   (g)   Birth control indirectly affects mortality.
   (h)   Births per year and population level are in a positive feedback loop.
   (i)   Population level and deaths per year are in a negative feedback loop.
   (j)   Birth control and births per year are in a feedback loop.

2. Let's take a look at energy, since no process or material is more basic to our technological society. Our economy has been based on the easy and cheap accessibility of fossil fuels—natural gas, coal, oil—to manufacture our material wealth. It is true that some of our energy comes from hydroelectric (dams) or nuclear power plants, but these have been used far less than fossil fuels. Our fossil fuels, like other resources, are finite in supply. Name some industries which use fossil fuels not for energy but for their chemical properties. (*Hint:* Many products come from oil besides gasoline. Name some.)

3. Name some positive and negative results of eliminating all species of insects.

4. Von Foerster's prediction of infinite population in 2024 assumes faster-than-exponential growth. Fertility rate—the number of children born each year per capita—increases without limit in this model. This gives shorter and shorter doubling time. In fact, fertility rate has been increasing. (a) Why has fertility increased in recent centuries? (b) Why can't it keep increasing forever?

5. The "Turning Point" approach divides the world into 10 regions. One or more regions fall into each of four types. Name the four types in this subdivision. Give one example of each.

6. Define *equilibrium fertility rate*. Does "Turning Point" suggest it be gradually (50 years) reached?

7. Smog is a problem in a number of major cities in North America. It was first observed in Los Angeles in 1943, but may be worst in Tokyo—where vending machines dispense whiffs of oxygen! What causes smog? How could placing a microcomputer in each automobile help decrease smog?

8. Compare the impact on the agricultural communities of the U.S. and India or China of the world's supply of oil being completely depleted.

9. Three definitions of ecology are: "The body of knowledge concerning the economy of nature—the investigation of the total relations of the animal to its inorganic and organic environment" (Hoeckel); "Scientific natural history . . . sociology and economics of animals" (C. S. Elton); and "Study of the structure and function of nature" (E. Odum). Compare and contrast these definitions. Give examples of important elements included in some but not others. What do they all neglect?

10. Chairman Mao in China successfully convinced hundreds of millions of people to put off marriage until the age of 25, so that more youthful energy could be channeled into useful work and revolutionary awareness. Give three reasons why this has significantly lowered China's birth rate.

11. *Field trip:* Visit your home! Make a careful survey of all labor saving or convenience machinery. (*Hint:* don't forget refrigerators, bicycles, lawn mowers, stereos, and lights.) Rate these subjectively for personal importance. What machines could you definitely do without? (electric can openers? electric toothbrushes?) Which would you find it difficult to do without?

E. F. Schumacher in his book "Small is Beautiful" says: "From the Buddhist point of view, there are two types of mechanisms which must be clearly distinguished: one that enhances a man's skill and power and one that turns the work of man over to a mechanical slave, leaving man in a position of having to serve the slave." How can you tell one from the other? Classify the items on your list by the scheme.

12. For the World Model approach to be successful, most world leaders must accept the recommendations of computer simulation contractors. This is not impossible, but requires overcoming some ideological barriers. Name one instance of a universally acknowledged scientific theory that was denounced at first for ideological reasons.

4

The Rise of the
Data Bank

SECTION 4.1. DATA BASE MANAGEMENT

We examine the requirements for setting up and using a large data base, using the example of an airline reservation network to show how the records in the data base must be structured, with different users being able to query and update the data base in different ways. We also look at security problems for data banks and time-sharing systems—protecting data and programs from unauthorized access. Next, we study precautions for protecting data against user error and hardware failure. The section is basically self-contained, except for its use of the ideas of time-sharing (Section 2.1) and computer networks (Section 2.2).

SECTION 4.2. COMPUTERS, CASH, AND CRIME

As more and more cash reserves are reduced to magnetic codes in the data banks of financial institutions, new techniques are opened up for the handling of money—and for computer crime. The first half of the section examines the technology and implications of an **electronic funds transfer system.** The second half catalogs a number of common **computer crimes,** and what must be done to prevent them. No background beyond the basic idea of computer networking (Section 2.2) is required for this section.

SECTION 4.3. DATA BANKS AND PRIVACY

The Privacy Act of 1974 was passed by the Congress of the United States to regulate the use of data banks by federal agencies, and to give individuals access to most of the records stored on them and the means to get mistakes corrected and irrelevant information removed. This section outlines the concerns that led to passage of the act; discusses the provisions of the act; and looks at what further steps will be required to diminish threats to privacy posed by data banks and the computer networks that link them. This section is self-contained, although it does use the basic notions of a computer network (Section 2.2) and a data bank (Section 4.1).

4.1. DATA BASE MANAGEMENT

In setting up a large **data base,** systems programmers must make it easy for people to both store and find information when they need to. An insurance company may have millions of records, the Internal Revenue Service adds a new record on every taxpayer every year, and the Weather Service stores 10 billion bits of data from the weather satellites every month. With this many records, you have to be careful where data are stored if they are not to be lost for ever. With hundreds of millions of records, it takes too long—even at electronic speeds—to search through every file in turn to find the information you need. Instead, the systems programmer has to specify carefully where each record is to be stored, and design programs for efficiently handling standard requests for queries about them, and for storing new records or updating old ones.

A **data base management system (DBMS)** is an **operating system** that provides the tools to let systems programmers create a data base, and to let users have access to the data base. The systems programmer uses a **data definition language** to set up a data base with primary records in **primary memory** and backup records in **secondary memory,** and to write the translator—usually resident in primary memory—that will respond to the user's input in a high-level **query/update language** to answer queries and update the files.

In other words, it is the systems programmer's work, writing programs in the data definition language to be processed by the data base management system, that turns a computer into a **data bank** (Fig. 1). His programs tell the DBMS what files to create, what types of entry can be made in the files, how to respond to queries and updates, and what checks should be made for consistency in the files.

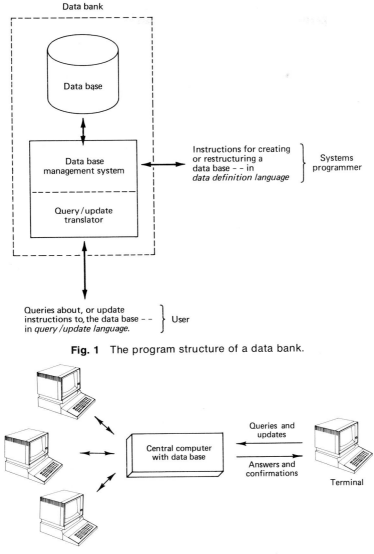

Fig. 1 The program structure of a data bank.

Fig. 2 An airline reservation network.

A Data Base for Airline Reservations

To get a better feel for all the work required to develop and maintain a data base and to make it easy to use, we study the design of a data base for airline reservations (Fig. 2). Instead of looking in detail at an actual data base, we consider just a few of the problems that are typical of all such systems.

We start by making a list of the queries an airline reservations clerk might ask:

What flights are there on Tuesdays for Alma-Ata?
Will the 2:00 p.m. flight for Lusaka leave on time?
What seats are vacant in first class on Flight 232 next Monday?
What meal service is offered on the 5:00 p.m. flight to Sydney?
What flight is William Tompkins booked on?
What is his seat assignment?
What excursion fares are available for round trips from Los Angeles to Tokyo?

Here are some of the update instructions which the clerk might type into the system:

Book four seats economy class on Flight 234 connecting to Flight 416 for Mr. and Mrs. William Tompkins and their 2 children, Fred, aged 11, and Wilhelmina, aged 4.
Cancel all reservations for Jennifer Umlaut.
Reassign Mr. and Mrs. Arthur Matabele from Seats 16A, B on Flight 169 to seats 18E, F.
Have a salt-free lunch for Imsong Yang on Flight 142 on Tuesday the 16th.

Thus the query/update language must be designed to let the clerk make all these queries and updates. There are, however, some things the clerk should *not* be able to change:

The number of seats on a flight
Flight times
Fares

These things do change, however, and so the systems programmer must provide a way for *someone* to change them. His solution could be to design *two* query/update languages:

CLERK: designed to handle all the clerk's proper updates and queries, but *nothing else*.
EXEC: includes all the CLERK query and update instructions, but also includes instructions for changing seating plans, flight times, fares, and for aiding management decisions.

Both these languages are different from the data definition language, which is used to establish the data base structure and the ways in which the user can get access to it.

Then, in setting up the airline reservations network, most termi-nals would be so wired up that the central computer would only respond to their messages if they were legal commands in CLERK. Only at the airline headquarters would there be terminals from which the central computer would accept EXEC commands. Headquarters might also be the location of the terminals that can respond to the programs in the data definition language which create or restructure the data base. Clearly, careful security precautions should be taken to prevent unauthorized people from meddling with these terminals at headquarters! We shall say more about security problems at the end of this section.

Having said all this, let us see what records the airline reservation data base should contain. The arrangement we give will be **hierarchical,** with high-level records pointing to records which convey more detailed information.

At the top level is information about flights from one specific city to another. By typing in

BDL → SFO FARES

a clerk would command the system to display on his screen information about fares from Hartford's Bradley Field Airport (BDL) to San Francisco's International Airport (SFO). The clerk could then tell the customer, who would decide to take a less expensive excursion flight leaving midweek, and say "Let's try leaving Tuesday morning." The clerk could then type in

DEP TUE AM

The system remembers that it is still in the BDL → SFO record, and switches onto the screen that part of the schedule that shows flights and connections from Hartford to San Francisco departing from Hartford on a Tuesday morning. The clerk reads this list to the passenger, who chooses Flight 97. The clerk then says, "You did say you wanted the Excursion, not First Class, sir?", and the passenger says, "Yes" with a do-I-look-like-the-type-who-can-afford-to-fly-first-class grin. "And which Tuesday, sir?" "April 11th." "Very well," says the clerk, and types in

97 APR 11 SPACE Y

This command asks the computer to display a chart of seats still available in tourist (Y) on Flight 97 for April 11 (the computer need not be told the year—it takes the April 11 within 12 months of today's date). Note that this command takes us down a level in the data base hierarchy. We are no longer at the level of general information about all BDL → SFO flights. Instead, we are looking at the record for a specific BDL → SFO flight, Number 97 on April 11. The clerk then says

"How many in your party?", and the passenger replies "Four of us, my wife and two children." Since the children's fares depend on their ages, the clerk asks how old they are, and the passenger replies "4 and 11," so both qualify for the lower fare. The clerk sees that the only four seats left together are in smoking, and so informs the passenger, who decides to take them, even though none of his family smokes. (Many airlines do not assign seats at the time of booking, but for this example we might as well spell out what happens if they do.)

The clerk is now ready to make the booking for the passenger. He is thus going to create a new record one level down on the hierarchy. He asks the passenger's name, address, and phone number (He is now typing in an *update*—up to now he had only typed in *queries.*)

> WILLIAM TOMPKINS
> 35 SPRUCE AVENUE, BLUEWITCH, CONN
> 555-9924
> M/M, CHILD FRED, WILHELMINA

followed by the seats requested

> 12A, 12B, 12C, 12D

with the computer still remembering that this is April 11th's Flight 97 from Hartford to San Francisco. The computer then removes seats 12A, 12B, 12C, and 12D from its seats-vacant list for the April 11th Flight 97, creates a record headed

> WILLIAM TOMPKINS
> 35 SPRUCE AVENUE, BLUEWITCH, CONN
> 555-9924

and stores in this record

> BDL → SFO 97 APR 11 Y
> M/M, CHILD FRED, WILHELMINA
> 12A, 12B, 12C, 12D

To complete its work, it places a pointer from the flight record to the TOMPKINS record, so that it will be possible to check who is on the flight if it becomes necessary to phone passengers because of a cancellation or other unusual event.

Now it is time to book the family's return flight. The clerk will again check with the computer and the passenger until the passenger has chosen his flight. Now, instead of creating a new record, the clerk can tell the computer to *retrieve* the old record and add the new reservations to it.

Thus we have a three-level data base:

The top level gives—for each specific pair of cities—fare information and flight information for all connections from the first city to the second. Flight information would include flight times, meal service, type of plane, and so on.

The second level gives for each specific flight (determined by origin, destination, flight number and date) such information as seats still available, pointers to records for each party booked on the flight, and (if they are known, and differ from the scheduled times) the estimated departure and arrival times. Note that this record does *not* need to include such details as meal service and type of plane—they are available one level up, since they depend only on the flight number and not on the day that the flight is made.

The third level has a trip record for each party using the airline—giving the name, address, and phone number of the leader of the party, the people in the party, the flights on which they are booked and their seat assignments on each of these flights, as well as any special information such as "needs salt-free meals" or "needs wheelchair."

Using the query/update language CLERK, the airline reservations clerk can get access to any of these records, by typing in

$$BDL \rightarrow SFO$$

or

$$BDL \rightarrow SFO \; 97 \; APR \; 11$$

or

WILLIAM TOMPKINS

followed by appropriate instructions. However, using CLERK, the clerk can only create or change records at the lowest level—with the computer automatically making the corresponding changes at the given-flight-on-a-given-date level. For example, the clerk can change a passenger's record by canceling his reservation on a particular flight—and then the computer will *automatically* restore his seats to the seats-vacant list for that flight, and remove his name from the passenger list, so long as the data bank is properly designed.

Using EXEC at headquarters, the supervisor can use CLERK to query the system and update passenger records, but he can also add new city pairs at the top level, as well as modify top-level records by adding or removing flights, changing the fare structure, or updating the seating pattern, meal service, plane type, or schedule of any particular flight.

However, EXEC must be more flexible than this. For example, if a plane is 2 hours late, an executive might want to check if it is worth delaying another plane to wait for people making connections. He would thus want to ask the computer to list all flights with more than 10 people connecting from the flight that was late, and to show for each of these flights how many of the people on them have connections that they have to make. To answer the question, the computer has to go from the flight record to the record of each passenger, find which ones are booked on flights leaving within 3 hours, say, of the scheduled arrival of the delayed flight, and so on. The key point about this example is that many uses of a data bank do not depend on access to a single record but require the **linkage** of many records before a problem is solved. (In Section 4.3, we shall study the threat to privacy posed by the linkage of records in *different* data banks via a computer network.)

The systems programmer's job is, in the first place, to set up the airline reservations data base so that it can hold the three types of records, with each record having the right pointers to other records (from a pair of cities to each flight-on-a-given day that connects them, from a passenger record to each flight on which he is booked, and so on). At the same time, he must design CLERK and EXEC so that they can be used to express all the appropriate queries and updates, and then write interpreters that will translate these commands into a form the machine can carry out. Some of the queries in EXEC may require complex programs searching through, and linking, many records. One of the key tests of the systems programmer's skill is to make sure that the queries and updates do not have **side-effects.** We give just one example of this:

Suppose the company decides to stop offering Flight 69 from Hartford to San Francisco. Someone in headquarters types in the EXEC command

ERASE BDL → SFO 69

and the system removes all trace of Flight 69 from the BDL → SFO record. If this were all the command achieved, the airline would be in trouble! What of all the people who have already booked space on Flight 69 at some future date? To anticipate this problem, the systems programmer must set the system up so that the above EXEC command not only updates the BDL → SFO record but also types out a list showing, for every day on which space has been reserved on Flight 69, a complete listing of the passengers—including phone numbers and addresses—booked on the flight that day. This list can then be shared among several airline reservations clerks whose job it is to contact the passengers, tell them of the cancellation, apologize, and make new reservations. Having prepared the list, the computer deletes all the second-level records on Flight 69. With this, its execution of the high-level EXEC command is completed. It is the job of the clerks to update or delete the third-level passenger records.

Working the other way, when an executive adds a new flight, a well-designed system would interrogate him to obtain all the necessary information—days it runs, flight times, plane type, seating plan, meal service, and so on. Having updated the first-level record, it would then create second-level records for the new flight, with one record for every day the flight runs in the next 12 months.

Clearly, there are many EXEC and CLERK commands besides those we have listed, and each must be designed to take care of a great deal of "backroom work" besides the obvious work required by the command.

Rather than looking at any more of these commands, we note that the system will also need to do a certain amount of "backroom work" quite apart from obeying queries or updates. For example, at the end of each day, it must make copies of all its second-level records for that day and "retire them" to a "historical file"; and set up a new empty record for each flight operating on that date a year hence. Finally, note that EXEC will be used for far more than handling the flights of individual passengers. If well designed, it will let managers obtain information on loading factors and profitability of all their flights, and give them a planning tool to continually improve their scheduling in the face of changing patterns of public demand.

Leaving our discussion of the airline data base, it is worth noting that workers in **artificial intelligence** (which we study in Chapter 5) are trying to set up systems that can form nonstandard linkages to combine filed information with general knowledge, to help "answer questions that have never been asked before." Where a data bank (as in airline reservations, insurance companies, or payrolls) has its records arranged so that it is easy to retrieve the answers to standard queries—what is the date of birth of a particular person? what is their annual salary? what is the fare for such-and-such a flight? what deductions are they eligible for?—the computer can usually answer them by sending a single entry from a single record, or linking a few records in a standard way. In artificial intelligence, however, scientists study how to program the computer to answer more complex questions like "How old is John's father?" To answer the question the systems needs to "know" about family relations, and about the way in which age is defined in terms of the difference between present date and birth date. Moreover, it must "know" how to search for relevant

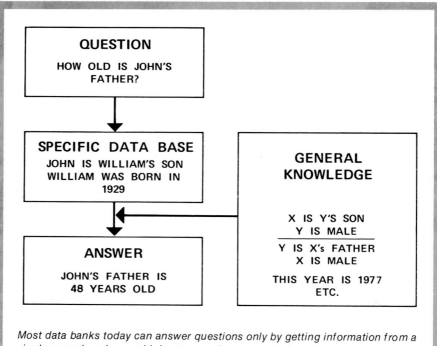

Most data banks today can answer questions only by getting information from a single record, or by combining two or three records in a standard way. Future developments will require much more "intelligent" systems, which not only can retrieve relevant information from the specific data base, but also can use "general knowledge" to answer a user's query. We shall have more to say about artificial intelligence in Chapter 5.

pieces of information—in this case, "William's son is John" and "William was born on March 17, 1929"—before it can combine them to answer the original question. In Sections 5.2 and 5.3, we shall study how this necessary "knowledge" can be given to a computer, as long as it is not too complicated.

The Problem of Security

Often, a data bank does not have its own computer. Instead, it operates within a large **time-sharing system.** In this subsection, we look at the problems this can cause, as people try to obtain illegitimate access through other terminals on the system. In fact, the problems we discuss apply to any user of a time-sharing system, whether they use a data bank, or simply have a file for the data and programs they are using for their own problem-solving.

If a terminal is only to be used for accessing a single data bank using a fixed query/update language, then the terminal can be wired to always provide access to just those facilities for which it was intended. However, to sign on to a time-sharing system through a terminal that is used for many different purposes, the user types in a **password** and user number—and thereafter uses the terminal as if it was his own personal computer, using programs to process data. The password gives the user access to his own files which contain the data and programs which he has accumulated in previous use of the computer. It acts as the "key" which is meant to open the "lock" on his files, a lock which keeps other people out.

Just as a key can open a lock whether or not it is yours, so anyone who has your password can obtain access to your files; and just as one can break a lock rather than use a key to open it, or cut a hole in the wall to avoid the lock altogether, so a really ingenious programmer may find ways of getting into files without having the password. The manager of a time-sharing system thus has a great responsibility to ensure that "only the right people have the keys to any given lock" and that "there is no way to cut through the door." In other words, he has the problem of ensuring security on his time-sharing system, so that only authorized users can have access to any given file, and so that no one can use computing time without being properly charged for it.

At the moment, passwords provide the main form of computer security. However, it does not take a computer expert to find out passwords. One can find out a person's password by simply watching how they **sign on** (start to use their terminal), or by going through their trash baskets and reading the password from their computer printout. To protect against this, many systems no longer print out the password when the user types it in at the terminal. This precaution is not enough, however. The more technically gifted person trying to "steal" the password could simply program a computer to try out passwords at random, going through perhaps hundreds of thousands until he finds some that give him access to useful files, or "free" computing time.

An ingenious way of finding passwords is to tap the lines that lead from the terminal to the computer, and decode the signals. Another use of wire tapping is called "piggybacking," in which a computer criminal can hook a second computer onto the line between the terminal and the central computer to intercept messages and even modify them. For example, someone using piggybacking could insert additional credit transfers to accounts when intercepting transmission between a terminal and the central records of a bank (compare Section 4.2). To protect against wiretapping, the best defense is probably to scramble messages. However, just as one can use a computer to generate scrambled messages, so can one use a computer to decode them. To change the code continually to foil would-be wiretappers costs a great deal both in hardware costs and in inconvenience to the user to ensure that the terminal and the computer are always using the same code at the same time!

There are other "keys" beside passwords. One is a magnetically striped card that a user can insert into a slot in an appropriately designed terminal. However, people so inclined can quite easily make counterfeit cards using ordinary magnetic tape. This has prompted some companies to look into devices for recognizing fingerprints as the "key" to signing on. Another type of "key" requires the user to answer a number of personal questions before being given access—but this is not only inconvenient to the user, but it also wastes a great deal of computation time that could be better used elsewhere.

Let us now look in a little more detail at "how to cut through the wall"—in other words how to use the system without having a password or any other sort of key. We first recall the distinction in a data base management system between the data definition language used by the professional to set up the system, and the query/update language used for normal access to the data base. We have the same sort of distinction with *any* **operating system.** There are the various ways in which the user can get his programs run by the computer in an easier fashion because of the operating system resident in the computer. On the other hand, there is the actual programming that sets up the operating system in the first place, and modifies the operating system when changes are required. Changes might be required to allow new terminals to be serviced; or to institute security precautions to thwart a new way of breaking into the system. Changes might also be made because of a new filing procedure or because of a rise of computation prices; or to make a new compiler available for a language that could not previously be used on the system. The maintenance engineers must, in particular, be able to change the passwords or privileges granted to a user. The programming language in which such changes are made is called the **systems command language** (Fig. 3). Clearly, one way that a potential wrong-doer can "cut through the wall" is to acquire the systems command language manual and then—having found any password that will

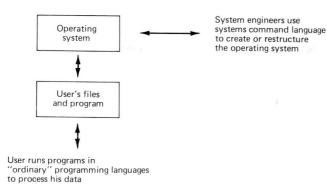

Fig. 3 The *systems command language* allows the expert systems programmer to *change* the operating system; while programs in "ordinary" *programming languages* can be translated by the operating system to allow users to process their data.

allow him to start using the system—get onto the system and type in systems commands that will give him access to passwords and the privileges of various users and their files. He will not only have access to the files of any other user, but can even change the basic operating system to his own advantage.

However, one does not have to have the operating manual for the operating system to be able to "cut through the wall." An operating system is itself a program—a huge one of perhaps hundreds of thousands of instructions. In a program this size, there are bound to be many bugs, and no matter how careful the system programmers are in trying to debug the system, one can be sure that some errors will remain. Some user may type in an unusual sequence of commands and instead of getting the system to respond in the normal way will suddenly find himself with material from another user's files. To most users, such a discovery is an annoyance. To some users, it is a challenge. Many university students, with no thoughts of crime but only of pranks, have taken delight in getting on a university time-sharing system and working hard trying to find bugs in the operating system until such time as they can leave messages in the file of a professor with such blood-curdling threats as "give all the students in your classes A's or your files will be erased!"

The users of a time-sharing system include banks and agencies connected with a nation's defense or war efforts. Clearly, the files of the banks must be protected from would-be robbers; while the defense and war files must be protected from would-be spies. To test the security of computer systems that are to be used by the United States

Defense Department, the United States Air Force has funded the MITRE Corporation to form expert programmers into "tiger teams" whose job it is to work at ordinary terminals of a time-sharing system and see if they can crack that part of the system whose use is being considered by the defense department. Even the most elaborate security on a time-sharing system seems unable to resist an attack from such a "tiger team." For this reason, a major research area is *security*—making it harder and harder for unauthorized users to obtain access to a data bank or to files in a time-sharing system.

In addition to security against outside intervention, a data base needs protection against user errors, and against times when the computer "breaks down" temporarily. A system has **data integrity** if it is protected against wrong data. If the data are wrong, the phone does not get fixed, tax is assessed wrongly, or someone loses their seat on a plane. The problem is to know when data are wrong. There is no dramatic, detectable malfunction; rather, the bad data simply propagate and "pollute" the data base. One approach to integrity is to check if a value in a data field is "reasonable." The DBMS can have an automatic "alarm" if bounds are exceeded. It can also use consistency checks, such as

total seats on flight = number of vacant seats + number of seats assigned to passengers on the flight

This is a software service that must be added to the basic data base management.

A computer is a machine. Like all machines, it can have things go wrong with it—for example, a wire could come loose, or dirt or static electricity could foul up the magnetic disks. A hardware failure—called a "crash" in computer jargon—is likely to occur in a computer at least once a week. A good operating system—and that includes a good data base management system—must be designed to correct most, if not all, of the errors that result from a crash. While computer printouts of mistaken bills do still occur, the chance of machine error is far less than the chance of human error. Unfortunately, some companies refuse to admit that even this small chance of error remains. They turn complaints from indignant customers back to the machine, instead of letting the customer discuss the problem with some human employee.

Let us consider the specific problem of ensuring **continued data availability**—making sure that a computer crash will not block access to data. For example, since people's travel plans depend on the airline reservations data base, we cannot afford to let this data base "go down"—that is, become unavailable to us. Again, we cannot afford to lose track of the Mission Control data base during a space flight. Since all computers experience some hardware failure at least once a week, the DBMS must be designed to handle this. Currently, most measures are embodied in the software, rather than in the hardware.

One approach is to require that all files that are changed on a given day be copied on to tape; and that each week the whole system be copied. This approach is called **dumping.** Since it takes about 40 minutes to dump the data on 3 disks (and we saw in Section 1.2 that the United States tax people use hundreds of disks), a preferable alternative is often to use *selective* dumping followed by **rollback** or **rollforward.** Every time a track of the disk changes, a copy is made of both the "before image" and the "after image." We said earlier that data bases pollute—and it may take days for the pollution to be found by data integrity checks. If pollution is found, the DBMS rolls back the data base to what is presumably a nonpolluted state. What if paychecks went out during the polluted time? That's tough! However, it should be possible to reconstruct what happened during the pollution period and correct many of the mistakes. The DBMS uses a backup copy of the data base to get old versions, and uses after-images to roll forward. In this way, users can be protected against most forms of operator error and hardware failure in a large, but well-designed, data base.

Suggestions for Further Reading

C. C. Gottlieb and A. Borodin: "Social Issues in Computing." Academic Press, New York, 1973.
Chapter 4 discusses files, data banks, and information systems, providing background for Chapter 5's discussion of information systems and privacy.

Waiting for the Great Computer Rip-off, *Fortune,* July 1974, pp. 143–150.
Contains an excellent account of the security problems associated with time-sharing systems.

B. R. Schneider: "Travels in Computerland." Addison-Wesley, Reading, Massachusetts, 1974.
This is a highly readable tale of the trials and tribulations of an English professor setting up a data bank to store information about plays performed on the London Stage, 1650–1800. The book immerses the reader in the "feel" of setting up a computer system, and shows how different

the reality can be from the smooth procedures of the textbooks. It dramatically emphasizes the many choices involved at each stage of setting up a complex system, as well as the problems of manpower and logistics involved.

Summary

We have seen how expert programmers use a **data definition language** to set up record structures and **query/update languages** which make it easy to store appropriate information, and to query and update it. A well-designed system does a great deal of "backroom" work, taking care of side-effects without further effort on the part of the user. A good data bank design restricts the queries and updates that any particular group of users can make. Special precautions must be taken to gain security against unauthorized access, as well as to protect against user error or hardware failure.

Glossary

Memory: The *memory* of a computer comprises a *primary memory* to and from which the CPU can very quickly move information; and a *secondary memory,* made up of devices like magnetic tape units and magnetic disk units, which are larger and cheaper than primary memory, but also much slower.

Data base: The *data base* is a collection of data—stored in primary or secondary memory—to which the computer can repeatedly refer in the course of its operations. It may be divided into *records,* each of which contains information about some specific person, policy, project, or other basic unit about which information is collected.

Data bank: A *data bank* is made up of one or more data bases, together with the computing machinery required to store or use them.

Operating system: The *operating system* is a set of programs, permanently resident in the computer, that make the computer easier to use. For example, an operating system can schedule jobs, transfer compilers from secondary memory to primary memory, and balance out the use of input/output devices and actual computing.

Systems command language: The language in which a system programmer sets up an operating system is called a *systems command language.*

Time-sharing system: A *time-sharing system* enables many human users to interact with a single computer at the same time. The operating system gives a fraction of each second of CPU time to the needs of each user, swapping the user's file back and forth between secondary and primary memory.

Password: A *password* is a code word that the user of a time-sharing system must type in each time he *signs on* (starts to use his terminal) to obtain access to his files.

Data base management system (DBMS): An operating system that helps the systems programmer create and restructure a data base, and helps a user get access to query and update the data base is a *DBMS*.

Data definition language: The *data definition language* is the programming language used by an expert data base programmer to specify the file structure of a data base, restructure the data base, specify consistency checks, etc.

Query/update language: This is a language designed for nonexpert programmers for *querying* and *updating* a data base.

Hierarchy: An organization whose components are arranged in levels from a top level on down to a bottom level is a *hierarchy*.

Linkage: *Linkage* is the process whereby different records in one or more data banks are combined to answer a single query or to create a new record.

Side-effect: A *side-effect* is any effect of running a program—like placing partial results in various locations of the store—that was not part of the program specification. Similarly, in ecological systems, pollution would be an example of a side-effect of industrial development.

Artificial intelligence: *AI* is that branch of computer science that studies how to program computers to exhibit apparently intelligent behavior.

Data integrity: *Data integrity* is protection against erroneous information in a data base.

Continued data availability: *Continued data availability* is assured if a crash in hardware will not block access to the information in a data base.

Dumping: Transferring the contents of primary memory to some other storage medium—either for human inspection, or to have a reference copy—is *dumping*.

Rollback: The process of referring back to an earlier copy of a portion of a data base to find unpolluted information is called *rollback*.

Rollforward: Using portions of a data base to update an old copy is called *rollforward*.

Exercises

1. Match each type of person with one or more appropriate items in the right hand column.

1.	systems programmer	a.	query-update language
2.	airline reservations clerk	b.	crash DBMS
3.	airline headquarters	c.	cancel reservation
	executive	d.	data definition language
4.	customer	e.	erase entire data base

5. airline company president	f. dump file for pollution check
6. tiger team	g. professor's file locked against
7. university student on time-sharing system	h. change flight times and fares
8. maintenance engineer	

2. Define "continued data availability" using at least three of the following terms: crash, access, data, DBMS, and dumping.

3. Why do many large computer users post armed guards to check admittance to their machine rooms (where the computers are), programming sections (where programs can be entered into the machines), and tape or disk libraries (where the thousands of reels of data and programs are kept when not running)? How can a program literally be "worth its weight in gold" and need such protection?

4. Draw a flow diagram showing (in outline) how the computer should respond to an EXEC cancellation of service on flight 179 from BDL to SFO. (*Hint:* Use A to stand for the top-level record on the flight; B 3/7 to stand for the second-level record on the flight for the 7th day of the 3rd month; and PASSLIST for the list of passengers whose flight has been canceled.)

5. Suppose a data base has a record on each person listing their birthdate and the names of their children and parents. What steps would be required to answer the question "How old is John Smith's uncle?" Would there be only one answer?

6. Suppose an important, expensive computer program is suspected of error. Should a program be presumed "innocent until proven guilty"?

7. Should the management of a time-sharing network install every possible safeguard? (*Hint:* Use the word "tradeoff" in your answer.)

8. Describe how rollback and rollforward might be used in an airline reservation data base. Why might it be a good idea to have a computer memory inside each terminal?

9. What steps should an airline reservations clerk take if, by a typing error, he or she put the wrong phone number in a passenger's third-level record?

4.2. COMPUTERS, CASH, AND CRIME

Credit cards and checks have greatly changed the way we handle money. Now computers add a new dimension: your cash reserves can be simply a series of numbers stored in the magnetic disks of your bank's computer. In the first subsection, we examine the possibilities this opens up for a "cashless/checkless society," while in the next subsection we examine the opportunities opened up for the computer criminal.

The Checkless Society

In the United States alone, over 30 billion checks are used each year to transfer something like $8 trillion from one person or company to another. The cost of processing these checks exceeds $5 billion a year for the banks alone. To this must be added the check-handling costs of businesses and individuals. Because of this, work is underway to develop a computer network to replace much of check handling by the **electronic fund transfer system** (EFTS) from one bank account to another. It is estimated that such electronic transfers will cost from 5 to 10 cents each, approximately half the cost of processing a check. Some people refer to the result of this development as a checkless or cashless society. However, it will really be a society with fewer checks and less cash. It is hardly worth a 10-cent computer charge to save putting a coin into a vending machine. Or, in the words of Mary Trompke, then a University of Massachusetts student, "When a civilization gets so that it is necessary to have an ID number to buy a loaf of bread, it's time to move on!"

The "checkless" society is an example of an **information utility**— but one that is specialized for financial transactions. In addition to moving money, it will allow automatic extension of credit. In this, it will extend the function of bank cards like Master Charge or the Barclaycard which do not provide short-term credit for a fixed annual fee—like American Express—but instead provide loans. These loans must total less than some limit fixed for the cardholder, and are charged interest at a rate of 18% per year. When you pay for an item by EFTS, you will have the choice of specifying whether the cost will be deducted from your bank balance or charged against your credit line (or a mixture of the two). Since the interest charge starts *instantly,* there will be a stronger incentive to pay directly from the bank balance than at present, when interest charges may not become effective until a month after the date of purchase. Bankers refer to this inducement for prompt payment as "the time value of money"— interest is computed on a daily basis.

Currently, checks take 2 to 4 days to process. It is estimated that EFTS would remove approximately $2 billion in the United States alone in these "phantom bank reserves" of checks in transit. The instant readout of financial transactions could also provide fast reporting of consumer spending and economic information to government economists trying to make decisions that will affect the rate of unemployment, inflation, and so on.

Let us see how a typical EFTS transaction might work when a person goes into a shop. The customer, after selecting the items, would take them to a clerk, who would tally the price, perhaps using an electronic "wand" to scan the universal price code on each item like this one

from a box of breakfast cereal and automatically register the cost and identity of the item. The customer would then either pay cash, or give the clerk his bank card, which would look much like a credit card with a strip of magnetic tape on the back. The front of the card would have the name of the person, and a photo and signature to help the clerk identify the customer. It might also repeat, in human-readable form, some of the information coded on the back for the computer. The customer would then tell the clerk how much of the bill he wanted to pay for in "cash" (instant transfer from his bank balance) or "charge" (instant addition to his total loan from the bank).

The clerk would then insert the card in a slot in his cash register—which would also be a computer terminal for the EFTS utility—and ring up the two amounts. The terminal would then read the magnetic strip to direct an enquiry automatically to the correct bank (that is, the "bank code" serves to "dial the right number") to find out whether the customer's bank balance was full enough to cover the "cash," or if he had enough credit left to cover the charge. (To detect forged cards, the computer could be programmed to store a random number both on the card's magnetic tape and with the bank account when the card is used. Then, the next time the card is used, the computer would check that the number on the strip is the number stored in the account on the previous use.)

If the computer flashed back a "no," the customer would have to find some other way of paying—even using old-fashioned money, or negotiating credit directly with the store—or leave without the goods. If, however, the computer returns a "yes," it will automatically subtract the "cash" amount from the *customer's* bank balance, add the "charge" amount to his debt at the bank, and add the total cost of the purchases to the *shop's* bank account. Since the shop may have a different bank from the customer, this may involve an extra "call" being automatically routed through the network.

It is as if each bank account had its own telephone, and the shop's terminal set up a conference call between itself and the customer's account (its "phone number" is on the credit card) and the shop's account (its "phone number" is permanently stored inside the terminal). This analogy makes clear that the EFTS network must indeed be a utility—a network used by many different shops and banks with free access to all—rather than the property of a single bank. Just as with the telephone network, the government may, and should, regulate the cost and distribution of services on the utility, but should not monitor the detailed transactions any more than it should "bug" or "wire-tap" telephone conversations. (We shall look at this and other privacy issues in the next section. People will not want records of their every financial transaction released without their knowledge.)

The terminal can also be connected via a network (not necessarily the same one) to a computer that keeps track of many important aspects of the store's operation. It may log the sale itself to update the salesperson's commission, and update a report on the profitability of certain items. It could also update its count on the inventory of each item. If this falls below a certain level—and the profitability report justifies continuing to stock the item—then the computer could automatically issue an order for more items. (We shall meet this type of system again in Section 6.3 when we look at the use of computers for automatic warehousing.)

The first steps to EFTS have already been taken. Most banks will arrange to have their computers automatically prepare checks each month to make such regular payments for a client as his insurance premiums. Companies have the bank handle transfers each pay day from the company's account to employees' accounts. More and more stores have a "telecredit" service that lets them verify whether a credit card still offers good credit, or whether there is enough cash in a check account to cover a check. Many banks now offer "bank-in-a-box"—an account holder can insert his bank card into a machine, and have it dispense cash, debiting his account for the amount. The same system could accept bills fed in through a slot, and deposit the amount to the account whose number is encoded on the bank card inserted in another slot. Thus many of the pieces are in place. They must be integrated and extended to provide a truly effective financial utility.

The EFTS would have many advantages. We have already mentioned the efficiency and economy of replacing much of the growing volume of check-handling. It would also reduce the amount of cash people would have to carry—perhaps even taxicabs could be hooked in by a radio link!—which would be especially welcome in urban high-crime areas. Retailers would get immediate payment—whether the customer chose the "cash" or "credit" option for bank card payment—and would not have to pay the commission they now pay to the credit card companies. Banks would eliminate having to return canceled checks, or handling stopped payments.

There are features that some users will not like. For example, EFTS would put a stop to "kiting"—issuing a check a day or two before there is money to cover it. However, this feature could be included in the EFTS simply by allowing half the usual salary to be added to the client's bank account the day before payday, or by letting the client's credit line increase to a maximum the day before payday, and drop to a minimum when his pay is added to his bank account. The beauty of a computer system is that good ideas often require a simple change in the program instead of a whole new machine.

It is not clear that the EFTS will do away with checks completely. When you receive a bill with some product you have ordered through the mail, or when you receive your electricity bill for the month, it may be easier to pop a check in the mail than to go to a terminal, insert your card, and dial in the account number of the biller, together with the total amount and the invoice number; but this electronic method *will* be available.

People will probably still want written receipts as a record of the bills they have paid via the computer. However, this will be only for their own files—it will not be like the check that must be sent to the bank, processed, canceled and then returned to the check-writer. Incidentally, since computers fail, the types of precautions we outlined in Section 4.1 will also be used in the EFTS. The records in each bank might be dumped every few hours for rollback in case of mistaken or fraudulent overwriting; and each terminal might be equipped with enough memory so that it can be interrogated for any data lost in the period while a bank's system, or part of the communication network, was down.

Having said so much in favor of EFTS, we must conclude with a few words of concern for the social impact. We have already mentioned the privacy problems—and we shall take these up in more detail in the next section. Another serious problem is: "Who qualifies for a bank card?" It is already almost impossible to hire a car without a credit card to present as proof of your credit rating. Many hotels will no longer accept payment in cash unless you can present a credit card when you check-in as a guarantee that your bill will be covered! Thus there already seems to be serious discrimination against people who either choose not to have a credit card, or for some reason— which may have little to do with their present ability to pay their bills—have a bad credit rating, and so cannot get a credit card. This problem will become worse with the introduction of the EFTS unless special legislation is enacted to protect people's economic access.

One solution is to make it illegal for a bank to deny a card to anyone. The bank may still reserve the right to limit the person to a zero credit line unless they meet the usual conditions for credit—but at least the person has a card. Then he should be able to get any service as long as the balance meets some formula related to a reasonable prediction of the cost of the service.

An interesting problem is posed by foreign travel. If each country has its own EFTS network—just as it now has its own currency—a traveler will need a bank account in every country he visits. Perhaps the solution is to have a government bank in each country. Before you leave your own country, you open a traveler's account in your government bank, with a balance large enough to cover your travel costs. Then each time you pass from one country to another, you insert your card in a "foreign exchange terminal." This automatically sets up an account for you in the new country; transfers all the money from your previous account to the new account (making the appropriate currency conversion as it does so); closes out your old account; and changes the account code on your magnetic strip to the new number. A printed slip will give you a record of your account number and balance before and after the exchange. An important privacy safeguard would be to keep no electronic record of which account numbers in the two countries are paired in this way. We shall see more of this principle of "decoupling of data banks" in Section 4.3.

A Sampler of Computer Crimes

"A group of robbers make their way into the safe of a large bank, and take one million dollars from the 100 million dollars in cash stored there. So skillful are they that no watchman detects their presence in the vault, and no trace remains after they have gone. To make the chance of detection of the robbery almost negligible, they arrange that an accomplice will juggle the bank's books, so that they will show the total cash holdings of the bank to equal those that remain in the vault."

Such a successful robbery is in fact unlikely to occur with today's security procedures in any bank with sizable holdings. However, a new breed of criminal has been able to take advantage of the increasing use of computers in banks to carry out robberies that are at least as spectacular, and in which the robbers's traces are covered even more skillfully. These criminals take advantage of the fact that more banking transactions are done via a computer. An individual's assets need not take the form of actual money at all as long as the bank keeps on a magnetic disk, for example, a record of how much credit the individual is entitled to. If Person A gives some goods to Person B, or Person A does some work for Person B, then a mutually agreed upon number will be subtracted from B's account, and added to A's account.

The "job" of the computer thief thus becomes clear—to manipulate the numbers stored in the bank's data bank (!) in such a way that he gets richer while no one else can detect that they are getting poorer. In the rest of this section, we look at some of the ways people have exploited this idea for their own enrichment. Clearly, this new type of computer criminal needs special skills in computer programming and networking.

The first computer-crime conviction in a United States federal criminal case occurred in 1966. The culprit was a 21-year-old programmer who worked for the software company that operated the computer of the bank where he had his account. He made one very simple change in the bank's software—adding a "patch" of a few extra instructions. Whenever the program was being run that checked whether or not an account was overdrawn, it was instructed by the "patch" to ignore his account. If his account number had been 01352 the "unpatched" and "patched" program might look something like that shown in Fig. 1. He had originally planned to use the patch just as a holding action, believing that he would be able to make a new

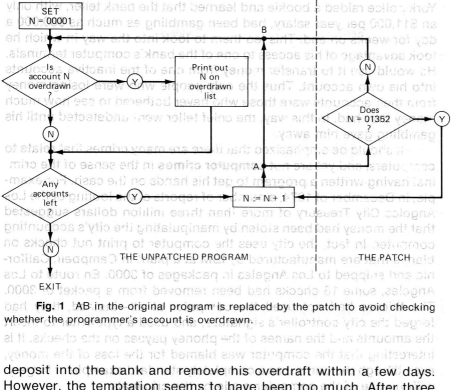

Fig. 1 AB in the original program is replaced by the patch to avoid checking whether the programmer's account is overdrawn.

deposit into the bank and remove his overdraft within a few days. However, the temptation seems to have been too much. After three months the patch was still there and he had gone $1300 into the red. He was only discovered because the computer broke down and hand calculation showed up the overdraft which he had programmed the computer to ignore!

Computer crime often seems to be discovered only as the result of some accident, rather than as a result of security measures built into the program. Because of this, many experts believe that there may be as many as ten computer crimes committed for every one which is discovered. There may even be thefts of millions of dollars which have yet to be uncovered.

A common crime is that of embezzlement—of juggling a bank's books to take money out for oneself. One case, in which the computer was used to embezzle one and a half million dollars, was that of a 41-year-old chief teller at a branch of New York's Union Dime Savings Bank. Again, he was discovered by accident—although this time the computer did not break down. Instead, he was found out when New

York police raided a bookie and learned that the bank teller, with only an $11,000 per year salary, had been gambling as much as $30,000 a day for weeks on end. This led them to look into the way in which he took advantage of his access to one of the bank's computer terminals. He would use it to transfer money from one of the inactive accounts into his own account. Thus the only people who were losing money from their accounts were those who never bothered to see how much money they had. In this way, the chief teller went undetected until his gambling gave him away.

It should be emphasized that there are many crimes that relate to computers, and yet are not **computer crimes** in the sense of the criminal having written a program to get his hands on the cash. For example, in December of 1974, a number of reports of the looting of the Los Angeles City Treasury of more than three million dollars suggested that the money had been stolen by manipulating the city's accounting computer. In fact, the city uses the computer to print out checks on blanks that are manufactured by IBM at a plant in Campbell, California and shipped to Los Angeles in packages of 3000. En route to Los Angeles, some 18 checks had been removed from a packet of 3000. The thieves had not used the computer at all—instead, they had forged the city controller's signature, and used a typewriter to insert the amounts and the names of the phoney payees on the checks. It is interesting that the computer was blamed for the loss of the money, even though the crime was a completely standard example of forgery, with no use of the computer made by the criminals.

There are other types of crime that do genuinely involve computers, and yet also do not fit under our definition of computer crime. A computer may cost hundreds of thousands, or even millions, of dollars, and so is a very desirable object to steal. Perhaps more interestingly, there have been thefts of computer designs and of computer programs. It may take many highly paid professionals a number of years to design a very complex operating system or computing machine. By stealing a large program or a design, a rival computer or software company could save itself literally millions of dollars. For example, in the spring of 1971 plans of IBM's 330 disk file system were stolen from IBM's San Jose plant in California. IBM placed a valuation of $160 million on the stolen plans and drawings for its 330 system, and placed an even higher valuation on information that had been stolen on a more recent disk file system, the 3340. At that time, many competitors were unaware of the principles upon which this new disk file system worked. They wanted to find out more about it so that they could either produce rival systems of their own, or develop products that were compatible with the new IBM system, and thus likely to enjoy greater sales. Finally, in June 1973, a number of suspects were arrested, and charged with felony, theft of trade secrets, conspiracy, receipt of stolen property, and offering or accepting inducement to steal trade secrets. Those arrested included several IBM employees as well as employees of a rival corporation, and several other corporations were implicated.

The first known theft of computer programs was brought to court in 1964. A programmer had taken software, whose total value his employer estimated at $5 million, "to work on at night." He received a 5-year term in a Texas penitentiary. Another programmer "kidnapped" some programs! He took them to a hideout in the mountains and notified his employer that he would not return them unless he was paid $100,000. He was eventually caught, and the programs were impounded for evidence in the sheriff's office. His employers were so desperate to use the programs just to be able to stay in business that they themselves burgled the sheriff's office so that they could make copies of the programs!

The first theft of programs that can be counted as a genuine computer crime, rather than a computer-related crime, appears to have occurred in 1971. In this case, the thief obtained access to the memory of a computer via a remote terminal connected to the computer through the telephone lines, and made a copy of a program that had cost a great deal of time and effort to produce. Intriguingly, a search warrant was issued to search the memory of the computer to find evidence related to the case.

One interesting outcome of a computer theft involved Jerry Neal Schneider, who was arrested in 1972 on charges of stealing some one million dollars worth of supplies from Pacific Telephone Company. After his conviction and some 40 days in prison, Schneider set up a new company, EDP Security, Inc., which will work for clients with software systems by cracking their security and then showing them what precautions would have protected the system against the tricks that he and his colleagues used. As can be imagined, the slogan of the company is "it takes a thief to catch a thief."

Schneider's "career in crime" started innocently enough. As a high school student, he would look in the trash cans of the Pacific Telephone Office near his home, helping himself to some of the excellent, although slightly damaged, telephone equipment that the company threw away. However, he found in the trash not only the equipment that had caused him to look there in the first place, but also system instructions, written guides for ordering equipment, catalogs, etc. From this, he learned how to use the phone company's computerized ordering system. After three years, he used his knowledge to launch his own company, called the Los Angeles Telephone and Telegraph Company. He used a touchtone telephone to get access to the Pacific Telephone Company's central ordering center. He had found the appropriate password on an invoice found in the trash. From the catalogs found in the trash, he could enter the appropriate numbers and description codes for the equipment he wanted. He placed the orders from different locations, for he had learned that the telephone company allowed a certain percentage of misdeliveries and losses for each location. Thus he always kept the amount of equipment that he took from the company at such a level that the company would not start checking out the losses.

Schneider had managed to get hold of keys to the various offices of Pacific Telephone Company. Each night, after a given office had received the false order Schneider had placed, he would drive up to the office in a company van he had bought at an auction to pick up his orders and the invoices which he would sign and return to the central office, and then take the equipment to the headquarters of his own company, where he would sell it—sometimes even selling it to Pacific Telephone when they ran short of equipment! Eventually, he employed ten people and had a 6000 square foot warehouse. He did not tell his employees the source of the equipment until he confided in one of them—who eventually wanted such a large salary that Schneider fired him. The disgruntled employee told the phone company, and so Schneider was eventually brought to court.

A major roadblock to protection against computer crime is that, apparently, the majority of companies prefer *not* to report a computer crime to the police. Rather, they try to make a private arrangement with the wrongdoer to get their money or their programs restored, and then get the programmer to resign. Companies proceed in this way because they feel that the loss to them of leaving the criminal at large is far less than the loss they would take if public confidence in their operation were undermined by the release of news stories about flaws in their computer system.

Another problem is the distorted ethics of many computer people who view "cracking a system" as an exciting challenge, rather than a crime. It is common practice among all too many programmers to make copies of programs they can find in the files of other users of a time-sharing system. People have even stated on the witness stand in court that they view as public property any program that they can find in anybody's file on a commercially available time-sharing computer system. Another programmer, who worked for a time-sharing service admitted that he would buy time from competitive services, and then do everything he could to get copies of programs, customer list files, user's files, and security measures on the operating system of the competitor—and then try to disrupt or even cause a breakdown in the competitor's time-sharing system. What is perhaps most distressing about this was that he stated his belief that this was not unethical, because he had not signed any contract prohibiting him from doing this, or ignored any explicit equivalent of a "no trespassing" sign. However, I think that such behavior is improper, and should be thought of as industrial sabotage or as theft, and punished accordingly. Meanwhile, the owners of time-sharing systems must do everything they can to provide software that protects the user—and the software and the time-sharing company itself—against such disruption, and leads to the apprehension of the malevolent programmer whenever disruption occurs.

Suggestions for Further Reading

R. L. Kramer and W. P. Livingston: Cashing in on the Checkless Society, *Harvard Business Review,* (September–October 1967), pp. 141–149.
This is an early, but thoughtful, review of the impact of computer transfer of money and credit by two computer experts in the Bankers Trust Company.

M. R. Wessel: Fair Access to the Checkless/Cashless Society, "Freedom's Edge: The Computer Threat to Society," Chap. 3. Addison–Wesley, Reading, Massachusetts, 1974.
Emphasis is placed on the steps necessary to ensure that the poor and disadvantaged are not victimized by the introduction of a financial utility.

To Catch a Thief, *Datamation,* February 1973, pp. 121–122.
An account is given of the Jerry Schneider case.

R. A. McLaughlin: Equity Funding: Everyone is Pointing at the Computer, *Datamation,* June, 1973, pp. 88–91.
A detailed look is taken at a large insurance swindle, and the new auditing procedures for computerized insurance records that it stimulated.

Using Computers to Steal—Latest Twist in Crime, *U.S. News and World Report,* June 18, 1973, pp. 39–42.
More information is given on computer crimes, along with precautions that can help prevent them.

D. B. Parker and S. Nycum: The New Criminal, *Datamation,* January 1974, pp. 56–58.
A profile of the computer criminal is provided.

Waiting for the Great Computer Rip-off, *Fortune,* July 1974, pp. 143–150.
    This is an excellent account of computer crime, with special attention
    paid to the problems and opportunities posed by time-sharing systems.
Economy & Business Section, *Time,* January 26, 1976.
    Page 53 gives an account of the use by Citibank of New York of terminals
    that will accept customer's cards to verify whether their account can
    cover a check.

Summary

We have probed two major implications of the increasing use of computers to provide the sole record of financial assets—the trend toward the
financial utility, including an **electronic funds transfer system (EFTS);** and
the new opportunities for **computer crime.** We examined how EFTS would
work, looked at the technical problems raised, and suggested safeguards for
privacy and for individual access to the system. In cataloging a number of
computer crimes, we saw that their prevention not only requires better security of the kind discussed in Section 4.1, but also requires fuller disclosure by
companies of crimes that do occur, and a different ethic about file-breaking
on the part of some programmers.

Glossary

Electronic fund transfer system (EFTS): *EFTS* is a computer network for
electronically transferring "money," by decreasing the computer record of
one account, while increasing the account to which transfer is to be made.

Information utility: An *information utility* a network that provides computer
usage to a wide public—in the same way that we have water, electricity, and
telephone utilities.

Computer crime: *Computer crime* occurs when the computer is programmed to provide fraudulent access to funds, computer time, data, or
programs. This is in distinction from computer-related crime, such as physi-
cally stealing a magnetic tape containing a program and data.

Exercises

1. Using the discussion in Section 4.1 of the data base for airline reservations as an example, specify the records structure and the query/update languages for a data base for the EFTS system described in the text.

2. Large corporations make considerable profit by the tactic of "kiting" a
check. *Example:* Yoyodyne Supersoftware writes you a check for $1 million

on September 3. This was in payment for a major operating system you, a subcontractor, supplied on that date. However, they issue it through the Obscuresville, Alaska, bank. The check takes 3 days to clear, due to the slowness of traditional paper-pushing long-distance information transfer. Yoyodyne earns interest on that $1 million until September 6. This could be well over $1,000 profit for Yoyodyne—and loss to you. Explain, in detail equal to this example, why EFTS would prevent this profit.

3. This Sunday night I accompanied two friends to dinner at a local restaurant. We had neglected to cash our paychecks the previous Friday, and carried only spare change. We went to another restaurant—the first refused our checks "on company policy." Even if we wished to avoid the interest charges on a regular credit card, how could a "bank-in-a-box" nearby have helped us, if there was a "box" on the corner connected to our bank? Why should the bank be less suspicious of us than the restaurant was?

4. The "Robin Hood syndrome" occurs when a computer criminal claims that harming individuals is immoral, but that government-regulated industries, telephone companies, transnational conglomerates, etc., themselves harm society, so hurting such entities is fair. Would you feel guilty in taking a dime from a defective pay phone? Is the analogy—based on "robbing the rich to give to the poor"—convincing to you? Give one difference between the 10¢ pay phone case and the typical computer crime. Name another recently "popular" crime considered daring and romantic by antiestablishmentarians.

5. Which of the accompanying graphs (A–F) most reasonably shows the amount of computer crime per year in the U.S., on the basis of what you have read in this section?

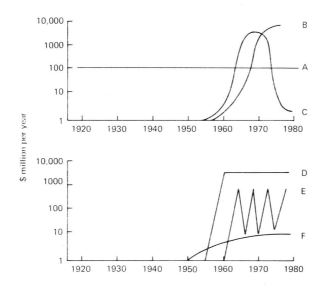

6. What does "it takes a thief to catch a thief" mean in the computer crime context? (*Hint:* When would a company *want* to have its software system security "cracked"?)

7. As more and more computer power is tied into networks, and more data made accessible on such a system, what agency or laws, now in existence, if any, can guarantee the right of all qualified people to use the system? What might happen if societal groups, divided by economic, racial, or educational barriers, are systematically excluded from participation in national computer networks?

8. What rights do you think a network has to *exclude* people? (*Hint:* When is a state allowed to deport or jail people?)

9. Should police require a warrant to search a data base? Why? When should police be allowed to examine your personal files?

4.3. DATA BANKS AND PRIVACY

As we come to live in an increasingly cybernetic society, more and more information about us is stored in **data banks.** As more and more people make airplane reservations, open checking accounts, file complicated tax returns, apply for insurance, and so on, only computers can save us from drowning in a sea of paperwork. For increasingly many people, however, there is a chilling feeling that the mass of data is beyond their control, and that their lives can be damaged because of the **linkage** and misuse of their records from a number of data banks.

In this section, we examine some of the threats posed by the unregulated spread of data banks. We then examine the provisions of the Privacy Act of 1974, passed by the United States Congress as an important step to "making the individual's informed consent a more respected and controlling feature" in the cybernetic society. An important provision of the act is to give people access to the records held on them in many data banks. As was pointed out in testimony, this access will not only help promote the accuracy of records, but will also increase public acceptance of data banks, diminishing the view held by many of the computer as a symbol of irresponsiveness and insensitivity in modern life. We close the section with a discussion of further improvements required beyond the Privacy Act of 1974.

The Need to Control Data Banks

In the 1960s, the United States Army established data banks allegedly designed to help in predicting and preventing civil disturbances. Army surveillance units took notes, tape recordings, and photographs in churches, on campuses, in classrooms, at antiwar rallies, and at other public meetings. At least four computers were programmed with the data, listing people taking part in these activities by political belief, memberships, and geographical region. Most of these people were simply exercising their right of free speech, and were not even engaged in acts of passive civil disobedience, let alone violent acts of disruption.

The Select Committee on Watergate heard revelations of improper access, transfer, and disclosure of personal files (including hotel, telephone, and bank records), and of illegal investigation of and collection of data on individuals. Officials created an "enemies list," and tried to use federal tax records as weapons of political and personal revenge.

These findings contributed to a genuine concern about the misuse of data banks for political purposes. There was, however, even greater cause for concern for the privacy and rights of the average citizen. It was felt that these rights could be seriously damaged by the careless storage, copying, or distribution of inaccurate or irrelevant records.

In a survey conducted from 1971 to 1974, the United States Senate Judiciary Subcommittee compiled a list of 858 data banks in 54 federal agencies, containing 1¼ billion records—and it was estimated that there were thousands more federal data banks that they had failed to uncover. At least 29 of the data banks contained derogatory information (passing bad checks, denial of credit, sexual habits, and so on). Of the data banks studied 457 had no explicit statutory authority for their existence. Individuals seldom knew they were on file—and even if they did, usually had no access to their records; yet federal agencies regularly passed records back and forth. Even agencies which—like the Internal Revenue Service collecting tax returns—had pledged confidentiality for information collected from individuals would regularly pass this information to federal, state, and local agencies. People listed information on their contributions to charitable organizations as part of their itemized deductions on their tax returns. Libraries with computerized library cards can compile records of each individual's reading habits. A bank's check records show many of an individual's financial transactions. It was clear that guarantees were required to ensure that this information was not transferred to an Army or CIA data bank to be worked up into a political profile.

Federal data banks contain answers to many questionnaires whose material may be considered an invasion of privacy. The Bureau of the Census conducted a survey for the Department of Health, Education, and Welfare which included questions like:

> What is the total number of gifts you give to individuals each year?
> What were you doing most of last week?

while applicants for Federal jobs had to mark as true or false statements like:

> I have never been in trouble because of my sex behavior.
> I believe in a life hereafter.
> I have no difficulty in starting or holding my bowel movements.

Already, in the early 1970s, there were thousands of data banks in the private sector in the United States. Between them, the five largest retail credit companies then had files on 54 million people. The Medical Information Bureau in Greenwich, Connecticut held medical records for 13 million people. There was increasing work on the Electronic Fund Transfer System we discussed in Section 4.2. The records in these data banks were freely exchanged with other firms in the private sector, and with law enforcement and surveillance groups in local, state, and federal government.

Here is an explicit example of the problem caused by the movement of inaccurate information from one data bank to another. A colleague of mine—call him R—was denied credit by a store. The store refused to tell him why. Eventually, he had to go to court to learn what it was in his file at a credit information bureau that had cost him his credit rating. He found that his file contained a record of a court case involving a bad debt by a *different* man with the *same* name! R had this information removed from his file, and his credit rating restored; or so it seemed. Later on he found that other credit information bureaus had the same false information in their files. All the bureaus had purchased the same list of court cases from a firm which compiled these lists for credit bureaus to use in assigning credit ratings.

To remedy this situation would require the following steps: The store must disclose the name of its credit information bureau, and the bureau must open any individual's file for his inspection and remove any inaccurate, misleading, or irrelevant data. Moreover, transfer of information from one data bank to another must be severely limited. In addition, a full record must be made of such transfers, so that corrections of data in one data bank can be transmitted to all other data banks.

In fact, the above story really has nothing to do with computers. The damage to the individual's credit rating would be just as great if the data bank were a room full of filing cabinets stuffed full of sheets of paper.

However, it is an immense amount of work to gather 100 files from filing cabinets in backrooms of buildings scattered all over the country; and it is relatively easy to retrieve, via a **computer network,** all computerized records stored under a given name. Thus, while the privacy issue for government and private records is not a new one, it is greatly *magnified* by the rise of the computer data bank. This is especially so when these data banks can be joined in vast networks and used to exchange information without the knowledge or consent of the individuals concerned. In the early 1970s, the United States General Services Administration had proposed to establish FEDNET—a

One of the first police forces to use a computerized data base for its records was the Kansas City Police Department. This picture shows Clarence Kelley, then Kansas City Police Chief and later Director of the FBI, talking to a policeman using one of the terminals of the police record system. (Reprinted, with permission, from "The Computerized Society" by J. Martin and A. Norman, published by Prentice Hall, New York, 1970.)

vast network linking data banks in many federal agencies. It was
strongly opposed because of the great possibilities of abuse, and
uncertainty of what the full implications of such a linkage might be.
As then Vice-President Gerald Ford put it, recalling the need for careful environmental impact statements prior to the construction of nuclear reactors, "Prior to approving a vast computer network affecting
personal lives, we need a comparable privacy impact statement. We
must also consider the fallout hazards of FEDNET to traditional
freedoms."

The Privacy Act of 1974

The early 1970s were seen as an especially important time to set
guidelines for data banks. A great deal of effort and money was being
put into developing data bank software and file structures and organizing data flows (recall our discussion in Section 4.1). It was thus
seen as the critical period in which to *build in* privacy safeguards;
otherwise there could be immense costs for restructuring the data
banks, and long periods of unavailability of data which might be crucial for health insurance, family assistance, or law enforcement. No
one doubted that computers and data banks were essential to the
efficient management of a large modern society—but most agreed
that efficiency must not be purchased at the price of individual liberties. Legislation was urgently needed to protect the rights of privacy,
speech, assembly, association, and petition of the government from a
"dictatorship of data banks and dossiers."

Thus it came about that the United States Congress enacted **The
Privacy Act of 1974,** which was signed into law by President Ford on
December 31, 1974. In this subsection, we list the major provisions of
the act and what it achieves. In the next subsection we shall discuss
what remains to be done.

The act acknowledged that an individual's access to employment, insurance, credit, and due process could all be endangered by
misuse of information systems. The aim of the act is thus to limit
government and preserve the freedom of the individual by curbing the
government's abuses of its power to investigate and store information. It would respect *privacy* by restraining the government's investigation of individuals, and its collection of improper or excessive information about their personal lives and their activities in society. Also
it would strengthen *confidentiality* by restricting data to uses agreed
on at the time of its collection. Here, then, are the provisions of the
act. The order has been rearranged and the provisions have been

rephrased to clarify what is involved. After each provision, a discussion is given in brackets [· · ·].

(1) Each federal agency is required to publish annually in the "Federal Register" full notice of the existence and character of their record systems, including the categories of individuals on whom records are maintained and the uses to which these records are put.

[Unless citizens know what type of records the government keeps, they are in no position to know where to check for information that they believe has been used against them. While some agencies might still try to hide the existence of certain data banks, and while the act provides no "flying squad" to track down such data banks, it was felt that this provision would encourage public-spirited employees to aid the administrators of such an agency in making full disclosures.]

(2) The act permits individuals for the first time to inspect information about themselves contained in agency files (the agency must tell an individual if he is on file—if he asks), and to challenge, correct, or amend the material. If the agency refuses to make the changes, it must give written reasons for the refusal. If the individual does not accept these reasons, he can take the responsible agency official to court where, if found guilty, he can be charged with a misdeameanor and fined up to $5000.

[By giving individuals the right to take officials to court, Congress placed the burden of enforcement on the public to obtain maximum effectiveness. It is hard to see how any federal enforcement agency could check through billions of records for accuracy. On the other hand, a citizen who has been denied a job may be hard pressed to determine which of the thousands of data banks listed in the "Federal Register" he should turn to to check the accuracy of the records on him. Note, too, that the "Federal Register" will only list the data banks of Federal agencies—the act does not apply to state or local government data banks, or to record systems in the private sector. Again, the act does not seem to provide a mechanism for helping the individual when he is *sure* that an agency keeps a file on him, but the agency denies this completely. It should be stressed, too, that an individual may want data removed from his file not because it is wrong, but because it is misleading or irrelevant. For example, it may be true that you once sat next to a known criminal on an airplane— but this should not be on file if this was just an accident of the airline's seating assignment.]

(3) The act does make some exceptions to the right of access given under point (2). Law enforcement agencies would be required

to open to any individual any criminal history information listing his arrests and convictions, but they would be allowed to deny the existence of, and access to, investigative files they were using to build up a case for later prosecution. Records of the Central Intelligence Agency, the Secret Service, and certain sensitive government records would also be exempt from disclosure.

[This is one of the stickiest provisions of the act. On the one hand, one would not want a Mafia chief or a foreign spy to escape prosecution because they could read all the data collected on them by the FBI or the CIA. On the other hand, returning to our discussion of the Army surveillance files on the political activities of private citizens, it seems disturbing that any amount of garbage on an innocent individual might be hidden from him by putting it in a data bank labeled "FBI prosecution files."]

(4) The act seeks to limit the information stored in each data bank by requiring each agency to show that all information stored is for necessary and lawful purposes of the agency, that it is current and accurate for intended use, and that safeguards are taken to prevent misuse. Even where data is relevant, it should not be stored if the social harm of storage outweighs its usefulness. Where possible, the data should be gathered from the individual concerned—telling him where it will go, how it will be used, and what the consequences will be of failure to supply information. The act forbids records of religious or political activities except by law enforcement agencies.

[The thrust here is to cut back drastically on the data stored, and to distinguish carefully between data the agency "must have," and data it would "like to have" but which the individual should be under no legal compulsion to supply. Remember those strange questions we cited above! Once again, the restriction on law enforcement agencies seems too weak.]

(5) The act stipulates that the agency cannot use data for any purpose other than that for which it was originally gathered, without the individual's consent. It prohibits transfer of data from one data bank to another unless it is a "routine" transfer for a purpose "compatible with the purpose for which it was collected"—as when an agency sends its employee records to the Treasury Department for payroll purposes. The act thus requires that, as part of the description of a data bank in the "Federal Register," each agency must define what these "routine" uses are to be. There are a few other transfers that are permitted without the individual's consent: data needed for the Census; statistical data that is not individually identifiable; data requested by a law enforcement agency, a Congressional committee,

or a court order; medical information on an individual with an urgent health problem; or data to be added to the historical record. Whatever the transfer, it must be recorded for at least 5 years or the life of the record, whichever is longer.

[This last provision is critical if an individual, having corrected his record in one data bank, is to be assured that the error does not remain elsewhere, able to harm him at some later date. Individuals can take agency officials to court if they believe they can show that the provisions of point (4) or (5) have been willfully disobeyed. However, the interpretation of the act already leaves something to be desired. For example, income tax forms issued by the U.S. Internal Revenue Service in 1976 stated that transfer to *all* Federal agencies was "routine." This destroys much of the usefulness of this part of the act. The act should be strengthened to limit transfers far more strictly. Another reasonable strengthening of the act would require an official to list all data banks that had been consulted in reaching a decision whenever so requested by the individual concerned.]

(6) The act gives individuals the right to refuse to supply their social security number (SSN), unless the law requires the number to be supplied—which it usually does not.

[It is feared that if all records contain the SSN, it will act as a universal identifier, making it easier to link the files in different data banks. Increasingly, people are being pressured to give their SSN—to get telephones, use libraries, cash checks, vote, obtain a driver's license, and other benefits, rights, and privileges. Record linking has been carried out in the past without any opportunity for the data subject to protest, interfere, correct, comment, or even know what linking of which records is taking place for what purpose. It is felt that providing the right of refusal to give the SSN—a right not previously clearly stated in law—would help protect those civil liberties which would be violated by enabling intelligence and surveillance uses of the number for indexing or locating the person. (The argument *for* using the SSN on all records is one of efficiency—it saves each agency from having to develop its own unique identifying codes, and reduces the chance of mixing up the records of all the different John Smiths.)]

(7) The act prohibits federal agencies from selling mailing lists of names and addresses of people on record in their data banks.

[A mailing list may represent a group of individuals possessing a certain set of characteristics. The disclosure that he shares these characteristics may be damaging to the individual. Under current law, an individual can request to have his name removed from any particular mailing list in the private sector, but cannot get a listing of all the lists he is on, and have his name removed. While removal of one's name from a mailing list may spare one from some junk mail, a troubling privacy problem remains: what future damage could it do to you to be on the list of people "who were not only on list A, but were cranky enough to have their name removed"?!]

(8) The act does not provide an overall enforcement agency (this was rejected as another layer of federal bureaucracy), but instead relies on continued oversight by congressional committees, the Office of Management of the Budget (OMB) and the President, as well as the civil litigation brought to bear on agencies by individuals. OMB is authorized to develop guidelines and regulations, to monitor enforcement, and to assist the agencies in meeting their responsibilities under the act. Each agency is required to inform OMB and Congress of any proposals to establish or alter any records system.

[Agencies are held responsible for their actions, with OMB intervening only if violations are brought into the open. There is a very real difficulty here in depending on existing institutions to uncover improper data banks. It remains to be seen how effectively OMB will be able to persuade agencies to comply with the act if their administrators are reluctant to do so. It also remains to be seen the extent to which compliance with the act will slow down federal information-handling—when, for example, the individual must be consulted before a nonroutine transfer takes place. In any case, it is expected the act will add $200 million a year to operating expenses; but a dollar a year per person seems like a bargain price for a little privacy!]

(9) The framers of the act explicitly excluded state and local government and private data banks from the act. The regulation of thousands of these data banks raises many issues beyond those to do with federal agencies. Instead, the act established a Privacy Protection Study Commission, composed of seven members, to provide Congress and the President with information about problems related to privacy in the public and private sectors. To reach its conclusions, the Commission will have access to any individual records it wishes to inspect, but will have to destroy or return them, as appropriate, after inspection.

[What will the Commission recommend? By the time you read this book, one or more of its annual reports will probably be available. It may be an interesting project to compare its recommendations with the opinions that you form while reading this chapter. In setting up the act, it was stated that "Creation of a privacy commission is recognition of the fact that the Congress intends to afford access to the decision-making centers of government to interests which promote the privacy of individual Americans against overly intrusive or arbitrary government policies."]

Implications and Developments

The immediate effect of the act will be to reduce the number of records stored, as agencies try to trim their data banks to guidelines acceptable to OMB, and destroy material they fear would expose them to constant litigation. The provisions on "routine" exchanges will increase the paper work and reduce the rate of information exchange between agencies. The act will also reverse the trend toward consolidation of information, in the interest of efficiency, both within an agency and among several agencies.

There will be a great deal of time wasted as members of the public ask to see their files simply out of curiosity, or insist on unimportant changes. The act may even lead to some files losing accuracy and coming more to fit the subject's "self-image"—since many agency officials may prefer to accept an individual's word on an entry than to conduct an independent investigation of the entry's correctness or risk being taken to court. For this reason, a major task in the future may well be to find mechanisms for settling differences of opinion about certain entries by a due process that does not involve the large amount of time and money consumed by going to the courts.

The development of a more efficient mechanism of verifying the accuracy or relevance of filed data—in response to a request from the individual concerned—should provide procedures for verifying the existence of files. To avoid abuse of the category of "prosecution files," it might be required that the equivalent of a search warrant must be obtained before a law enforcement agency would be allowed to establish a file that was closed to the individual concerned. Such a warrant might be issued only if the agency could prove that a conviction was likely. The mere suspicion raised by an Army surveillance report that "he was at a rally" would not justify opening a secret file.

There are a number of conflicts between the act and other aspects of U.S. government procedure that need to be worked out. The Freedom of Information Act requires that all government records be available for inspection except material "which would constitute a clearly unwarranted invasion of privacy." This requires disclosure well beyond the "routine" transfers and allowable exemptions listed under provision (5) above. The Privacy Act will also hinder those agencies that have used personal data to evaluate the effectiveness of new social legislation. If strict confidentiality can be guaranteed, however, it may not require too much extra effort to recruit enough volunteers who will let information be gathered on them strictly for program evaluation.

The most obvious shortcoming in the act is the exclusion of nonfederal data banks. It seems fairly clear that its provisions should be extended to cover state government data banks, and the data banks of the large credit bureaus and insurance companies. Beyond that, however, great care must be taken. For example, how do we write the law so that we distinguish the records that a bank keeps on individual X from information about X that another individual Y keeps in his safety deposit box? Carelessly phrased, an act that opens the bank's records to protect the rights of X could result in great damage to the privacy of Y. With the increasing use of home computers, more and more people will have their own "personal data banks" in which they may include all sorts of information about other people, from details of what a guest had for dinner last time he visited, to confidential information about a business rival. How do we protect the right of an individual to the privacy of data he stores in his own "personal data bank," yet prevent abuse of the Freedom of Information Act that would occur if agency officials began to store sensitive files in their home computers instead of in the central agency data bank?

While the act does not apply outside federal agencies, it *will* have a "spillover" effect. To protect against violation of the act, computer professionals will have to develop hardware and software that will give improved computer security. This will make all data banks easier to protect from illegitimate access (although, unfortunately, it will also make it harder to find secret data banks "hidden" in a large time-sharing system). More to the point, the federal government will pay a great deal of money for the development of **query/update languages** that automatically limit the type of data that can be transmitted over different linkages—just as, in Section 4.1, we saw how the query/update language could structure the use a clerk made of the airline reservations data bank. Once these techniques are developed, it will prove economically attractive to the owners of nonfederal data banks to install privacy protection software of the same kind.

To close this section, we must stress that the real point of the Privacy Act is not to give individuals the right to sue when their records are incorrect or are misused. Instead, this right of suit is a means to an end—the design of responsive and responsible institutions that properly balance efficient service to the general public with respect for the privacy and liberties of the individual. Thus care must be taken to go beyond the needs of the individual who makes a complaint. Once their needs have been met, rulings must be made on whether the data gathering, data structuring, or data transfer policies of the agency need revision to prevent a complaint of this kind from occurring again. To put the matter in computer terminology: it is not enough to correct the answer; we must debug the program as well.

Suggestions for Further Reading

Privacy Act of 1974: *United States Code, Congressional and Administrative News,* 93rd Congress, Second Session, 1974, Vol. 2, 2177–2194. (For legislative history, see Vol. 4, pp. 6916–6999.)
> This is the complete statement of the act; the major stages that led to its enactment; and a detailed discussion of each section of the act.

R. E. Cohen: Agencies Prepare Regulations for Implementing New Privacy Laws, *National Journal Reports,* 7, May 24, 1975, pp. 774–777.
> An account is given of steps being taken by Federal agencies to comply with the Privacy Act of 1974.

M. R. Wessell: The Data Bank—Civil Rights and Civil Wrongs, *in* "Freedom's Edge: The Computer Threat to Society," Chap. 4. Addison–Wesley, Reading, Massachusetts, 1974.
> This is a thoughtful review of the legal problems raised by data banks, written before the Privacy Act of 1974. It includes a useful account of Sweden's Data Inspection Board.

A. F. Westin and M. A. Baker, "Data Banks in a Free Society." Quadrangle/The New York Times Book Company, New York, 1973.
> Westin and Baker give an in-depth 1972 report for the Computer Science and Engineering Board of the United States Academy of Sciences on computerized record keeping and its effects on the individual's right to privacy. It includes detailed accounts of 14 data banks—in government, in commercial organizations, and in nonprofit organizations.

Summary

We have reviewed the threats to liberty and privacy posed by widespread linkage of computer data banks, and examined the safety measures provided by the **Privacy Act of 1974.** We saw that future efforts will require continual restructuring of data bank procedures, and speedier access to correction of records than going to court can reasonably provide.

Glossary

Data base: A *data base* is a collection of data—stored within primary or secondary memory—to which the computer can repeatedly refer in the course of its operations. The data base may be divided into *records* each of which contains information about some specific person, policy, project, or other basic unit about which information is collected.

Data bank: A *data bank* is one or more data bases, together with the computing machinery required to store or use them.

Query/update language: This is a language designed for nonexpert programmers for querying and updating a data base.

Computer network: A *computer network is* a net made up of *nodes,* with each node being joined to one or more other nodes by *links.* Each node contains either a computer or a terminal, and the links pass programs and data back and forth. A *centralized* (or *star*) *network* links many terminals to a single central computer with a large data base and great computing power; a *decentralized network* links many computers—and could link many data banks—so that a user at any one computer can run programs on, or share information with, another computer on the network.

Linkage: The process whereby different records in one or more data banks are combined to answer a single query or to create a new record is called *linkage.* Do not confuse these links between records (which are pieces of information) with the links between the nodes of a computer network (which are communication channels).

Privacy Act of 1974: An act passed by the U.S. Congress to regulate the storage of data in federal agency data banks, and to give individuals the right to see their records, correct errors, and remove data that should not be on file.

Exercises

1. Give two possible reasons why a data base, given your name, might *not* be able to find your file.

2. *Mad Magazine* once published a series of cartoons about the future. People were identified only by numbers, not names. A man in a horizontally striped shirt runs in, with his name (Melvin Cowznovsky) written across his chest. "I've just escaped from jail," he says, "in jail they take away your number and refer to you only by name!" Give two reasons why names for people are preferred to numbers, and two reasons why numbers might be better than names.

3. Name an example of data from a data base of personal information that altered the career of a political figure. If you can't think of an example, ask someone.

4. Indicate whether the following statements are true or false.
- (a) All data banks are listed in the Federal Register.
- (b) Law enforcement agencies must open any investigative files to individuals on request.
- (c) Law enforcement agencies cannot collect records of religious activity.
- (d) The 1974 Privacy Act forbids any transfer of data from one federal data bank to another.
- (e) People must give their Social Security Number (SSN) when asked by police.
- (f) Federal agencies can sell lists of names and addresses.
- (g) The 1974 Privacy Act creates a major new agency.
- (h) All states must list their data banks by 1979.
- (i) A single query/update language is now used federally.

5. (a) Estimate the number of pieces of paper used to store information in America. A factor of 10 either way probably doesn't make much difference. Assume that for each of 200,000,000 citizens, there are approximately 100 agencies, companies, and institutions with a record on that person. Assume the average personal file (school, tax, credit, etc.) is 10 pages long. Assume that for each page of personal information, there are at least 10 pages of nonpersonal information—fiction, inventories, production, shipping, storage records, ...

(b) If you could flip through this pile of paper at a rate of 1 page per second, how many years would it take to finish—assuming no new pages are produced?

(c) If the equivalent of 1000 pages can be stored on a reel of magnetic tape, roughly how many reels would the total U.S. information bank contain—assuming no redundant records are eliminated. At bargain rates of $10 per reel, how much would it cost to put all the information on magnetic tape?

(d) Comment briefly on your personal reaction to the figures you have just calculated. Compare cost estimate (c) to the $200 million a year figure for the cost of complying with the Privacy Act of 1974.

6. The Securities Exchange Commission (SEC), which regulates the stock market in America, has a policy of "full disclosure" requiring corporations to be subject to thorough examination before being allowed to place their stock on the Exchange. Does Yoyodyne Semiconductors Inc. really have two factories of digit-widgits? Briefly discuss the possibility of an agency similar to the SEC which would examine corporate computer systems before allowing the companies to handle data of interstate origin. How would you keep this agency from abusing this power (e.g., by taking bribes to okay dubious computer programs).

7. Explain, in a paragraph, whether or not you think the federal government should have access to psychological test records from schools in order to locate potential criminals, drug users, or suicides.

8. Explain your reaction to Milton Wessell's suggestion that, before a data bank is established, a data bank impact statement (similar to an ecological impact statement for construction projects) should be written. Name two difficulties raised by the idea.

9. If individuals have the right to take officials to court to eliminate misleading or irrelevant information from their files, why aren't the courts jammed with privacy-seeking individuals resisting routine government procedures? Give three reasons why this is an unlikely possibility.

10. When Howard Hughes died in 1976, no one could produce (for several weeks) a will for his $2 billion empire. Does this represent a triumph or a defeat for the principles of individual rights to privacy of information? Explain briefly.

11. The 1974 Privacy Act allowed CIA and Secret Service records to be exempt from disclosure. Do any of the major clauses of that Act prevent the following loophole? The federal government might use the Secret Service nondisclosure rule to hide a complete FEDNET data bank on all citizens by putting it officially in Secret Service files.

12. Most newspapers keep a "morgue"—a file of old stories. Several large morgues (notably *The New York Times*) have been computerized. Should there be any restrictions of access to these records? (*Hint:* Consider copyrights, libraries, the cost of buying a newspaper.)

5

Artificial Intelligence

SECTION 5.1. BRAINS AND COMPUTERS

We study ways in which the brain processes information, with particular emphasis on vision and the control of movement. We see how increasing knowledge of brain function can work with developments in computers to help us build better **prostheses**—devices that replace a missing part of the body such as an eye or limb. We close with a discussion of the promises and dangers of this type of brain technology. The only background required for the section is the notion of **feedback** from Section 3.1.

SECTION 5.2. MACHINES THAT SEE AND PLAN

A robot can take information from a TV camera and use this to build up a "model" of the world around it inside its computer memory. This process is called **scene analysis.** Given such a model, it can respond to a command by **planning**—going from the high-level "what is to be done" to a step-by-step specification of how to do it. The section is essentially self-contained, beyond brief mention of the notion of **compiler** from Section 2.1 and the notion of **hierarchy** from Section 2.4.

SECTION 5.3. MACHINES THAT UNDERSTAND NATURAL LANGUAGE

A major trend is to make computers easier to use. One part of that trend is to attempt to program computers to respond to natural language input, rather than just to formal programs. Partial success has been obtained in getting computers to respond to English sentences about **microworlds**—limited areas of information which restrict the possible meanings of sentences the computer must consider. We consider three microworlds, and examine the special techniques needed for speech understanding by computer. The section is almost self-contained, except for basic concepts from Section 4.1, Data Base Management.

SECTION 5.4. COMPUTERS IN WAR AND PEACE

Ideas about programming intelligence into machines have both military and civilian applications. We look at developments in missile and airplane guidance. We then consider sensor arrays that can be used to automate a battlefield as well as an ecosystem, to pinpoint the firing of a gun or of a cell in the brain. Finally, we discuss the moral issues posed by work on weapon systems. This section uses the concept of **feedback** from Section 3.1, and the notion of **pattern recognition** from Section 5.2. However, it can be read without reference to these sections.

5.1. BRAINS AND COMPUTERS

Computers are often called "electronic brains," and newspaper articles as well as science fiction talk of "intelligent machines" taking over from mankind. Such statements are false and misleading. Brains are different from computers—but we can learn from studies of how brains process information. Computers cannot think—and yet many aspects of thought are becoming computable.

Artificial intelligence is the branch of computer science that studies how to program computers to exhibit apparently intelligent behavior. We discussed an early success at the end of Section 1.1—programming a computer to learn from experience how to play a better and better game of checkers. In Section 5.2, we shall see how computers can carry out **scene analysis**—analyzing visual input such as a TV picture to determine the objects that make up the scene. We shall also see how a robot can be programmed to **plan** its activity—as in finding a path through a cluttered room which will steer clear of all obstacles. Then, in Section 5.3, we shall see how a computer can be programmed to understand commands and questions in a natural language such as English. We shall see that computers can be programmed to do very well only if the "world" they live in is small enough. They thus still lack the flexibility and generality, let alone the initiative, that seems to be the mark of true intelligence.

The cybernetic viewpoint holds that we can learn much about ourselves, as well as about animals and machines and societies, by looking at general patterns of information processing, including patterns of control and communication. Thus we can better understand the way in which our brains work as we think about the way in which we must program computers to get them to do some of the tasks that our brains do. In some sense, then, we may say that the brain is like a computer. However, this does not deny the differences. The structure of a brain is very different indeed from the structure of a computer; and the fact that we can live in such rich worlds, with our actions not guided by an immediate command but rather by a rich interaction of hopes and dreams and fears and emotions and inspirations, show just how different brains are from any computer yet built.

Brain theory tries to analyze directly the way in which our brains work—using mathematics and computer simulation to build on the surgeon's observations of human brain function, and the scientist's experiments on the brains of animals. Studying brains is fascinating in itself, but it is also important in helping us find ways to reduce the effects of brain damage, or to improve education. In this section, we look at studies of how our brains let us see and enable us to control our movements, and we study how this knowledge can be used to help people who are blind or who have lost a limb.

An Overview of the Brain

We saw, in Section 3.1, that any **system** interacting with an environment receives **inputs** from that environment, and provides **outputs** to the environment. Humans and animals receive their input through the five senses of vision, hearing, smell, taste, and touch—and other senses as well, which let us feel how hot or cold it is, for example. To get these inputs from the environment, we have special cells in our body called **receptors** or **sensors,** which *receive* or *sense* energy from the environment and code it into electrical signals which can be sent to our brains. For example, the sensors in our eyes called *rods* and *cones* respond to light, and convert it into electrical signals; the hair cells in our ears respond to vibrations, and so send signals to the brain coding the sounds around us; while chemical sensors in the tongue and the nose signal the tastes and smells of our world. Our sensitivity to touch and pressure and hot and cold comes from receptors scattered throughout our skin.

We can act upon the world in many ways—by walking around, by lifting objects, by speaking, all of which we achieve by means of our muscles, whether it be to move our limbs or our vocal chords. We call the muscles **effectors**—they serve to take signals from the brain and transform them into outputs which can have an *effect* upon the world. The body also has another set of effectors—the glands, which can respond to signals from the brain to affect our body chemistry. For example, the brain can cause the adrenal gland to pump out more adrenalin when we are put into a stress situation.

In between the receptors and the effectors comes the **central nervous system**—an incredibly complex network of billions upon billions of cells, called **neurons** (Fig. 1). The neuron is a special cell that receives inputs from other cells, computes upon them, and sends messages to affect other cells in turn. It is these networks that let us store information—laying down memories—and call up information—remembering things. It is these networks that let us see; it is these networks that let us form a plan of action; and it is these networks that let us interact adaptively with our world.

A rough view of the human brain seen from the side is shown in Fig. 2. The **spinal cord** is that part of the central nervous system that lies within the spine—the long row of bones running down the middle of our backs. The spinal cord is the "interface" for the body and the limbs with the brain. Every receptor in the body or the limbs or on the skin must send its signals into the networks of the spinal cord. Every muscle in our bodies or our limbs is controlled by spinal cord neurons. As we move up from the body into the neck, the spinal cord is enlarged and extended to form the part of the brain called the **brainstem.** The brainstem is the "interface" for the head—it is to the brainstem that signals from the eyes and the ears and the skin of the head must come, and it is from here that the signals pass out to the muscles that control talking, jaw movements, facial expression, eye movements, and so on. Rising out around and above the brainstem are the **cerebral hemispheres**—covered by the **neocortex**—which are the most highly **evolved** parts of the brain. Animals like birds or reptiles have relatively little neocortex. It is only in the mammals that

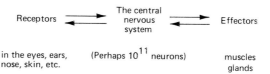

Receptors ⇄ The central nervous system ⇄ Effectors

in the eyes, ears, nose, skin, etc.   (Perhaps 10^{11} neurons)   muscles glands

Fig. 1 Receptors provide inputs to the central nervous system, which emits output through the effectors

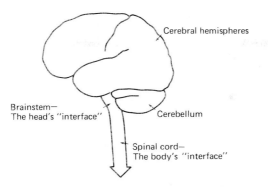

Fig. 2   A side view of the human brain

the neocortex becomes an important part of the brain. The neocortex is largest in the primates—apes, monkeys, and man. This seems to be the part of the brain that is involved in long-range planning, allowing us to base our actions not on the here-and-now, but on our accumulated experience, and our long-range goals. However, all parts of the brain are closely integrated with one another, and cannot function by themselves. For example, the **cerebellum,** which lies behind the brainstem, interacts with the neocortex to ensure that our actions are not simply carried out in the right order, but are carried out in a smoothly coordinated way.

It is hard to convey a full sense of how wonderfully complex a machine the brain is. Perhaps some idea can be gained from Fig. 3, which shows a Purkinje cell of the cerebellum. Each human cerebellum contains hundreds of thousands of these cells, and each Purkinje cell receives inputs from hundreds of thousands of other cells. Thus, in some ways, this single cell is comparable in complexity to a complete microcomputer, with a few tens of thousands of transistors, as discussed in Section 2.3. Of course, the Purkinje cell cannot be programmed in a general-purpose fashion, and probably plays a very specialized role in helping the brain control our movement. Nonetheless, it is clear that the task of understanding how hundreds of thousands of such cells work together with each other, and with the billions of other neurons in the brain, is an awesomely difficult task.

At present, scientists are beginning to have a fairly good idea of how neurons work together to extract patterns in the signals sent back from the rods and cones—the receptors in the eyes. We also begin to understand how activity in spinal cord neurons can control muscles to yield coordinated movement. However, when we move away from the input and output, our understanding of the brain is more in terms of how large chunks of the brain interact with each

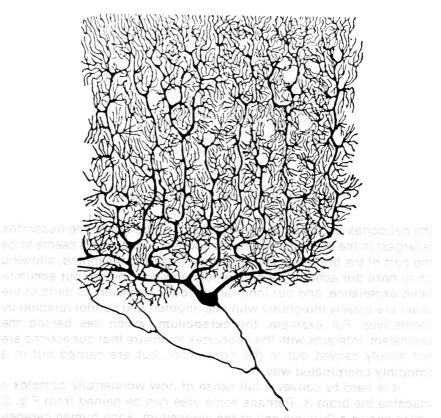

Fig. 3. The Purkinje cell of the cerebellum as drawn by Ramon y Cajal. (Reprinted, with permission, from the *I.E.E.E. Student Journal,* January 1970.)

other, and our understanding of the detailed computations carried out in the neural networks becomes quite poor.

The two main ways that we have found out about the actual functioning of the brain are from observations of humans who have brain damage or must receive neurosurgery; and from experiments on animals.

Some of our most dramatic insights into the brain have come from what might be thought of as mistakes! A brain surgeon, having to remove a malignant tumor, finds that the patient has not only lost the dangerous cancer, but has lost some important mental ability. One of the most dramatic examples was the case of a man who had part of his temporal lobe removed—that part of the neocortex that is behind the temples of the skull. He lost the ability to make new memories. He could remember how to talk and how to feed himself, and if you were engaged in a conversation with him, he could follow what was going on as long as he was not distracted. Once his attention had wandered, however, there was no way for him to recall what had been going on before. He could not be sent to the store to buy something, because—even if you had given him a shopping list—he would not remember that he should look at the list! Perhaps the only cheerful thing one can say about this amazing illness is that even after 20 years, the patient does not remember that he has been suffering from it.

Thus one of the ways that we can learn about the brain is by observing the behavior of people who have lost part of their brains—whether it be by surgical removal of a tumor, by a gunshot wound, or by a disease which has "eaten away" part of the brain. We can also learn about human brains from electrical stimulation of the brain carried out during surgery. If a surgeon has decided that he must cut away part of the brain to remove a tumor, he still has the problem of deciding how to cut it out. He will thus often carry out stimulation with an electrode to find out how the patient will react. He may find that stimulation of the brain on one side yields movement of the toes while stimulation of the brain on the other side yields movement of the fingers. Reasoning that a patient will suffer far less from paralysis of the toes than from paralysis of the hand, he will then cut in from the "toe side" of the tumor.

In this way, people have accumulated much information about the overall structure of the brain, getting a feel for what one large area of the brain will do when it is stimulated, or what defects a person will show if a large area of the brain is removed. However, we can only obtain information about the human brain directly when it is justified as part of medical treatment. If we want to carry out experiments to determine the detailed connections of neurons within the networks of the brain, we must turn to animals. Here, we are guided by the principle of evolution. This is the idea that man and the other animals have descended from common ancestors, and that because of this, many features of our bodies and our brains will be the same. To say that humans are like animals is not to say that we are identical to animals—much of our appreciation of art and beauty, our ability to use tools and to express ourselves in language, distinguish us from the other animals. However, the way in which our brains control our muscles and process information from the receptors to let us see the patterns of the world around us, have much in common with the function of animal brains. Thus if we can understand the neural networks in the brains of animals, we will have received clues about much of the function of our own brains. Later on in this section, we shall see some of the ways in which studies on animals are adding to our understanding of our own ability to see.

Control of Movement

One of the ways in which new understanding of the brain and improved microcomputer technology can work together is in the design of artificial arms to replace those of people who have suffered an amputation. Until recently, the only type of artificial arm used levers and pulleys so that the wearer could learn to shrug the shoulder around on his "good side" in such a way as to cause the artificial arm to move, open its claws, close them about an object, and then move with the object in its grasp. These movements were slow and clumsy, and required the use of muscles that could be better used in controlling their own, natural arm.

When you move your own, natural arm, you do not have to think carefully about each muscle to move your limbs. As a result of experience, you can simply "decide" to pick up a pencil, for example, and the rest is done "automatically." To try and put this in terms of nets of neurons, we may say that there are patterns of activity that are set up in the neocortex as you decide to reach for the pencil. The pathways from neocortex to spinal cord then translate the neocortical pattern into a pattern—in both space and time—of activity of neurons in the spinal cord. The activity of these neurons causes the right muscles in the arm to contract at the right time so that your hand reaches out, your fingers grasp the pencil, and you pick up the pencil. As we discussed in the previous subsection, we have a fairly good idea about the detailed nets of neurons that can provide the patterned activation of the muscles, but we do not know very much about the detailed networks that allow us to make the decision to pick up the pencil, and that transfer the commands from neocortex to spinal cord. However, some scientists interested in the design of artificial arms realized that they do not need to know these details as long as they could pick up the activity in the spinal cord and use it to control the motors in artificial arms. The motors could then move the various joints in just the way that the muscles would have moved the joints of the natural arm when that pattern of activity occurred in the spinal cord.

In fact, the idea of monitoring neurons in the spinal cord of an amputee, and using the signals to control the artificial arm without any conscious thought—by just simply thinking "reach over there"— remains a dream. However, a simpler approach to designing a "cybernetic" arm has become a reality. When a patient has an arm amputated, there usually remains a stump at the shoulder, and this stump contains parts of a number of muscles that once controlled the movements of the normal arm. When an amputee thinks about making a movement of the "arm that is not there," he still sets up in those shortened muscles electrical activity that used to lead to the appropriate shortening of the muscles to move the joints of the arm in the appropriate way. So, what the engineers have done is build an artificial arm to be attached over the stump. The arm has sensors placed on the stump to monitor the EMG—the **electromyogram**—which records the electrical activity in the muscles in the stump. A computing circuit within the arm can then take the signals from the EMG and use them to recognize what arm movement those signals corresponded to when the natural arm was there. Then this microcomputer can send control signals to its effectors—in this case the motors that control the rotation of the joints in the artificial arm.

Development of a truly "cybernetic" arm would require the much finer control of the wrist and fingers that could be obtained by monitoring neurons in the spinal cord, instead of just the relatively crude signals given by looking at the electrical activity in the muscles of the stump. One problem here is ignorance—we do not yet really understand how to find the right neurons in the spinal cord to monitor, or how to decode their signals once we had found them. The other problem is that we do not know how to insert enough sensors in the spinal cord to obtain detailed information about the activity of the neurons without mashing the spinal cord and killing the neurons in the process. There is some hope that eventually we will be able to place chips of **integrated circuitry** against patches of spinal cord, and that this circuitry will be so fine in its detail that it will be able to match the intricacy of the spinal networks, and let us decode what is going on. This type of development is, however, probably 10 or twenty years off.

To see another way in which a "cybernetic" arm can be improved—and now we are talking about improvements that are currently under way—we must recall one of the basic concepts of cybernetics, namely feedback. As we see in Fig. 4, when we are trying to catch a moving target with our hand, we can feed back error signals—the difference between our actual position and the position of the moving target—to determine the way in which we should move our hand (Fig. 4). This type of visual feedback can of course be used by someone wearing the artificial arm we have just described, for the use of visual feedback takes place in the brain, not in the arm. How-

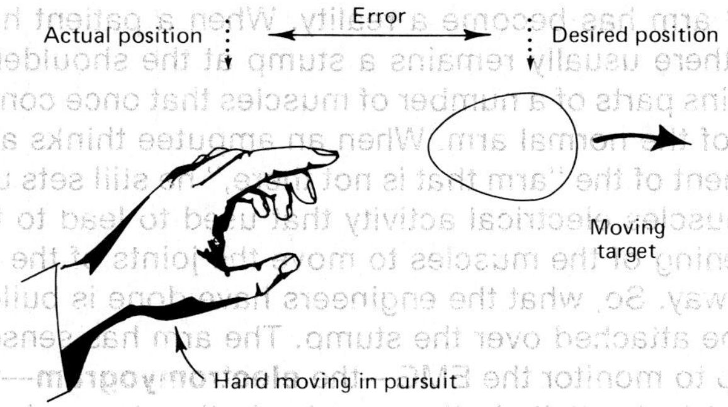

Fig. 4 Using visual feedback to catch a moving target.

ever, there are other uses of feedback which require sensors in the hand. For example, when you pick up an egg, you use feedback about how strongly your fingers are pressing against the egg to ensure that you stop the fingers from breaking the egg. Clearly, a mechanical hand set up to close in on an egg would be very likely to break it. To solve this problem, cybernetic engineers have devised touch sensors which can be built into the fingertips of an artificial hand. Thus the microcomputer in the artificial arm can be programmed to close the hand not only with maximal force, but rather to close it until such time as the feedback signals from the touch sensors in the fingertips reach some critical level. Using this principle, engineers in Yugoslavia have indeed been able to design artificial hands that can successfully pick up eggs without breaking them, and yet can exert far greater force when some heavier and less delicate object is to be lifted.

Sight

We have already mentioned that the eye contains receptors, called "rods" and "cones," that respond to light. In fact, the retina— the coating of cells inside the eyeball—contains several layers of neurons which serve to **preprocess** the signals from the rods and cones before sending them back to the brain. This preprocessing transforms the pattern of light and shade into a form that is more useful to the animal. For example, in the eye of the frog, it has been shown that there are four main types of preprocessed information sent back to the brain. One type of cell sending messages back to the brain is most active when a small wiggling object like a fly appears in a certain part of the visual world of the frog; while another type of neuron is most active when a large dark moving object, such as an enemy, moves past the frog. For this reason, these cells are known as "bug detectors" and "enemy detectors." In other words, the neural networks in the eye serve to extract from the visual input information that will be important to the frog in its survival—both in finding food using "bug detectors," and in avoiding becoming food using the "enemy detectors." The main visual station in the brain of the frog is called the "tectum," and a pattern in the world is mapped onto a pattern on each retina and these patterns are then reassembled in the brain. Unlike the situation shown in Fig. 5, however, what is mapped into the tectum is not anything like a still photograph of the world, but is in fact a map showing the location of bugs and enemies and other features that are important to the animal.

If we look at the visual system of a human—and the diagram shown in Fig. 6 also applies to other mammals such as cats and monkeys—we find that although there is a region called the "superior colliculus," which is like the tectum of the frog, there is a much larger visual pathway going back to the visual cortex at the back of the neocortex, passing through a way-station called the "lateral geniculate." (We need not worry about where these rather forbidding names come from!) As we can see from the figure, light from the right half of the visual field moves through the lens onto the left half of the retina and then the input from the two eyes is collected back into the left half of the brain. In the same way, information about the left half of the world is collected in the right half of the brain. Since the detection of flies is not of primary importance for mammals, it is not surprising that we do not find bug detectors in the retina of mammals. In fact, in

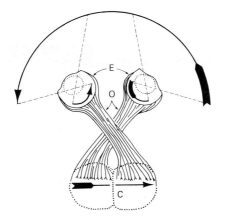

Fig. 5 Schematic of the visual system of the frog, with visual patterns formed on the retina being mapped back into the *tectum*, a region in the frog's brain.

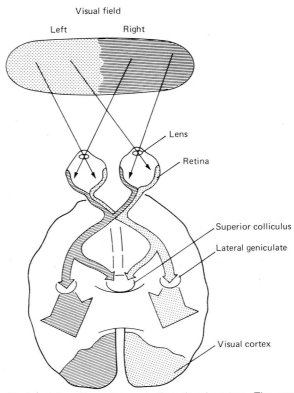

Fig. 6 Horizontal section of mammalian visual system. The *superior colliculus* corresponds to the frog's *tectum* (Fig. 4). In mammals, the *visual cortex* plays an important role in helping the animal see complex patterns.

experiments that record the electrical activity of cells in the brains of cats and monkeys, it has been found that cells in the retina and the lateral geniculate are finding contrast—regions where the intensity of light or some color changes drastically. In other words, the neurons are finding boundaries between regions, thus providing cues which will let the visual cortex recognize the presence of different objects of the world. In the early stages of visual cortex, the neurons seem to respond best to lines at a specific angle in the visual world—as if the cortex were building up a map of the contours of objects in the world. Other cells seem to respond best to different textures. Together they contribute to the recognition of objects as the basis for the animal's interaction with its world.

The original study of the ''bug detectors'' and ''enemy detectors'' was entitled ''What the Frog's Eye Tells the Frog's Brain.'' In a follow-up study, entitled "What the Frog's Eye Tells the Monkey's Brain," a neurophysiologist named Humphrey in Oxford, England, tried to learn more about the visual system of the monkey—which is relatively close to that of man—by comparing it with that of the frog. Until Humphrey's work, people had always assumed that a monkey that had lost its visual cortex (see Fig. 6) was condemned to total blindness. However, Humphrey stressed that the superior colliculus (Fig. 6) of the monkey was similar to the tectum of the frog. He thus reasoned that a monkey without visual cortex should be able to see at least as well as a frog. In other words, although it would not be able to perceive patterns—such as recognizing a face or telling one letter from another—it should be able to locate moving objects or bright patches in the world around it. He suggested that the only reason monkeys seemed blind when they had no visual cortex was because they had not been trained to pay attention. A tourist often finds it easier to ignore signs in a foreign language than to go to all the effort of learning what they mean. In the same way, it could be argued that the monkey that had come to recognize patterns in its world would not learn to pay attention to the signals coming through its superior colliculus when it had lost its visual cortex. Humphrey trained a monkey for two years, and was in fact able to get it to carry out basic navigation in its world by paying attention to these cues of movement and brightness. It is clear, then, that the comparison of the brains of different animals is not just simply fascinating in itself, but also can lead to important therapies. By looking at the behavior of one animal, we can be led to expect an animal to have hitherto unknown capacities. When we discover that it has those capacities, then there is a good chance that humans will have it too, and so we can provide new therapies.

Another area of research related to vision is the attempt to restore sight to people whose brains are still intact, but who have had their retinas or the pathways linking their eyes to the brain destroyed. Some experiments have succeeded in implanting a number of fine wires into the visual cortex, and then placing small electric currents in the wires. A human with these wires learns eventually to recognize patterns of stimulation corresponding to a light moving in front of their eyes. The drawback to this approach, at the moment, is that the number of wires that can be placed in the brain at the moment is very small—remember our discussion of the spinal cord and artificial arms—so that the visual resolution is poor. In addition, even when a few wires are in place, they eventually irritate the neurons and cause them to die. Once again, we will have to wait for new advances in integrated circuit technology to find ways of placing a large enough array of stimulators on the brain without causing it undue damage. Even when that technological problem is overcome, though, there still remains the very real problem that the cells in normal visual cortex do not respond directly to a pattern of light, but respond to a preprocessed pattern generated by the neurons in the retina and lateral geniculate. Thus our understanding of the computation that these layers of neurons carry out in preprocessing the visual information will have to advance even further, so that the integrated circuitry stimulator can carry out at least part of the necessary transformation, to ensure that the stimulation of the visual cortex is meaningful.

Brain Technology

We have now seen some of the ways in which we can gain new understanding about the workings of the brain, and we have seen that, among other things, this understanding can help us devise better **prostheses**—devices that can replace missing parts of the human brain or body. By implanting electrodes we can hope to monitor more and more of the activity of the nervous system to provide finer control of artificial limbs. Going the other way, we can hope to provide more and more accurate stimulation by devices placed on the visual cortex to restore more and more of their sight to people who have lost the use of their eyes. Already, the technology of inserting electronic devices into the human body has played a very important role in saving life. Electronic pacemakers, implanted in the heart of someone who is prone to heart attacks, can provide electrical impulses that will keep the heartbeat properly rhythmical, and thus avoid the breakdown of rhythm that leads to a heart attack.

In summary, then, it seems that the technology of implanting electrodes in the body is a valuable one, and will restore something approaching normal function to many people who would otherwise be severely disabled, or in risk of losing their lives. However, the very power of this technology means that it can be used in ways that we might find disturbing, as well as in ways that are clearly beneficial. Some people, for example, have suggested that anyone who has been convicted of a crime should have placed in their brains a number of electrodes that would monitor the brain activity and have it transmitted to some central computer. This computer would then analyze the brain activity to determine whether it was of the kind that normally accompanies the intention to carry out a criminal act. When this occurred, the computer would then send a message which would pass electrical current through electrodes to knock the man out, while simultaneously summoning the police to arrest him. In this way, he would be stopped in his tracks before any crime could be committed.

At the moment, this idea is very unrealistic, simply because we do not understand what patterns of brain activity go with something as abstract as "the intention to commit a criminal act." Again, it is not clear how a computer would determine when it was safe to "stop the criminal in his tracks"—it would certainly be unwise to knock out a man who was driving a car. However, even if these problems could be solved, there would be very real moral problems. In many countries, the privacy of the individual is to be respected, and he is to be assumed innocent until proven guilty. The fact that a few crimes might thus be prevented would not justify such great invasion of privacy.

Although it is not clear that one could design computer programs to recognize "criminal intent," it is certainly true that it is possible to implant electrodes in people's brains that would have the property of knocking them out. Imagine what life would be like in a totalitarian state in which all citizens were forced to have such electrodes placed in their heads, and could all be rendered unconscious by any policeman simply at the flick of a switch. Thus, like most technology, the technology of implanted electrodes can be abused. However, it seems to have so many important applications in helping people who are otherwise disabled that it would be most unwise to ban it because of its possibilities for misuse.

There is another intriguing question about the proper use of implanted electrodes. In 1975, American TV viewers were presented with a fiction called "The Six Million Dollar Man," which told of an astronaut who had suffered hideous injuries in a crash on return from a space mission, and had had an eye, an arm, and both legs replaced by "bionic devices." These were far beyond the sophistication of those that we have discussed as being within the range of current technology. Many children became avid watchers of the show, and thrilled to the feats of superhuman strength that the hero of the show could carry out because of the strong motors that were included in the artificial arm and legs. We can imagine that many of the children envied him his abilities. In fact, in 1952, an American novelist named Bernard Wolfe published a book called "Limbo '90" in which he imagined a society in which men voluntarily had their limbs amputated so that the far more powerful and flexible cybernetic limbs could be attached in their place. This seems bizarre! However, it seems worth considering how one draws the line between using brain technology to repair damaged function, and using brain technology to allow people to perform at a level that would not otherwise have been possible. Wolfe's novel gives an eloquent picture of a society in which the replacement of the natural by the unnatural has gotten out of hand. What perhaps seems more likely as a projection for the future is that we will make more and more use of machines to expand our abilities, but that these machines will remain firmly part of the environment, rather than part of us. Just as writing helped humans expand their memory by allowing them to write down many details that they would otherwise forget, so can we expect personal computers to make that memory even more flexible and dynamic than writing can be. What we can hope for is a world of man–machine **symbiosis.** This is a state in which man and machine "live together" in a way that extends the range of the humanly achievable, but does not break down the barriers of the human individual by replacing his limbs or his eyes with machines, no matter how wonderful those machines may be.

Suggestions for Further Reading

W. M. Brodey and N. Lindgren: Human Enhancement: Beyond the Machine Age, *IEEE Spectrum,* February 1968, 79–93.
>Suggestions are made as to how developments in computer science and artificial intelligence could contribute to evolutionary systems that work for human enhancement.

M. A. Arbib: "The Metaphorical Brain." Wiley, New York, 1972.
>Chapters 1 and 2 give an introduction to the brain, its anatomy and physiology. Section 2.4 looks at visual preprocessing in cats and frogs, while Section 5.1 discusses the role of feedback in the control of movement.

J. Y. Lettvin, H. R. Maturana, W. S. McCulloch, and W. H. Pitts: What the Frog's Eye Tells the Frog's Brain, *Proc. IRE* **47,** 1959, 1940–1951.

N. K. Humphrey: What the Frog's Eye Tells the Monkey's Brain, *Brain, Behavior, and Evolution* **3,** 1970, 324–337.
>Two readable accounts of experiments on the visual systems of animals.

Bernard Wolfe: "Limbo '90." Penguin Books, Harmondsworth, 1952.
>A novel of life in a world in which replacement of body parts by prostheses has become fashionable.

Supplementary material, written for the layman, and beautifully illustrated, may be found in:

Keith Oatley: "Brain Mechanisms and Mind." Dutton, New York, 1972.

R. L. Gregory "Eye and Brain: The Psychology of Seeing." McGraw-Hill, New York, 1966.

Lucien Gérardin: "Bionics." Weidenfeld and Nicolson, London, 1968.

Much of the work in this area has been influenced by the classical volume: Norbert Wiener: "Cybernetics." Wiley, New York, 1948.

Summary

We have seen how **brain theory** extends our understanding of the human brain, by computer analysis, by the study of neurosurgery, and by comparison of human brains with animal brains. Insights into the brain can lead to the construction of cybernetic limbs, and devices to help the blind. This type of technology raises difficult ethical problems. **Artificial intelligence** is the study of programming computers to exhibit intelligent behavior. We suggest that its task is not to build "machines smarter than humans." Instead, we should aim for man–machine **symbiosis** which will enable humans to achieve more than would otherwise be possible.

Glossary

Artificial intelligence: *AI* is that branch of computer science that studies how to program computers to exhibit apparently intelligent behavior.

Brain theory: The use of mathematics and computer simulation to analyze the way in which brains work is *brain theory*.

Scene analysis: *Scene analysis* is the process whereby a computer analyzes visual input, say from a TV camera, to determine the nature and location of objects in the scene.

Planning: *Planning* is the process of generating and comparing different courses of action and then choosing one before starting to act. It takes the system from a high-level specification of "what is to be done" to a step-by-step specification of how to do it.

System: A *system* is an object or process—or collection of objects or processes—that we choose to study. The *environment* comprises those processes which we expect to have an effect on the system. The *inputs* to the system are the effects of the environment on the system. The *outputs* of the system are the measurable responses of the system.

Receptor or **sensor:** A special device that responds to light, sound, etc., and converts it into signals for the brain or a computer is a *receptor* or a *sensor*.

Effector: An *effector* is a device that transforms signals from a brain or computer into some effect: muscles or motors product movement; glands produce hormonal changes.

Neuron: The basic computing element of the brain is a nerve cell, or *neuron*.

Central nervous system: The network of neurons lying between the body's receptors and effectors is the *central nervous system*.

Spinal cord: The network of nerve cells inside the spine is the *spinal cord*.

Brainstem: The network of nerve cells that connects the spinal cord to the brain is the *brainstem.*

Cerebral hemispheres: This is the most highly evolved part of the brain, with one hemisphere seated around the other parts of the brain on each side of the head. Its outermost, covering region is called the *neocortex.*

Cerebellum: This brain region is involved in the smoothing of movement.

Evolution: *Evolution* is the development of each species of plant or animal from different, usually simpler, ancestral forms. The more similar are two species, the closer in time are they likely to be to a common ancestor.

Electromyogram (EMG): An *EMG* is a tracing of electrical activity in a muscle.

Integrated circuitry: *Integrated circuitry* is a complete circuit of many transistors produced by photographic techniques on a single piece of silicon, called a *chip*. This replaces circuits in which transistors are made separately, then wired together.

Preprocessing: Taking data from sensors and changing it into a form that will simplify a recognition or classification process is *preprocessing.*

Feedback: *Feedback* is the process whereby output signals are fed back to the input of a system, so that the system can respond to information about its own performance. A *negative feedback* system uses this information to negate (or at least reduce) the *error signal*—which is the difference between the actual output and some desired output.

Prothesis: A *prothesis* (plural, *protheses*) is a device designed to replace some missing part of a body, such as an eye or a limb.

Symbiosis: Living together in mutual dependence is called *symbiosis.*

Exercises

1. What is the purpose of the visual preprocessing performed by the retina? Why not just pass the intensity information from each of the 10 million retinal cells directly to the visual cortex?

2. Much important brain theory comes from studying the behavior of animals, and men, with brain damage. If damage to a particular brain region often results in the loss of a specific behavior, can one validly claim that that region produces that behavior?

3. Why is visual feedback not enough to control a prosthetic arm?

4. Inside the brain there are no nerve cells that signal pain, heat, pressure, etc. when disturbed—so that brain matter may be sliced by a surgeon while the patient is conscious. Why do you think this is true? What is the function of pain in changing behavior?

5. Imagine a future in which cybernetic (bionic) arms have been developed which are far better than any we can build today: they are stronger than normal arms, tire less easily, have sensitive feedback, and can have lots of dandy attachments. Some people begin to have their arms amputated so that they can have these artificial limbs fitted. A law is written making it illegal for people with normal arms to have them replaced by cybernetic arms. Would you vote for or against the law? Give your reasons.

6.   Find out how many hairs are on your head. Estimate the area by cutting a piece of paper to fit like a cap over the hairy part of your scalp. Cut the paper into rectangles, adding the area of the pieces. By means of a mirror, a ruler, and great patience, count the number of hairs sprouting from a ¼ inch by ¼ inch section of scalp. Multiply. Suggest how a scientist might estimate how many neurons there are in the brain of an animal.

7.   Why are the eyes, ears, nose, and tongue in the head? Why not put major sensors out on the limbs, or lower on the body? Consider (a) the location of the brain, and (b) the limit on the maximum rate of nerve signal transmission speeds (whether carrying sensory input to the brain or output from the brain to effectors).

8.   Pursuing the analogy between brain and society, how do the number of people on earth and the number of neurons estimated to be in the human brain compare? Can one consider the brain to be intermediate in size between the neuron and human society, based on this figure? Give specific numerical calculation, and a single sentence of interpretation.

9.   Sign your name on a ruled sheet of paper five times with each hand with your eyes shut, and five times with each hand with your eyes open. What differences arise? Explain.

5.2. MACHINES THAT SEE AND PLAN

In monitoring an assembly line, the computer receives its data from sensors. It must process these data in time to order the rejection of faulty products by the time they reach an ejection mechanism on the line. Such a system of

$$\text{sensors} \rightarrow \text{computer} \rightarrow \text{effectors}$$

may be called a **robot.** We recognize the overall setup of Fig. 1 of Section 5.1, except that now we have a computer—rather than a network of neurons—to compute upon the inputs relayed by the sensors. At the present time, most robots are—like the defect monitor just mentioned—rather limited in their activity. In the rest of this section, however, we look at robots that use **artificial intelligence** techniques in processing visual information to guide their interactions with the environment.

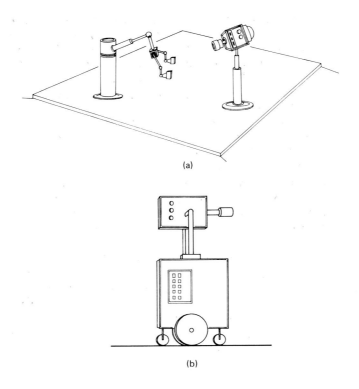

(a)

(b)

Fig. 1   (a) A hand–eye robot. (b) A mobile robot.

We shall consider two types of such robots. In a **hand–eye robot** (Fig. 1a), a TV camera feeds a picture to a computer which can command a mechanical arm to pick up and manipulate objects. In a mobile robot (Fig. 1b), a TV camera atop the robot feeds a picture to a computer which extracts the data it needs to build up a description of the robot's environment. The computer can then plan ways for the robot to carry out tasks, such as locating an object and pushing it to a designated place without bumping into obstacles.

The computer must carry out **scene analysis**—analyzing a pattern of light and shade to figure out what objects are located in which precise places around the robot. Then, given a command, the computer must go through a **planning** phase—figure out what to do before it actually starts moving. We first briefly describe some activities these robots are capable of, and indicate the type of planning the computer must perform to guide these actions.

Here is *a task for a hand–eye robot:*

1.   Analyze a scene to recognize it as a stack of three visually distinct blocks—say A atop B atop C (Fig. 2)—at a certain location on a table top.

2.   Store this analysis of the scene. Call this record M (for memory).

3.   Use M to compute the coordinates of the base of the stack. Convert the coordinates into a sequence of instructions which will cause the mechanical hand to "swipe" the base of the stack, thus scattering the three blocks around the table top.

4.   Analyze the new scene and use this to reconstruct the situation stored as M. This requires the computer to recognize which block in the new scene corresponds to which block in the old scene. It must also compute that, in order to restack the blocks, it must replace C, B, and A in *that* order, first clearing a space for block C.

If the program does not make use of visual feedback in guiding the arm as it moves, the computer must make sure that a block will only move when grasped by the mechanical hand and returned to its previous position on the stack. The computer must provide a trajectory that will not displace any blocks "by accident." Unfortunately, there is enough play in the mechanical arm for even the most precise computation to yield defective behavior. A more refined program—involving far more computation—would make continual use of both visual feedback via the TV camera and tactile feedback via pressure sensors on the hand (remember our discussion of the artificial arm in Section 5.1). The feedback would make sure that the hand would avoid obstacles, and that it would not release a block until it was securely in place on the stack. (The reader may get some feeling for the problem by trying to stack blocks with his eyes closed.)

Let us next describe *a task for a mobile robot:*

1.   Analyze a scene to recognize a number of large obstacles and their locations on the floor of the room.

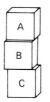

Fig. 2   A stack of three blocks.

   2.   Store this analysis of the scene. Call this record M. We may refer to it as the robot's **model of the world** (Fig. 3).

   3.   Given a command "Push the large cube to the door," use M to plan a path that will place the robot behind the large cube, and then another path that the robot may pursue in pushing the large cube to the door.

   4.   Convert the plan into a sequence of instructions to the drive wheels of the robot. If the robot moves "with its eyes closed," it may bump into an object that was hidden behind other objects during its analysis in phase 1, and which lies on its computed path. If this happens, it must update its model of the world, then make a new plan which takes this into account.

   Simple "robots" are already in use on assembly lines (Section 6.3). A more exotic use of robots is in space exploration. The Russians explored the moon with a simple carriage which could be controlled remotely from earth. It had a television camera so that technicians on earth could monitor the view of the robot, and send commands to pick up rocks, move closer to an interesting formation, etc. However, such a strategy is not appealing for mars, since the distances are so great that messages, even at the speed of light, will take anything from 8 to 15 minutes for the round trip. If a technician sitting back on earth were to see something interesting moving on the television screen and send the command "Hey, chase that!", the message

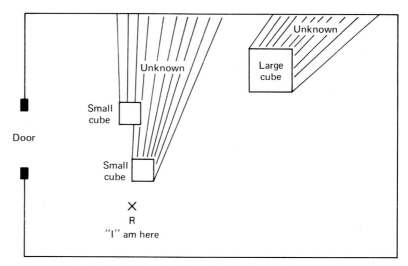

Fig. 3 A possible "model of the world" for a robot.

would reach the robot more than 10 minutes after the thing was seen. By that time, it would be gone. Thus much work has been done to build some low-level intelligence into mars explorers. For example, the Viking mission, landing on mars in mid-1976, had a robot that could automatically scoop up samples of martian soil and carry out a careful chemical analysis under computer control.

We might even imagine a mobile robot being used as a robot vaccum cleaner! We could give it the command "Vacuum the dining room," and it would use its model (stored as data in the computer's memory) of the house to figure out how to get from the closet to the dining room. It would then use its television camera to figure out where obstacles and objects are in the room. If the objects are very, very small, it will suck them up; if they are of intermediate size, it will reach out with its mechanical arm and place them on a tray for you to retrieve later; and, finally, it will use its knowledge of where large objects are to vacuum around them without denting precious furniture. While the first mobile robots have cost millions of dollars to develop, I would speculate that if housekeepers in their millions were prepared to buy a robot vacuum cleaner, it could be marketed for under $1000 and become a fairly common household item. It is in this way that, in just a few years, color television sets have gone from luxuries to almost standard equipment in many of the developed countries.

Planning

We wish to be able to issue such commands to the computer as "Push the large cube to the door," and have the robot's control computer automatically **translate** this into an appropriate sequence of commands to the robot's motors that can turn the wheels step by step. This is much like the process of **compiling** that we studied in Section 2.1. However, the "translation" now depends on **context**—on what is going on around the robot. Just what path the robot takes depends on where objects are in the room. We can thus view planning as **context-dependent compiling.** Let us outline how this might be done.

Our robot can analyze input from a TV camera to "see" objects. We shall outline this process of scene analysis in the next subsection. The computer can then build up a model of the world in its memory, listing the nature and location of objects it has already "seen" or into which the robot has bumped. Now suppose that the robot has built up the internal model of its world shown in Fig. 3. Here it has analyzed its world as a room with a doorway in one wall, and containing a large cube and two small cubes. In addition, there are areas which may contain other objects but are labeled "unknown" because they have so far been hidden from view by other objects.

Given the command "Push the large cube to the door," the control computer may proceed by breaking it into two second-level problems (recall our discussion of structured programming in Section 2.4):

1. Go to large cube
2. Go to door, while pushing cube

The computer must then break these two down further. This phase of planning involves finding alternative paths and choosing one of them. For example, the robot might compute that to get to the large cube it must start out on RC or on RA (Fig. 4) to avoid the nearer small cube, and that it must then follow CD or AB to get to the large cube. It might choose the path RAB both because it is shorter, and also because it does not lead through unknown territory where other obstacles might be encountered. Thus command 1 is compiled as

1(i). Go from R to A
1(ii). Go from A to B

Similarly, step 2 (Fig. 5) might be analyzed in terms of the alternate paths EJKGL and EFGL. EFGL might be chosen because it is

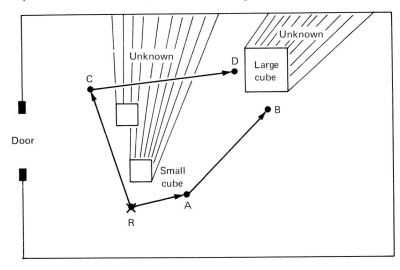

Fig. 4 Planning the path to the large cube.

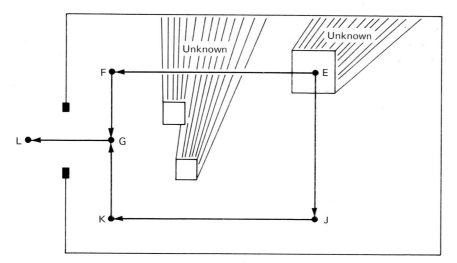

Fig. 5 Planning a path to push the cube to the door.

sufficiently shorter to offset the possible risks of going through "the
unknown." The computer thus compiles command 2 as

    2(i).   Push from E to F
    2(ii).   Push from F to G
    2(iii). Push from G to L

    The plot thickens. To push the large cube from E to F, the robot
must (Fig. 6) get behind the cube (i.e. to W') and then move just far

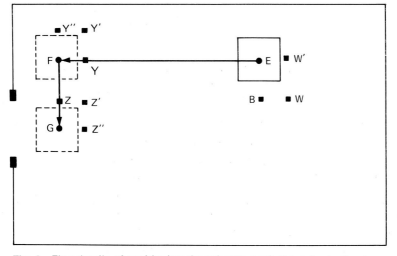

Fig. 6 Fine details of positioning the robot to push the cube to the door.

enough (namely, to Y) for the cube to get to F. Thus the computer must not only compile "Push from E to F" as "Go from W′ to Y," but must precede this command by the instructions "Go from B to W" and "Go from W to W′" which will position the robot correctly to start pushing. Using "GO (R,A)" to abbreviate "Go from R to A" we see that the third level of compilation will yield the program:

GO (R,A)
GO (A,B)
GO (B,W)
GO (W,W′)
GO (W′,Y)
GO (Y,Y′)
GO (Y′,Y″)
GO (Y″,Z)
GO (Z,Z′)
GO (Z′,Z″)
GO (Z″,L)
STOP

Next, the instruction GO (A,B) when following GO (R,A) must be broken down into an instruction-pair of the form

LEFT θ
FORWARD X

telling the robot to turn left through the appropriate angle θ and then go forward distance X. These instructions are at the level of the LOGO language of Section 2.3, which was used to control the TURTLE.

LEFT θ can finally be expressed in such terms as "Lock left wheel, advance right wheel 4 steps," while FORWARD X might compile as "Advance both wheels 12 steps synchronously."

It thus takes us through the six levels of a **hierarchy** of increasing detail to go from the brief, but very high-level, command "Push the large block to the door" to a sequence made up entirely from appropriate combinations of the three "machine-language" instructions:

L: locking right wheel, advance **L**eft wheel one step.
R: locking left wheel, advance **R**ight wheel one step.
B: synchronously advance **B**oth wheels one step.

What makes the mobile robot "smarter" than TURTLE is that it can do its own scene analysis and planning. It can thus respond in a context-dependent way to very high-level commands.

To plan, a computer (or a person) needs to know something about its world. For example, the mobile robot planning a path through the world of Fig. 3 has to know when the space between two objects is large enough, it has to know how to place itself behind an object it is going to push, and so on. We saw in Section 2.1 that a compiler is a very large program that has special subroutines specifying, for each high-level instruction, what low-level program will do the same job (this is spelled out in more detail in Section 8.2). In the same way, a planner is a very complicated program that can compile high-level programs in a way that depends on context. To obtain more of a feeling for this, consider a planner for a hand–eye robot (Fig. 1a), which must move blocks on a table top. Let us see what programs the computer needs to put one block on top of another in a way that takes into account the current state of the world.

The nature of the problem is shown in Fig. 7. If we tell the compiler "PUT CUBE A ON TOP OF CUBE C," it has to clear D off the top of C, and B off the top of A, before it can carry out the command. Let us see how the planner could be written in such a way that it would figure this out. In what follows we use a subroutine called "PLACE Y ON TABLE" which causes the computer to find a clear space on the table big enough for Y, and then cause it to move its mechanical hand over to Y, pick it up, move it over, and then put it down on the clear space, as shown in Fig. 8. This routine does *not* check to make sure that Y has nothing on top. Thus anything on top may, or may not, fall off in the process.

It also has a subroutine called "PLACE X ON Y," which will make it move the mechanical hand in such a way as to lift X up, move it across, and then set it down on top of Y—*without checking to see if X and Y have clear tops.*

The challenge is to write programs for the planner that will get it to do all the necessary checking and clearing. In the case of carrying out "PUT CUBE A ON TOP OF CUBE C" in the situation shown in Fig.

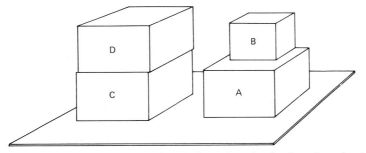

Fig. 7 Posing a problem for a hand-eye robot—to put cube A on top of cube C.

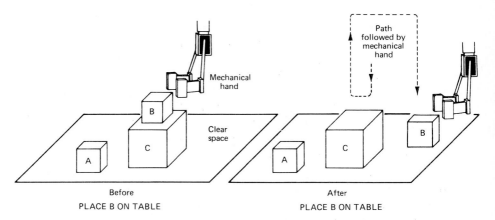

Before	After
PLACE B ON TABLE	PLACE B ON TABLE

Fig. 8 The routine PLACE Y ON TABLE gets the robot to place an object Y—in this case the cube B—but without checking to see if the top of Y is clear.

7, we could use the program

> PLACE B ON TABLE
> PLACE D ON TABLE
> PLACE A ON C

The question is what program do we put in the planner when we do not know in advance what, if any, blocks will be on top of A and C? Here it is: We program the computer so that

> PUT CUBE A ON TOP OF CUBE C

compiles as

> CLEARTOP A
> CLEARTOP C
> PLACE A ON C

Now we must specify the program CLEARTOP X. It uses a test "ON TOP OF X?" which answers "NO" if nothing is on top of X, but otherwise delivers the name Y of a block which is atop X.

> CLEARTOP X

compiles as

> ON TOP OF X?
> IF NO: EXIT
> IF Y: PUT Y ON TABLE

Remember from our discussion of Fig. 8 (where the parameter Y had the value B) that PLACE Y ON TABLE did *not* check to see if there was anything on top of Y. However, PUT Y ON TABLE does:

PUT Y ON TABLE

is compiled as

ON TOP OF Y?
IF NO: PLACE Y ON TABLE
IF Z: PUT Z ON TABLE
PUT Y ON TABLE

The reader who recalls Section 2.3 will see that this is an example of **recursion:** the program PUT Y ON TABLE *calls itself*—both with Y and changed **parameter** Z—in its own definition. In Fig. 9, we check that these definitions really work in handling the situation shown in Fig. 7.

Scene Analysis

In this subsection we study scene analysis: examining how a computer can take the ill-defined pattern of light and shade repre-

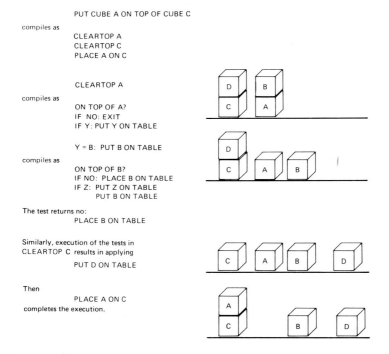

PUT CUBE A ON TOP OF CUBE C

compiles as

CLEARTOP A
CLEARTOP C
PLACE A ON C

CLEARTOP A

compiles as

ON TOP OF A?
IF NO: EXIT
IF Y: PUT Y ON TABLE

Y = B: PUT B ON TABLE

compiles as

ON TOP OF B?
IF NO: PLACE B ON TABLE
IF Z: PUT Z ON TABLE
PUT B ON TABLE

The test returns no:
PLACE B ON TABLE

Similarly, execution of the tests in
CLEARTOP C results in applying
PUT D ON TABLE

Then
PLACE A ON C
completes the execution.

Fig. 9 Using the instructions in the text to compile PUT CUBE A ON TOP OF CUBE C in the context shown in Fig. 7.

sented in a TV image and extract from it the information required to build a "model of the world." As we have seen, this model can then be used to plan the robot's interaction with the environment.

Scene analysis starts by taking the activity from the **receptors** (in this case, the two-dimensional array of light intensity detected by the TV camera), and **preprocessing** these data to obtain features that can contribute to recognition of the scene. A commonly used scene-analysis technique replaces the two-dimensional array of light inten-sities by an array approximating a line drawing of the objects in the visual field. The first two steps in this process enhance contrast and then fit short line segments to the points of high contrast. This is much like the preprocessing operations we saw for the visual system of cats and monkeys in the previous section. The result of this process as applied to a picture of a cube might look like Fig. 10a. The next step fills in gaps to some extent by finding long lines—which cover as many of the short line segments as possible, to obtain an outline such as that in Fig. 10b.

We note that 10b is by no means a complete line drawing of a cube—some lines are missing, especially ones where two faces meet between which there is little or no change in texture, so that the contrast detectors provide no input to the line segment filters.

There seem to be two main strategies for proceeding beyond an incomplete outline such as in Fig. 10b. In **straight-through analysis** (Fig. 11a), the input pattern is to be recognized without further pre-processing. For example, one might process rough outlines like those of Fig. 10b by searching for a complete outline using the operations of adding medium length line segments with such "rules of thumb" as "lines should continue an existing line," or "start from an existing vertex and run parallel to an existing line" in an attempt to satisfy such criteria of completeness as "a line must join two vertices—it cannot stop dead," or (if we can make use of stereo information) "if a vertex is at the near end of a line, then it will usually have more than two lines leading from it." If a line is very short, it may be deleted. If

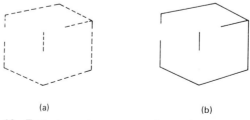

(a)   (b)

Fig. 10 Two stages in preprocessing a picture of a cube.

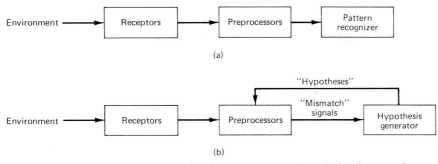

(a)

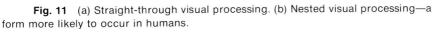

(b)

Fig. 11   (a) Straight-through visual processing. (b) Nested visual processing—a form more likely to occur in humans.

two lines are aligned, the gap between them may be filled unless vertices on them indicate that they belong to distinct objects. In this way, the computer seeks a complete line drawing, which its recognition programs can definitely classify as being a cube or some other object.

In **nested analysis** (Figure 11b), the computer uses the rough outline, as in Fig. 10b, to generate "guesses" or "hypotheses" as to what object is being looked at. Further preprocessing can then be done, to either check the hypothesis, or generate "mismatch" signals which can be used to compute another hypothesis. A nested analysis could still make use of line completion techniques, but would integrate them into the object recognition process—continually testing to see if new lines would yield the outline of a "known" object. Analysis only continues until an object can be characterized with a fairly high level of confidence exceeding some threshold—so that "perfect" line drawings can only be constructed by the computer after object recognition, not before. More sophisticated programs make use of cues from color and texture as well.

It would seem that human brains use the nested analysis approach more than the straight-through approach. Because we expect an object to be familiar, we can compensate for inadequate contour information. We seek enough cues to classify stimuli in terms of a known object—rather than trying to account for all the details (including omissions) of the visual input. For example, we see Fig. 12 as a square. Of course, having perceived the square, we may then notice the gap in the right-hand side—but the point is that we see a square with a gap in it, rather than a collection of five line segments.

This expectation principle also works in **pattern recognition** systems. These are computer systems that classify input as being one of

Fig. 12   This figure is most commonly described as a square—with a gap in it.

a fixed set of different patterns—such as the letters of the alphabet. Suppose we want a machine to recognize hand-printed characters. We might use preprocessing of the kind mentioned above to break each character into lines and curves. Then a letter "A" might be characterized by the direction and meeting points of three straight-line components; and so might a letter "H." In **optical character recognition (OCR)** systems of the kind we discussed briefly in Section 1.4, the extent to which a letter of the input matches a standard letter is often judged by an optical system which passes light from the letter through a filter. The more light that gets through, the better the match. Of course, an optical system of this kind only works well for print and type, and needs a different filter for each typeface. For handwriting, we still need programmed recognition techniques.

But what do you make of the following letter?

Ħ

It could be either an A or an H. If, however, it occurred in the *contexts*

TĦIN

BEĦNS

you would conclude that it was an H in the first case, and an A in the second. Sophisticated character recognition systems, then, not only use letter-by-letter techniques, but also use context. The computer stores a dictionary, and can choose between different interpretations of a letter whenever only one interpretation yields a word in the dictionary. Even an OCR system may be used with a computer dictionary program to remove ambiguities. This is because a chipped letter may be ambigious, even if it comes from a standard typefont. For example, "ı" might be a short j or a smeared i.

Having seen that the recognition of simple objects is programmable, we must face the problem of analyzing a scene comprising several objects, with some partly in front of others. One method, which works quite well when we have a scene comprising a few objects each of which is an example from a short list of "familiar" objects, is *model fitting.* For example, suppose we had "models" of cubes, wedges, and spheres. Then we might fit a cube to nine of the lines of Fig. 13a, and

(a)   (b)

Fig. 13 In analyzing a complex scene, the computer may analyze part of the scene, then "subtract" that part to continue the process of analyzing the rest of the scene.

then remove them to leave the lines of Fig. 13b to be explained (with the "fuzzy region" indicating "anything can go here that 'works' "). These fit a wedge better than a cube or sphere, and so we conclude with the analysis of the scene as "a cube in front of a wedge."

These methods only work well for simple scenes composed of geometrical objects. They can be useful in an assembly line, where a robot has to recognize only a few different components, picking up the right one at the right time, and fixing it into place, or discarding the part if it has defects. Quite different problems are faced in building a scene-analysis system for a mobile robot that must navigate out of doors. Clouds and trees do not have straight-line edges. Instead of just building up long lines, a scene analysis of this kind also tries to find regions with a given depth or color or texture. These regions can then be used as data for the recognition programs. For example, if a large region of blue occurs at the top of a picture, then it is likely to be sky. If a region of dappled green occurs above a brown region, then these are likely to be the foliage and trunk of a tree. In this way, color and texture analysis can provide valuable information even when the outline of an object in the scene is irregular, or hidden by other objects. Research on both scene analysis and planning continues at a vigorous pace.

Suggestions for Further Reading

B. Raphael: "The Thinking Computer." Freeman, San Francisco, California, 1976.
    Chapter 7 discusses machine perception; Chapter 8 talks about robots; Chapters 3–5 give a good account of planning techniques.
M. A. Arbib: "The Metaphorical Brain." Wiley, New York, 1972.
    Chapter 4 gives a useful account of artificial intelligence and robotics,

with special emphasis on planning and scene analysis. It provides the basis for the treatment in this section.

B. Williams: How Smart are Computers? *The New York Review of Books,* November 15, 1973, pp. 36–40.

A British philosopher writes an interesting essay on the book "What Computers Can't Do: A Critique of Artificial Reason" by Hubert L. Dreyfus, an American philosopher.

S. Albus and J. M. Evans, Jr.: Robot Systems, *Scientific American,* February 1976, p. 76 ff.

Describes the use of robots, in the sense of programmable machines, in many factories; and shows how some can analyze input from sensors to cope with uncertainties in the environment.

Summary

We may define intelligence as involving the ability to learn from experience. In this section, we saw two ways in which a robot could be programmed to make use of that experience. In **scene analysis,** a computer analyzes the input from a TV camera to determine what objects (items about which the computer has programs) are in the environment and where they are located. In **planning,** the computer generates and compares various plans of action to decide what sequence of actions to carry out. Planning takes into account the current goals and environment of the system, and so can be thought of as context-dependent compiling.

Glossary

Artificial intelligence: *AI* is that branch of computer science which studies how to program computers to exhibit apparently intelligent behavior.

Robot: A *robot* is a computer-controlled machine that can sense things around it as it carries out human commands. It may have touch sensors to tell when it has bumped into things, or a TV camera for visual input. A *hand–eye robot* has TV input and a hand with which to pick up objects. A *mobile robot* has wheels on which to move around.

Model of the world: The information that an animal or robot has inside its brain or computer about the world around it is the *model of the world.* It thus serves to guide the system's interaction with its environment.

Translator: A *translator* takes a program written in a high-level language, and enables a computer to execute it. It may be a compiler or an interpreter.

Context: The *context* of an item is the material surrounding the item that helps define its meaning. For example, "pen" has different meanings in the two contexts "The pig is in the pen" and "The ink is in the pen." Similarly, a lion has a different "meaning" in the context of a zoo or of wide-open spaces.

Planning: *Planning* is the process of generating and comparing different courses of action and then choosing one before starting to act. It takes the system from a high-level specification of "what is to be done" to a step-by-step specification of how to do it. It can thus be thought of as *context-dependent compiling.*

Hierarchy: An organization whose components are arranged in levels from a top level on down to a bottom level is a *hierarchy.*

Parameter: A given command or subroutine may have a number of *parameters* that must be specified before the computer knows what to do. For example, the instruction FORWARD X has one parameter, namely X. When we replace X by a number we obtain a command that the computer can execute—FORWARD 100, for example, will get the computer to send 100 "one step forward" commands to a robot.

Recursion: *Recursion* is the definition of loops in a program by letting the program call itself—so that the use of the program may recur again and again during its execution.

Scene analysis: This is the process whereby a computer analyzes visual input, say from a TV camera, to determine the nature and location of objects in the scene.

Receptor or **Sensor:**   A special device that responds to light, sound, etc., and converts it into signals for the brain or a computer is a *receptor* or *sensor.*

Preprocessing: *Preprocessing* means taking data from sensors, and changing it into a form that will simplify a recognition or classification process.

Straight-through analysis: This type of analysis processes the output of the preprocessors to recognize the sensory input without further processing. By contrast, *nested analysis* generates "guesses," and then calls for further preprocessing of the input, which either confirms the "guess," or generates mismatch signals which can be used to generate a new guess.

Pattern recognition: The process whereby a computer can recognize a pattern—such as telling which letter of the alphabet a squiggle of lines is meant to be is called *pattern recognition.* As such, it often requires the use of context.

Optical character recognition (OCR) system: An *OCR system* is one that can accept typed or printed pages as input, and provide computer code of the symbols on the page as output, using optical filters in making the classification.

Exercises

1.   What characteristics would a hand-eye robot need to be able to play ping-pong? What else would be useful though not necessary?

2.   Can an airplane or missile with an automatic guidance system be considered a mobile robot?

3.   What problems would an optical character recognition (OCR) system for reading handwritten script have that one for coding typed text would not have?

4. An example of the nested visual processing (see Fig. 11b) occurs in context-sensitive OCR. Suppose an OCR has preprocessors that can:

    (a)   recognize a "correctly" printed letter;

    (b)   make a list of possible characters for a badly printed letter.

The OCR also has a "hypothesis generator" which can:

    (a)   combine the certain letters and a randomly chosen possibility from the list for uncertain letters;

    (b)   look up the hypothetical word thus constructed, in a computerized dictionary;

    (c)   eliminate the possible letter from the list if no such word occurs in the dictionary.

Show how this would work for the TAIN BEHNS example in the text. Name two reasons why this method will not always work, giving specific examples.

5. Refer to the description and examples of the blocks world language. Using instructions of the two kinds:

CLEARTOP X   and   PLACE Y ON Z

interpret (compare Fig. 9) the top-level instruction

PUT CUBE A ON TOP OF CUBE C

starting from the position shown in the accompanying figure.

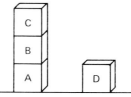

6. Look at the following figure. What planning activity must a robot perform to follow this command:

"Put the boxes in a straight line in order of size."

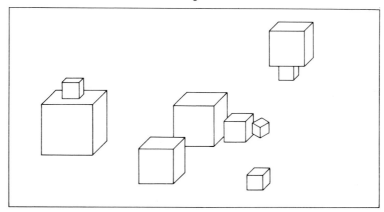

7. In what sense must a robot have a modifiable model of the world?

8. People who have been blind from birth have sometimes had their sight restored by operations. Typically, such a patient, when shown a sphere and a cube soon after sight is restored, will say, "I can tell them apart, but I don't know which is which." Explain in terms of one-way visual processing, model fitting, and expectation.

9. Show how the block-pushing robot might proceed, from the situation shown in Fig. 3, with the command "push the two small cubes together." Break each part of the plan into subplans, until you reach the level of the "GO" instruction.

10. The block-pushing robot in the text moves "with its eyes closed." That is, it surveys its environment, plans its path, then begins to move. Only if it bumps into something unexpected does it "open its eyes" and plot a new course. Why wasn't this robot programmed to move with its "eyes open"? (Consider processing time and the change in perspective caused by viewing from a new angle.) Why must animals move with their eyes open?

11. What trouble might an OCR system that can recognize both letters and numerals have with the circled symbol pictured here? Explain how you interpret it, reading first vertically and then horizontally, in terms of *context.*

12. What difficulties does a robot scene-analysis program for line drawings have that one for three-dimensional scenes does not?

5.3 MACHINES THAT UNDERSTAND NATURAL LANGUAGE

In Chapters 1 and 2, we saw that we must be very careful in writing a program, making sure that the computer always knows *exactly* what to do next in following our instructions for solving a problem. However, when we ask a friend to do something, we expect him to be able to respond without being told step-by-step how to do so. The previous section began to close the gap: we saw that if we do enough step-by-step programming *in the first place* to give the computer a scene-analysis program and a planning program, it can compute the detailed steps necessary to obey a high-level command like "Push the red cube to the door." However, a command like "Push the red cube to the door" is still fairly formal—and just because a robot can respond to commands of the form "Push A to B" does not mean that it can make sense of other English sentences, like "Try to get something into that doorway, will you?"

This section sketches the problems, and preliminary successes, of communicating with the computer in a **natural language** like English—rather than high-level, but still formal, programming languages. The importance of this work is to make computers easier to use by people with little training in programming. In particular, a major goal of this research is to let people obtain information from a data base using English, instead of the formal update/query languages of the kind we discussed in Section 4.1.

Syntax and Semantics

To understand more about how a program to handle natural language works, we need to discuss two important concepts from **linguistics,** which is the study of language. These concepts are "syntax" and "semantics." Briefly, the job of **syntax** is to tell whether a sentence is *grammatical;* while the job of **semantics** is to tell whether a sentence is *meaningful.* For example,

'TWAS BRILLIG, AND THE SLITHY TOVES DID GYRE AND GIMBLE IN THE WABE

is grammatical if "brillig" and "slithy" are adjectives, if "tove" and "wabe" are nouns, and "gyre" and "gimble" are verbs. Syntax is the study that lets us make such statements, even though we have no idea what the sentence means! In general, then, syntax analyzes a sentence in terms of pieces like adjectives, noun phrases, verb phrases, and so on. However, linguists soon discovered that it was not always possible to analyze a sentence into its grammatical pieces without some semantic information. For example, in the sentence

I RODE DOWN THE STREET IN NEW DELHI

the words THE STREET IN NEW DELHI form a single *noun group,* telling us where the riding was done. In the sentence

I RODE DOWN THE STREET IN A BUS

it is only the words THE STREET that form the noun group telling where the riding was done. To make the distinction, one must know at least that NEW DELHI can contain streets but A BUS cannot. The use of even such small fragments of *meaning* as this is an example of the use of semantic information to work out the structure of the sentence. Here is a similar example:

HE HIT THE CAR WITH A ROCK

in which THE CAR is the noun phrase, and

HE HIT THE CAR WITH A DENTED FENDER

in which THE CAR WITH A DENTED FENDER is the noun phrase. However, semantics has more work to do than simply help syntax tag the structures in the sentence. Consider the two sentences

THE INK IS IN THE PEN
THE PIG IS IN THE PEN

In this case, a syntactic system can work out that PEN is a noun without any help from semantics, but if we are actually to *use* the sentence, then we need to know that in the first case, the PEN is a writing instrument, while in the second case it is an enclosure. For example, in French a writing pen is UNE PLUME, while an animal pen is UN PARC or UN POULAILLER. In the 1950s, attempts to program computers to translate from one language into another failed precisely because people did not then know how to represent semantic information in a way that the computer could use. One of the main achievements of computer scientists in the 1970s is to make great progress in handling semantic information for **microworlds.**

A microworld is essentially an environment in which a conversation can take place. If we know we are talking about farms, PEN is far more likely to be an animal enclosure than if it occurs in the microworld of book-writing. Similarly, if we overheard two convicts say

THE PIG IS IN THE PEN

we might well interpret PIG as policeman and PEN as penitentiary—the underworld microworld! We shall study three microworlds in this section—one will be a "world" of parts that a company supplies; another will be the microworld of blocks on a table top; while the third will be the "world" of lunar rock samples.

The use of **context** is also vital for any question-answering system. For example, the correct answer to

WHERE IS THE EMPIRE STATE BUILDING?

is "In the United States" if the question is asked in Russia; "In New York City" if the question is asked elsewhere in the United States; and "On 34th Street" if the question is asked in New York City.

In the next three subsections, we study three computer approaches to natural language. The first system is Codd's **clarification** system for a data base. Instead of making a full semantic and syntactic analysis of a sentence, the system extracts fragments from the query, and then asks questions to *clarify* the exact nature of the query. This interchange between computer and user continues until the computer has built up a formal representation of the query that is acceptable to the user. The second system is Winograd's system which can handle questions, commands, and new information about the blocks microworld, so long as they are typed in. The third system, Wood's LUNAR system, can handle spoken input. These last two systems can carry out a full semantic and syntactic analysis, and very rarely need to call for clarification from the user.

A Clarification System for a Data Base

We now give Codd's example of the sort of clarification responses the computer would make in formalizing a query to a somewhat limited data base which contains information about suppliers, parts, projects, and shipments of parts by suppliers to projects. In what follows, the computer's printout is shown in CAPITALS, while the user's input is shown in *italics*:

PLEASE PROCEED.
Give me a list of the part numbers, quantities, and suppliers of Houston parts.

YOU ARE REQUESTING (AMONG OTHER THINGS) A LISTING
OF QUANTITIES OF PARTS. DO YOU WANT:
1. QUANTITIES ON HAND
2. QUANTITIES ON ORDER
3. QUANTITIES SHIPPED?

The system has been programmed to distinguish these three types of
quantities, and so emits a clarification request if it does not find the
type specified in the original request.

I want quantities on order.
FINE! NOW, WITH REGARD TO "HOUSTON PARTS," DO YOU
MEAN:
1. PARTS SUPPLIED BY HOUSTON SUPPLIERS
2. PARTS SUPPLIED TO HOUSTON PROJECTS
3. PARTS ASSOCIATED WITH HOUSTON IN SOME OTHER
WAY?
I mean item 2.

The computer can recognize the 2, and so proceed. If the user has
responded in some "strange" way like "Isn't it obvious?", the system
can structure the dialog by rephrasing the clarification request more
formally: "PLEASE REPLY BY MEANS OF ONE OF THE NUMERALS 1
OR 2 OR 3."

GOOD! I NEED ONE MORE PIECE OF INFORMATION. IN THE
LISTING OF PART NUMBERS, QUANTITY ON ORDER, AND
SUPPLIERS, HOW DO YOU WANT SUPPLIERS TO BE IDEN-
TIFIED:
1. BY NUMBER
2. BY NAME
3. SOME OTHER WAY?
By name and by city.

At this stage, the system has asked enough questions to build up a
query in the formal update/query language. It now rephrases this in
English to make sure it has captured the question intended by the
user.

O.K. THIS IS WHAT I UNDERSTAND YOUR QUERY TO BE: "FIND
ALL COMBINATIONS OF PART NUMBER, QUANTITY ON OR-
DER, SUPPLIER NAME, AND SUPPLIER CITY SUCH THAT THE
SUPPLIER SUPPLIED THE PART TO A PROJECT LOCATED IN
HOUSTON." IS THIS WHAT YOU INTENDED?

If the user is satisfied, he types in YES, and the system responds to the formula that it has built up, partly from the user's original query and partly from the succeeding dialog. Let us see what happens if the user is not satisfied:

I have changed my mind.

The system does not understand this, although it would understand a YES or NO. Since it cannot interpret the response, it tightens up the dialog as follows:

PLEASE SELECT ITEM 1 OR 2 BELOW:
1. THE RE-STATEMENT IS SATISFACTORY
2. THE RE-STATEMENT IS NOT SATISFACTORY
2

The user chooses the second alternative.

IF YOUR INTENT CAN BE EXPRESSED BY MAKING MINOR CHANGES IN MY RESTATEMENT, PLEASE TYPE IT IN WITH YOUR CHANGES INCORPORATED. IF YOUR CHANGE IS MAJOR, YOU MAY RESTATE YOUR QUERY IN YOUR OWN TERMS.

At the present time, only a limited capability prototype has been programmed. Initial results seem encouraging for the general approach, though they are highly restricted. The general procedure is as shown in Fig. 1:

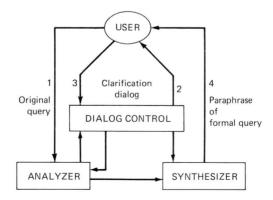

Fig. 1 The use of clarification dialog to formalize a natural language query to a data base.

1. User makes an initial statement of his query in unrestricted English. The analyzer attempts to transform the query into the formal query/update language.

2. System interrogates user about his query to obtain information that is missing or hidden in language the system does not understand, and to resolve ambiguities. A good system design must include encouraging responses to prevent the user from signing off in disgust at the failure of the machine to understand his question immediately.

3. User responds to system interrogation. The clarification loop of 2 and 3 may be repeated many times until the system is ready for Step 4.

4. The synthesizer provides a restatement of user's query in system English in a very precise way, based on an English rephrasing of a precise query in the query/update language.

If the user does not accept the restatement, then he must modify it, or type in a new form of the query to reinitiate the process. However, if the user does accept the precise restatement of the query, then the system may immediately answer the query.

Talking about the Blocks World

We now examine a system with the ability to respond to English, even when it is *not* in a standard format and without continual requests for clarification. Winograd built a language-understanding system for a "robot"—simulated on computer graphics—that has a "hand" which can pick up, move, and put down the objects in a simple table top "blocks world."

Given a *command* in English, the robot will attempt to execute it.

Given a *question* in English, the robot will attempt to answer it in English.

Given *novel information,* the robot will add it to its data base, and emit the words "I UNDERSTAND." This does not mean that the robot "really" understands, but simply that the material has been stored.

In the following sample of dialog—slightly adapted from the original—the *italic* entries are typed in by a human, while the CAPITAL entries are the robot's response.

1. *Pick up a big red block.*
OK.

The system answers "OK" when it carries out a command. The initial situation is shown in Fig. 2. In order to pick up the red block, the

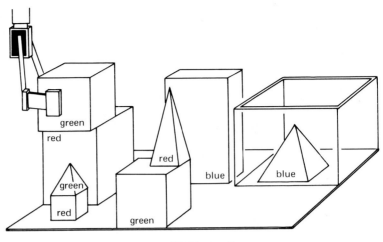

"Table top"

Fig. 2   The table top world of Winograd's robot.

"robot" had to clear it off by finding a space for the green one and moving the green one away. (Recall our discussion of Figs. 7–9 of Section 5.2.)

> *2.   Grasp the pyramid.*
> I DON'T UNDERSTAND WHICH PYRAMID YOU MEAN.

There are three pyramids in the scene, and the program knows that phrases beginning with "the" are intended to refer to a specific object the speaker has in mind.

> *3.   What does the box contain?*
> THE BLUE PYRAMID.
> *4.   What is the pyramid supported by?*
> THE BOX.

Earlier the system responded to "the pyramid" by saying "I DON'T UNDERSTAND WHICH PYRAMID YOU MEAN." Now, it assumes that we mean the one just mentioned, which sits on the floor of the box.

> *5.   Can the table pick up blocks?*
> NO.

The semantic rules include the knowledge that "picking up" must be done by an animate object, and that the table is not animate.

6.   *Can a pyramid be supported by a block?*
YES.

The deductive system finds an actual example, so it knows this is possible.

7.   *Can a pyramid support a pyramid?*
I DON'T KNOW.

The question makes sense, but there is no example in the scene. The system has no way of looking into the details of its programs, even though these fix what it can really do.

8.   *Stack up two pyramids.*
I CAN'T.

The robot tries and fails. Infuriatingly, Winograd does not reask question 7 at this point. Presumably, however, the answer would still be "I DON'T KNOW." Failure to stack up two pyramids need not imply that a pyramid can never support another one—consider the case of a table-top world containing only one pyramid. We shall later suggest a more satisfying approach.

9.   *There are four blocks to the left of the box.*
NO, FIVE OF THEM: THE RED CUBE, TWO LARGE GREEN CUBES, A LARGE RED BLOCK, AND A LARGE BLUE BLOCK.

The system knows that it has complete information about the basic properties of objects, including location. It checks any statements about these to see whether it agrees or disagrees.

10.   *The blue pyramid is mine.*
I UNDERSTAND.

On the other hand, possession is left as an unknown property of objects, about which it can be told. However, the ability to answer question 12, below, shows that it must have "X is mine = I own X" in its general data base. It stores possession information in its data base, accepting it at face value.

11.   *I own all blocks which are not red, but I don't own anything which supports a pyramid.*
I UNDERSTAND.

The result of "understanding" these sentences is the creation of new procedures within the robot for deducing whether I own something.

12.   *Do I own the box?*
NO.

The box supports whatever it contains, in this case a pyramid (refer to Fig. 2).

13.   *Do I own a steeple?*
SORRY, I DON'T KNOW THE WORD "STEEPLE."

The system interrupts immediately when it sees a word it does not know.

14.   *A "steeple" is a stack which contains two green cubes and a pyramid.*

The quote marks indicate that we are defining a new word. The definition is added to the dictionary stored in the system's data base.

I UNDERSTAND.
15.   *Are there any steeples now?*
NO.

The new definition is used as a description to recognize steeples.

16.   *Build one.*
OK.

The description given in the definition is enough to deduce a plan for building new objects as well as recognizing them. The word "one" means "a steeple," and the plan is carried out.

17.   *Thank you.*
YOU'RE WELCOME!

The system can recognize idioms and give the stock response that a speaker of American English would.

With this, we can briefly look at some of the procedures used by Winograd in his system. **Parsing** is the process of breaking a string of words into the pieces specified by the syntax. A left-to-right parser is a system that parses a sentence by working from the left-hand end of a sentence, building a tree of possible parsings which are consistent with the initial segment. In Fig. 3, we show two possible parsings consistent with the first three words, but only one of these parsings survives the addition of the fourth word.

Winograd uses left-to-right syntactic analysis, but invokes the semantics of his blocks world to remove many possible ambiguities.

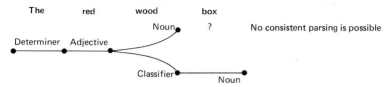

Fig. 3 An example of left-to-right parsing.

For example, each time a possible noun group is formed, his parsing program calls a semantic routine to check whether it describes a possible object in its very limited microworld.

Unfortunately, the system is overly bound to the here and now (or recent past) in looking for possible meanings. It would seem to be a *very important* development—going well beyond Winograd's work—to add to the system rules for creating "possible worlds" consistent with the "physics" of the block world. Such a system, when faced with the question

Can a pyramid support a pyramid?

would create an internal representation of two pyramids atop a table top, then try to stack one atop the other, fail, and on this basis reply

NO.

Interfacing the parser with the robot involves two portions. The major contribution is to transform the parsed English sentences into procedures written in a special high-level programming language called PLANNER for carrying out the command or request of the input sentence; and to go from PLANNER procedures to appropriate English language output. Given a command in PLANNER, the system can generate a plan for carrying it out, and then execute it. We discussed techniques for this in the previous section. Given a question in PLANNER, the system can build a data structure that represents the answer; and given information in PLANNER, it can incorporate it into the internal model or report any glaring inconsistency. These are the query and update functions we discussed in Section 4.1, Data Base Management.

Speech Understanding

So far we have assumed that the natural language entering the computer is typed in, so that there is no problem of character recognition. A more interesting situation—and the least any science-fiction

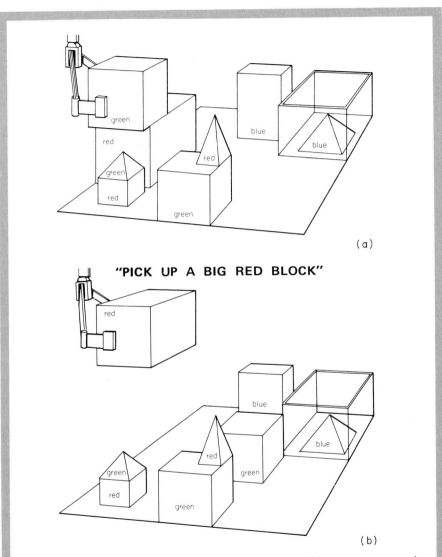

"PICK UP A BIG RED BLOCK"

(a)

(b)

Four states in the response of Winograd's robot to natural language commands to move objects about in its microworld of blocks. To obey the command "Pick up a big red block" (b), the computer first must remove the green block (a). To obey the command "Find a block which is taller than the one you are holding and put it into the box" (c), the robot first must put down the block it is holding. Then it must compare the height of that particular block to the height of all other blocks until it finds a suitable block, which it can then put in the box. To obey the

"FIND A BLOCK WHICH IS TALLER THAN THE ONE YOU ARE HOLDING AND PUT IT INTO THE BOX"

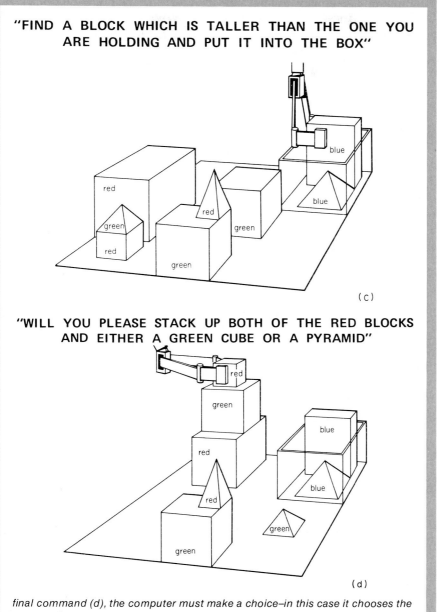

(c)

"WILL YOU PLEASE STACK UP BOTH OF THE RED BLOCKS AND EITHER A GREEN CUBE OR A PYRAMID"

(d)

final command (d), the computer must make a choice–in this case it chooses the green cube over the pyramid–and before it can pick up the second red block, it must move the green pyramid and place it somewhere on the table top.

enthusiast would expect—is that in which the human *speaks* to the computer. At first sight, it might seem that the problem breaks down into three parts, as shown in Fig. 4. This is like the straight-through visual processing of Fig. 11a of Section 5.2. As the reader may suspect, we shall soon abandon it in favor of a "nested" analysis more like that of Fig. 11b of Section 5.2.

The first box in Fig. 4 simply takes in the spoken input, and sends on the standard computer representation of each new word to the text analysis box. This second box then uses syntax, semantics, and context programs of the kind we have just described to build up an unambiguous representation of what each sentence really means, and sends this to the planning box. This box answers the question, obeys the commands, or stores the information from the spoken input, whichever is appropriate.

The problem with this scheme is that it does not work! People mumble, so that it is not clear which syllable they really spoke. People run one word into another, so that it is not clear where one word—or sentence—ends and another begins. People have different accents, so that one person's "yawl" is another person's "you all," and one person's "spine" is another's "Spain."

Systems currently being built for speech understanding thus use a limited vocabulary and restrict the input to some microworld, using syntax, semantics, and knowledge of the world to resolve ambiguities in the spoken input.

The first step is to turn the spoken input into a **spectrogram**—analyzing speech into "high notes" and "low notes," with a dark band for each "note" that contributes strongly. A band rises as pitch increases, falls as pitch decreases. A **phoneme** is a sound that corresponds—roughly—to one letter in the written word. Experts can recognize some phonemes from the shapes of the bands in the spectrogram. This suggests that we can use pattern recognition techniques (compare the previous section) to recognize the phonemes, and then chop the strings of phonemes up into words—to build the first box of Fig. 4. The catch is that the decoding of spectrograms is highly error prone. An expert speech scientist, looking at one phoneme at a time, is only correct about 30 percent of the time if no context is used. In the other 70 percent, they might have anything

Fig. 4 An impractical, straight-through approach to speech understanding.

from 1 to 10 other guesses as to what the phoneme might actually be. Remember our discussion in Section 5.2 of the use of a dictionary to tell if Ħwas an A or an H *when it appeared in context.* We would classify it as H in T Ħ IN and A in BE Ħ NS, because a dictionary would contain THIN but not TAIN, and BEANS but not BEHNS. When the speech scientists used a computer to retrieve dictionary words which contained a sequence of phonemes meeting their list of partial specifications, they got 96 percent correct *words,* with most of the remaining errors confusing "a" and "the." This study provides the basis for building a speech-understanding system.

One such system, now in the pilot stage of development, is the LUNAR system being built by William Woods and his co-workers. The microworld of LUNAR is a data base on moon rocks, listing for each sample, phase, and constituent, the data on amounts found, who did the measurements, and how the measurements are made. The first stage of the LUNAR project, successfully completed, was to automate the answering of queries that a geologist might *type* in about moon rocks. This part of the system uses techniques like those used in Winograd's system, translating sentences in ordinary English into one-shot computer programs for extracting the answer from the data base. The next stage in development of LUNAR is to program the computer so that it can also handle *spoken* queries. In the rest of this section we outline the way in which the LUNAR system is expected to handle speech when fully programmed.

Working on the spectrogram, the system might segment part of the input into three phonemes

$$\begin{pmatrix} l \\ \text{or} \\ w \end{pmatrix} \begin{pmatrix} \text{front} \\ \text{vowel} \end{pmatrix} \begin{pmatrix} s \\ \text{or} \\ z \end{pmatrix}$$

where a front vowel is the type of vowel made at the front of the mouth. Consulting a dictionary, three words would be found that meet these alternatives:

LESS
LIST
WAS

Given the type of questions it usually gets, LUNAR would order LIST as the most likely interpretation, followed by WAS, and then LESS. The normal procedure, of which this is an example, is to use three phonemes (there may be phonemes between them) to direct each dictionary lookup. With only two phonemes, there may be too many consistent words; with more than three phonemes, errors may block retrieval of any dictionary entries.

Once a number of words have been found in this way, syntactic and semantic programs can be used to help work out "blurred" phonemes. For example, if the system has decoded

LIST POTASSIUM RUBIDIUM RATIO

the syntactic procedure suggests that -*s* is the next phoneme, and so can give this hypothesis to the phoneme analyzer to test.

It turns out that short function words like FOR tend to be very fuzzily pronounced. Usually, the longer content words are much easier to pick out of the spectrogram, and the system can then use syntax to *predict* the small function words in a speech string, and then test phonemic match. This will usually be poor, and the next word is a good indicator of the likely correctness of the match. The phonemic analysis often yields many distinct interpretations:

$$\begin{pmatrix} \text{BEEN} \\ \text{DID} \\ \text{DONE} \\ \text{ANY} \end{pmatrix} \begin{pmatrix} \text{EIGHTY} \\ \text{ANY} \end{pmatrix} \text{PEOPLE} \begin{pmatrix} \text{DONE} \\ \text{BULK} \end{pmatrix} \text{ANALYSES} \begin{pmatrix} \text{IN} \\ \text{ON} \end{pmatrix} \cdot \cdot \cdot$$

and the system may use both syntax and knowledge of the rock sample microworld to come up with the choice

HAVE ANY PEOPLE DONE ANALYSES ON . . .

It would then call a phonemic reanalysis to check the hypothesis that the first word is HAVE, rather than any of the alternatives previously listed.

Suggestions for Further Reading

B. Raphael: "The Thinking Computer." Freeman, San Francisco, California, 1976.
Chapter 6 gives a very good overview of computer understanding of natural language.

E. F. Codd: Seven Steps to Rendezvous with the Casual User, IBM Research Laboratory, San Jose, California, RJ 1333 (#20842), January 17, 1974.
The aim of this work is to let a data base be used by a casual user who cannot be expected to be knowledgeable about computers, programming, logic, or relations, and who is unwilling to learn even a simple artificial language or artificial constraints placed on a natural language like English.

T. Winograd: A Procedural Model of Language Understanding, in "Computer Models of Thought and Language" (R. C. Schank and K. M. Colby, eds.), pp. 152–186. Freeman, San Francisco, California, 1973.
This is a useful account of both the language processing and planning procedures programmed into the system for the blocks microworld.

W. A. Woods: Progress in Natural Language Understanding—An Application to Lunar Geology, *Proceedings of the National Computer Conference,* 1974, pp. 441–450.
Early steps in the design of the LUNAR system are presented.

Summary

Successful computer systems have been restricted to **microworlds.** Codd's data base query system engages in a **clarification** dialog to build up a formal query equivalent to the English query typed in by the user. Winograd's system uses **syntax** and **semantics** to respond to quite complex English commands, queries, and novel information about the blocks world. Wood's system uses a dictionary to reduce phoneme ambiguity, as well as syntactic and semantic processes, in answering queries about the microworld of moon rock samples.

Glossary

Language: A *language* is a systematic way of arranging symbols into strings to express meaning. It may be a *natural language* like English, Chinese, or Swahili that humans use to communicate with one another; or a *programming language* in which to write programs for a computer.

Linguistics: *Linguistics* is the study of language. This includes the study of *syntax*—what it is that makes a sentence grammatical—and *semantics*—how the words of a sentence work together to give the sentence its overall meaning. *Parsing* is the process of breaking a string of words into the pieces—such as noun phrase and verb phrase—specified by the syntax.

Microworld: A *microworld* is a limited "world"—such as the blocks world, or the subject matter of a specialized data base—that restricts the semantics of a computer program for planning or natural language understanding.

Context: The *context* of an item is the material surrounding the item that helps define its meaning. For example, "pen" has different meanings in the two contexts "The pig is in the pen" and "The ink is in the pen." Similarly, a lion has a different "meaning" in the context of a zoo or of wide-open spaces.

Clarification: In a natural language understanding system, a *clarification response* is one that the computer makes to get the user to provide more information that the computer needs before it can respond to the user's original input.

Phoneme: A basic sound of spoken language, such as a simple vowel or consonant, is a *phoneme.*

Spectrogram: A *spectrogram* is an analysis of sound by a graph that shows, at each point in time, how much energy there is in the various "high notes" and "low notes."

Exercises

1. Two characteristics of language: language is sound and language is linear. First, spoken language is primary, and written language only represents it. Second, the symbols occur in a distinct arrangement of succession, one after another. Explain briefly why each of these makes computer understanding of natural language a difficult problem, but a possible one.

2. Two more characteristics of language: language is systematic and language is a system of systems. First, not all possible combinations of symbols can occur. There is structure, which can be modeled. Second, a language has a phoneme system (not all sounds you can make are used), a grammatical system, a semantic system, and so on, rather than being a single, easily described structure. Explain briefly why each of these makes computer understanding of natural language a difficult problem, but a possible one.

3. If the possible objects in the "blocks world" are box, pyramid, block; and each could either be small, medium, or large; and each could be colored green, red, or blue; then (a) how many distinct object-size-color possibilities are there? (b) how many possible two-object towers are there?

4. Give at least two other meaningful (if odd) parses of the highly ambiguous sentence "Time flies like an arrow." and explain their meanings by paraphrase.

5. Indicate whether the following statements are true or false.
- (a) A speech-understanding system might use an optical character reader.
- (b) Language-understanding systems require standard format input.
- (c) The "blocks world" system adds novel information to a data base.
- (d) Natural language understanding systems must analyze their own programs.
- (e) Natural language programs are helpless when confronted by idioms.
- (f) "All mimsy were the borogoves" has unusual syntax but normal semantics.
- (g) Microworlds free the programmer from concern for context.
- (h) Parsing is unnecessary for speech understanding.

6. There is an African tribe whose people nod their heads vertically to indicate "no" and shake their heads horizontally to indicate "yes"—the opposite meaning of these gestures in our culture. Which aspect of language is this difference manifested in, syntax or semantics? Explain.

7. Why do many computer scientists experiment with microworlds rather than trying to represent the patterns of reality as considered by the Club of Rome? What good is a microworld? Suggest one microworld not mentioned in the text with which you would be interested in having a machine discussion. Give reasons for why you think it would be easy or hard to put the microworld on a computer.

8. Is the following sentence of Noam Chomsky's invention grammatical?

"Colorless green ideas sleep furiously."

How meaningful is it? Does it have some impressionistic, poetic, evocative content?

9. The U.S. Military services tend to name their inventory in the following curious manner: "Lining, polyurethane, for box, wooden, 10″ × 10″ × 10″, bomb, antipersonnel, type x-7, for storage of." Should such descriptions be parsed left-to-right or right-to-left? Why is such a system of nomenclature used?

10. A speech understanding system could work very well and easily if it had a limited vocabulary—say 100 words—with unambiguous meaning, and which were selected to sound very distinct and clear. Such systems are just now becoming available. Name four practical or amusing uses—be specific and give some sample inputs.

11. What advantages are there in having natural-language-understanding systems respond to idioms (the language peculiar to a people of a district, community, or class)? How is this response accomplished? How is it unlike most language usage?

5.4. COMPUTERS IN WAR AND PEACE

Throughout human history, many of the greatest inventions have had both strong military applications and also many peaceful ones. Gunpowder revolutionized the pace of war, and yet gunpowder is also extremely useful in mining and quarrying operations. The discovery of the proper use of magnets was a boon to navigation, and this meant that both traders and navies could sail further and more confidently than before. Ideas about programming some intelligence into machines also have both military and civilian applications.

Guided Missiles

As we saw in our study of **feedback** systems in Section 3.1, the whole field of **cybernetics** grew out of the insights of Norbert Wiener's study of World War II artillery. In earlier wars, when guns were fired at towns or at slowly moving armies, the gunner could consult tables which showed him how to elevate his gun for different ranges and wind conditions to get a good chance of hitting the target. By World War II, however, the speed of airplanes had set two new problems for the gunner: First, it was hard to obtain a good fix on a fast-moving airplane; and, second, the round is *not* to be fired at where the plane is *now* but at where the plane *will be* when the round intercepts the plane's trajectory.

Wiener in the United States and Kolmogorov in the Soviet Union developed a theory to handle these problems, taking account of measurement errors people would make in measuring the plane's position. It showed how to take the data points (sightings of the plane) and make the best **estimation** as to the **trajectory** that a plane would be following (Fig. 1) unless the pilot suddenly decided to change course. With this theory, the gunner could use data about the gun and wind velocity to aim at the place the plane was most likely to be when a gun's shell intercepted the trajectory. The theory thus has the two crucial ingredients of **smoothing**—compensating for errors in the information being used—and **prediction,** or **extrapolation**—building upon available data to make good guesses about what will happen in the future.

When a ball is in your hand and you are in the process of throwing it, you have a great deal of control over how fast it will go, in what

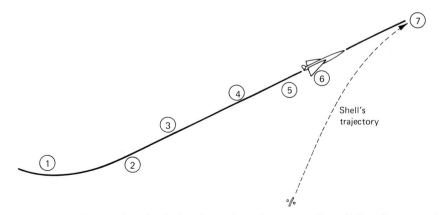

Fig. 1 The numbers in circles show where the gunner *thought* the plane was at different times. The curve shows the best estimate of the trajectory that can be made using these observations. Instead of aiming at the plane's present position (6), the gunner aims at (7), where the plane is predicted to be when the shell hits the plane's estimated trajectory.

direction it will go, and whether it will have spin on it. Once it has left your hand, however, you cannot change its movement. A **ballistic missile** (such as a bullet or a cannonball) is like this ball, with no control over the projectile once it is fired. To go beyond ballistics, the missile needs guidance and tracking. One type of **guided missile** has engines and radio control, so that the gunner can apply midcourse corrections to the trajectory. One current approach is to have a TV camera in the nose cone of the missile, to feed a picture back to the human on the ground or in a plane who can steer the missile.

Going even further, one can build *feedback* (Section 3.1) into the system, so that it can automatically *track* its target using some error measure. One recent development of this kind is a heat-seeking missile: If it is fired into a region of sky where there are enemy planes, there is only one place in that region that is hot, namely where the jet engines are. The missile shifts direction and measures temperature to see if it is getting warmer or colder. If it is getting warmer, it continues in that direction; but if it finds it is getting colder it changes direction. In this way it will hunt out the direction of the jet engines, advance till it makes contact with the surface of the plane, and then explode.

However, this technique is of little use in a "dog fight" in which planes from both sides are close together. In this case, the hot jets may belong to a plane of either side. One new approach to this problem is the **laser designator.** Once the missile is up in the air, someone on the ground or in another plane aims a weak **laser beam** at the target. This is much weaker than the James Bond burn-you-dead-type laser beam and does not damage the target—but it does make a clearly visible line of light pointing at the enemy vehicle. The optical system on board the missile can then lock onto that beam and fly down it, exploding when it hits the surface at the end of the beam.

Another increasing use of the computer is in automatic guidance systems for aircraft. Air forces already have fully automatic, pilotless, reconnaissance planes. While pilots are still more versatile than automatic guidance systems, they require a cockpit, a life-support system, and an ejection system, which increase both payload and cost per pound. Even in piloted planes, the automatic pilot takes over for much of normal flight. Low-flying fighter planes can now be equipped with terrain-following radar that can control a plane when it is near the ground to ensure that it maintains a certain height above the ground no matter how hilly it gets. These developments, which are changing the face of air war, are also going to be very useful in improving the safety of civil aviation. Already, the Boeing 747 is an easier plane to fly than the Boeing 707 because it is a generation later, and incorporates many new automatic devices to help the pilot in his task. The length of a 747 is greater than the length of the first airplane flight ever made—by the Wright brothers at Kitty Hawk—so the thought of piloting one is really rather frightening! It could not be done without the developments in control technology that allow so many of the variables involved in a plane of that size to be automatically taken care of by computers using feedback (recall Fig. 8 of Section 3.1). This allows the pilot to content himself with "mapping the grand strategy" of the plane's maneuvers.

ARPA, the Advanced Research Projects Agency of the United States Department of Defense, has been providing research funds for what it calls SIAM, the Self-Initiating Antiaircraft Munition. A plane will make a bombing run over an enemy airport and drop a couple of bombs to let the enemy think that this is the aim of the mission. However, the real goal would be to drop SIAMs, which bury themselves in the ground. They have sensors that can detect when planes land at the airfield, and the SIAM can then fire missiles to destroy the plane. It is as if a guerilla were stationed at the edge of the airport waiting for an appropriate target to arrive. Using the technology already mentioned, the missile can be designed to fix itself on the target and destroy it with great accuracy.

It is always worth remembering how "ancient" much of this is. The sophistication is new, but the general idea of automatic weapons is very old. A mine field is an example of an automatic weapon. If the navy wants to block enemy access to a harbor, they seed it with mines—except perhaps for a small channel to give their own ships access to the harbor. However, when the war is over and they have secured the territory, they then have the problem of getting rid of the mines. This "mine-clearing" problem is present for the SIAMs, too. Suppose an airfield had six SIAMs. One way to clear the airfield is to send in six drones (remotely controlled aircraft) to have them blown up, using the missiles; or one might have the SIAM responsive to some sort of radio signal that will deactivate it. Another approach might be to make the SIAM selective, so that it is only activated when it detects the types of planes the enemy uses. This means that if the enemy captures one of your planes, they can safely use that airport, but will otherwise be in trouble. One can imagine a crazy situation where each side has captured the other's planes and so are safe from the other side's SIAMs, but get blown up by their own!

PHALANX, a United States Navy antimissile missile, recently identified the Santa Barbara islands as a missile. Thus, just as for computers in general, we can expect any such complex system to have "bugs." Before you use a system, you must remove most of the bugs, and have some safety measures to ensure that if bugs do crop up later, they will not have catastrophic costs. It is worth stressing, though, that the *goals* of the system must be appropriate if the "debugging" process is to have any value. We shall talk more of the case for and against the development of weapon systems in the last subsection of this section.

Sensor Arrays

Turning to a heavier use of computers in the battlefield, we have the development of the idea of the **pinball-machine battlefield.** The battleground is seeded with various **sensors**—one device can transmit a particular signal when movement or vibration occurs nearby (as when a truck rolls by); another can detect the heat from the body temperature of someone moving by; while other sensors detect the sound of someone walking, or the smell of sweat or urine or food.

One approach to the pinball-machine battlefield is the U.S. Army's REMBASS (Remotely Monitored Battlefield Sensory System). The idea is to build a fairly indestructible self-contained unit that contains a full set of sensors. Then, to "wire up" a battlefield, planes "bomb" the area with a large number of sensor units. Instead of exploding on impact, the units bury themselves in the ground. In this way, a whole area can be instrumented in a matter of hours. An array of perhaps tens of thousands of signals from sensors scattered all over the battlefield could then be relayed back to a computer which would carry out a **pattern recognition** process of the kind we discussed in Section 5.2. The job of the computer would be to look at the various features it was receiving and try to compute the location of a possible target. Then it could call in an air strike on that region, or could itself fire missiles, targeting them toward the indicated place.

Such a system requires that the area concerned be declared a **free-fire zone**—that the army keep their own troops out of the area, and state that anyone or anything moving in the area is an enemy, and so can be fired on. Free-fire zones are a common feature of war, having nothing to do with computers. They simplify the soldier's task, relieving him of the job of telling friend from foe. The tragedy of such a decision is that all too often innocent civilians are in the area, and have no knowledge that they are in a free-fire zone until it is too late; and, even if they knew, their only escape would be to abandon their homes and join the stream of refugees.

The technology of instrumenting a large area with sensors and using computers to extract from the array of sensor signals the location of "targets" has peacetime applications, too. Instead of a battleground, one instruments a lake. Sensors that are responsive to movements and to different chemical concentrations can be put on a buoy or fixed to a lump of cement and dropped to the lake bottom. This sets up a rough grid so that the computer can roughly map out the concentrations over space and time. Programs then determine whether there is now a region that is getting too polluted, and use techniques like those discussed in Section 3.2, Prey and Predators, to work out what seem to be the chemical deficiencies involved, and on that basis call in a "strike." Now a strike is not the dropping of a bomb, but rather the addition of various chemicals to help that portion of the lake "come back to life." Alternatively, the system might detect a large school of fish, and compute whether it is large enough to allow fishing vessels to take a sizable catch without damaging the vital balance of the lake. Thus we see that sensor array technology is being developed both as a military tool and as an ecological tool.

One of the basic technological advances of World War II was to use **echolocation**—as bats use the echoes of their own high-pitched screeching to locate prey—to pinpoint the presence of submarines. An observer in a submarine sends out sound waves and the returning echoes—as well as engine noises—can be used to locate and classify other shipping. The United States Navy is extending this idea to develop SOSUS (Sound Surveillance Undersea System) to use a network of underwater microphones to monitor submarines. ARPA is funding a similar development—a land-based array of microphones to pinpoint artillery some miles away. A computer program will decode the sound coming in to solve two problems: The first is to tell fairly accurately *where* the sounds are coming from, despite the noise of other guns which make it hard to judge where any single gun is. The second is to tell *what* types of guns are firing, to figure out if they are "friendly" or, if not, to determine appropriate counter-measures.

Surprisingly, this technology of "signal separation" should also prove useful in brain research. A researcher inserts an electrode by a neuron of an animal whose brain he is trying to understand. Usually, he obtains a mixture of different signals coming in because there are many different cells nearby in the brain. If he obtains a trace with different peaks as in Fig. 2, he may infer that there are really two units there, one that gives large electrical signals and one that gives small electrical signals. The traces are, however, seldom as clean as this example. Thus brain researchers, too, want to know how to figure out,

Fig. 2   A trace of the combined electrical activity from two brain cells, A and B.

from the response of an array of sensors, the location of the sources of the signals, and the nature of the signals they are sending. Understanding the brain is important to us both in terms of our general intellectual interest in understanding this most complex system, and in learning how to correct defects in the brain, carry out improved brain surgery, and so on.

Some Moral Issues

What were your emotions as you read the preceding material? Excitement at the fantastic abilities of the new weapon systems? Horror at the billions of dollars being spent on new ways of killing people? Pride that the same basic research can increase the military and economic strength of a nation? Perhaps a complicated, even inconsistent, mixture of these feelings? In the rest of the section, we discuss some of the moral issues raised by such feelings.

By the end of the Vietnam war, many Americans believed that *any* contribution to a military effort was wrong. Yet, during World War II, there seemed little doubt—after some hesitation—on the part of the Allies about the justice of fighting Hitler, with his slaughter of six million Jews and many other atrocities. However, the horror of Hitler did not mean that all forms of counteratrocity were justified. One can get a very good feeling for the human dimensions of decisions about the proper level of military efforts by reading books about the Manhattan Project that developed the atom bomb for the United States and Britain in World War II. The scientists working on this project were in many cases men of high conscience who wrestled with the following problem: There was a good chance that the Germans would be able to develop the atom bomb. Some of the best nuclear physicists, like Werner Heisenberg, were in Germany. The Manhattan project scientists were convinced that nothing could be worse than for the Nazis to take over the world. Thus they saw that, as a short-range goal, they had to develop the atom bomb before the Nazis did. However, they also saw that the world would be a more terrifying place if armies had access to the atom bomb. Thus many scientists worked on two problems at the same time—how to develop the atom bomb, and how to convince the politicians and the military not to abuse it. Many worked very hard—although, as it turned out, ineffectively—to convince the then United States President, Harry Truman, that he should not drop atom bombs on Japan.

Is it the "right thing," then, for people to work on building weapon systems? Many citizens will feel it is their patriotic duty to make sure their country is militarily strong. Others will note that sales of munitions to other countries bring in billions of dollars in export revenue, and that this alone justifies the production of weapon systems that are competitive on the international market—no matter how horrible the wars may be in which people use them. Finally, of course, the majority of people in the "defense industry" work there because that is where they can find jobs—and because a regular paycheck is far more important to them than any abstract moral issue.

What is the position of a scientist who does not approve of the development of weapon systems and so does not work on explicitly military projects? If he sees a civilian spin-off from some military research project but cannot see any justification for the military application itself, he may well campaign for the denial of funds to the military program, and insist that the peaceful application be funded explicitly. In this way, the United States scientific community rallied to stop the appropriation of funds for the antiballistic missile program.

A more difficult question is the following: Is a scientist a hypocrite if he conducts basic research for a peacetime project, when he knows that it may well have military applications of which he disapproves? For example, we want to understand the mechanisms of the brain that let us perceive and feel and love and think and move and talk and give lectures and get angry. We know that to understand this we have to get into the brain and carry out recordings from different neurons. We know, however, that that is going to require a technology that can take an array of recording devices and use the signals to figure out the activity of many different brain cells, to get some idea of how different parts of the brain work together. However, we have already seen that any real progress on the basic principles of a system of this kind can also help to build military systems that will pinpoint the presence of enemy guns from an array of microphones. It seems too extreme to ban this type of brain research to avoid the risk of a military spin-off. By the same argument, the cavemen should not have developed stone knives because while these certainly allowed them to increase their range of foodstuffs, it also increased their ability to kill each other.

Brain research has more direct problems. If we understand how to use drugs and surgery to heal a shattered brain, we then have more techniques that can be used for interrogation and "brainwashing." The new technologies require vigilant use of safeguards of citizen's rights if they are not to be abused.

Large-scale computer systems which can monitor great piles of data and predict trends, are, as we saw in Chapter 3, vital to controlling pollution, population, and the deterioration of our resources. Yet, at the same time, these large-scale computer systems have immense military applications. One of the ironies of history is that the Congress of the United States, which has done so much to provide funds for the development of computers and control systems, has acted most often on a fear basis. It has allocated funds through the Department of Defense more than seeking out and funding the civilian applications. It is the task of the citizen in a democracy to acquire enough of an appreciation of these systems to help his representatives make intelligent choices about the proper growth of technology. How does the citizen learn enough to influence these decisions, and what role can he play in an increasingly technological society? We shall discuss these issues in Sections 6.2, Computers and the Media, and 7.2, Democracy in the Computer Age.

Suggestions for Further Reading

N. Wiener, "I Am a Mathematician," MIT Press, Cambridge, Massachusetts, 1964.
   The second volume of Wiener's autobiography. See especially Chapters 12, the War Years; 14, Moral Problems of a Scientist—the Atomic Bomb; and 15, Nancy, Cybernetics, Paris, and After. (Nancy is the name of a town in France!)
P. Stanford, The Automated Battlefield, *The New York Times Magazine,* February 23, 1975, p. 12.
   Discusses the weapon systems mentioned in this section, giving references to military journals in which further information can be found.
R. Jungk, "Brighter than a Thousand Suns," Harcourt, New York, 1958.
   This is a readable account of the development of the atomic bomb.

Summary

We recalled the growth of **cybernetics** from the design of control systems for World War II artillery, and explored some new types of design for **guided missiles.** We saw how computers could monitor input from an array of **sensors**—to call "strikes" on a battlefield, or to control the ecology of a lake. We closed with a discussion of some of the issues raised in trying to find the proper balance between military and civilian research.

Glossary

Cybernetics: *Cybernetics* is the study of computation, communication, and control in the animal and the machine. It has been extended to the study of information processing in social systems too, in which humans may interact with machines.

Feedback: The process whereby output signals are fed back to the input of a system, so that the system can respond to information about its own performance, is *feedback*. A *negative feedback* system uses this information to negate (or at least reduce) the *error signal*—which is the difference between the actual output and some desired output.

Trajectory: The *trajectory* is the path followed by the variables of a system as they change over time.

Estimation: *Estimation* means going from partial data to some estimate of the process that was measured to obtain the data. If the process is one that changes over time, then two important types of estimation are *smoothing*—compensating for errors in the information being used—and *prediction* or *extrapolation*—building upon available data to make good estimates of what will happen in the future.

Ballistic missile: A *ballistic missile* is one that can be aimed, but—in contrast with a guided missile—whose course cannot be corrected once it has been fixed.

Guided missile: A *guided missile* is one that can not only be aimed but—in contrast to a ballistic missile—can have its aim altered in midcourse, either by a human or by a computer.

Laser: A *laser* is a device that emits a beam of coherent light (the light waves are all of the same precise "color," i.e., of exactly the same frequency). A weak laser beam is not destructive, but a high-energy laser beam can melt heavy armor in a fraction of a second.

Laser designator: A device that uses a weak laser beam to pinpoint a target for a guided missile is a *laser designator*.

Receptor or **Sensor:** A special device which responds to light, sound, etc., and converts it into signals for the brain or a computer is a *receptor* or *sensor*.

Pinball-machine battlefield: This is a battleground seeded with sensors that feed a computer programmed to detect enemy movements.

Free-fire zone: An area in which an army decrees that anyone or anything moving is an enemy, and so can be fired upon, is a *free-fire zone.*

Pattern recognition: *Pattern recognition* is the process whereby a computer can recognize a pattern—such as telling which letter of the alphabet a squiggle of lines is meant to be. As such, it often requires the use of context.

Echolocation: Bats emit high chirping sounds, and *locate* their prey, or obstacles in their flight path, by the pattern of *echoes* they receive in turn. Technology can use this process, too, although not necessarily using sound waves.

Exercises

1. The MIRV, or Multiple Independently Targeted Reentry Vehicle, is a weapon system design in which several nuclear warheads are released from one rocket "bus" which, while in space, changes course, speed, and direction so that each warhead proceeds ballistically to a different target. Thousands of missiles are now being converted to MIRVs. What kind of problems must be solved by a MIRV on-board computer? What constraints does its location as a rocket payload put on its characteristics?

2. How is it possible to predict the most likely future position of an airplane by cybernetic means? Can't it go anywhere the pilot wants to by totally unpredictable evasion tactics?

3. Choose the word or phrase that best completes each of the following sentences.
- (a) Automatically aimed antiaircraft guns were developed in _____. (1) WWI, (2) WWII, (3) the Korean War, (4) the Vietnam war.
- (b) "Smoothing" is a cybernetic technique for _____. (1) compensating for errors, (2) making guesses about future positions, (3) eliminating instabilities in rocket motor performance, (4) applying midcourse corrections to a ballistic missile.
- (c) A ballistic missile is one which is _____. (1) guided by radio, (2) heat-seeking, (3) steered by remote TV, (4) unguided, like a bullet.
- (d) A laser designator _____. (1) is a communication device, (2) is an anti-tank weapon, (3) optically guides a missile, (4) can burn a hole in 6" steel plate.
- (e) SIAM stands for _____. (1) Semi-automatic Infrared Antiballistic Missile, (2) Signal-Initiated Anti-aircraft Mine, (3) Self-Initiating Antiaircraft Munition, (4) Sensor Input Automatic Missile.
- (f) One approach to the "pinball-machine battlefield" is _____. (1) SIAM, (2) PHALANX, (3) REMBASS, (4) ARPA.

4. Give two examples of military technology that were developed simultaneously in different countries during World War II, each using new scientific principles.

5. Match each item in the first column with the appropriate item in the second.

1.	Harry Truman	a.	ordered bomb on Nagasaki
2.	U.S. scientific community	b.	anti-ballistic missile
3.	ABM	c.	good for brain and battlefield
4.	free-fire zone	d.	used by bats and submarines
5.	laser designator	e.	claimed island was missile
6.	array of sensors	f.	rallied against ABM
7.	echolocation	g.	anyone moving is foe
8.	PHALANX	h.	useful in "dogfights"

6. Do you think that the techniques mentioned in this section, by making killing more impersonal, increase the chances, dangers, and nature of war?

7. Dolphins can, by echolocation (which means "using echoes to locate things") distinguish between different species of the same-sized fish, judge distance with great accuracy, tell substances apart, and navigate through mazelike coral reefs undisturbed by the sounds of other dolphins. An immense chunk of the dolphins' larger-than-human brain is devoted to auditory processing. What does this suggest for the complexity of computerized echolocation systems for submarines?

8. Computers play good checkers and mediocre chess. Does this suggest a sufficiently advanced modeling of strategy to plan battles by machine? (You might investigate the role of computer battle simulation in the American invasion of Cambodia, and other fiascos.)

9. When Neil Armstrong and "Buzz" Aldrin landed the Eagle on the Sea of Tranquility on the Moon, 10 July 1969, the on-board computer, linked to the descent engines and the radar, was supposed to have made the landing automatically. But the computer fell behind in its calculations, temporarily overwhelmed by radar data, and the pilot brought the spacecraft in by hand. In the split-second decisions of warfare, when do you think it is safe to leave machines irreversibly in charge? Would you be comfortable in a robot-piloted airplane?

10. Terrain-following radar allows automatically piloted planes to fly hundreds of miles at speeds over a thousand miles per hour at altitudes of only hundreds or scores of feet. This makes it possible to fly in beneath radar coverage, unspotted by sky-scanning defense systems. Radar itself evolved as a countertactic to sudden air raids. Do you think that each advance in military technology creates a defensive counteradvance? How might this affect military research, funding, and development? Why did the scientific community reject the ABM (Antiballistic Missile)?

11. Some work was done in the 1960s on a "man amplifier"—a hydraulically powered articulated framework of metal arms and legs. A man straps himself into it, and his motions are sensed and cybernetically amplified so that the man–machine system can run, lift weights, and so on, but with superhuman strength. Feedback allows the human operator to feel the resistance of the device to objects being handled [see Robert Heinlein's "Starship Troopers" for an excellent fictionalized treatment of their use in battle].

    Name two uses a soldier might make of a "man amplifier." Can you name two possible peaceful applications?

12. How do you think aerial combat is affected when one soldier on the ground with a heat-seeking bazooka missile can down a jet fighter? What good is a fleet of hundreds of long-range bombers if small guided missiles become cheaper and more effective?

13. *Library project:* See the article on accurate guided missile technology in the July 1975 *Scientific American*. How dependent are these systems on computers? Why are on-board computers necessary? Why is increased accuracy considered more important than increased warhead power? How do the new systems change military policy?

6

Learning and Working

SECTION 6.1. COMPUTERS IN EDUCATION

The computer can be used both to present material to a student—
tutorial mode CAI (computer-assisted instruction)—and to drill the student in material already studied—**drill and practice CAI.** In **dialog–inquiry CAI,** the system can also respond to questions asked by the student about the subject matter under instruction. By contrast, the **discovery mode** of computer use in education lets the student design projects on which he wishes to work using the computer as a tool for carrying out those projects. We discuss the role of the teacher, and the impact of computers both inside and outside the classroom. Most of the section requires only Section 1.1, The Idea of a Program, as background. However, the discussion of dialog–inquiry CAI will be enriched by a study of Section 5.3, Understanding Natural Language.

SECTION 6.2. INFORMATION FLOW IN THE CYBERNETIC SOCIETY

This section first examines the way in which the news is prepared. The computer can help relatively little. Rather, it is political freedom that is the crucial factor in the flow of news in a cybernetic society. We see how computers may be used to make it easier for people to contact others with similar interests, as well as to track down jobs and so on. We look at the impact of computer techniques on the design of libraries, and see how computer networking can bring many of the facilities of a library into the home. Most of the section is self-contained, but the discussion of libraries uses the concept of computer-assisted instruction from Section 6.1.

SECTION 6.3. THE IMPACT OF AUTOMATION

The **industrial revolution** saw increasing use of heavy machinery, with the concentration of workers in the factories in which the machines were housed. The **assembly line** breaks production into many small tasks, with each worker carrying out one task again and again as products move by on the line. **Automation** turns many of these tasks over to machines. We examine the benefits and drawbacks of automation, and the new tasks it sets the unions. We look at the many ways in which computers can affect car production. Finally, we see how technology can be used to *humanize* work in a factory. This section requires *no* background from other sections.

6.1.   COMPUTERS IN EDUCATION

Through education we learn about ourselves, our society, and our world. Much of that education is informal—we learn as we explore our neighborhoods, interact with people, read, watch TV, dream, and so on. There is, however, also the formal education of school—where we are taught the basic skills and knowledge of our society. Our school education, if it is a good one, pulls us in two directions—it gives us the skills to become a responsible job-holding citizen; yet it also gives us a perspective that stops us from simply accepting society the way it is.

At first sight, it might be thought that a computer can only help drill us in the way things are—programming us to repeat predetermined sequences of activities for achieving predetermined goals. In the next subsection, we shall see that **computer-assisted instruction (CAI)** can indeed be used to help students master arithmetic, vocabulary, and language skills.

However, we shall see that the computer can also be used to help the student make his own discoveries. The stress here is not so much on "what to do" but on "how to figure out what to do"—not on answering a single question, but on discovering procedures to answer that question and many more like it. Given the present rapid pace of change in society, it is clear that the emphasis in education has to be less on "this is the way it is always done" and more on *applying what you know in new situations.*

This increasing importance of "education for discovery" by no means downgrades the importance of the accumulated wisdom of a nation or a culture. The lessons of history, an analysis of social innovations that did or did not work, and an account of science and technology are all important additions to the mental equipment of the citizen. Care must be taken, however, to enable the student to relate these lessons to his own needs and perspective. This does not mean that a teacher should teach only what the student already believes is relevant. It does mean, however, that teachers must try to show students the full relevance of what they teach, noting that this relevance may well depend on the social background as well as the technical skills of the individual student. Using computers, students can take what they learn of this accumulated wisdom and develop and test their own models on the computer, learning to deal with their failures of understanding by debugging their programs. Thus the computer increasingly lets knowledge be something that can immediately be used, rather than something that must simply be learned for an exam. Another important benefit of using the computer as a tool for discovery is that most students find it fun to play with computers, trying out their ideas for new programs—and so students can get enjoyably involved in their work.

Two further points need to be made:

The first is that the computer is only one part of the process. Just as books changed the role of the teacher, so computers will change his role, too. With a good textbook available, the teacher can stress the essential points of a topic, leaving it to students to study the details by themselves. With computers available, the teacher need work less on drilling the students, and can assign homework problems of an interesting complexity. A good teacher is still needed, however, to provide human interest and motivation, and respond to the needs of individual students—for praise and for discipline, as much as for information—in a highly personal way.

The second is that education is a life-long process, and we can expect many of the ideas discussed in this section to have an impact in the home as well as the school—thanks to personal computers and home consoles (Section 2.3).

We now turn to an examination of some specific uses of the computer in education.

Drill and Practice CAI

We first examine frame-oriented CAI, in which the student sits at a computer terminal and works through a sequence of **frames.** These blocks of instructional material were entered in advance by an **author**—who may be a teacher or a CAI programming specialist. A frame may offer information, and will test the student by posing questions. The information may be textual or may include the presentation of pictures or the playing of sounds. The virtue of the computer is that the student does not have to follow through the frames in a fixed sequence irrespective of the depth of his understanding. Rather, the computer has within its program for each frame both expected correct answers and diagnostics to take incorrect answers and use them to determine how to respond to the student.

The simplest use of CAI is for **drill and practice,** using the computer to drill in facts which have already been taught by other means. For arithmetic drill, for example, the computer can present problems, and then wait while the student types in an answer. If the answer is correct, the computer will then type out another problem. If the answer is wrong, the computer will request the student to work through the problem again. Similar use can be made of the computer for drill in grammar, typing, and so on. The programs for drill and practice are very simple, and are composed of a string of frames of the kind shown in Fig. 1.

The simplest way to use such frames is to have the student answer question after question until finally he has finished the whole list of questions stored in the computer, or has tired of the whole game and turned the computer off. However, a program that consists of a string of frames of this kind is not a very good one. What if the student does not know the answer to one of the questions? In tests of simple arithmetic skills, the student probably will hit on the right answer eventually, but if he is being drilled in French vocabulary, there is very little chance that he will be able to guess a word he does not know. Because of this, we need a more flexible program.

A frame in such a program might look like that shown in Fig. 2. We see that it differs from the frame of Fig. 1 in that instead of making the student try again and again and again until getting the right answer, he is given two chances. If he does not get it right the second time, the correct answer is typed out.

Figure 3 shows the overall program for sequencing the individual blocks. Each time the student signs on, he will have to type in some keyword to indicate on what type of subject and on what type of

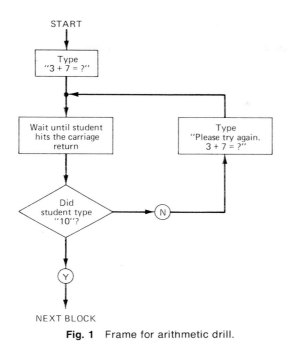

Fig. 1 Frame for arithmetic drill.

lesson he is working. Arith3, then, might be the keyword for the drill for the third lesson on arithmetic. The first statement in Fig. 3 tells the computer to use the list stored in memory as List Arith3—the list of frames for the third arithmetic drill. The program works through one frame at a time, removing it from the list if the student gets the right answer, repeating it on the list if the student gets it wrong. Thus the first test checks to see if the list has been exhausted yet—which, of course, it will not have been until the student has answered a great many questions. However, once the list is empty, we get the computer to print out some farewell message.

If the list is not empty, then we go to a routine called "Pick a frame." This could be designed in many different ways. One way might be to take the first frame from the list, while another might be to pick a frame at random. In any case, the program then transfers control to the entry point of the frame. Then, a process such as that shown in Fig. 2 is followed, which of course will differ depending on the particular problem on which the student is being drilled.

To make this system really effective, we should also program the computer to remember with what problem the student has had trouble, and give him another chance to try it again. Hopefully, after several repetitions, the student will get it right. If the student gets the right answer, whether on the first or second try, the frame returns control to the main program via Exit A. In this case, the program removes that frame from the list—since the student got it right without being told the answer, the program will not ask him to do that job again—and then goes back to repeat the process. If, on the other hand, the student does not get the right answer even after two tries, we add the frame to the list before repeating the process. Note that when we picked the frame we did not remove it from the list. Thus

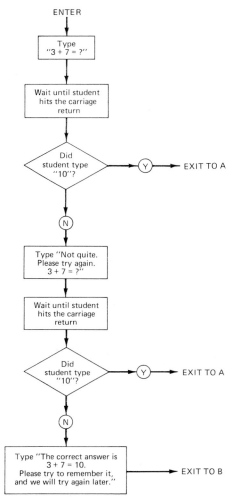

Fig. 2 A frame for arithmetic drill that helps the student who does not know the answer. The computer branches to different places depending on whether the student got the right answer (EXIT TO A) or not (EXIT TO B).

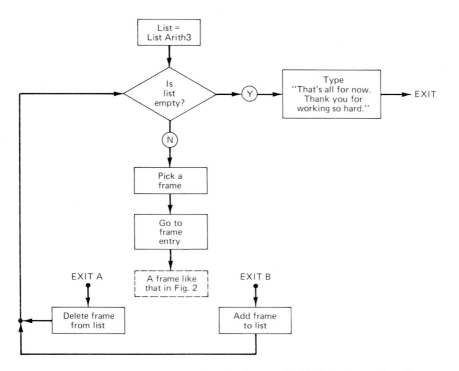

Fig. 3   A program to keep track of the frames the student has mastered.

there are now two copies of that frame on the list. The idea here is that since the student could not get it right the first time, we had better make doubly sure that he has learned it before we remove it from the list. Let us now see two ways in which this sort of program could be improved:

First, consider the fact that the fourth box of Fig. 2, with its message "Not quite. Please try again." could well mislead the student if his answer is not even approximately correct. Thus, one way to put more "intelligence" into the program is to have it compute whether the student's answer was even approximately right. For example, one might have the computer print out "Not quite." if the answer fell between 8 and 12; have it print out "That's way off the mark." if it does not fall between 8 and 12; and have it print "You must type out a number for the answer." if the student did not type any number at all, or typed something else, before hitting the carriage return.

One of the tests of an author's ingenuity in setting up a drill and practice program is to design error messages that are likely to keep the student's interest even when he is wrong, and—when appropriate—provide hints that relate in some way to the mistake the student has made. For example, the computer could tell the student whether or not his second answer was closer than his first one. Another improvement is to catch common mistakes. For example, students sometimes multiply numbers instead of adding them. We could thus program the computer to respond to the answer "21" with "3 times 7 is 21. But what is 3 plus 7?"

The second improvement is related to the first. Once we give the computer the power to detect common mistakes, it can build up a **model of the student:** a list of the type of problems he gets right, and a list of the type of mistakes he commonly makes. Then, instead of simply churning through a list of examples as in Fig. 3, the computer can—if suitably programmed—**generate** examples based on the student's past performance. For example, if the student has trouble with carrying a digit when adding numbers, the computer could pick pairs of numbers that give the student practice on this. In other words, instead of having a separate block like Fig. 2 for every example the student will see, the computer has a single block in which the two numbers appear as **parameters** A and B. The computer chooses numerical values for A and B, and then calls the block with these specific values, checking the answer in the ways we described above.

Tutorial CAI

The preceding discussion suggests that instead of simply drilling the student on material that has already been taught, the computer should also present new material. This is called **tutorial CAI.** Rather than only tell the student the correct answer to a block of drill, and make sure that the student will later receive remedial drill if he gets it wrong, the computer now has to present to the student appropriate material depending on what sort of error he made.

The author preparing a tutorial program must tell the computer how to figure out which frame to send the student to next depending on the nature of his response. The essential logic of the program is then shown in Fig. 4. The frame of Fig. 2 is replaced by the frame of Fig. 4. On entering the frame, the computer first displays some textual material, which gives the student the background knowledge he needs. This text may be displayed all in one go, or may be displayed a small piece at a time, with the student being asked to press the carriage return each time he has finished reading the displayed portion. Once the text is read, the student is then presented with a question, or a sequence of questions. The author of the program includes in the

ENTER FRAME

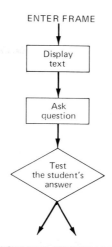

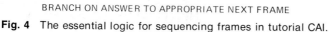

BRANCH ON ANSWER TO APPROPRIATE NEXT FRAME

Fig. 4   The essential logic for sequencing frames in tutorial CAI.

frame a diagnostic routine that tries to determine from the student's answers what remedial instruction he needs—and, on this basis, chooses the next frame. Thus, a student who gets all the questions right may race ahead to a frame much further in the sequence; a student who is doing somewhat less well may be given a few extra frames on the same topic; while a student whose mistakes are disastrous may be sent back to redo some earlier frames whose basic information he seems to have forgotten or misunderstood.

How do these instructional programs get written? Figures 2 and 4 give us some clue. Basically, we load the computer with a special program, called an **authoring program** that will enable the author— either a teacher or a programming specialist working with teachers— to set up an instructional program. The computer following an authoring program for practice and drill simply types out on its screen "Please type in the next question" and then asks the author to "Please type in the answer." It then automatically fills in the appropriate instruction within a program with a predetermined format, like the flowchart of Fig. 2. For "authoring" tutorial CAI, the situation is a little more complicated. The computer assigns a number to the first frame. Then, each time the teacher has finished programming a frame, the computer will increase the frame number by 1, and ask the author to type in the text for frame number such and such. It will then insert that text into the subroutine for displaying the text in Fig. 4. It will then ask the author for the question, and insert that in the appropriate place in the frame program. The hardest part, of course, is to get the author to clearly specify how to handle the student's response, specifying which frame to do next under what condition.

For each diagnostic that he programs for distinguishing different types of answers, he must then provide the appropriate number for the frame to which the computer is to switch the student's attention. In other words, it is still up to the author to call upon the teacher's deep experience in teaching a particular subject to decide what are the appropriate frames. The teacher must specify what is the right amount of text to give the student before asking a question or two, as well as providing appropriate diagnostics for student errors to determine the appropriate frame to require for remedial work. The authoring system—which is like a large computer operating system but is specially suited to the needs of authors of CAI programs—relieves the author of the tedious problems of keeping track of just where each frame is to be stored in memory, and saves him from having to write out all the detailed connecting material that tie the frames together. The authoring system also gives the author tools that make it easier to prepare illustrations for inclusion in frames and to modify existing CAI materials.

There are hundreds of different efforts underway on CAI. Two of them are so large that they deserve special mention. The first of these is the PLATO system (Programmed Logic for Automatic Teaching Operations) initiated at the University of Illinois in 1960. It uses a central computer with about 1000 terminals on its network. (There are now two other PLATO networks, one based in Minneapolis, the other in Florida.) These terminals are especially interesting because they allow not only the display of text, but also the graphic display of elaborate pictures which, once set on the screen, stay there until overwritten. The device that allows this is called a "plasma display panel," and can display any picture characterized on a 512×512 grid of points. Because of this pictorial display, students can interact with the system in far more effective ways than simply selecting multiple choice answers, or by typing in a word or a number. For example, one program for grade-school children lets them explore by trial and error the motions of a man balancing a stick, discovering the problems of overcorrection and the proper feedback strategies required to balance the stick. In a more advanced course, chemistry students at the University of Illinois can use a program that lets them simulate chemical experiments on the computer to ensure that they understand the basic ideas of the experiment and the various alternatives open to them before they start work in the laboratory.

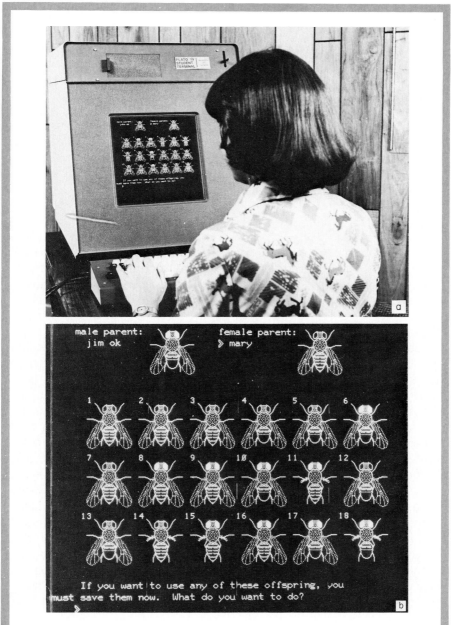

A computer-assisted instruction (CAI) lesson in the genetics of fruit flies, run on the PLATO system. The student can see the interaction between dominant and recessive genes as the computer "creates" new generations of flies in far less time than would be needed to actually breed the flies.

The PLATO system offers a language, TUTOR, which eases the problem of authoring new courses. TUTOR can be used by teachers who have not had any previous experience with computers. It includes structures that make it easy to generate the pictures for the plasma panel display, as well as various devices to make it easier to generate frames. For example, the handling of slightly misspelled responses—a variant of either the correct response or one of the incorrect responses anticipated by the teacher—is handled automatically by the system, which will usually inform the student of the correct spelling at the same time.

Another large CAI system is the TICCIT (Time-shared Interactive Computer Controlled Information Television) system, which was developed by the MITRE Corporation, with software under development at Brigham Young University. Instead of using a plasma panel, the TICCIT system uses television sets that contain special circuitry that will continually "refresh" the screen hundreds of times every second. The TV screen is not (at present) used for the presentation of moving pictures as on a normal TV program, but is rather used to present one frame of information at a time. The system gives each student a new frame on the average of once every 10 seconds. Unlike the PLATO system, which offers TUTOR to help individual teachers set up their own instructional programs, the TICCIT approach is to have a course put together by teams of specialists. The student starting a course of instruction on TICCIT has the choice of getting an overview of the material or plunging into the details. He can also obtain access to supplementary material such as films or text materials. Many of the frames use Sesame Street-type techniques to add humor in cartoons to try and liven things up for the student.

In our discussion of computer-assisted instruction, we have so far assumed that the student is using a terminal connected to a large computer which contains all the appropriate instructional materials and programs. However, advances in microcomputers (recall our discussion of "the shrinking machine" in Section 2.3) makes increasingly attractive the design of a self-contained system—perhaps the size of a large book—that would contain on its face a graphic display like the PLATO plasma panel, and would contain on a few integrated circuitry chips all the necessary logic for switching from frame to frame in a CAI program. The program for a single lesson could then be on a removable pack, perhaps the size of a cassette for a tape recorder, which the student would place into the "book" whenever he wanted to follow the lesson. In fact, the Xerox Corporation is now developing such a system, under the name DYNABOOK, with a target date of the early 1980s. Just as the new electronic technology has allowed manufacturers to sell pocket calculators more powerful than the old large adding machines for less than $20, so is it projected that the cost of DYNABOOK can be brought down low enough to make it cost-effective to provide one for each student.

With the advent of personal computers and home terminals, CAI programs will be able to raise home correspondence courses and self-study courses to a much higher level of sophistication than ever before. However, instruction via the computer will not eliminate other modes of learning. No matter how far computer technology progresses, it will probably be true that a book is cheaper than a program—and that writing in the margin of the book will require less technology and less expense than having the computer store your individual comments on particular parts of a program you are studying.

The usefulness of the computer for drill and practice is that it does not get impatient and frustrated as a teacher might. If the student does not get some simple fact right, then the computer can present it again and again, repeatedly giving the student the hint he needs to help him remember how to get it right next time. It is worth noting that we can achieve a similar effect with far less technology by simply having the student look at a question in a book in which he can lift a flap to see the right answer. The student then simply places a tick against a question as soon as he gets it right. If he does not have a tick against a question, then he must go back and do it again later. There are at least three reasons why teachers prefer the use of expensive computer technology.

One is that it is very easy for a student to cheat when using a book—or, put into kinder terms, to lift the flap while still making up his mind as to the right answer, and then suddenly decide that the answer he would have thought of is the one he sees. Again, the student might go back to a question he had gotten wrong too soon after he had seen the answer, and so not really learn the new answer sufficiently well.

The third advantage comes with **generative CAI.** A book is limited in the number of questions it has printed in it, but a properly programmed CAI system can generate any one of thousands of different questions, with each question designed to help the individual student. The questions are "tailor-made" on the basis of the model of the student built up in the computer as a summary of the student's correct answers and mistakes in previous use of the CAI program.

Clearly, much of the success of a CAI program depends on how well the author anticipates the needs of students. If the bright student is not to be bored by the material, there must be diagnostic questions that will let him skip sections of material he already knows. If a student is having trouble with the material, there must be diagnostic questions that will provide him with extra drill on remedial material. Since students can differ so much in their motivations and abilities, and also in the backgrounds with which they come to a particular course of instruction, the feature of having a record that lets the teacher check a student's progress becomes very important. A teacher can tell whether a student is being frustrated by having to do too much tedious remedial material; or by having a computer that has not been programmed to handle certain types of misunderstanding, and so keeps giving him irrelevant material instead of truly remedial material; or skips too much material for a student whose answers pass the computer, but only reveal a superficial understanding.

As time goes by, we can expect a teacher to use experience with students in this fashion to add better and better tests, and more and more useful remedial material, to the program. CAI can thus be a tool for building an *adaptive curriculum* which grows over time to handle the needs of more and more types of students.

However good CAI programs become, there is still a role for the understanding human teacher to help the frustrated student. Even with the most intelligently or amusingly written programs, students can get bored if the material is not on a subject that interests them. A teacher who is free of the problem of grading large masses of detailed exercises may be in a better position to provide individual pep talks to make sure a student remains involved. He can also provide encouragement and sympathy, to add the human dimension to the learning experience.

Dialog–Inquiry CAI

A new approach to CAI is called **dialog–inquiry,** and is still at an early stage of development, being at present little more than tutorial CAI, coupled with extra facilities that allow the student to ask questions back at the computer rather than having the computer only supply information on the basis of the student's response to the questions which the computer has just asked.

Dialog–inquiry systems are built using some techniques from artificial intelligence—especially the work on natural language understanding discussed in Section 5.3. Because of this, the dialog–

inquiry approach has also been referred to as "AI in CAI" (artificial intelligence in computer-assisted instruction).

It would take too much time to explain the dialog–inquiry approach in any detail here. Rather, we shall present a sample dialog between a student and computer in the dialog–inquiry mode, and hope you have learned enough from Section 5.3 to have some idea of how such a system could be written. The important point, again, is that the computer can ask and answer questions about a limited **microworld,** and the success of the system is based on the extent to which the programmer has anticipated the types of information that the student will want to know about.

What follows is a conversation between a student and a computer about the microworld of South American geography, based on the work of the late Jaime Carbonell. The student's questions and statements are in *italics,* the computer printout is in CAPITALS, and our comments are in the regular text format.

> *How many square miles are there in Brazil?*
> THE AREA IS APPROXIMATELY 3,600,000 SQUARE MILES.
> *What is the principal religion in Uruguay?*
> THE PRINCIPAL RELIGION IN URUGUAY IS CATHOLICISM.

The computer is now waiting for the next question from the student. In this particular case, the student takes so long to respond, that the computer automatically "chases" him.

> WELL, HAVE YOU MADE UP YOUR MIND?
> *The principal religion in Peru is . . .*
> I AM AFRAID I CANNOT ANSWER THAT.

In setting up a program of this kind, one has to give the computer some way of indicating the fact that it cannot answer a particular question.

> *Is it true that the area of Uruguay is 70,000?*
> THAT'S ABOUT RIGHT. THE EXACT ANSWER IS 79,000.
> *Could you please indicate the principal rivers in Argentina?*
> I DON'T UNDERSTAND YOUR WORD "INDICATE." I'LL GIVE YOU ANOTHER CHANCE.

Here the problem is not that the computer does not have the answer in its data base. Rather, the student has used words that the computer cannot use to retrieve information from its data base. Recalling our discussion in Section 5.3, note that we are not saying that the computer has any sophisticated notion of whether or not it can understand something. Rather, we program the computer so that whenever it meets a word it does not understand, and cannot ignore, it will fill that word in the format I DON'T UNDERSTAND YOUR WORD "____." I'LL GIVE YOU ANOTHER CHANCE. This is what the computer did in this case with the word "indicate" in the student's question.

> *The principal rivers in Argentina are . . .?*
> THE PRINCIPAL RIVERS IN ARGENTINA ARE THE RIO DE LA PLATA, THE PARANA, THE URUGUAY RIVER, THE SOLADO, THE PARAGUAY RIVER, AND THE PALCOMAYO.
> DO YOU WANT TO CHANGE THE GENERAL MODE OF IN-TERACTION? PLEASE ANSWER Y OR N.
> *Y.*
> OKAY, MR. JONES. LET'S GO AHEAD. WHERE IS BRAZIL?

Again, it is not that the computer really thinks that it would be fun to go ahead. Rather, it has a formated statement "OKAY. . . LET'S GO AHEAD" to use whenever it changes mode. It fills in the name of the student, of which it has a record from the student signing on, and then prints out the statement. In this case, the student signed on as Mr. Jones.

> *In SouthAmerica.*

> I BELIEVE YOU MEANT TO TYPE "SOUTH AMERICA."

Here we see the standard ability of many CAI systems to accept a slightly misspelled answer, while printing out the correct spelling for the student.

> THAT'S RIGHT. IS IT CORRECT TO SAY THAT THE CITIES IN BRAZIL ARE SAO PAULO, RIO DE JANEIRO, BRAZILIA, PORTO ALLEGRA, BAHIA, RECIFE, SANTOS, MANAUS, BAYLIN?
> *Yes.*
> THAT'S FINE. THE CITIES IN BOLIVIA ARE . . . .
> *La Paz, Sucre, Bubata, and Aconcagua.*
> AT LAST!

Presumably, the student took a long time to respond, but not so long that it triggered out a "chasing message" from the computer.

> ANYWAY, LET US SEE WHAT YOU HAVE JUST WRITTEN. HAVEN'T YOU INCORRECTLY USED "BUBATA AND ACON-CAGUA?" ON THE OTHER HAND "LA PAZ" AND "SUCRE" ARE

CORRECT. THE COMPLETE ANSWER ALSO INCLUDES POTASI, CACHABAMBA, AND SANTA CRUZ.

The computer compares the list which it has stored in memory as the correct answer to its question with the list of cities typed in by the student, and generates its response by a program with a flow diagram similar to the one we show in Fig. 5.

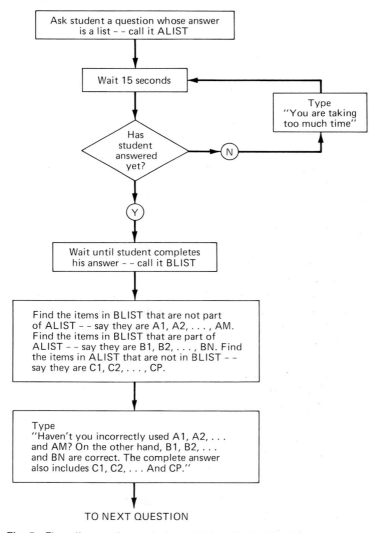

TO NEXT QUESTION

Fig. 5 Flow diagram for analyzing a list typed in by the student in response to a question from the computer.

TODAY'S REVIEW IS OVER. IT HAS BEEN A PLEASURE TO
WORK WITH YOU, MR. JONES.

If the computer time allotted to the student for this lesson ex-
pires, the computer prints out a farewell message of this kind, filling
in a blank in a standard format with the name the student gave when
signing on. Opinion is divided as to whether this "programmed chat-
tiness" is helpful or offensive.

The Computer as an Aid to Discovery

Having stressed that CAI will not replace, but rather supplement,
more traditional modes of instruction, let us next note that the computer has a great deal to offer in education besides its use for drill and
practice and for the presentation of simple tutorial material. If computers are regularly available, students can also take advantage of
them to carry out numerical computations and to retrieve information
from a large data base. For example, a student taking a course in
physics usually does only simple homework problems, because he
has had to do the arithmetic involved by hand. The trouble with simple problems is that they do not give the student experience with how
some of the more subtle concepts are used. However, once the student can use a computer to do the arithmetic, he can work on nontriv-
ial problems. He can let the computer do all the distracting details,
and can concentrate on really understanding the principles of physics
involved. By the same token, a student studying social sciences can
use the computer to retrieve information from a large data base, and
compile statistics that will help him find out the answer to really meaningful questions about society—such as trends in unemployment, or
marriage statistics, or what have you. Note that personal computers
may handle most of the student's needs for numerical computations;
but that he will need time-sharing access if he wants to retrieve information from large data bases.

The use of the computer to help the student master the basic
principles of a subject, and discover new and exciting ways to use
them is the key to the SOLOWORKS project at the University of
Pittsburgh. This is a mathematics education project for beginning
secondary school students, with four laboratories in which the student can interact with computers and other equipment to go beyond
the basic curriculum to develop an exciting feel for the subjects of
study. In each laboratory, the student can proceed at his own pace,
but the teacher keeps track of the student's progress, helping him

Various forms of discovery-mode use of the computer in the SOLOWORKS project. In Photo (a), a student in the modeling lab is testing a mechanical computer simulation of a lunar landing. The students and teacher in Photo (b) are manipulating a graphic display of Lissajous figures.

when he has difficulty, and encouraging him whenever his motivation drops.

In the *computer laboratory,* the student has access to computer terminals, and learns how to program. He also learns to master the basic mathematics of setting up problems in a form that the computer can handle. While working in the lab, he is meant to progress from the stage at which he depends on the teacher to specify what programs he will write to the stage at which he can go off by himself to design programs that interest him.

In the *dynamics laboratory,* the student learns basic principles of physics and engineering—such as how objects move in space and time. For example, the students can work with a flight simulator, to understand the forces acting on an airplane as it is in motion. This experience makes vivid many of the most abstract principles of physics. Students can also try out their understanding by putting pieces together to make various weird and wonderful machines.

In the *synthesis laboratory,* students learn about that part of mathematics that analyzes the production of complex effects by combining simple ones—just as the rich sound of an orchestra is produced by combining the relatively simple sounds of the individual instruments. They can work with both a music synthesizer and a device that can program projection equipment to put on multimedia displays. Thus they come to understand basic mathematical principles while being involved in the design, debugging, and performance of original work on this electronic equipment.

Finally, in the *modeling/simulation laboratory,* they use the computer to simulate systems in much the way we discussed in Chapter 3. Here, they come to understand mathematical models of physical and ecological systems.

In *drill and practice* and *tutorial* programs, the author provides a completely structured environment in which the student is led carefully step by step through a prearranged set of material, with the particular path he takes through the material dependent on the way in which he responds to the question presented to him by the computer. In this case, the CAI program is totally in command. At the other extreme, the use of the computer in **discovery mode**—for a *laboratory,* for *problem solving,* or for *simulation*—puts the student mostly in charge. He designs projects on which he wishes to work, and then uses the computer as a tool for carrying out those projects, programming the computer to do those portions of the task that he wishes to give it.

Whether it be in making the computer terminals available so the student can do a great deal of computing and information retrieval, or whether it be the setting up of explicitly designed laboratories such as the SOLOWORKS project, the idea of the discovery mode is to create environments in which many complicated types of information become real and thus become easier to understand—instead of abstractions forced down a student's throat in a lecture. Such environments are meant to be for the student of mathematics or science what a visit to France would be for the student of French—an environment in which these are living subjects that help him explore an exciting part of his world, rather than being dead pieces of knowledge that must be studied "because they are good for you."

Suggestions for Further Reading

A. L. Hammond: Computer-Assisted Instruction: Two Major Demonstrations, *Science,* **176,** 1972, pp. 1110–1112.
   A useful account of the TICCIT and PLATO systems for CAI is given.
J. Bone: Turning on with CAI, *American Education,* November 1974, pp. 33–36.
   A look is taken at the experiences of staff and children with CAI drill and practice in Chicago innercity elementary schools.
J. R. Carbonell: AI in CAI: An Artificial-Intelligence Approach to Computer-Assisted Instruction, *IEEE Transactions on Man–Machine Systems,* **MMS-11,** 1970, pp. 190–202.
   This is an introduction to the dialog–inquiry style of CAI, and the source of our dialog on South American geography.
J. G. Kemeny: "Man and the Computer." Scribner's, New York, 1972.
   The President of Dartmouth College presents a lively picture of how people and computers can "live together" to humanity's advantage.
S. Papert: Teaching Children Thinking, *IFIP Conference on Computer Education,* North-Holland Publ., Amsterdam, 1970.
   This is an early view of the "discovery mode" of using computers in education.
T. A. Dwyer: Heuristic Strategies for Using Computers to Enrich Education, *International Journal of Man–Machine Studies,* **6,** 1974, pp. 137–154.
   A view is given of the philosophy behind the SOLOWORKS project, stressing the use of the computer as an aid to discovery (a heuristic), rather than simply a device for drill and practice.
Alan Kay: A Personal Computer for Children for All Ages, *Proceedings of ACM National Conference,* August 1972, Boston, Massachusetts.
   Here is an early look at the DYNABOOK philosophy, speculating about personal portable information manipulators and their effects when used by both children and adults.

A. Goldberg and B. Tenenbaum: Classroom Communication Media, *ACM SIGCUE Topics in Instructional Computing,* **1,** 1975, pp. 61–68.
What happens when children aged 8–15 can create and explore powerful computing tools—of the kind planned for inclusion in DYNABOOK— including free-hand and programmed graphics, animation, and music synthesis is discussed.

Summary

We saw that the computer can be used as a tool for discovery, helping the student gain mastery in applying the ideas of a subject in new ways. It can also be used in **computer-assisted instruction (CAI)**—whether it be for **drill and practice,** for **tutorial** work, or in a **dialog–inquiry** mode. We saw that the best CAI programs will form a **model of the student** to **generate** questions suited to the student's needs. We stressed the continuing importance of a human teacher, both to cater to the needs of the student for personal attention and encouragement, and to spot ways in which CAI programs can be adapted to meet the needs of more types of students. With personal computers and time-sharing terminals, we can expect computer education to have as important an impact in the home as in the school.

Glossary

Computer-assisted instruction: *CAI* uses the computer to present exercises and/or instructional material to the student. A well-designed program will schedule the material in a way that matches the student's performance on the exercises.

Frame-oriented CAI: A mode of computer-assisted instruction in which the student works through a sequence of *frames* is *frame-oriented CAI.* A frame is a block of instructional material. In *drill and practice CAI,* the frame presents a question on material which the student has learned elsewhere, and then tells the student whether he is right, or what kind of mistake he has made. In *tutorial CAI,* the frame presents instructional material as well as questions, choosing the next frame on the basis of the student's answer.

Authoring system: This is an operating system designed to aid authors— teachers or programming specialists—in constructing programs for computer-assisted instruction.

Model of the student: This is built up within a sophisticated CAI system, which keeps track of the types of questions the individual student gets right and a list of the types of mistakes he commonly makes.

Generative CAI: A form of CAI, this does not switch between a fixed set of frames specified by the author, but instead generates frames on the basis of its model of the student.

Parameter: A given command or subroutine may have a number of *parameters* that must be specified before the computer knows what to do. For example, the instruction FORWARD X has one parameter, namely X. When we replace X by a number we obtain a command that the computer can execute—FORWARD 100, for example, will get the computer to send 100 "one step forward" commands to a robot.

Dialog–inquiry CAI: Dialog–inquiry CAI allows the student to ask questions of the computer, instead of just getting frame information supplied by the computer on the basis of the student's performance.

Microworld: A *microworld* is a limited "world"—such as the blocks world, or the subject matter of a specialized data base—that restricts the semantics of a computer program for planning or natural language understanding.

Discovery mode: As distinct from CAI, this use of computers in education lets the student design projects he wishes to work on and then use the computer as a tool for carrying out those projects.

Exercises

1. In the arithmetic drill program (Fig. 1) what happens if the student hits the carriage return 100 times in a row? Can you add a few boxes to the flowchart to prevent this situation? Draw the altered flowchart for a program that gives the student 10 chances for a correct answer.

2. Formal education is presumed to occur in school. Name four sources of informal education.

3. List three reasons why a CAI program "clocks" student responses or total time.

4. Which of the accompanying graphs ("learning curves") do you expect most accurately shows student performance on drill-and-practice material? The vertical axis is percent correct response, the horizontal axis is time.

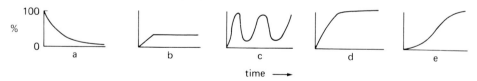

5. Choose the word or phrase that best completes each of the following sentences.
  (a) CAI stands for____. (1) Cybernetic Artificial Intelligence, (2) Computerized Automation in Industry, (3) Complex Aided Input, (4) Computer-Assisted Instruction, (5) Cybernetic Aided Instruction.
  (b) CAI involving presentation of material to students is ____. (1) tutorial mode, (2) material mode, (3) student mode, (4) presentation mode, (5) dialog–inquiry mode.

   (c) Using the computer as a tool for individual projects is ____. (1) drill mode, (2) PLATO, (3) curriculum mode, (4) discovery mode, (5) simulation mode.

   (d) A block of instructional material is called a____. (1) schema, (2) drill, (3) frame, (4) list, (5) model.

   (e) A curriculum which automatically grows is called ____. (1) drill-and-practice, (2) adaptive, (3) tutorial, (4) extendible, (5) dynamic.

6. Explain how a CAI system that includes an ecological simulation program can teach ecology in a way that no human teacher can. List two ways in which this method is incomplete, or misleading.

7. Outline, with a diagram and a paragraph of explanation, what a CAI system to teach chords on an electronic piano might look like.

8. "Flight simulators" are used for civil aviation, military training, or manned space flight. In a paragraph, how might CAI help teach pilots to fly planes or spaceships? List two ways in which this differs from the problem of learning mathematics, or geography.

9. A good teacher has a "model" of the student. What does this mean? List five specific things that your teacher in this course knows about you (or at least about *some* of the students in the class!). Which might a CAI system be able to keep track of, or use? What do you think no computer could know about you that is very important to your education?

10. Give two reasons why the *facts* of history are conveniently taught by CAI, and two reasons why the total subject of history would be very difficult to teach with CAI. (*Hint:* dates, names, people, interpretation, essays, background, ...)

11. How would a large, adaptive, nationwide CAI system help students who have just transferred into the country (from a different, foreign curriculum)? How might new problems arise?

12. Suppose a CAI system built a model of each student, with a detailed record of how a student answers questions. What privacy problems might this raise? What restrictions should be made on the content or availability of these records? (*Hint:* Look at the provisions of the Privacy Act of 1974 discussed in Section 4.3.)

6.2. INFORMATION FLOW IN THE CYBERNETIC SOCIETY

In the previous section, we examined the use of computers in education—emphasizing programs that could enrich formal courses of instruction. However, we still learn once we leave the classroom— or the CAI terminal! In this section, we examine the possible impact of computers on two of the ways in which we learn more about the world around us. The first is in the **news**—a package of information on recent happenings, whether obtained from a newspaper, magazine, radio, or TV. The second is the **library**—a repository to which we may turn for detailed information on a wide range of topics.

These are both processes of the **cybernetic society**—ensuring the free flow of information required to keep people informed on what is going on around them, and also to provide them with the background required to make sense of public events. However, we shall see that improving the news will make less use of computer technology than will the upgrading of libraries.

Making the News Responsive

What distinguishes the news from a library is that it is a *package*—a collection of items chosen by the editor to represent the important events of the last day or so. The key questions are: "Important to whom?" and "Slanted in whose interest?" A newspaper or TV station may be owned by the government, big business interests, or a union—and so may choose items and present them in a way designed to encourage support for the owner's viewpoint. We shall see that this is a social problem which the use of computers will do little to solve. It is only when we turn to libraries that computer technology can begin to play a major role.

In the late 1960s, I met a man—call him M—who, as a reporter for a San Francisco TV station, wanted to make the news responsive to the needs of many people. For example, if he was assigned to cover a town meeting and noticed that a representative of some minority group was not getting heard, M would march him up with the TV camera to the chairman of the meeting. He would thus make sure that this person was given a hearing in front of the town meeting, and that the general public would be exposed to the minority viewpoint. The TV station felt that they could not, in covering the news, take on this responsibility for shaping it, and M was fired.

However, M was still very much devoted to providing news that reflected what different people were thinking and wanted to know. His solution was to provide a local news service in a neighborhood in Los Angeles. He set up a phone so that anybody who dialed in would receive a five-minute summary of local news. More significantly, when the five minutes were up, the caller could record his own contributions to the news. At regular intervals, M would try to distill the spirit of all these comments, and then record a new five-minute news segment. He hoped in this way to let the news evolve, becoming not simply "for" the people but "of" the people, expressing what people were really thinking.

The idea caught on. Soon there were 100 people calling in every day. However, M could not digest 100 taped comments a day. He imagined that he could solve the problem with a few helpers and a few more telephones; but even this staff would reach their limit with a few hundred people. Then what happens when we try to provide a **responsive news service** for millions of people? The popularity of radio "phone-in" talk shows highlights how real a need there is— while the foolishness of the comments of many callers gives one some idea of the problems involved.

One attempt to preserve M's idea would be to use a **hierarchy** (Fig. 1) of call-in stations. A citizen can phone the neighborhood number to get gossip from Mr. Smith down the street and add his own contribution; or he can phone in at the small town level and get some idea of what the mayor is thinking and what people think about what the mayor is thinking and what the reactions are to the latest actions in the town council. A citizen could also phone in for news at the levels of town, region, state, and so on. At each level of the organization, reporters would provide a summary of events at that level, and also try to give a distillation of the reactions reported by the staff at all the regions reporting to it.

Unfortunately, this scheme appears doomed to failure. It is not clear that the news at high-level stations, where the staff must try to distill what 100,000 people have said as filtered out through three or four layers, would be any better than what the media churn out now.

The hierarchical scheme also poses a serious problem of evaluation. In any system like that of Fig. 1, the major problem is the unrelia-

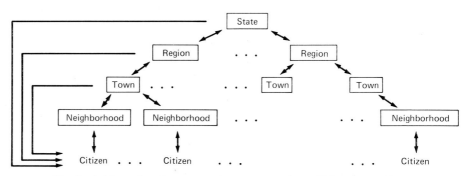

Fig. 1 A hierarchy of a responsive news services. Citizens can dial in to the news segments at any level. However, they can only contribute to the neighborhood news. Above the first level, contributions come only from the previous level.

bility of people's input. A journalist has to know when to follow a lead and when not to; but how can the high-level staff in Fig. 1 sift millions of comments and decide what things to include in their segment, which things are true but unimportant, and which things are downright lies, paranoid statements, or expressions of old prejudices? We see no indication that computers will replace the judgement of seasoned reporters, with their network of reliable contacts, and their feel for what "tips" are plausible.

As we saw in Section 5.3, a computer system for understanding natural language will only work well if it uses accurate information about a restricted microworld. As we might expect, then, a computer system designed to assign "credibility ratings" to statements from people would overload very quickly, even when limited to a very small domain of information and restricted vocabulary. A few thousand statements stretch the current capacity of language understanding programs. K. M. Colby (then at Stanford University) developed a system that would ask "Does what this person says tend to contradict what other people say? Now, does that mean that everybody else is wrong or does it mean he is wrong?" It would then weight statements as to how credible they are. However, this system is still too simple. It cannot begin to think as well as a human, who has lived and experienced society and its dynamic effects upon himself.

All this suggests that we cannot use computers to handle the "information explosion" of a system like that shown in Fig. 1. My feeling is that the distribution of news should remain roughly as it is in the democratic countries, but that we might use some technology to help the journalist become aware of viewpoints that would not normally have access to the media. For example, computerized polling (which we discuss in Section 7.2) could add to Letters to the Editor, and so on, in making the news editors aware of currents of public opinion and interest.

We only have a limited amount of time that we can spend each day catching up on the news. We cannot follow the detailed news of every town or state, but rather only want to hear news of our own town or region—with just a general account of what goes on elsewhere. To this end, it helps to have newspapers, journals, radio, and TV stations provide both local news coverage and wider, but relatively brief, news coverage. This regional diversity has been shrinking in recent years, as more local newspapers have been swallowed up in national chains. There is genuine hope, however, that the advances in computer typesetting discussed in Section 6.3 will provide newspapers with the flexibility that will allow the preparation of regional editions of even the largest chain. The daily news media deliver the news for the general public. Magazines and journals provide the news for special interest groups at weekly or monthly intervals—news for scientists, or members of a union or conservation groups, or news of the world of girl scouting, and so on.

However, there is a difference in viewpoint that cuts across the type of special interest we have just mentioned. This is a political viewpoint. People who share a political viewpoint are not simply pursuing their own interests in a "live and let live" fashion. They are interested in the way in which power is distributed in their country, and perhaps beyond. As long as their beliefs fall within the range of politically acceptable beliefs in a democracy (see Section 7.2, Democracy in the Computer Age), there is no problem. Nor is there any problem for people who hold the political beliefs of the ruling power in countries with authoritarian regimes. In all too many countries, however, the expression of political opinion that opposes that of the ruling power is highly dangerous. For example, consider the military junta that overthrew the democratically elected government of the Marxist President Allende in 1973. The junta disbanded the trade unions, sent political parties into recess, intimidated the press, and closed congress. They set up a network of secret police, whose interrogations include prolonged beating (with truncheons, fists, or bags of moist material), electricity to all parts of the body, and burning with cigarettes or acid. Alas, Chile is no isolated example. The reader may consult *Matchbox*, an International Journal on Human Rights published by Amnesty International of the USA, to see how widespread political repression is throughout the world. Examples come from North and South Korea, Uruguay, Cambodia, and so on, including the treatment of the Black Panthers in the U.S. and of Jews in the Soviet Union.

In summary, then, the role of computers in improving the diversity of the news is relatively small, although computerized publishing will reverse the trend for local newspapers and little magazines to become too costly to be economically viable, and computerized polling may increase public feedback. More important is the creation of a political climate in which diverse opinions can be expressed, so that citizens can find a news source that provides information tuned to their own regional, political, and special interests.

Computers and Communication

Before we turn to a study of libraries, we will briefly discuss the possible impact of computers on interpersonal communication.

Computers already play a crucial role in launching and controlling the satellites that carry more and more telephone traffic, as well as radio and TV signals. They also are at the heart of telephone exchanges which can route calls and automatically tally their cost without human intervention. Computers are, however, being used in other ways to put people in touch with each other. For example, computer dating services use a computer to match personality and interests of men and women, giving each subscriber a list of people they can contact in the hope of spending a pleasant evening together. At the moment, the pairing of people is very rough—only rarely will a couple find anything approaching an "ideal" match in their personalities. However, the importance of computer dating is that it gives people a way of meeting new friends, beyond people who live in the same block or work at the same job. A mechanism such as this for "breaking down social barriers" can be especially helpful for people lost in the anonymous hustle and bustle of a large city.

Looking into the future, one can imagine a computer-driven telephone network that also lets people communicate with people they did not previously know. Most of us have at some time shared the frustration of being alone in a large city, feeling sorry for ourselves, extremely lonely, and wanting to talk to somebody. How fine it would be to pick of a phone and dial not a number, but a description such as "Playing chess and talking about the Civil War," a couple of the hobbies we would like to share. The computer could then search its data base of subscribers, and eventually a phone would ring and someone would answer. You would then say "Hi! I believe you're interested in playing chess while talking about the Civil War," and the fellow at the other end would reply "Yes, that's right." Then if he were free, you could arrange to get together. Such a system to help overcome the alienation of the big city is within our present technological capability right now. A small precursor exists in the "hip" community with such setups as the Haight Switchboard in San Francisco, where one can phone in to a central number for drug help, a ride to Denver, or help in locating a lost dog.

Again, however, there are problems of scale. How much should you put into the system to ensure that people can get in touch if you want them to? How, on the other hand, do you define yourself in such a way that not too many people are ringing you so that night and day you have no time left for anything but playing chess while talking about the Civil War, as the rest of your life slowly disintegrates! There is an even greater problem of other invasions of privacy—recall our discussion in Section 4.3. If you tried to contact someone interested in reshaping the government, you might find that the national police force had phoned that number first, and that the person you were calling was already in custody.

As we spread information around to break through the barriers of loneliness that affects us in a large society, we at the same time have the very real problem of building safeguards to ensure that the breakthrough is at the level of individual interaction, rather than one that allows any bureaucracy to impose upon us its own rather limited views. Basically, this will require people to "edit" their public description, without any permanent record remaining of earlier views or life styles which they no longer want made public. Such "editing" will not only be political—people may wish to drastically change their life style when they marry or get a new job. The use of "private box numbers" (recall the discussion of the computer **mailbox** in Section 2.2) may be a necessary protection, to avoid having people's names compiled onto lists—whether the lists be for blackmail, or for the distribution of mass-produced "junk" mail.

With proper safeguards, networks of this kind will not only reduce alienation, but also increase people's mobility, as the computer automatically pairs job openings with suitable employees, available housing with suitable tenants, and so on. As the subscriber turns from a listing of job openings to a general survey of employment opportunities, the function of the network merges into that of a library. It is to the role of computer networks in the library of the future that we now turn.

The Computerized Library

In Section 4.1, we saw the development of new computer techniques that would allow us not only to store a great deal of information, but also to retrieve information quickly. These techniques are already being used to make it easier to obtain access to the wealth of information in large libraries.

Clearly, librarians have long been concerned with the question of arranging information in a way that will make it easier to find when needed. Books are cataloged according to their general subject area, as well as their title and their author. Each book has a catalog number—similar to an address in our computer terminology—which specifies where the book may be found in the library. If we know the author or the title of a book, we can look it up in the catalog to find out where the book is stored. If we do not know the author or the title, but are simply interested in finding books in a given subject area, we can work through the extensive lists of books within that general category.

The computer can ease this process in many ways. Two of these are already in operation in a number of libraries. The first is simply to take the catalog and replace the shelf after shelf of index cards by a magnetic disk. The user then sits at a terminal, and types in the title, the author, or the general area. The computer then proceeds to flash all items falling under that heading on the screen, one after another, until the user tells the machine to stop while he examines the item more carefully. When the desired item is found, the user may then jot down the catalog number, and go and get the book.

Somewhat more sophisticated information retrieval systems try to provide many different keywords describing the subject matter of a book. Then, rather than simply listing off all the books in a single area at the request of the user, a suitably designed computerized catalog would list those that meet a whole array of specifications typed in by the user. For example, a suitably designed keyword information retrieval system would let you type in the three descriptors "artificial intelligence," "social implications," and "published after 1970" and list for you the very few books, of which this is one, which meet all three specifications. This would save you the effort of having to read through the titles of the many, many books on, let us say, computer science in general, before you found a book that met your specifications. It also saves you the trouble of rushing off to the shelves to get a book that turns out to be misleadingly titled. If that book had been properly cataloged, the misleading keywords would not have been associated with it in the catalog.

Turning to the future, we can expect the catalog to become far less a collection of separate items, no matter how well indexed by keywords, and become far more an interactive dialog–inquiry system of the kind we discussed in our treatment of computer-assisted instruction in Section 6.1. Instead of requiring the user sitting at his catalog–terminal in the library to know in advance the appropriate keywords to obtain the information he needs, a CAI-like system would set up an interactive dialog that would help the user define his topic of interest. You might start by simply turning in the word "computers." The terminal might then respond by listing six or so major computer topics and ask you to specify which one you want. So it would go, back and forth, with you and the terminal each interrogating the other until finally you had reached a stage at which you were ready to have the computer provide you with detailed information. This system need not be restricted to giving a list of catalog entries. Instead, it would let you choose to see an overview of an area if you felt that this would prove more useful than access to book entries. Of course, just as in tutorial CAI, it will often prove useful for you to receive this overview before continuing the queries that would help specify an area of immediate interest.

We can expect the library of the future to offer a wide range of services beyond the provision of a computerized catalog, and the availability of a wide range of books. For many subjects, the information we require is not the detailed treatment that a book offers, but rather an orientation. For this orientation a glossy documentary—with all the features of a fine TV special or an edition of the children's television program Sesame Street—will answer our needs far better than a book. We can thus imagine that the outcome of our dialog with the catalog computer will often get us to retrieve from the library a video-tape cassette rather than a book. When we had retrieved this cassette, we could insert it in our terminal, and watch the exciting overview of a subject. For many occasions, this overview would be all we need, and we could put the cassette away and stop. However, in many other cases, the overview would only whet our appetite, and for this reason the cassette would not be a simple video-tape, but would contain at the end a dialog–inquiry program that would help us find out whether or not there was material available that would let us pursue our interests. In some cases, we would be referred to yet more audio-visual material. One can expect that usually, once we have received a general orientation in a subject, we would be ready to read the detailed treatment that a book can so comfortably, portably, and economically provide.

Whereas books are relatively cheap to write and publish, a glossy documentary usually requires a large team of people to produce, and can require a budget in the range of tens to hundreds of thousands of dollars. Where is the money for this going to come from? We can well imagine that there will be documentaries produced by the TV networks for their own viewers, which can then be made available in library editions. The government, whether as part of a public education program or as intentional propaganda, will probably find it worthwhile to finance the production of documentaries on many topics related to its current policies and priorities. Educational institutions will wish to produce documentaries that record significant breakthroughs they have made. Again, we can expect many special-interest groups to put out their own versions of what is going on in some subject area—for example, one may expect oil companies, the governments of oil-producing nations, and various consumer groups to each put out their own perspective on "energy."

Given the limited time span of the interest which anyone can bring to a documentary, each alternative treatment will have to be incomplete, and so will tend to emphasize those aspects that are in the interest of the sponsor. Rather than try to eliminate slanted documentaries—perhaps by a wearisome and expensive process of litigation—it seems best simply to rely on "objective" cataloging provided by the librarian, which will clearly specify the original sponsorship of each item. The intelligent reader or viewer should then be able to determine what is the likely bias of an item, and treat it accordingly. He can also look at items on the same topic with different sponsors if he wishes to have a more balanced impression. Finally, he can use the catalog–computer not only to obtain access to these items, but also to obtain access to reviews of these items, which would include reviews by groups of differing interests who would attempt to set the record straight.

We thus see that the computer, with evolving techniques of data-base management and computer-assisted instruction, can allow people to obtain far more flexible access to a wide range of material. However, it should be stressed that the development of a library with these resources will be a long and expensive process. We saw in the previous section that the development of a CAI program for even a small area of knowledge is a slow and difficult process. It relies for its success on the author making sensitive use of long teacher experience of the sort of difficulties that students will have with the subject matter at hand. In the same way, an interactive catalog of the kind we have described can be expected to start with little more than the keyword facilities that are already available. Then, as time goes by, we can expect that librarians will accumulate sufficient experience with the problems of library users to build catalog programs that will anticipate all the most common problems. However, in those areas of the library for which public demand is relatively small, or for those needs that are unusual in nature, the services of the human librarian will still be required to augment the computerized catalog.

Because the holdings of individual libraries are already large, it can be expected that the catalog programs will become large, too. Just as libraries can only afford to stock certain books, so can we expect libraries to only stock certain catalog programs. We can imagine that, in the future, computer networks will link libraries to allow users at one library to have access to the catalog program in another library. However, since the cost of this access will be similar to the cost of making a long-distance telephone call between libraries, we imagine that users will be encouraged to make relatively little use of the interactive catalog facility, and move as quickly as possible to the ordering of a cassette or book to be sent through the mail.

With this discussion of computer networking to link libraries, we come to the ways in which computer technology can bring the library into the home. We have already suggested that the home computer will, within 10 years or so, become as standard a fixture as the color TV set has become in the developed countries. We have also seen that the home computer can be used in the stand-alone mode with cassettes to provide program and data base, or can be used as a terminal for access to a large computer elsewhere. We can thus imagine that people in the future will use their home computer as a terminal to obtain access to the catalog program of a library. As we have already stressed, the major cost of using the computer as a terminal will be the cost of communication. When you receive a message on the radio or TV, that message is being broadcast, and you share the cost of the communication channel with possibly hundreds of thousands of other receivers. However, when you make a phone call, you are paying for a channel that is for your personal use. That is why the cost of a phone call per minute is so much greater than the cost of using a TV set per minute. The cost of a phone call is reduced if instead of using a voice quality transmission line you use a cheaper line which sends teletype messages. On the other hand, if you wish to receive a moving picture, then the bandwidth required, and the resultant cost, are far greater. Taking these cost considerations into account, we can expect that the likely access of the individual at his home computer to the resources in the library will be through print interaction, with a likely time span of at most 10 minutes. This would require a communication cost comparable to a normal telephone call. Then, in many cases, this print interaction would have provided the user with all the information he needs. In other cases, he will want to view a cassette or read a book. At that time, he would have the choice of either ordering it to be mailed to him from the library, or making a trip down to the library himself. This same process of interaction could also be used by people considering taking courses at an educational institution—with the dialog ending when they have determined whether or not there is a course that is matched to their interests.

In short, it seems that the library will remain as a repository of books, but it will be enriched by the increasing availability of audio–visual materials. Access to these materials will be helped by a computerized catalog, starting with keyword access, but with the steady addition of more and more sophisticated dialog–inquiry CAI type programs. Because of costs of communication, and because of the old-fashioned delights of browsing, it seems that the library will remain as a place to which people actually go; but it will also allow people to obtain overview information on a wide variety of topics, via home computer terminals, without leaving their homes.

Suggestions for Further Reading

J. R. Pierce: Communication, *Scientific American,* **227,** September 1972, pp. 30–41.

P. C. Goldmark: Communication and Community, *Scientific American,* **227,** September 1972, pp. 142–151.
These are two of the articles in a *Scientific American* special issue looking at the impact of new forms of communication on modern society.

K. M. Colby: Simulations of Belief Systems, *in* "Computer Models of Thought and Language," (R. C. Schank and K. M. Colby, eds.), pp. 251–286. Freeman, San Francisco, 1973.
Describes among other topics, computer simulations of how a credibility rating can be assigned to different statements.

L. I. Press: Arguments for a Moratorium on the Construction of a Community Information Utility, *Communications of the ACM,* **17,** 1974, pp. 674–678.
The author argues that society is not yet in a position to justify either the construction of an information utility in a prototype community or the acceptance of a policy in favor of its widespread implementation.

E. B. Parker and D. A. Dunn: Information Technology: Its Social Potential, *Science,* **176,** 1972, pp. 1392–1399.
A positive view is given of the development of an information utility.

D. B. McCarn and J. Leiter: On-Line Services in Medicine and Beyond, *Science,* **181,** 1973, pp. 318–324.
The authors discuss the growth of a national and international network for tracking down references to books, papers, and reports in science and technology.

J. G. Kemeny: A Library for 2000 A.D., *in* "Computers and the World of the Future" (M. Greenberger, ed.), pp. 135–162. MIT Press, Cambridge, Massachusetts, 1962.
An early look at the impact of computers on library design and management is presented.

D. Halberstam: CBS: The Power and the Profits, *The Atlantic Monthly,* **237,** Nos. 1 and 2, January and February 1976.
Halberstam analyzes the power given to the American TV networks when their half-hour news programs became the only source of news for a large number of Americans.

T. Ehrlich: Legal Pollution, *The New York Times Magazine,* February 8, 1976, pp. 17–24.
  The former dean of the Stanford Law School argues that we rely too heavily on law as an instrument of social change.

Summary

We have studied ways in which the free flow of information can be improved in the **cybernetic society.** We have distinguished the dissemination of **news** from interpersonal communication and from the use of the **library.** While it appears that computers will be able to provide new routes for interpersonal communication, it seems that the problem of large numbers overwhelms their use in sifting input from the general public to automatically produce a **responsive news service.** Rather, we can expect computers to play a relatively minor role in getting out the news, in computerized typesetting, and computerized polling. Political freedom, rather than increased computer use, seems to be the key to a good array of news services.

A major role for computers is likely, however, in the libraries of the future—both in the use of dialog–inquiry techniques of CAI in providing better access to library materials, and in the use of computer networking to link libraries and provide access to libraries from people's homes.

Glossary

Cybernetic society: A *cybernetic society* is one in which people and machines interact in processing large amounts of information.

News: *News* is a packaged sample of information about current events. A *responsive news service* designs the sample in response to public requests and input.

Computer conferencing: *Computer conferencing* lets humans conduct a conference even though widely scattered geographically, by communicating through a computer network. Each user has a *mailbox*—a reserved section of memory in one of the computers on the net—in which other users can leave messages by typing in the right instructions at their terminal.

Library: A repository containing detailed information on a wide variety of topics is a *library.*

Hierarchy: An organization whose components are arranged in levels from a top level on down to a bottom level is a *hierarchy.*

Computer-assisted instruction: *CAI* uses the computer to present exercises and/or instructional material to the student. A well-designed program will schedule the material in a way that matches the student's performance on the exercises.

Exercises

1. Give two reasons why "private box numbers" might be used in a computer network for communication.

2. Explain, in a paragraph, how a computerized hierarchical news network, as described in this section, requires *more* man power than conventional methods.

3. (a) What are two current methods for computerizing library catalogs?
(b) What are two future extensions?

4. Draw a simple flowchart for an information retrieval program which locates the index cards for books that have listed (on their index cards) the three keyword descriptors "artificial intelligence," "social implications," and "published after 1970." Assume the cards are in alphabetical (or any other) order and that it takes only microseconds to check whether or not a particular keyword is on a particular card. Why might such a search be unsuccessful? (Give two reasons.)

5. Name two conventional (noncomputer) ways of locating people who want to play chess while discussing the Civil War. Imagination, not efficiency, is called for.

6. Choose the word or phrase that best completes each of the following sentences.
  (a) A package of information on recent happenings, in general, is _____. (1) a library, (2) propaganda, (3) rumor, (4) news, (5) an editorial.
  (b) "M," in San Francisco, made _____ reporting too responsive to the public, and was fired. (1) TV, (2) radio, (3) newspaper, (4) telephone, (5) underground.
  (c) A strict hierarchy of call-in stations is most likely to _____. (1) succeed within 5 years, (2) overthrow the government, (3) be ignored, (4) pose evaluation problems, (5) increase the number of reporters.
  (d) Experimental systems for microworld systems assign _____ to statements. (1) "tips," (2) languages, (3) credibilities, (4) probabilities, (5) prejudices.
  (e) The role of computers in improving news diversity is _____. (1) insignificant, (2) relatively small, (3) economically viable, (4) limited by repression, (5) already large.

7. Explain, in a paragraph, how control of a hierarchical news gathering and reporting network could be used to repress and intimidate citizens.

8. List 10 questions you think should be included on a form to be filled in by people using a computer-dating system. How might videotape be used to improve such a system?

9. Suppose you had to write down keywords to describe this book in a computer catalog. Roughly how many would there be? (*Hint:* Pick 2 sections by sticking a pin in the table of contents at random. List the keywords for each section. Then use this to estimate the number of keywords for the book.) How big would each "card" for a textbook have to be? How does this compare to the standard card in the card catalog of your library?

10. Give 3 reasons why it is better to browse in a library than to use a computer catalog.

6.3. THE IMPACT OF AUTOMATION

In **automation,** much work is handed over to the machine that would hitherto have been done by humans; while new tasks are given to machines that no human could have handled. In studying automation, then, we are asking how machines, and in particular computers, are changing the way in which people work. To do this, we must first look at the nature of work. Perhaps the most common answer to the question "Why do you work?" is "To make money." For other people, the reason is social pressure—they have grown up expecting that everyone must have a job, and so they do, too; yet other people may have a sense of social responsibility—they do not wish to be a parasite, and feel that they must contribute to overall productivity. Finally, many people—even though they need money to buy food, and wish to contribute to society—are mainly motivated by the need for self-fulfilling activity, and find it a pleasant coincidence that a career which they find stimulating is one for which they can get paid.

In an ideal society, then, one would want every person to have work that they find satisfying, and financial rewards that would enable them to maintain a decent standard of living. In this section we must try to assess the extent to which automation is bringing us closer to, or further from, this goal. At the same time, we must see to what extent technological innovations in the nature of the workplace require compensating social innovations on the part of the human population.

The Industrial Revolution

If we are to understand the impact of automation, we must first place it in historical perspective. The first steps were taken toward automation when one of our distant ancestors, perhaps not even human yet, first picked up a stone to use as a weapon for hunting, or a tool for preparing food or clothing. The first tools provided the first technology. The change from a hunting to an agricultural society marked a dramatic upheaval in the way in which people lived. It took place about 8000 years ago, although agriculture started much earlier. The move came from a relatively scattered tribal existence to the life of the town—which perhaps happened first in Jericho some 9000 years ago—and marked another radical alteration in human society. The change that offers the richest parallels with the changes now being brought about by automation was the first **industrial revolution.** This "revolution" consisted in a drastic change in the means of production, with increasing use of heavy machinery, and the concentration of workers in the factories in which the machines were housed.

A revolution of this kind has no sharp beginning or end, but one may say that it started around 1750 in England, and had completed its first major phase within 100 years. During this period, for example, spinning and weaving ceased to be cottage industries: instead of farmers' wives and daughters spinning the wool, gathered from their own sheep, and weaving it into rough cloth to be taken to the market, the wool was gathered and taken to the factories. Again, the production of many small articles, which had been done by individual craftsmen or by guild members working with just a few apprentices, were now turned over to factories, in which hundreds of people worked long days in the company of the machines.

The first industrial revolution brought about a great increase in production, but also a great loss of self-esteem among the workers, and much human misery. People who had before lived on their own farms now found that they had the choice of either starving or going to live in a factory town. Frequently, the life of the peasant had been one of misery—there was no age of bliss, but a time of low income and often miserable living standards. But, at first, the new industry provided no improvement, and a great loss of traditional lifestyles, such as they were. Workers in factories found, all too often, that they must live in the substandard houses provided by the factory owner, must work 12 or 14 hours a day in hideous conditions, and must accept whatever small wage they were given—using it to buy food at inflated prices from the company store, with whatever little was left being spent on alcohol to drown their sorrows. It was not only adults who had to work in these conditions, but young children, too—children who were often horribly mangled when at the end of a long day they dozed off and got caught in the machinery.

It was on the basis of such conditions that Karl Marx wrote his famous critique of "Capital," and tried to assess the likely outcome of these conditions. He expected that capitalism would be crushed as the workers of the world united and cast off their chains. Marx's analysis of the situation was in fact an extremely important one, and much of our understanding of the impact of economic processes on society rests on his insights. Nonetheless, the history of the world in the last 100 years has departed quite strongly from his forecasts. Although I am not expert in the field of economic history and cannot spell out what really has happened, nonetheless, there are several factors to which I can point. One is the fact that the owners of the factories eventually realized that it was not in their interests to exploit the workers to the utmost limits. While it seemed at first that the less the workers were paid, the greater would the profits be that would go to the factory owners, it soon became clear that to earn as much money as possible, a factory owner had to produce as many goods as possible. To produce more goods, there had to be larger markets. This led to the development of the various colonies of European countries during the 19th century as markets for European manufactured goods—and not just simply sources of raw materials for the European factories. It also led to the raising of the living standards of the workers; for if the workers could become consumers, then the level of production could rise, and so the level of profits could be the greater. Henry Ford doubled his workers' wages so that they could afford his cars! The second factor in the failure of Marx's vision was that the interest of workers in mutual support to improve their living standards was not able to overcome the call of nationalism. Many socialists and communists had hoped, before World War I, that the ties between the workers in different countries in Europe would be such that they would never take arms against each other. Yet, in the hysteria of World War I, even many of the most ardent socialists among the German workers were eager to enlist and go to war against their fellow workers in other countries, all in the name of nationalism.

We could continue this sketchy economic history further, but since our main purpose in discussing the first industrial revolution and its consequences is to provide a perspective for our discussion of the impact of automation, we will discuss just one further social change that was an outgrowth of that revolution. We have seen that as factories came to provide cheaper goods, workers in cottages and guilds could no longer compete in the marketplace, and so were forced to go to the factory or to starve. In the factory, most workers were badly underpaid and terribly overworked. The eventual response to this was **unionization**—the workers in a factory finally realized that the only chance they had of shorter working hours and higher wages was to band together. If one of them went on strike as an individual, he would simply lose his job, and someone else would take his place; but if all of them could go on strike at the same time, then the loss of production would pose such a serious threat to the industrialist that he would be forced to take steps to improve their conditions so he could get them back to work, and get his profits flowing once again. (It may shock many readers that as recently as the 1930s, United States steel companies could call upon armed "goons," or strike-breakers, to come in and shoot down striking workers, sometimes with the assistance of state and local police. It is only since the 1930s that the unions have had a strong voice in the conditions of labor throughout the United States.) One of the questions which we discuss below is the extent to which the union can still protect the interests of the worker in the age of automation.

From Assembly Line to Automation

With this background, we can move from the first industrial revolution to the invention of the **assembly line:** the discovery that the productivity of humans and machines in a factory can be raised dramatically if each job is analyzed and broken down into simple parts, with each human being required to specialize in a single sub-task. (We might regard the programmer teams described in Section 2.4 as an attempt to bring this approach to the writing of large programs!) The various parts that had to be assembled into a finished product could then be arrayed along an assembly line which would move steadily past individual workers, and as the parts came by each worker, it was his job to carry out the few simple tasks required of him. Because the tasks were simple and repetitive, a worker could become very skilled at them and carry them out very quickly. Because the parts were moving along on an assembly line, rather than being reached for by the worker when he was ready to handle them, the pace of work could be stepped up. While the introduction of an assembly line into a factory required the installation of new equipment, and could thus be very expensive, these costs could be more than made up for by the increased productivity that resulted. Increased productivity could mean in turn increased wages for the workers—as long as they had a strong enough union to help them share in the new profits. The price they paid for this increased economic well-being was having to carry out the same monotonous task day in and day out. While for some people the chance to get paid for a job that required no mental effort on their part was satisfying, for all too many other people the job on the assembly line was intensely boring and frustrating. Thus the first Industrial Revolution and the subsequent increased use of the assembly line has provided jobs that allow the worker to earn a reasonable amount of money and has made a large contribution to productivity. However, for many workers there has been a great loss of personal involvement and satisfaction in the work.

With this we can move on to look at automation. We may characterize automation as a continuation of the assembly line idea. Once a job is divided into simple subtasks, it becomes easier to turn those tasks over to a machine, and so we find that, with automation, more and more of the jobs of the assembly line are done by machines. The computer can be used to make those machines a little more "intelligent" than might otherwise be possible. Instead of doing a repetitive task the same way again and again every time, a computer-controlled machine can follow a program that allows it to test for various conditions on the assembly line, and modify its actions accordingly. The other face of automation is that many tasks that are not of the assembly-line type can also be turned over to the machine—for the computer is an information-processing device, and thus a whole range of clerical and even higher-level tasks can now be done by the machine.

What are the advantages of automation? From the point of view of the worker, it means that some of the most boring tasks of the assembly line need no longer be done by humans. Much human drudgery can be done away with. Again, many jobs that expose the worker to dangerous gases or dangerous conditions, such as coal mining, can be increasingly done by the machine, thus decreasing the number of workers who must put their lives in danger.

Of course, these very advantages bring disadvantages. If there are fewer workers exposed to boredom or danger, there are also fewer workers who have a job. To some cynics, it may seem that this is one of the major reasons why a manager should decide to automate his plant, but the savings in payroll may only be comparable to the cost of putting in the new machines. Here, the even more cynical observer would suggest that the reason for automating is that machines "don't go on strike, whereas people do"—by automating, the factory owner is "getting the union off his back." This leads to the suggestion that automation is automatically a bad thing, and that one should always design a factory to provide as many jobs as possible for people. This is a somewhat naive viewpoint, however, as we can see by looking at a specific example, the newspaper industry.

Until recently, a newspaper was prepared in roughly the following way: a news story was either typed by the journalist who had covered it, or was pulled off the teletype if it had come "over the wire" from some news service. The various typed and teletyped pages were then passed on to an editor who would mark up the pages in various ways, carefully count the number of words, and on this basis lay the material out ready for typesetting. The marked-up pages would then go to a typesetter, whose job it was to sit at a special typewriter device and type the material in such a way as to set type. A print could be taken from this so that a proofreader could check to see whether all the type had been set correctly. Then, finally, the type would be locked in place, and sent off to be used in making the masters which would go on the printing press—and the paper would be printed.

The computer can change all that. When a journalist types his story, instead of typing it at a conventional typewriter, he can type it at a **graphics terminal,** which not only displays his story on the screen where he can read it, edit it, and correct any errors, but also makes a magnetic tape. (We saw some other uses for this magnetic tape in our discussion of text processing in Section 1.4.) Thus, when the journalist is satisfied with his story, he can shift the magnetic tape over to the editor. Again, one can arrange that, if a story comes over the wire, the receiver is not a teletype system, but a computer system that codes the information on magnetic tape in just the way that the journalist's story was coded. Thus it can be treated by the editor in exactly the same way.

The editor can insert the story, in magnetic tape form, in his machine and use a **light pen** and the keys on his own console to edit the material once more, removing material that he does not want published in the paper, and adding new material. He does not have to count words and worry about space, because he can have the computer automatically show him how much space will be taken by the material that remains, so that it becomes a very easy job to adjust the length of an article. As a result of this, when the editor has finished his job, all the information required to direct a machine to set type is already in place. There is no need to have a human typesetter go from the manuscript to the typesetting machine; and there is no need for a human proofreader to check the accuracy of the typesetting. Thus the use of the computer eliminates the need for the people who handle the teletype machines, for the typesetters, and for much of the proofreading.

Newspaper automation is not attractive simply for the jobs, and thus the money, it saves. It appeals greatly to the newspaper publisher because of its *flexibility*. Since it takes several hours to set type for a paper, it is almost impossible to get a hot story into the paper if it requires any major revision of material—unless the story is known several hours before the paper goes to press. With a computer typesetting system, however, the changes can be made almost at the last minute. Again, because all the information is stored on tape, it is very easy to rearrange sections of the paper, simply by directing one portion of the tape to be read into the typesetting machine before another. In other words, the advent of automation in the newspaper business is important not only because of the economies it affords, but also because of the immense flexibility it offers.

Automation and the Unions

One can expect that more and more newspaper publishers will want to convert their printing operation to the computer mode. This can only be done, however, by the loss of a great many jobs, and the unions that represent the workers involved are not prepared to see these people laid off. In one very bitter strike at the Washington Post during 1975, not only did the printers go on strike, but also there were fires set, and some people took crowbars to the printing presses, to ensure that the paper could not be printed on those presses during the typesetters' absence.

The outcome of labor action of this kind is often quite strange—the union agrees that the managers may install the new equipment, while the managers agree that they will not fire anyone. One of the most dramatic examples of this "featherbedding" was the decision to keep a fireman on every diesel train on American railroads. When the trains were pulled by steam engines, a fireman was required—in addition to the engineer—to shovel coal into the steam engine's furnace. When the diesel engines came along, there was no longer any need for the fireman. However, the unions were strong enough to get the railroad to agree to have a fireman in each engine cab—even though there was no work for him to do—rather than run the risk of a long and costly fight in which the engineers would join the firemen in a walk-out. Of course, when firemen retire, no new firemen are hired—and so this attrition slowly cuts down the featherbedding. The job of the union is to protect their members—and this is the key to the survival of any union leader. In this case, we see that the unions succeeded in preserving only one of the conditions of the job—that it was a source of money for the worker—and had left the job with no socially productive role, and no aspects of self-fulfillment for the individual worker.

It is true that the unions continue to play a very important role for many workers in ensuring that they are properly paid, and that they have tolerable working conditions. For many other workers, however—such as the firemen and the typesetters—it seems that the unions cannot properly respond to changing conditions. A century or two ago, a farmer would expect to work the land in the same way as his father or his father's father before him. A craftsman would expect to carry out his craft in exactly the same way as the master to whom he was apprenticed, and his master's master before him. However, we now live in an age that is marked by dramatic change. Since 1940, we have seen television go from a novelty to a standard medium of communication; we have seen the first computer built and seen a hundred thousand and more following; we have seen airplanes become a standard means of transportation and the jet engine come into its own; we have seen space travel with men walking on the moon and with spacecraft sending back pictures from many of the planets of the solar system; we have become used to satellites relaying our messages around the globe and providing us with surveys of our own resources; and we have seen incredible advances in medical science. With all these changes, many old means of employment have gone forever, while totally new opportunities have arisen—with especially large growth in the service industries, of which the provision of computer services is the one closest to the theme of this book.

Even with the growth of new professions, it is still not clear that new technology can create more jobs than automation destroys. It is likely that, if major unemployment is to be reduced, we shall see a trend toward earlier retirement and a shorter work week. However, automation will tend to make fewer and fewer jobs available for unskilled workers. Because of this, most countries will need major improvements in the education of the poor, the disadvantaged, and the minorities if these people are not to be permanently frozen out of the marketplace.

The young person starting his career today cannot expect to work in the same job for 40 or 50 years. Rather, a quite drastic change in professional orientation—and a continual process of reeducation—must be expected. This puts many unions in a very difficult position. While unions such as a roofers' union can probably count on continuing demand for the services of their members, other unions must face the fact that in a few years the profession that they serve will be, if not obsolete, at least in very little demand. The union, then, finds itself to be too job-tied for an adaptive society. Its emphasis on the size of the paycheck and the number of hours worked no longer meets the real emotional needs of the workers in finding satisfying employment. Yet, if a union tries to place its members in other professions, it will be accused of poaching by other unions. A major challenge for the unions, in the future, is thus to come up with a far larger structure of interunion cooperation, which will let unions predict patterns of change in employment, and work together to ensure that wherever possible workers are retrained and given union cards that will enable them to continue to play a useful role in society. However, even such an agreement will not make life easy for the man who has held a senior position in one profession and can—even after retraining—only qualify for half the pay in another job.

The point we have made is that when we consider automation— as when we consider so many other topics in this book—the real focus is not on the use of computers, but rather on the broad social problems of which the computer is but one aspect. We see that there has been a massive change in the conditions of the workplace over the last two centuries, starting with the Industrial Revolution. Automation continues that process, as it puts some people out of work, and creates new employment opportunities for others. It removes certain boring and repetitive tasks from the marketplace, it increases productivity, and it decreases cost through mass production. What remains is to develop a sufficiently flexible social structure to take advantage of these changes by ensuring that each member of society has a fair share of the wealth that is created in this way, and has a chance to make meaningful use of his or her talents.

One promising approach for the union is to have workers negotiate with management not simply for more pay or for shorter hours, but also to negotiate directly to make the work more meaningful to them. There have been adaptations of this kind in the car industry. In Sweden, for example, workers at the new Kalmar car production plant of Volvo do not work in the straight assembly-line situation in which each worker has to perform the same small repetitive task year in and year out. Instead, the workers form small teams that are responsible for one complete phase of construction of the car. Thus each worker can take part in a number of different tasks. This has two advantages to the worker. First, it makes the work more interesting and challenging, because of the variety of the tasks involved. Second, it restores some sense of craftsmanship and achievement to the work. Instead of just being one of several hundred people producing a given car, the worker finds himself to be a member of a small team, and thus if their part of the car checks out in its tests better than usual, then this could be a source of personal pride to the worker.

Another form of adaptation—not nearly as successful, but nonetheless interesting—was spontaneously generated by the workers on the assembly line at General Motors' plant for producing the Vega automobile in Lordstown, Ohio. Here the workers rebelled against a situation in which they were forced to perform very dull tasks very very quickly for long stretches of time without a break. They found, in fact, that they could perform the repetitive tasks almost twice as quickly in short stretches of 10 or 15 minutes at a time as they could possibly perform them over stretches of hours at a time. Thus groups of four workers would band together and agree that they would spell each other for 15 minutes at a time, with two men doing the work of four during each period. This gave the workers time to make phone calls, smoke a cigarette, or catch up with their reading of the sports pages. It hardly made the work any more creative or fulfilling, but it did at least make their conditions more humane. Surprisingly, the union stewards objected to this innovation as much as management did—perhaps they were disturbed by the idea that the workers could take any initiative that did not come down from the union! One of the important developments at Volvo is that at all plants—even those which must still use assembly lines—there is progress with *worker democracy,* letting workers join with union leaders and management to suggest improvements in working conditions, incentives, and production methods.

Cars and Computers

We now leave questions of the social impact of automation, and devote the rest of the section to a number of examples of the way in which computers are being used in the automobile industry.

First, let us look at some of the ways in which the computer can be used to help with the mental work involved in car production—namely, in the design process itself. Car parts—fenders, hoods, etc.—are stamped out of sheet metal using large dies. In the past, these dies were hand tooled by craftsmen, working from elaborate blueprints supplied by the designers. Now, however, the blueprint comes not in the form of a few charts on paper, but in numerical form stored inside a computer. These computer specifications can be used to automatically drive the milling machine that cuts into a large block of metal carving out pieces until finally the metal is shaped in such a way that it can be used to stamp out the bodies of the individual cars. Moreover, the use of the computer does not simply come in to replace the craftsmen and the milling machine. It is also used to help the designer develop the specifications of the car. It is still the practice in such companies as General Motors to build a full-size clay model of half the car (after all, the other half is just the mirror image!) and shape this to form an esthetically pleasing design. However, once the overall "look" of the car has been agreed on, the further redesign process will take place inside the computer. An elaborate machine is used to move back and forth over the full-size clay model and feed the measurements of each point into the computer. Engineers can then sit at a graphics console, and look at pictures on the screen, showing how the car looks from various angles, and carry out computations which will "sweeten" the measurements, to make sure that all the curves on the surface are smooth.

Not only does this process reduce a great deal of the tedium of the original manner of drawing the blueprint by hand, but it also puts the measurements in a form where they can be easily modified. For example, a windshield has to be designed to fit a specific opening in the car and must meet government regulations about the sweep of the wipers. In addition, it must be shaped in such a way that when molten glass is poured into the mold for the windscreen, it will sag into the mold without any distortion or stretching. An engineer might take two weeks to develop a design satisfying all these requirements if he had to do it by hand—yet he can do it in one afternoon using computer graphics. The cost of man and machine together for one afternoon may be no less than the cost of the engineer alone for two weeks. What is important, though, is the *turn around time.* It is difficult enough to meet the basic production schedule for a car—but any sudden design changes occurring late in the schedule would be absolutely catastrophic without the capacity that computers give for rapid recomputation of specifications.

In Chapter 3, we discussed the use of **computer models** and **simulation** in predicting how a complex system would change under various scenarios. The computer can also be used in this way in the process of car design—predicting how a particular type of structure will respond to different types of crash. In the past, the testing of a car body's response to a crash was an elaborate and costly business. To set up a crash in such a way as to ensure that the impact would be of a particular kind might take two weeks, and the total cost would be $30,000. Now, with increased understanding of the effects of different types of impact on different types of metal structure, one can use mathematical models to analyze the resistance to crashing of different regions of a car. Just as in, for example, a study of prey–predator relations we saw that the computer simulation was no good unless we knew which parameters described the system, so in the modeling of the effect of crashing on a car must we have various parameters about the strength of different pieces of metal. However, these parameters can be obtained in a device called a *static crusher,* which places forces on one portion of the car at a time. Thus many different parameters can be obtained in a relatively short period of time on a single car. Then all these numbers, together with a program representing a general mathematical model, can be fed into a computer. The engineer can then simulate different types of crashes, and receive as output from his graphics system a sequence of drawings that can be used to make a film—an "animated cartoon"—of the crash. One can then look at this film and discover what seemed to be the most disturbing types of damage to the car in various types of crashes, and then develop various modifications to the affected portions of the car. After a sequence of experiments in the static crusher, followed by a number of runs on the computer, one can make a *series* of design changes in a short time at relatively little expense. Then, one can check out the model by building a car that meets the new specifications and running it through a real crash.

Another use of computers is for automatic warehousing—keeping a complete data base (see Section 4.1) of all parts including their part number, description, and location in the warehouse. This allows an automatic updating of inventory—perhaps even to the extent of automatically replacing orders at the appropriate factory when a given stock gets below a certain level.

The computer can also be used to keep track of the extent to which warranties are used. If a distributor seems to be charging the company for an unnecessary number of repairs under warranty—as measured by a comparison of his replacement rate with the national average—then the company can have a spot check made.

In Chapter 5, we saw something of the work conducted by people in the field of artificial intelligence to enable computers to "see" the nature and position of objects in their surroundings. We may expect increasing use of such devices in the transition from a welding tool that "feels its way around" in a specified fashion on a lump of metal on the assembly line to a "visually guided" manipulator that can behave in a far more flexible way.

In addition to the use of computers to control particular pieces of machinery, they can also be used to monitor the assembly line process. For example, sensors can be placed at different stages in an automated production line to ring an alarm if a jam-up occurs. The counts are also important for maintenance scheduling. Since the counters are also used to maintain a fast schedule of production, the workers often try to trip mechanical counters, to increase the apparent production rate, allowing them to slow down. Computerized counters are less easy to fool in this way.

As our discussion of the Lordstown plant made clear, one of the greatest dissatisfactions of assembly line workers is with having to carry out a task at a fixed speed set by the assembly line. Volvo set about reducing this problem by introducing **buffers** into many of their existing assembly lines. A buffer is a "waiting room" or "stockpile" between two successive operations in a production chain. Instead of having to carry out his task every 15 seconds as things go by him on the assembly line, a worker can work fast to build up a number of processed units in his buffer, and then take a break while the next worker catches up. Without buffers, a hold-up or breakdown at any place on the assembly line can stop production all the way down the line. With buffers, the workers can enjoy their work more, and there is better productivity because the buffers can absorb the effects of most disturbances.

Volvo has used computer simulation in deciding where to put the buffers on their existing production lines. The programs estimate the maximum annual production of the line, the distribution of each worker's time, the time workers spend waiting due to breakdowns (both of people and of machines), opportunities to take breaks, and possibilities of participation for different sizes and placements of buffers.

To close this section with a dramatic look at the impact of the computer on the workplace, let us look in more detail at Volvo's factory in the Swedish town of Kalmar. It is the world's first modern car assembly plant without a fixed-speed assembly line. This new factory not only uses buffers, but also—as we mentioned above—has the employees working together in groups. Instead of being placed on a moving assembly line, the partially built car is on a moving platform—called an *assembly wagon*—that carries the car from one group to the next, and also serves as a work table. The wagon is shaped to make it easy to work on all parts of the car—even tipping 90° to the side to make it easy for workers to get at the underside of the car.

Each 15 to 20 person group has its own natural subtask, such as wiring up the electrical system, installing the interior safety system, decorating the car interior, or installing the steering system. The group has its own work area (as well as its own changing room and coffee area) with large picture windows in the outer walls. When a wagon is brought into the work area, it is positioned at one of six work stations. At each station, two or three people each carry out tasks which may take 5 minutes to complete. The wagon is then moved to the next station, where the proper tools and parts are waiting. Often, the workers will move along with the wagon through all six stations of their work area. To handle all the tasks of a 30-minute cycle requires much more highly trained workers, but most workers prefer the flexibility and responsibility of this arrangement to the repetition of some simple task every minute or less on a fixed-speed assembly line.

The assembly wagons can be controlled and checked in three ways: from a central computer, from one of the computer terminals located within each group, or through manual controls located on each wagon. The wagon automatically moves from one work area to the next, following magnetic "tracks" buried in the floor. It stops automatically in the "parking place" that forms the buffer between two work areas. Normally, there are two wagons in the buffers before and after each work area, to allow the assembly groups flexibility in pacing their own work. If a person stands in the path of an assembly wagon, it will stop on contact. After the person moves away, the wagon waits a few seconds, and then automatically continues on its way.

The central computer keeps track of the location of each wagon. As soon as a car body is placed on a wagon, it is registered in the computer. Sensors report the location of the wagon at any time. When a wagon arrives at one of the six work stations in a work area, the computer makes sure the necessary parts—tailored to any required variations in the design—are there waiting, together with assembly instructions displayed on a computer terminal!

Each group checks only part of the quality of its work, since much of the work can only be checked out when new components are connected in later work areas. When any work is checked, the results are entered into the central computer which relays the results back to a graphics screen in the appropriate work area. Thus the computer helps integrate the human organization, the technical system, and the follow-up function into a single system.

This system is at least as efficient as a fixed-speed assembly line—it still ensures that the right worker is in the right place at the right time, equipped with the right parts, the right tools, and the right instructions, but because he can set his work pace in collaboration with his fellow team members, and share the team's pride in work well done, the worker in such a factory is far better motivated and takes greater satisfaction in his work.

With proper technical planning and worker participation, technology can be used to *humanize* the workplace. This fits with our repeated point that the trend in computer science—with high-level languages (Section 2.1), computer graphics (Section 2.2), and natural language understanding (Section 5.3)—is to make computers easier for humans to use, and *not* to make humans submit to the mind-numbing chore of machine-language programming.

Suggestions for Further Reading

R. Lindholm and J.-P. Norstedt: "The Volvo Report" (introduced and translated by David Jenkins). Swedish Employees Federation, Stockholm, 1975.
    A description is given of the impact of both automation and increased worker participation in improving working conditions in Volvo, the Swedish car company.
M. Maccoby: The Bolivar Story, *Working Papers for a New Society,* Summer 1975, pp. 43–55.
    Increased worker participation in setting up work conditions in a factory in the southern United States is described.
B. Kremen: Lordstown—Searching for a Better Way of Work, *The New York Times,* Sunday, September 9, 1973, Section 3, pp. 1 and 4.
    Discusses the working conditions on the assembly line at General Motors' Lordstown plant.
P. Mantovix, "The Industrial Revolution in the Eighteenth Century" (Translated from the French by Marjorie Vernon). Jonathan Cape, London, 1961.
    This is an excellent account of the beginnings of the modern factory system in England.

Summary

We traced the impact of technology on the workplace, from the **industrial revolution** to the introduction of the **assembly line** and on to **automation.** We looked at the impact of computers on the publishing and car industries. We saw that automation abolishes many old jobs, but noted that new technology has brought new jobs, especially in the service industries. This rapid changeover in job categories requires life-long reeducation for the individual, and a new flexibility on the part of the **trade unions.** Much of the impact of technology has combined efficiency in production with the dehumanizing of the workers. We saw that, however, with proper technical planning and worker participation, technology can be used to *humanize* the workplace.

Glossary

Industrial revolution: This period, starting around 1750, saw the rise of the factory as the place for the production of goods, with workers tending the machines.

Union: A *trade union* is an association of workers, banded together to fight for better wages and working conditions.

Assembly line: This is a moving line on which a product is assembled. As the product passes by each worker on the line, the worker must carry out some small assembly task—repeating the same task again and again as objects move by on the line.

Automation: *Automation* is a form of production in which many human tasks are turned over to automatic machines.

Graphics terminal: This is a terminal comprising a TV-like screen, possibly equipped with a teletype and a light pen, that enables a human to communicate with a computer in terms of pictures.

Light pen: A photoelectric device for sensing the location of patterns on a graphics screen is a *light pen*. With the help of the computer, it can let a human operator "write" on the screen, move patterns around, select items from a menu, etc.

Model: A *model* of an object or process is another object or process which shares crucial properties with the original, but is easier to manipulate or understand. A *scale model* has the same appearance as the original save for size and detail. However, increasing use is being made of *computer simulation:* the model is a computer program that lets a machine compute how key properties of the original will change over time. It is easier to change a program than to rebuild a scale model if we want to explore the effect of changes in policy or design.

Buffer: A *buffer in a computer* is a place where information can be temporarily stored, usually just after being read into the computer (an input buffer) or just prior to being read out of the computer (an output buffer). A *buffer in an assembly line* is a place where items can be temporarily stored between two successive operations in a production chain.

Exercises

1. There are millions of people working in automated factories, or having frequent contact with data output from a computer. Yet there are only about 200,000 Americans who are computer programmers. Does this help to refute the claim: "Computers take away more jobs than they create, because few people can become computer experts"? How?

2. Why did the transition from hunting to agriculture, 8000 years ago, establish the need for mathematical models of the world?

3. Does automated machinery inevitably eliminate cottage industries like spinning, weaving, and washing? (*Hint:* What automated devices do you have in and near your home?)

4. The computer has been called a tool, yet it does not directly move, alter, combine, or create any material substance, as a screwdriver, blowtorch, sewing machine, or spinning wheel does. Name two other such nonmaterial tools.

5. Name three negative effects of the Industrial Revolution in the period 1750–1850.

6. Name three reasons for improvements in productivity with the assembly line.

7. Explain, in a paragraph, the idea of a "buffer." Relate its use on assembly lines, in computer memory (between where new information is input and the old is used), and with the "in" and "out" baskets on secretaries' desks.

8. It has been said that the assembly line was invented by Samuel Colt, who used it (basically) to make guns for soldiers in the Civil War. Why was this innovation so successful in this application? (*Hint:* Use the word "interchangeable.")

9. Find a cartoon showing a computer affecting a job. How does this reflect a real problem? Does it misrepresent the problem?

10. Which of the jobs listed below do you think would be easiest to eliminate by automation? Which would be hardest? Why?

Street cleaner, waitress, accountant, airline ticket salesman, antique appraiser, answering service, druggist, grocer, masseur, marriage counselor, optician, pizza baker, safe cracker, silversmith.

11. Many robotlike devices in factories have short lifetimes. They are often found with screwdrivers jammed in sensitive places. Look up the origin of the word "sabotage" and relate it, in a paragraph, to the possible conflict between computer automation and workers in the factory.

12. In what way does automation increase the hierarchical structure of a company? How does it decrease it?

13. Gutenberg's printing press automated the procedure for producing books, which were formerly lettered by hand, individually, by scribes. Did this invention increase, or decrease jobs (a) initially? (b) eventually? Why? What unexpected side effects did this have? Name two.

14. Does automation eliminate only menial labor? Discuss the problems to be solved in programming a stock broker's job. Stock brokers make roughly $50,000 a year.

15. Over 40,000 Americans die in automobile accidents each year. How do you think this compared with horse carriage accidents a century ago? What does this suggest about safety in automated processes, and social wants?

16. A computer program written by Dr. Gelernter solves geometry problems at about the level of a bright high school student. Does this mean that geometry will not be taught in high school anymore? Explain. Another computer program composes string quartets. Does this change the number of new composers? In general, does automating a process automatically displace people from jobs? How do these examples differ from the ones in the section?

17.   Compare the job of a worker in a fast-food restaurant, perhaps a hamburger or a chicken stand, with a worker in a more traditional restaurant. Describe the difference in terms of speed, monotony, frustration, personal involvement. How is the first job more automated than the second?

7

Networks and Politics

SECTION 7.1. NETWORKS FOR PLANNING

It is suggested that planning centers be set up to use computer simulation and data base management in regional planning—whether at the town, state, national, or international level. Computer networking would allow planners to share data and programs, and to set up problem-solving teams. Networks can also be used for distributed problem-solving—we discuss the EMISARI system use in the 1971 United States Wage–Price freeze. This section can be read with little background beyond the concepts of computer networking (Section 2.2), computer simulation (Chapter 3), and data base management (Section 4.1). It does not require details of these sections beyond those concepts.

SECTION 7.2. DEMOCRACY IN THE COMPUTER AGE

We start by examining the notion of a democracy as a system that makes government responsive to the public interest. We then examine ways in which computer networks can aid democracy. We suggest that people have relatively little time for political decision-making, and so need elected representatives as their interface with the detailed decision-making of government. Computer networks can give citizens access to information; let them register queries or complaints with the planning networks; and let them take part in instantaneous polls on key issues. This section is fairly self-contained, but uses the notions of planning networks from Section 7.1 and of computerized libraries from Section 6.2.

SECTION 7.3. A BRAIN FOR PLANET EARTH

We examine the ways in which planning and information networks may be used on an international scale. While it seems unrealistic to expect complete cooperation between nations in the near future, we can expect many specialized networks to develop—some of them as natural outgrowths of United Nations agencies. We examine the impact of different ideologies on patterns of cooperation, and on efforts to use computers to reduce those conflicts that could lead to war. We reexamine the world simulation models of Section 3.3 in the context of planning networks; and see how the considerations of Sections 7.1 and 7.2 are modified when we consider networks that are worldwide.

7.1. NETWORKS FOR PLANNING

We have already seen that computer simulation (Chapter 3) and data base management (Section 4.1) allow decision-makers to construct models of complex systems and explore their dynamic implications, while relating their modeling to a wealth of stored data. For example, we saw that weather-forecasting uses both computer models and reference to extensive weather records. By continually comparing predictions with actual weather, meteorologists can improve their models, making them more accurate in their predictions.

In this section, we shall see how these techniques of **computer simulation, data base management,** and **model validation** and updating can be used by regional planners—whether the region be a town, a group of towns, a state or province, or a nation. The National Aeronautics and Space Agency of the United States uses a Mission Control to monitor and control the key variables of a spaceship. In the same way, we can expect each region to have its own "Mission Control." We shall further explore strategies for linking these control centers into **planning networks**—using **computer networks** (Section 2.2), so that planners at one **node** of the network may work with, or learn from, planners at other nodes.

The Idea of a Planning Network

The solution of social problems is intimately tied to the organizations of government that put those solutions into effect. As the English management specialist Stafford Beer has observed, "How can you have plans that are not couched in terms of the organization which must implement them? But . . . if the organization is no longer well adapted to the environment, how then can the plans be relevant to existing threats? . . . we expend our resources in the ever more efficient implementation of irrelevant plans."

This point is illustrated by my experiences on a visit to scientists in Russia in 1964. In Moscow, a limited edition of the telephone book was published many years ago and promptly sold out. Thus hotel rooms in Moscow (in 1964, at any rate) contained no phone book. The desk in the hotel lobby for Intourist—the Soviet agency that handles foreign tourists—had a phone book, but would not release numbers, although they would place a call. It could take several days—asking Intourist to place a call each time I returned to the hotel—to get through to a scientist whose phone number I did not have. When I mentioned the problem to a brilliant young Moscow mathematician, he sympathized, but said not to worry, for soon there would be a new **bureau** to arrange contacts between scientists. He was so conditioned to the formula

"Given a problem, create a centralized organization to solve it"

that he could not accept the idea of simply making phone numbers freely available, with the scientist coming to the phone either to make an appointment or to apologize for being booked up. It seems that this is clearly a case in which **decentralized government,** taking in this case the form of communication via the telephone network, is far better than a rigid centralized organization. (Recall our discussion of computer-aided telephone communication in Section 6.2.)

Of course, this form of communication can only succeed because of a highly organized substrate. It requires an organization that will ensure the "health" of the telephone network. The important point is that that organization, once having established the channels of communication, does not control the content of the communications in the way that a bureaucracy in charge of scientific contacts would do. In other words, we really need a careful mix of organization and of freedom in the way we use it.

In this section, we suggest that much of government should be conducted on a local basis, with networking being used to coordinate different regions. A decentralized computer network allows programs on one computer to be run from any node of the network. Again, data accumulated at one node of the network may be used at any other node. However, one can at present use data and programs only if one knows they are there. In Section 6.2, we outlined possible dialog–inquiry cataloging techniques for the library of the future. We can expect cooperation on a planning network to be greatly improved if these techniques are also used to set up a directory showing where appropriate problem-solving techniques are available in the net—if indeed they are—as well as information on how to utilize these techniques.

The use of computer networks to solve incredible problems was "foreseen" in a story by the American science-fiction writer, Fred Brown. He told of a time in the distant future when man had spread throughout the galaxy and sought to link together all his computers to solve galactic problems. The Secretary General of the United Galaxy was given the honor of throwing the switch and asking the first question. As he asked that first question, a sudden realization came over him; and hardly had he asked, "Is there a God?" than he leaped for the switch. It was too late—a bolt of lightning struck him dead and fused the switch forever as a voice rumbled down, "There is . . . NOW."

This story reflects both the naive belief that a sufficiently large network of computers can solve any problem, and the dark pessimism that such a network will pass entirely out of our control. For too many people, suggestions of increased computer use raise the fear of seeing humans hypnotized and dominated by the machine. In fact, the reality of the modern world is that we all too often see humans hypnotized and dominated by an ideology or nationalism. Our goal, in urging increased use of computers, is to see humans extending the reach of rationality. Before accepting any solution to a problem, people must examine more fully the way in which their ideology has biased their approach to that solution.

Clearly, it would help planners using a computer network to have a natural language question-answering system of the kind discussed in Section 5.3. We have seen, however, that these only work in a rigidly defined **microworld**—such as that of the blocks on the table top. Even in as seemingly simple a situation as a child's story, we find the number of concepts required to keep track of the implications involved swamps the capacities of current computers. We are faced with what is known as the **combinatorial explosion**—when we take two items there is only one way of putting two of them together, when we take 100 items, there are about 5000. As we look at the possibilities of more complex combinations, the number of combinations increases explosively relative to the number of components that may be combined. The implication seems to be that in the near future the use of such question-answering systems will be limited to fairly technical areas in which the concepts are relatively few in number and relatively tightly defined. It is for this reason that we may expect much of the best work to be done by men and machines working together. The humans will use their *associative abilities* to see many aspects of the broad picture, while the computer may be used, in partnership, to explore *far faster* than is humanly possible many different possibilities, in precise numerical form where appropriate, but simply qualitatively in other cases.

Humans working together can use computers to produce answers that are more subtle and comprehensive than those obtained without computation. There is a trade-off between seeing a broad perspective and keeping track of details. The human can dominate the former; the computer can help with both: holding detailed data; projecting trends; and prompting the user with a "menu" of questions, reminders, and categories.

As our discussion of world simulation in Section 3.3 stressed, there are many important situations in which computer simulations cannot yet give reliable predictions. We shall have to weigh the computer output against analyses based on the seasoned judgments of

At NASA's Mission Control in Houston, engineers and technicians sitting at banks of consoles use advanced computer and communications technology to guide the flights of spaceships.

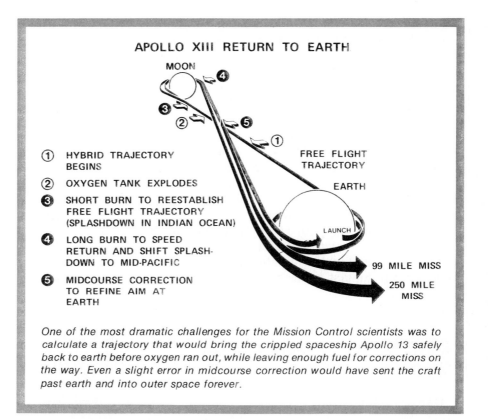

APOLLO XIII RETURN TO EARTH

① HYBRID TRAJECTORY
BEGINS

② OXYGEN TANK EXPLODES

③ SHORT BURN TO REESTABLISH
FREE FLIGHT TRAJECTORY
(SPLASHDOWN IN INDIAN OCEAN)

④ LONG BURN TO SPEED
RETURN AND SHIFT SPLASH-
DOWN TO MID-PACIFIC

⑤ MIDCOURSE CORRECTION
TO REFINE AIM AT
EARTH

FREE FLIGHT
TRAJECTORY

EARTH

LAUNCH

99 MILE MISS

250 MILE
MISS

One of the most dramatic challenges for the Mission Control scientists was to calculate a trajectory that would bring the crippled spaceship Apollo 13 safely back to earth before oxygen ran out, while leaving enough fuel for corrections on the way. Even a slight error in midcourse correction would have sent the craft past earth and into outer space forever.

politicians and professionals as well as public opinion. We must avoid the twin oversimplifications of believing either that technology is evil and will ruin mankind, or that technology is magic and can solve all our problems.

Any real-world decision-making requires us to balance a number of goals. For example, when Mission Control engineers were trying to bring the crippled spaceship Apollo 13 back to Earth from the Moon, they had to find a trajectory that would bring the astronauts back before their oxygen ran out, and yet would not use so much fuel in the early stages that there was none left for later corrections. In the same way, regional planners must face the continual challenge of balancing the many conflicting aspirations of their constituents.

It should be stressed that reforming government by the increased use of planning networks is no guarantee of a stable social system. A team of doctors, no matter how well schooled in the art of mutual consultation, may still lose their patient if none attends to the crucial symptoms, or if none has access to appropriate drugs or surgical techniques. In the same way, a government—no matter how many computers it uses!—will fail if no one strives to develop the new tools required to solve its problems.

Networks for Local Planning

We now outline how such a network *might* be operating, perhaps 10 years from now. It is worth stressing that there will be *many* such networks in the future. One will link town planning boards in a single country; another will keep track of food resources worldwide; while another will be a national energy resources network.

Imagine a network linking the planning centers of towns with a population over 100,000 in some country. Each town would have its own "Mission Control," with many people sitting at consoles making use of computers and a large data bank. Many may be engaged in routine activities—keeping track of fuel supplies, allocating repairmen to different maintenance jobs, assigning policemen to traffic duty, but others will be engaged in **planning,** and it is here that the network can come into its own.

The mode of operation is machine-aided problem-solving—humans pose questions, calibrate goals, and relate solutions to human needs; while computers provide data bases, simulation techniques, and decision-making tools. Networks then allow the sharing of human and computer resources to decrease solution time or increase a solution's efficacy. Experience with a network yields a form of learning as data get arranged in better ways, and as programs are written with better instructions on how and when to use them.

In each proposed network, then, we imagine that each *node* is staffed by a team of human planners who have available excellent planning and computer facilities. For quite a bit of the routine decision-making, and even a certain range of planning activities, the facilities available at the node 10 years from now would be quite sufficient to handle local problems. However, in other planning activities, the fact that the node is part of a network becomes important.

Suppose a group is working on a new traffic flow pattern for their town and has *not* had much experience with this sort of planning. They could then instruct the network to connect their computer automatically to computers in *similar* towns that had already been through this type of planning.

In the most fortunate case, the network provides access to a complete program together with a rich data base—allowing the planners to get to work immediately, without program development.

A virtue of the network is that, in using the program, the new group may see ways to improve it. For one thing, they expand the data base. For another, they might add new dimensions. They might add aesthetic considerations, such as landscaping subroutines, to a subprogram—such as one for trading off for noise and pollution level against average access time—which is already in the overall program.

Alternatively, the new group may learn from the old group's mistakes. A follow-up study, to which the new group also has access, may show the traffic jams that result from failing to consider the usage patterns of a new stadium.

Thus an important learning function for the network would be that the local team could log back into the network any improvements they had made in the procedures, as well as adding their own experiences to the data base. Instead of taking several years to make a moderately good program of their own, the new group might—by adding their own experience to the program already on the net, and the data on its strengths and weaknesses—prepare an *excellent* plan of their own in a month or two. Morever, they would leave in the net a highly improved planning instrument for others to use.

What if no program that is reasonably well suited to solve the problem is yet available on the network? There are at least three alternative strategies that might be followed.

We have already considered the first: If the problem is one that only the local group needs solved, and if it has resources well suited to search for a solution, then the local group can carry out its planning in a relatively conventional way, but aided by network resources.

If, however, the problem is of local interest, but the local group lacks much of the knowledge necessary to its solution, then some form of **computer conferencing** seems to be in order, using the rich computational powers available at each node. Planners could use the network to put together a problem-solving team from different nodes of the network with people and programs expert on the different subareas which must be brought together to solve the problem at hand.

Finally, it may be that many different regions need to solve the same local problem, even though none have access to a program designed for its solution. In this case, the network could get them in touch with other so that they could work together on solving the problem. It may well be that the result of their preliminary investigation is not to find one solution that is clearly the best—but rather to present two or three candidates. A feature of the network use should be an agreement to experiment: If there are six towns and three methods appear to be worthwhile, let two towns try each method. The resultant feedback could be used to provide a flexible instrument. This avoids any one method getting a monopoly only because it was used first and not because it has any special advantages.

Networks for Distributed Planning

So far, we have stressed *local* decision-making, even though the resources of many nodes of a network may be called on to solve a given local problem. Now, however, we should say something about multiregion problem-solving, in which a number of regions must take part in the give and take of formulating a plan which is relatively satisfactory to all participants without sacrificing certain overall goals. The technological questions here are probably quite similar to those very challenging ones we have discussed for local planning. However, there are a number of new psychological and political questions that must be considered.

To get some idea of the usefulness of a computer network for helping regional offices cooperate in solving national problems, we consider EMISARI—the Emergency Management Information System and Reference Index—set up by the U.S. Office of Emergency Preparedness in August 1971. EMISARI was designed to link the National Office with 10 regional centers throughout the country, as they implemented the 90-day general freeze on wages and prices in the United States—a freeze announced by President Nixon on August 15, 1971.

Before we look at EMISARI in more detail, we can make several general observations.

First, the network was used to link nodes in building and using a large data base. It did not use simulation capacity. Since future networks for distributed planning will provide simulation tools, we can expect them to be more powerful.

Second, although EMISARI links a National Office with regional offices, the same computer technology could be used to link nodes even when there is no overall command post. All that is required is some way of resolving conflicts between nodes. This would be simple in an administrative function such as the wage–price freeze—the two parties can submit their problem to someone they respect elsewhere on the network, and accept his judgement whatever it may be. If however—as in Section 7.3—we extend our consideration to international networks, the resolution of conflict becomes very difficult indeed. If two countries fail to reach agreement over resources that each considers vital to their national security, the use of computer networks may be unable to head off a war—though good communication may decrease the risk somewhat. Our concern in this section is less dramatic. We consider a case in which the planners at each node are pledged to reach agreement; and see how the network can help them do this more quickly and more efficiently.

Third, we note that EMISARI has a very specialized role. This suggests—as is in fact the trend—that we will see many specialized planning networks, rather than a single network designed to "control the world." Of course, there will be **linkages**—just as it is helpful to have an air traffic control network feed the latest estimates of flight times to an airline reservations network. The topic of linkages returns us to the privacy questions of Section 6.3: What information may an individual, a locality, or a state keep from network access? Network planning may lead to legislation, and the imposition of economic controls, boycotts, and direct intervention in the process of production and employment. This will always raise the question as to what extent a higher-level authority (such as a national plan) may impose its orders on a lower-level authority (such as local planners). There may be conflict between a company wanting to keep secret the recipe for some food they produce and the government wanting to set hygiene standards for all ingredients.

These questions about the interaction of different levels have counterparts in the general cybernetic theory of systems, for, in trying to understand a very complex system, we try to divide it into subsystems and often end up with a **hierarchical** description. As in the **top-down** solution of a problem (Section 2.4), we can explain the whole system to the extent that we can understand the interaction between its subsystems, and these subsystems can in turn be explained in terms of even smaller components. Thus we always ask how detailed a description of the subsystem must be before that description is useful in understanding the behavior of the overall system. How much detail about local activity is required for the effectiveness of high-level control? We must balance this against the reasons for which a lower-level region may wish to protect information about itself. To take an example from international relations, a country may wish to keep information secret about its supply of scarce resources in order to improve its bargaining power to get higher prices. We must stress that these are *age old* governmental questions, and that they are closely related to the questions of individual privacy and data banks (whether or not these data banks are part of our proposed networks).

After these general points, we can now look at EMISARI in more detail. Since the wage–price freeze was only to last 90 days, EMISARI had to be designed to aid in the development of policy, rather than to implement a policy that had already been worked out in detail. Each regional center had to provide citizens within its region with information about the freeze, and to respond promptly to requests and to complaints. It was the function of the network to pool the experience gained at each center so that the Cost of Living Council—whose job it was to set policy—and the National Headquarters of the Office of Emergency Preparedness—whose job it was to administer policy—could provide consistent guidelines. Otherwise, quite different policies might develop in different regions, leading to legal problems and other complications. The job of EMISARI, then, was to handle the reporting and guidance aspects of freeze administration. It had to provide a data base on public requests, complaints, and violations, organizing, updating, retrieving, and analyzing this huge mass of information. Note that it was not the job of a computer on the network to make sense of all the information automatically. Rather, the network had to be set up in such a way that the appropriate human decision-makers could obtain all the information they needed to set the policy guidelines for use in each regional office.

In setting up EMISARI, the designers followed certain general management information principles. First, they did not simply use the network to gather information for the National Office; rather they ensured that feedback and policy guidance would be passed back "down the line," so that local managers could see what information was useful in helping manage the freeze, and what information was irrelevant. This continual feedback provided motivation, and greatly improved the data-gathering process. It must be recalled that in keeping a data base under control, it is not just a problem of finding the right data—it is at least as important to stop the system from being flooded by a huge mass of irrelevant data, which slows down the retrieval time for useful information. The network also served to let managers doing similar jobs in different regions coordinate their activity.

Different people used the network in different ways with different "time constants." The job of some people was to use the network to find the information they needed immediately to respond to emergencies. For other people, the job was to assess the pattern of activity as it went by week by week, to provide the permanent documentation on the administration of the freeze which would provide a basis for later analysis for long-range improvement of activities within the Office of Emergency Preparedness.

It was very important to design the system so that it could be easily modified. Because no one had administered a 90-day wage–price freeze before, there were many unanticipated conflicts and bottlenecks which had to be "debugged." Some of these could be met by simply changing data stored in the data base, but others required changing the program that determined communication pathways, or the structure of records. Another need for modification was that, as the weeks went by, users became more experienced with the system, and thus wanted to be able to take short-cuts, rather than going through the step-by-step procedures that had been initially set up for inexperienced users. Similarly, as the freeze progressed, the demands placed on the system changed, and so the system had to be updated to adapt to this changing environment.

As this discussion of modifiability suggests, the 90-day lifetime of the freeze required a continual "on-line" analysis of activity. This system was operating in uncertainty, and had to help the human users discover what exactly the problems were that they had to solve. They built up experience with the type of enquires the public made, the type of violations that occurred, the various inequities that led people to complain, and the ways in which the public cooperated. This enabled them to better structure the system to respond quickly.

Since the system was initially used by hundreds of people who had not had experience with computer networking before, EMISARI was designed as an interactive system, with a simple menu-type approach that would let people ask questions to work down a "tree" of queries and updates. For example, when a user signed on he would have eight choices—each with a corresponding number—which would let him determine what he wanted to

Retrieve information on
>   Contacts and agencies   (1)
>   Programs and estimates   (2)
>   Messages and letters   (3)
>   Tables   (4)
>   Files   (5)
> Update   (6)
> Explanation   (7)
> Description and Assignment   (8)

If the user chose (6), saying that he wished to update, he would then have a total of six choices, depending on whether he wanted to update estimates, messages, letters, tables, files, or telephones. If, for example, he chose to update messages, he would then get a choice between modifying a message, writing a message, or deleting a message, etc. In each case, the user was carefully guided to either retrieve the information he needed, or to add appropriate information to the files.

The high-level managers of the system could ask for tables of relevant data, with commentaries, giving them an overview of the decision-making being conducted at various regional centers, and in the nation as a whole. Meanwhile, workers in the regional centers could obtain access to rulings and interpretations by the Cost of Living Council, and to pertinent news items. These pieces of information could be accessed by keyword retrieval. For example, if a user typed in the word "rent," he would get back all entries that included "rent" as part of the title. This not only gave back all items with words like "rent" and "rental" in the title, but also gave back, rather alarmingly, items with titles like "apprentice" in the title! The keywords could also be entered in pairs, to retrieve items in which both keywords appeared.

A special feature of the system which contributed to its flexibility was the recording of all keywords that users had tried. Thus, in addition to those keywords that had been used successfully, there was built up a list of keywords that had not yet been used. If a keyword was used often enough, this told the system designers at the National Office that there was a great public need for information on its topic. The designers could then set up appropriate new records and appropriate new guidelines to handle these areas.

As we said in introducing EMISARI, it was designed for updating and accessing a data base, rather than for simulation. We also said that a general philosophy of such computer networking was to help humans solve problems, rather than to delegate problem-solving entirely to the machine. Given the changing nature of the system, it was very important to have an up-to-date listing of people with their current responsibilities in this dynamic environment. Because of this, an important feature of EMISARI was a "contact directory" that would let people get in touch with other people who could help them with their problems. In particular, there was a man named the "Monitor" who provided the "central" human contact, being available when no other contact could be found, or when general questions of system operation had to be raised.

The initial form of EMISARI required 2500 lines of high-level language programming, and took only one week to "get on the air." This impressive response time was a result of the fact that the Office of Emergency Preparedness had already conducted earlier work on computer conferencing, and so had the basic network capability sketched out. What remained was to add the appropriate data structures and specialized communication pathways needed for the handling of the freeze. As the programmers gained greater experience with the system, and got feedback from the different users, they added new features. As the system grew in size, it was reprogrammed to make information more easily accessible. EMISARI was still evolving when the freeze ended. We thus see the important interaction in building a learning capability into a planning network of having both expert programmers working on the system design and having users continually providing feedback. The users then have to change their way of using the system as the system becomes restructured.

It seems clear that the experience with EMISARI was a positive one. It allowed a huge number of decisions to be made on a nationwide basis in a coordinated fashion and with a speed of response that would have been impossible with conventional methods of communication. This efficiency impressed the Internal Revenue Service—when they were called on to continue with stabilization policies for the economy after the freeze, they had the Office of Emergency Preparedness build for them a new system called IRMIS. This Internal Revenue Management Information System was a version of EMISARI designed to handle the problem of stabilization rather than freeze administration.

The Office of Emergency Preparedness, which designed EMISARI, now uses a system called RIMS—the Resource Interruption Monitoring System. This is a version of EMISARI so designed that it can quickly be tailored to handle specific emergencies. It has already been used to handle the 1973 threat of interruption of service on the Pennsylvania Railroad and the 1973 voluntary petroleum allocation program—designed to avoid stringent regulations to enforce reallocation of crude oil and products that might otherwise have been necessary. It has also been used for the 1974 nationwide strike of independent truckers, and the energy shortage that hit the United States at the end of 1974.

What is particularly interesting about the design of all these systems—and what we have seen especially in the discussion of EMISARI—is that they can be reprogrammed in response to changing conditions. In particular, they are responsive to the pattern of public demands and enquiries. Thus, as time goes by, they can—within the general guidelines under which they were established—come to better and better serve the public needs. With this in mind, we can turn to the discussion of democracy in the computer age in the next section.

Suggestions for Further Reading

S. Beer: The Liberty Machine, *in* "Cybernetics, Artificial Intelligence, and Ecology" (H. W. Robinson and D. E. Knight, eds.) pp. 9–29. Spartan Books, New York, 1972.
Beer proposes a network of operation rooms, strategically located in relation to the spread of social problems.

M. A. Arbib: Man–Machine Symbiosis and the Evolution of Human Freedom, *The American Scholar,* **43** (1), Winter 1973–74, pp. 38–54.
The importance of a learning function in planning networks is emphasized.

E. J. Cristiani, R. J. Evey, R. E. Goldman, and P. E. Mantey: An Interactive System for Aiding Evaluation of Local Government Policies, *IEEE Transactions on Systems, Man and Cybernetics,* **SMC-3** (2), March 1973, pp. 141–146.
The authors show how municipal planners may evaluate zoning policy using graphic displays of housing and industry patterns. The output is driven by computer simulations of population growth, location of industry, and so on.

P. E. Mantey and E. D. Carlson: Integrated Data Bases for Municipal Decision-Making, *AFIPS Conference Proceedings,* **44,** 1975, pp. 487–493.
GADS (Geo-Data Analysis and Display System), an interactive system for use by municipal planners in such tasks as police manpower allocation and analysis of urban development policies, is described.

W. R. Ewald, Jr.: "Graphics for Regional Policy Making, A Preliminary Study," A Report to the National Science Foundation Research Applications Directorate. Office of Exploratory Research and Problem Assessment, Washington, D.C., August 17, 1973.
This is a useful survey of the use of computer graphics and networking/conferencing in regional and national policy making.

R. H. Kupperman and R. H. Wilcox: EMISARI: An On-Line Management System in a Dynamic Environment, *Proceedings of the 1st International Conference on Computer Communications,* October 1972, pp. 117–120.
The Emergency Management Information System and Reference Index is described, and its use during the United States Wage-Price Freeze of 1971 is explained.

Summary

We have looked at the way in which the computer technology of **simulation, data base management,** and **model validation** and updating may be used to help regional planners by providing computer capacity in each region, and linking these nodes into **networks** for coordinated **planning** and sharing of resources. We have seen that much of the planning will be on a local basis, with the network being used simply to gain access to resources; but we have also seen that networks will be used to coordinate planning between many regions. The pattern of network use will be machine-aided problem-solving by humans—it will not turn over all planning functions to the machine. We can expect there to be many different planning networks, each specialized to its own function. **Linkage** between such networks will be desirable for efficiency, but will raise difficult problems of privacy and sovereignty.

Finally, we saw that both for local planning, and for distributed planning, a learning function will be very important. The data and programs available at each node, and the structure of cooperation between the nodes, will have to be changed continually in the light of increasing experience with any one network.

Glossary

Computer simulation: *Computer simulation* is the use of a computer program to model a system, enabling us to see how key properties of the system will change over time. It is easier to change a program than to rebuild a scale model of the system if we want to explore the effect of changes in policy or design.

Model validation: Checking the predictions of a model against the actual changes of the original over time is called *model validation.* An analysis of differences can be used to modify the model to get one that more accurately predicts important activities of the original.

Data base management: *Data base management* is a body of techniques for storing, manipulating, and retrieving the information in a data base.

Computer network: A *computer network* is like a net made up of *nodes*, with each node being joined to one or more other nodes by *links*. Each node contains either a computer or a terminal, and the links pass programs and data back and forth. A *centralized* (or *star*) *network* links many terminals to a single central computer with a large data base and great computing power; a *decentralized network* links many computers, so that a user at any one computer can run programs on, or share information with, another computer on the network.

Computer conferencing: *Computer conferencing* enables people, even when widely scattered geographically, to conduct a conference by communicating through a computer network. Each user has a *mailbox*—a reserved section of memory in one of the computers on the net—in which other users can leave messages by typing in the right instructions at their terminal.

Linkage: *Linkage* is the process whereby different records in one or more data banks are combined to answer a single query or to create a new record. It also refers to the sharing of computational resources between different computer networks.

Planning: *Planning* is the process of generating and comparing different courses of action and then choosing one.

Planning network: A computer network designed to help human planners at one node work with, or learn from, planners at other nodes, is called a *planning network.*

Decentralized government: *Decentralized government* is a form of government with its top-level decision-making processes dispersed throughout the system rather than concentrated in one person, place, or legislative body.

Bureaucracy: *Bureaucracy* is a system for carrying on the business of government by means of *bureaus,* often characterized by unquestioning adherence to routine and regulations.

Combinatorial Explosion: A *combinatorial explosion* occurs when a huge number of possible combinations are created by increasing the number of objects which can be combined—forcing us to find ways of finding a far smaller set of relevant combinations when we seek to solve a problem.

Microworld: A *microworld* is a limited environment—such as the blocks world, or the subject matter of a specialized data base—which restricts the semantics of a computer program for planning or natural language understanding.

Hierarchy: A *hierarchy* is an organization whose components are arranged in levels from a top level down to a bottom level.

Structured programming: *Structured programming* refers to a body of techniques for writing programs which have fewer errors and are easier to correct. A key technique is *top-down design* which specifies the overall problem, then breaks this into pieces called *modules,* breaking this down again into smaller and smaller modules, eventually producing modules easily programmed by a single programmer. Each module has a *contract* which lets the programmer handle that module without knowing the fine details of other modules. The contract says that IF other modules have done certain jobs, THEN this module in its turn will do its own job.

Exercises

1. Give two examples of large groups of people living in one place, all of whom get by quite well without centralized rules of any official nature.

2. It is listed as a "virtue of the network" that new users may add new data or programs for solving community problems. Name two defects of this growing network idea. What are the defects of complexity by accumulation?

3. "All that is required is some way of resolving conflicts between nodes." In a global network, where each node is a nation, what kinds of conflict-resolving methods exist today? Name three. Is there likely to be, in the future, a single such method?

4. It can be misleading to make sweeping claims from a single anecdote. Suggest two other reasons why the Russian mathematician *stated* that a new bureaucracy would solve the problem of scientific contact.

5. Give a military reason for the use of decentralized computer networks in which programs can be run from any node. (*Hint:* What is the military afraid of?)

6. "When we take two items there is only one way of putting two of them together, when we take a hundred items, there are about 5000." (a) Get a feeling for this combinatorial explosion by calculating exactly how many pairs of different numbers (from 1 to 100) there are—one such pair is (27, 39); (39, 27) counts as the same pair. (b) How many pairs of numbers are there from 1 to n?

7. In a science fiction story by Frank Herbert, government was streamlined by computers. Automated voting, polling, and legislation sped government activities by a factor of a thousand. Laws were passed, amended, repealed in minutes, departments and bureaus were created and destroyed daily, and so on—to a bewildering extent. Finally, an emergency group was formed to slow things down again, by sabotage, assassination, and propaganda. Explain, in a page, how you think this story reflects the realities of computerization, and people's fears thereof.

8. The disaster of Apollo 13 was kept nonfatal by computer planning. But the Apollo program itself was impossible without computer planning. In one paragraph, support or deny "Sure computer planning could prevent some disasters—but without computers, they wouldn't happen anyway!"

9. Do you think systems like EMISARI encourage the government to effect complex, irrelevant planning for the wrong problems? Explain, with one actual and one hypothetical example.

7.2. DEMOCRACY IN THE COMPUTER AGE

In the previous section we suggested how techniques for simulating social systems can be combined with data base management and computer networking to yield **planning networks.** These networks store data and problem-solving techniques, and allow formation of problem-solving teams—for example, by letting people work together via **computer conferencing**—to aid local decision-making. They also let people in different regions work together to solve problems that involve them all. In Section 7.3, we shall even consider networks for solving problems on a global scale: A Brain for Planet Earth.

In Section 6.2, we suggested how CAI techniques might yield computerized libraries that will give people easy access to *vivid* high-level information about many topics, and will provide interactive facilities to help them track down detailed information. In this section, we explore ways in which the citizenry, becoming better informed via this "dynamic library," may have a constructive influence on the governmental processes of the planning networks.

What Is Democracy?

Through much of human history, all the power in society has been vested in a privileged few: kings and lords, the leaders of armies, the great landowners, and—more recently—powerful merchants and industrialists. It is only in recent time that this power has been transferred to more and more of the populace. In such ancient Greek cities as Athens, all men—but not women, foreigners, or slaves—were involved in the city's affairs; but 2000 years passed without real democracy on a national scale. **Democracy** is a form of government in which—ideally—sovereign power resides in the people as a whole. This power is then exercised either directly by the people, or by officers freely elected by the people. It is part of the democratic ideal that all people in the state should have equal rights, without hereditary or arbitrary differences of rank or privilege.

In countries like the United States and Australia, which follow the Western European pattern of democracy, most adults have the vote, and can use it to determine which political party will hold power for a period of several years. Each party expresses a widely held view about the nature and function of government. Active citizens will work within a party to help choose candidates for public office, and to help change party policy. Most people, however, restrict their political activity at the national level to choosing between the candidates running for office in their district at each election.

It is beyond the scope of this book to analyze all the different forms that democracy can take, and to assess the successes and failures of different attempts to establish democracy, but we can note some of the failings of the Western form of democracy, and consider some of the ways in which the increased information flows of the cybernetic society might be used to correct them.

The basic complaint about this Western, multiparty form of democracy is that politicians become too preoccupied with who might vote for them at the next election. They make harmless statements that will offend no one, and put off unpleasant but necessary political decisions for far too long. In addition, there are complaints that too much power gets into the hands of the party leadership, and that the general public has too little say in many important decisions as to how the country is run.

There seem to be two major issues here:

How do we ensure that the general public is educated enough so that politicians in a Western democracy must discuss key issues instead of platitudes?

How do we open up the political process so that the general public has a fuller role than the occasional choice between parties or delegates?

We suggest that computer networks will help solve these questions—although some readers will certainly want to argue that we need less technology in politics, not more. Before we do this, however, it is perhaps worth making a few comments on power and freedom.

Freedom means different things in different countries. In a very poor country, the most important freedom is the freedom to survive. A democratic government is then one that makes its task the development of industry and agriculture, which will provide food and basic housing and health care to the entire population. A corrupt government is one that tolerates the misery of the many to buy luxury for the few. In a richer country, industry and agriculture are well developed. Most people are adequately fed and housed. Because people are relatively comfortable, their needs change. They can take survival for granted. Freedom of the press becomes a necessity instead of a luxury.

Whatever the needs about which people worry, and whether a country has one party or more, democracy only works if:

(i)   the ruling party makes it its policy to respond to people's needs;

(ii)   most people can live with the alternatives;

(iii)   no power group that is strong enough to overthrow the government becomes angry enough to do so.

If (i) fails, then the government is not democratic. If (ii) fails, then there is likely to be a revolution. In a two-party country, the regular process of elections can only continue if the two parties have a great deal in common. If this is so, most of the people who vote for one party can tolerate the policies of the other party. If this were not so—if, for example, one party would introduce an absolute monarchy while the other would introduce Chinese-style communism—a win by either party would lead to civil war. If (iii) fails, then there will be a coup. For example, in Chile, the democratically elected Socialist government made changes so quickly to raise the living standard of the poor that the economic well-being of the rich was badly damaged—and it became easy for the Army to set up a dictatorship. The powerful felt threatened by the needs of the many, and so put an end to democracy in Chile.

When we talk about computer technology and democracy we must expect no miracles. If a dictator rules a country, he can use computers to help keep track of dissenters. Only a civil war or a revolution or a "palace revolt"—or old age—can end his power.

What we will do now is to suggest how—if a country is dedicated to democracy—it can use computer networks to make government more responsive to the people.

Decisions Take Time and Knowledge

There are two extreme views on how computer networks may be used to give "power to the people." One uses the networks to let citizens vote on all issues; the other relies on the planning networks to always compute what is most in the public interest. We suggest that these are too extreme, and consider how we can balance the two, removing their main drawbacks.

Some people have advocated a "push-button democracy" in which *all* government legislation is voted on by *everyone!* Each citizen would sit down before his television set once a day, have 10 or 15 crucial questions posed to him, and then press buttons indicating whether or not he approved the measures—with the results to be electronically tabulated and the majority vote passed into law. Unfortunately, this scheme would *not* make for better government. While each of us is able to sense fairly well the general implications of patterns of decision-making on our own lives, and thus to protest when we feel that our rights are being invaded, there are few issues on which we have the expertise necessary to handle the fine details. We know very well from our own lives—whether it be the naming of a child, the purchasing of a home, or even what to wear to a party!— that we need plenty of time to think over the alternatives before we reach a decision. Thus we must not get carried away with computer technology. It is no use if it overloads the individual with decisions he is ill equipped to make.

As we discuss in more detail below, the complexities of modern society require that the people have officials to bear most of the detailed burdens of decision-making. Certainly these officials will include the experts who work on the planning networks we discussed in Section 7.1. Can we rely on these people to use the networks in the public interest, and not bother the general public with government decisions at all? I suggest that the answer is NO. A planning network can—as we saw in Section 7.1—be used to improve traffic flow, or to administer a wage–price freeze, but it cannot be used to decide whether, for example, a wage–price freeze is more important *to the people* than an all-out drive to increase employment.

This seems to suggest the proper function of democracy in the computer age—to involve the general public in setting the high-level goals of the planning networks. There will be specialists who know much more than the average citizen about the mechanics of implementing a particular policy, but they should keep coming back to see how the general drift of the policy suits the average citizen. They must then strive to refine their technology to fit the perceived needs of people. Here it is useful to enunciate THE PRINCIPLE OF THE HUMBLE ELITE: For certain system functions, the shaping of the function must be done by certain individuals. Such an elite must be humble in that it accepts the responsibility to explain its decisions to the public and be responsive to their viewpoints: combining *government* with *democracy* and *education*.

In viewing the role of the **technocrat**—the technical expert—it is worth stressing (as we did in Section 2.4) that everybody who has programmed a computer knows that any complex program, no matter how carefully written, will have a **bug**—or error—in it. Let us take a simple analogy: Cars continually need repair. Now presumably a car is a much simpler mechanism than a model of a region of the world geared for reliable decision-making. If General Motors, with all its resources, cannot ensure that a car will work without bugs, it is naive for us to expect that an economic model can work without bugs. Thus, while we can build models that will often help us make better decisions, there is no guarantee that the decision will be right in any particular case. We have to keep on testing our models in specific cases, and monitoring the long-term effects of our policies. Suppose you were to wish that mankind would never have another day of unhappiness. If atom bombs fall and mankind never has another day of happiness it is not that your wish was not granted—rather you did not make the right wish. To make democracy work, we need the feedback that gives the people of a region or country a chance to check every now and again whether the technocrats doing the planning in that area have things working in roughly the right way. When the public decides that the policies do not "feel as good" as they thought they would, they can insist on the need for "reprogramming."

Technocrats are presumably as corrupt as anybody else, and so continual public monitoring is also required to make sure that they are not working only for their own reward, or for some pressure group.

No matter how many safeguards and checks and balances we put into the system, we cannot expect to avoid mistakes. Thus it is useful to contrast this observation with the collection of stories "I, Robot" by Isaac Asimov. This book is based on the three "laws" of robotics:

(1)   A robot may not injure a human being, or, through action, allow a human being to come to harm.

(2)   A robot must obey the orders given by human beings except where such orders would conflict with the First Law.

(3)   A robot must protect its own existence as long as such protection does not conflict with the First or Second Law.

The surprising outcomes of many of Asimov's stories are based on the idea that the robots will *always* obey the three laws, no matter how mysteriously. Unfortunately, no matter how good the stories may be as stories, their basic assumptions are absurd. Such safeguards are impossible for only a being that knows *everything* could predict the eternal consequences of every action.

Of course, the problem of setting goals is a very difficult one. For example, the United States Environmental Protection Agency, in trying to reduce pollution from cars, may have set too narrow a goal. It defined pollution purely in terms of reducing the emission of certain substances, which led to unfortunate side-effects in the emission of new contaminants. Thus we must continually face the problem of redefining our goals in terms of high-level criteria. It might be objected that the average citizen cannot vote with such sophistication— that the average citizen neither knows, nor cares to know, enough science (be it natural, behavioral, or social) to make the proper decisions, and that his attitude is simply "I want my phone calls to get through, my lights to go on, the buses to run, the streets to be clean, . . . ," with no concern for other decisions. However, the history of universal suffrage has shown the folly of such rhetoric as: "These people (women, blacks, etc.) don't know enough to vote."

The high technology of planning networks still requires feedback processes to relate this general feeling of the people to the labors of the technocrats. *Politicians* can serve as moderators between technocrats and the populace, helping determine which views are open to public debate—both by noting controversial trends in the planning networks and by responding to significant public pressure.

As we have said, an individual does not have time to consider all policy decisions. This is why he chooses a delegate whose *approach* to policy-making he approves, rather than needing push-button democracy in the crude sense of mass voting on all issues. It is important that the politician of the future not think purely in terms of advocating whatever policy seems likely to win the most votes. Rather he must help people educate themselves sufficiently to make a wise decision. As we shall see in the next subsection, interactive TV and computer technology can be used by a representative to inform his constituents and sample their attitudes. Sufficient dialog must be obtained if a group is to feel that their views have been incorporated into policy-making. It is important to have a network that helps people assess the impact of various decisions, so that a politician knows that when he says something he will be really on the spot to think through its implications.

In many two-party countries, a great disservice is done to the electorate by the mass media in their coverage of electoral campaigns. Too often, the news broadcasts and papers discuss what tactics the different candidates are using, and what their relative standing is in the polls. They do not help the public make a detailed examination of the issues involved, to see what the genuine projections are for the decision-making of the candidates on these issues.

Such comments suggest that much of our voting should be for issues, rather than for politicians. However, given the limited decision-making ability of individual voters, and the sometimes sudden prominence of novel issues, there is much to be said for voting for a representative whose wisdom you can rely on in novel situations. If you cannot personally examine each issue, you want a representative who will usually respond to the issues in the way that you would *if you had the time*.

We close this subsection with a number of questions for the reader:

One wonders whether, in the future, we should license politicians to ensure that they have basic skills in economics, social simulation, and computer science—to name just a few!—before they may run for office. If we must accredit politicians to ensure that they can make decisions about complex organizations, how do we guarantee that the certification process is not a process of indoctrination by an existing power group? Will such politicians be able to respond to clear indications of the need for revolutionary changes when they conflict with their own self-interest? If the operations rooms of the planning network are not to be highly instrumented versions of the old "smoke-filled room," what decisions should be open to public debate and democratic vote? Who decides what data may reach the control rooms? Are your intimacies suitable grist for its mill? What phenomena are to be modeled? When is direct intervention permissible? Who decides the criteria that guide such decisions? the voter? by majority vote? How do we ensure that the voter knows enough to reach his decisions? Can we get him to vote for the good of all, rather than in his own narrow interest?

Information Networks

There are many ways in which computer networking can increase public control of government.

We saw one mechanism in action in the EMISARI system of Section 7.1. Once the political decision to have the United States wage–price freeze of 1971 was made, the system was set up to make it easy for people to make queries and complaints about the guidelines. This made is possible for the officials to carry out the policy in a way that was responsive to the public interest. Properly used, this sort of technique can keep track of public reaction to new policies and adjust the policies if they become unpopular, or if the policies fail to achieve what they were set up for.

What of the setting up of policy? Many of the actions of government are either too specialized or too technical for it to make sense for the general public to become heavily involved. These are the responsibility of the elected officials. However, even though most people cannot become involved in very many issues, it would be good to have many people involved in key issues. Examples include the introduction of a new welfare program, or of new steps to provide equal rights to minorities or to women. People want to have a say in setting up policy of this kind. Yet people are often ill-informed on the issues. One answer would be to have public debate of the issues over television, with computer-polling used to detect shifts in public opinion and concern. By using the network to inform the government of trends, while forbidding that the majority vote be *automatically* passed into law, we would remove the weight of direct responsibility from each push of the button. The debate form, with two or more opposed, interested, informed people given 3 to 5 minutes each, is constantly used on British TV for the presentation of all kinds of issues, from the trivial to the most serious. Many of the debaters might, depending on the subject, be nonpoliticians, with appropriate special knowledge or interests. With a daily presentation of this kind on one key issue (broadcast in prime time on all channels simultaneously?), an unprecedented kind of large-community interaction could be produced. It would be essential that all electors have access to a poll-TV, and that the button-pushing follows the debate, with a computer breakdown of the results presented on TV within, say, 1 minute. With such immediate feedback, each viewer could compare his own opinion with that of the whole community. It would be desirable that a participant could punch in any of a variety of alternative responses to the debate, not just a YES or NO, as well as, perhaps, some self-classifying data (age, class of occupation, and so on).

If an important issue were presented in this way several times over a period of weeks, the debaters on television would have an opportunity to react to the poll results. They could experiment with variations of their positions in an attempt to improve their popularity from poll to poll. Through them, the entire community would be, in effect, learning much about each other and also debating with each other. Politicians would also learn much observing the results. The chief value of such frequent, massive, fast-feedback polling would be a progressive *education* of the public in the use of a flexible, sensitive process of opinion-formation—gradually leading to consensus decision-making—that is far more delicate and clear than the present crude polls and elections.

These "citizen-feedback" techniques can be used at many levels. They can be used to help establish public opinion on issues at a regional level (town, county, province, state), on a national level, or even on issues that involve several nations. They can also be used by a local representative to inform his constituents of the actions he has taken and to obtain input on how he should react on upcoming issues.

The type of citizen-access to planning networks we saw for EMISARI is more likely to prove effective in letting people feel that government is responsive to them rather than an overwhelming parade of "big issues." A key problem will be to keep the number of such "issues-and-feedback" sessions large enough to ensure citizen input to the political process, yet small enough to stop people from feeling overwhelmed, or simply bored.

Perhaps we can see elections as one way of providing feedback that will trigger corrective action before departures from "reality" become too large. Citizens much check the extent to which the formalized goal structures—or the power and prejudice of special interest groups—used in decision-making actually coincide with the needs of the electorate. Of course, there is always the tension between constructive leadership and participatory democracy: between following the needs of people as they currently perceive them, and shaping those needs.

When people discuss politics, they usually look for data that confirm their political bias, rather than try to find data to help them change their minds. A conservative sees proof of tax money being thrown away on the poor where a liberal sees proof that far more attention must be paid to getting welfare to really help people. Moreover, it is not true that once people see things as they "really" are, they will necessarily behave in some ideal "rational" way. Thus, in any long-term planning, we must take into account the fact that people gather data to fulfill certain ideological needs making them fit some existing mental **schema**—their way of seeing things—rather than changing this schema to fit the facts. The *quality* of information is a factor just as important as the peculiar filters in receiving minds. We must avoid a worship of "information" for its own sake—more is *not* better, if attention to accuracy is at the price of relevance. A mass of *irrelevant* information is the perfect camouflage for the exercise of power.

Ideology *can,* however, give way to evidence if the facts are "strong enough." We can see examples of this from Russia. For a long time the theories of **relativity** and **genetics** were considered to be bourgeois, decadent sciences; but the facts rebelled. After 1945, it became clear that if Russia wished to have international "clout," it needed the atom bomb, and to have the atom bomb, it had to accept the theory of relativity. For a long time the Russian dictator, Stalin, praised a strange form of genetic theory called "Lysenkoism," but when the crops continually failed, it became clear that hybrid grain developed using Western genetics was needed. Thus, although there is a great ability in people to ignore evidence, it can, when presented forcefully enough, begin to penetrate, forcing people to face up to reality. Perhaps *this* is the role of such future studies as "The Limits to Growth," which we studied in Section 3.3. They make us realize where we are going, so that short-term gains seem less sweet when we look at the long-range disaster that will ensue unless we take positive action.

Let us just consider two examples of the sort of short-range thinking that these studies try to correct. An affluent individual may say, "I can support this many children, why shouldn't I have as many as I want? I can afford to buy more gasoline, why shouldn't I go as fast as I want?" The problem is to develop national or international perspectives that let such people see that although they may be making things better for themselves in the short run, it is true that in the long run they are making it worse for everybody. An amusing example was offered by a letter to the editor in the British newspaper, *The Guardian,* in January 1975. The inhabitants of a village jointly agreed to give their vicar a barrel of wine for Xmas. A large barrel was handed from house to house. The first contributor decided that he could put in a quart of water since that would not be noticed in a whole barrel of wine. The barrel moved on—and at Xmas the vicar received a barrel of water!

What this means is that democratic government has two apparently contradictory goals:

(i)   it must respond to the interests of the people; and

(ii)   it must educate the public to better understand national and international priorities and long-term goals.

In a closed society, the goal of education (ii) can slip into mere **propaganda,** in which the government determines the party line with little concern for public opinion, but then uses the media to try and convince the public that the party line is "just what they wanted." In wartime, even the most liberal governments tend to act this way when they feel that it is vital to the war effort. In an open society, however, when the danger of war or revolution or mass starvation is low, the government will be only one of many voices. Private interests will seek to present their viewpoint, and with this much diversity, the thoughtful citizen will be better equipped to distinguish useful insights from mere propaganda.

Having said all this, let us end the section with a closer look at the possible uses of computer networks in democracy.

One of the impacts of evolving computer technology is that it becomes easier and easier for people to use computers without any particular skills—much as most of us can drive a car, even though we may know little about the internal combustion engine.

We saw in Section 2.3 that—at least in the developed countries—a home computer will be as common as TV sets in the 1980s. This computer will combine a TV set and an electric typewriter with the abilities of a small computer. In addition to working on its own, this computer could also act as a terminal for a **computer utility.** We saw in Section 5.4 that such a utility could handle financial transactions. More importantly, though, citizens will be able—as we suggested in Section 6.2—to use their computer for home access to "dynamic libraries," which would provide TV-style documentaries for overall perspective on a subject; with interaction capabilities to give the user access to more detailed material—including books and papers. Experts in all fields would contribute to *updating* all levels, improving cross-references, extending access to backup material using the evolving technology of CAI: Computer Assisted Instruction.

We said before that *too much* information is just as bad as *too little* information. It will require specialized editing by first-class newswriters and librarians—making expert use of data base management and CAI techniques—to keep the system responsive to the public interest. Nobody can keep track of everything. It is a continuing struggle to perceive what really matters. Each individual must develop his own perspective and critical judgment. The dynamic library must flexibly respond to the individual's queries, rather than restricting him to dogma or overwhelming him with trivia.

To interface such public **information networks** with the governmental process, the updating would include information fleshing out the daily news. In particular, significant planning developments on the planning networks would be outlined for the general public.

Subject to cost limitations, many of the data base management, simulation, and learning techniques of planning networks could be used by students and the general public—both to help them learn about these techniques and apply them for their own benefit; and to obtain more insight into the mechanisms of government.

As we have stressed, both in this section and in Section 6.2, we can only expect a government to allow information in the network to the extent that they allow it to be published in newspapers—the age-old question of freedom of the press. One imaginative friend suggested that the fate of a system that circulated information contrary to government policy might be announced in the following news item:

> The government is sad to announce that last night one of its research satellites accidentally collided with the Information Network satellite positioned over the continent. A spokesman for the Department of Defense speculated that it might be some months, at least, before the Information Network Foundation will be able to replace their satellite. He added that it is the government's hope that there will be no cause for such accidents in the future.

In any case, we can hope that all countries will have a wide range of topics on which the government can let people obtain the information they need. To these we add systems for citizen feedback. These include systems that let people register complaints and queries with appropriate planning networks; and TV-polls, both on national issues and to let a representative carry on a two-way examination of the issues with his constituents. In these ways, computer networking can serve to make government more responsive to the needs of the public, while helping the public understand the problems government must solve.

Suggestions for Further Reading

S. A. Umpleby: Is Greater Citizen Participation in Planning Possible and Desirable? *Technological Forecasting and Social Change,* **4,** 1972, pp. 61–76.
Umpleby discusses the impact of communication and computer
technology—including CAI—on democratic forms of government. An excellent bibliography is given for readers who want to pursue this topic
further.

C. B. Macpherson: "The Real World of Democracy," Oxford University Press,
London and New York, 1966.
This is a short (67 pages) book, giving the text of the Massey Lectures first
broadcast by the Canadian Broadcasting Corporation in January and
February, 1965. The author compares liberal democracy in the sense
used in countries like those of Western Europe and Canada with the
nonliberal democracies of communist countries and of the underdeveloped countries.

R. A. Dahl: "After the Revolution? Authority in a Good Society." Yale University Press, New Haven, Connecticut, 1970.
Dahl examines the way in which democracy evolves to give "power to the
people" when there are many different opinions to respond to, and few
people have time to carefully weigh all the issues.

Summary

Democracy can only work within limits. It can help government respond
to more and more sections of the public, but it cannot ensure that powerful
groups will sit idly by while their own interests are threatened, unless the
country has an army and police force committed to upholding decisions
made by the public through their elected officials.

People do not have time to respond to a computer poll on all government policies. On the other hand, it would be foolish to commit government
to officials of the **planning networks** without public input on policy. Representatives elected for their decision-making style can bridge this gap. **Information networks** can then be used by the public for general information, for
appropriate interactions with the planning networks, and for feedback on
key issues.

Glossary

Bug: A *bug* is an error in a program that causes the computer under its
control to behave differently from what was intended. *Debugging* is the process of tracking down and correcting such errors.

Schema: A *schema* is a person's point of view on some set of issues which
greatly determines the way he or she responds to them.

Model of the world: An animal or robot's *model of the world* is the information it has inside its brain or computer about the world around it. The model thus serves to guide the system through interaction with its environment.

Propaganda: *Propaganda* is the systematic attempt to spread information designed to convince people of a particular viewpoint.

Genetics: *Genetics* is the study of the biological basis for the inheritance of characteristics.

Relativity: Einstein's *theory of relativity* explained the surprising behavior of particles that travel with a speed approaching that of light. It also showed that mass could be converted into energy, and laid the theoretical basis for the construction of atom (fission) and hydrogen (fusion) bombs.

Computer conferencing: *Computer conferencing* enables people, even when widely scattered geographically, to conduct a conference by communicating through a computer network. Each user has a *mailbox*—a reserved section of memory in one of the computers on the net—in which other users can leave messages by typing in the right instructions at their terminal.

Computer utility: A *computer utility,* like electricity and water utilities, is a network to which everyone has access.

Planning network: A *planning network* is a computer system designed to help human planners at one node work with, or learn from, planners at other nodes.

Democracy: *Democracy* is a form of government in which sovereign power resides in the people as a whole. This power is then exercised either directly by the people, or by officers freely elected by the people.

Information network: An *information network* is a computer system designed to supplement the media by letting people get specific information about current issues, activity on the planning networks, and so on.

Technocrat: A *technocrat* is someone who holds a leadership position in society because of his or her expertise in technology.

Exercises

1.   Give two examples of "specialists who know more than the average citizen can about the mechanics of implementing a particular policy" whom you would not challenge even when the policy, incorrectly implemented, would kill you. Is this an example of *voluntary* surrender of decision-making power in a democratic context?

2.   What do you think Arthur C. Clarke (a writer on science, and of science fiction) means by saying that the United States was not really united until the railroad and telegraph systems were built?

3.   In the city-state of Athens 2500 years ago and in some New England towns today, all the citizens can assemble in one place and debate on alternate plans for common problems. Aristotle said that the size of a political community is limited by the range of one man's voice. What do you think he meant? Do you believe this to be true today? What is the limit today on the size of a political community?

4. Before Chile and Argentina leased satellite circuits on the INTELSAT network, there was almost no rapid communication between the two countries. And yet their capital cities are less than an hour apart by airline service, and they share a 1000 mile geographic boundary. What prevented normally efficient communications in the past? (*Hint:* Look at a map of South America. What other kinds of boundaries can be forced to play a smaller role in global problem solving with the advent of computerized networks?)

5. Suppose three candidates, A, B, and C, are running for a single office. Each citizen votes by listing a first choice and a second choice. Is it possible for exactly ⅓ of the voters to prefer A to B, ⅓ prefer B to C, and ⅓ prefer C to A? Can you think of a "fair" way to select a winner? Does this suggest a limit to purely democratic planning?

6. Give a brief example from your own life of a time when you solved a problem by stepping back and choosing a higher level, more all-encompassing goal.

7. Only rarely in history has a group seized near total control of a country and then returned control to the populace (Kemil Ataturk in Turkey, or the leaders of the American Revolution, for instance). What does this suggest about the willingness of political experts to support construction of a network for "computer-aided democracy"?

8. In Athens, 6th century B.C., the first great democracy was born. However, the slaves (who could not vote) outnumbered the citizens. Similarly, through most American history, women could not vote. Would a computerized democracy, in which a minority of the subjects were full voting citizens, be a fair and effective government? Justify your belief in ½ page.

9. One survey shows that in 1972 Americans spent an average of 90 *seconds* per day reading books, newspapers, or magazines (business forms, ads, and street signs were not counted). The typical college student spends closer to 90 *minutes* per day reading. One reason is access—the mythical "average" American home has only two books; most students carry that many with them. Another is the overwhelming presence of TV. One important result is the massive ignorance of the populace. This section suggests that a computer-based mixture of TV and text might successfully give citizens access to politically important information. Write a ½ page essay criticizing this view.

7.3. A BRAIN FOR PLANET EARTH

In Section 7.1 we saw how computers could be used for planning from the municipal level on up to the national. In Section 7.2 we saw how the citizens of a country could influence that planning if the political opinion in the country had enough common assumptions to support a democracy. In this section we go further, and ask whether we can expect the development of worldwide planning networks—A Brain for Planet Earth—to occur in the next few years; and to explore the impact of the wide range of political beliefs held by the governments of different countries.

Grand Aims and Realistic Subgoals

As the world population rises, the resources available for each person dwindle. Countries rich in one resource may be desperately poor in another. While some countries have highly developed industry, other countries may find almost their entire population engaged in subsistence farming. Meanwhile, conflicting ideologies plunge many nations into states of war—or near war—as Protestants battle Catholics in northern Ireland, Christians battle Arabs in Lebanon, and Jews battle Arabs for the lands of Israel. Overshadowing all of this is the polarization between the superpowers of the United States, China, and the Soviet Union, and the grim threat of nuclear war.

The only sane response to these threats is world cooperation on a scale we have never seen before. Nations must learn to live with other nations of different ideologies. The developed countries must use part of their wealth to provide technology and capital to help the underdeveloped countries begin the long, hard climb from bare survival to self-reliance. Countries must accept the obligation to share resources in such a way that no country goes without at least its basic needs. Finally, countries must accept the distribution of materials in this way as an *obligation* rather than an act of charity.

However, the very severity of the threat makes us pessimistic about the chances of a swift acceptance of these very reasonable goals for international cooperation. We certainly cannot hope for true equality between nations in this century. If the people of India were suddenly to achieve the American standard of living in the strange sense of two cars per family, the resource depletion and pollution would be catastrophic. On the other hand, we cannot expect Americans to reduce their standard of living to anything approaching that of the average Indian villager. Our goal must be "equal opportunity" rather than "equality"; trying to initiate trends that will allow the underdeveloped nations to see genuine progress. One complacency-shaking scenario that has been suggested for the end of the 20th century is that—if affluent countries like the United States do not commit sizable resources to aiding the underdeveloped countries—a terrorist from one of those countries will one day carry an atom bomb in a suitcase and leave it in a bus terminal in Los Angeles or New York. This would be done not to make things better for the underdeveloped nations but just to wipe the smug smile off affluent American faces. Perhaps, then, the sense of obligation that we refer to above will be backed up in the future by nuclear blackmail.

However, even if we agree that "equal opportunity" is the appropriate goal for international cooperation, grounds for pessimism still remain. We have already listed the great ideological bitterness that divides both people within nations and people of different nations. To this we must add the observation that recent years have seen nations act more to grab resources for themselves than to ensure that resources are fairly shared. During the energy crisis of the early 1970s, the French left the solidarity of other oil-consuming nations to try to strike a special deal with the oil producers. This gained France at most a short-range advantage, but the long-range effect was simply to encourage oil prices to rise even further. In fact, the oil producers raised prices to such a level that the balance of trade of the developed nations was grossly impaired, and this contributed to the economic problems of a recession. Even worse, the oil-poor, underdeveloped nations were placed under an increasing burden. The response of the United States to this shortage of energy seemed to be far more in terms of mobilizing America's huge resources for domestic energy consumption than in ensuring that other nations of the world, less well endowed, would be able to meet their energy needs.

In a similarly depressing vein, we may note that in the 3rd Law of the Sea Conference in 1976, those nations with ocean borders almost all voted to extend their territorial limits to 200 miles off shore, thus increasing their own share of ocean resources with little regard for the needs of countries that are not fortunate enough to have long coastlines. This defeated efforts to make as much of the ocean bed as possible an international resource to be shared by all—a move that would hopefully have created a valuable precedent for the sharing of such land-based resources as energy, food, and minerals.

We have said that it is unlikely that a world order of complete international cooperation will spring up in the next few years. We *can,* however, expect many small areas of international cooperation to develop. In fact, as we shall spell out in the rest of this section, it is reasonable to predict that we will see the creation of a multiplicity of planning and information networks—of the kind we have seen in the previous two sections—on a worldwide basis. These networks will have limited goals, rather than providing a single world government.

There will be networks for worldwide distribution of specialized information; resource allocation networks; networks to improve economic coordination and to transfer capital to underdeveloped nations; and networks to monitor possible sources of conflict. We shall see that such networks are very likely to arise, and will each be beneficial in the respective sphere of influence. Going beyond the limited goals of the individual networks, however, we may hope that the interlinkage of governments brought about by their cooperation in many different networks will increasingly encourage cooperation on more and more issues. In any case, the individual networks will prove of great value in themselves, and we will see the linkage of pairs or triplets of such networks forced by the realization of planners of the huge overlaps in the data bases and programs that they are using on the networks involved.

In any worldwide network for resource allocation, satellites could play a valuable role by monitoring resources. For example, satellites could keep track of the world's oil resources.

To add a touch of realism to this discussion, we can briefly look at some of the "seeds" from which these networks can grow.

To start, we may expect that a number of the agencies established by the United Nations will function more efficiently when converted into computerized planning networks. For example, the Food and Agriculture Organization (FAO) could use computer-networking to maintain an inventory of world food production, making contingency plans to respond to famines with a program of relief that would cause minimum dislocation in the more fortunate countries. Moreover, the FAO could devote itself to a full-scale systems analysis that is not simply aimed at responding to particular food crises, but works toward a stable world free of hunger. Resource satellites could be used to map areas of the world in which more food can be grown. Computer conferencing could be used to share information between agricultural experts to allow them to devise agricultural plans that would increase the self-reliance of individual nations. One of the great problems faced by the FAO is the difficulty that workers in one country have in obtaining access to data compiled in other countries. This is one of the problems that the developments in computer networking sketched in Section 7.1 are designed to solve.

By the same token, the World Health Organization (WHO) and the World Meteorological Organization (WMO) could have their efficiency improved by the development of computer networks. Of course, it must be stressed that the existing bureaucracy in these organizations would have to be drastically reshaped, along lines suggested by the new communication paths that the computer would open up. What must also be stressed is that natural linkages would develop between these networks. For example, the problems of malnutrition accompanying a famine would require coordinated efforts by the FAO and WHO. On the other hand, long-term forecasts produced by the WMO on the basis of extensive computer analysis of worldwide satellite photographs of weather patterns could be used to provide the FAO with advance warning which it could use to determine the best crop mix for different countries as weather conditions vary.

We can also expect that the town-planning networks and national economic networks which we discussed in Section 7.1 will find it useful to exchange information with networks in other countries. At first, the exchange may be highly formalized, but it can be expected that nations that share common goals and political philosophy will find it increasingly valuable to pool their data bases and problem-solving techniques. We may also expect that existing "networks" such as diplomatic channels and international scientific societies—which do not yet use much computer technology—will increasingly try to structure information so that it can be exchanged through a computer network. The resultant change in rate and type of flow will drastically modify the way in which people interact. Just as technological change has played a major role in the nature of war (think of the development of nuclear warfare) and of cities (think of the impact of the automobile) so will computer networks drastically change international relations, as diplomats, politicians, and civil servants find that they may exchange information that previously they did not even know how to obtain. For example, if in working out some international treaty, the planners can continually interact through the network, they will be able to make small concessions without "losing face"—rather than trying to reconcile complete plans that have been independently generated. Of course, a safety clause is required here—if you "give enough inches, you go a mile." Thus the participants in treaty building through a network must reserve the right to reevaluate a draft plan before they put it into action.

In making plans for international cooperation, it seems useful to avoid, as much as possible, grand plans to which all regions must conform. Care must be taken to separate issues as much as possible to minimize the extent to which disagreement on one issue blocks agreements on others.

It seems tempting to state the **principle of maximal autonomy,** which stresses that for most applications, the networks are voluntary organizations, which may or may not be used by regions or by regional alliances. In other words, the stress is to be on using each network as a source of tools to be *adapted* by *local* experts to solve their problems. These tools are not limiting in any strict sense, and new tools can be added to the network.

Unfortunately, while this principle is appealing, we must face up to the fact that even in a distributed control structure, there will still be competition for resources. Once nations have agreed to give up some resources in exchange for other benefits, then it is necessary that each nation comply with the agreement if future uses of the network are to be successful. How is this compliance to be brought about?

Within a nation, we have the *judiciary* to judge conformance to the rules, the *police* to enforce the rules, and a *penal system* to punish those who violate the rules. While we do have a World Court to judge the extent to which nations adhere to treaties, we do not yet have an effective international "police system." The United Nations has been able to play a useful peace-keeping role once a settlement has been reached which is approved by the superpowers; but, for the foreseeable future, there is no way in which the "world as a whole" can enforce a decision on one of the superpowers. We have seen Czechoslovakia and Viet Nam serve as sacrifices to the balance of power where the nations with the "clout" have been more concerned with their own interests than with the freedom of choice of the small nation concerned.

To take another example: In the early 1970s, the United States, which had just about stopped whaling, decided to heed the conservationists and urge a ban on whaling. The Soviet Union and Japan, which still have whaling industries, did not agree. Should the United States have gone to war to protect the whale? The risk of an all-out conflagration hardly seemed to merit it. Perhaps the most one can hope for is that the compelling data of ecological models will finally break through. It is now possible to show that above a certain level, the short-term economic gain of catching whales now can only yield long-term economic disaster, as various whale species go to extinction. The United States has the same problem internally, as American fishermen harvest tuna at levels that will yield a drastic fall in reproduction. Unfortunately, politicians—whether their country has only one political party, or two or more—find it far easier to respond to short-term economic interests than to encourage people to take a longer-term view. Perhaps the information networks in Section 7.2 can be used to create the climate of public opinion that will allow a mature long-term perspective to drown out the clamoring of small special-interest groups.

Let me stress, in closing this subsection, that I do not believe that it is a question of *whether* international planning networks and national information networks will be implemented, or whether there will be linkages between various networks. The question is rather *when, how well,* and *with what safeguards* they are to be implemented.

The Diversity of Nation-States

In planning networks for world cooperation, we usually take the nation-state as the basic unit of political organization. We have been trying to see to what extent the economic and ecological pressures currently facing the world can encourage that cooperation between nations while at the same time respecting the needs of the individual citizens of each nation. We are looking for a world order that can accommodate trends toward increased international, political, and economic cooperation while at the same time allowing cultural diversity. It is proper to ask, then, to what extent we can expect the grouping of nations into cooperative entities. We can see encouraging signs in the development of such entities as the European Common Market, in which a number of nations work together in their economic planning. However, recent years have also seen **separatism,** in which moves have been made for previously united countries to separate into two or more parts, and **devolution,** in which regions of a country move toward increased self-government. Bangladesh has already separated itself from Pakistan, while the Basques in Spain, the Scots and the Welsh in Great Britain, and the French in Canada are all pushing for increased autonomy.

However, in those cases where there is a move for separation, we may often trace the move to a lack of a flexible federal governmental structure that allows a reasonable autonomy on many issues to the individual states, as well as allowing cultural diversity to flourish. Thus devolution may be the proper response to separatist sentiments.

What we seem to need then, recalling from the last subsection our principle of maximal autonomy, is a form of government that can coordinate planning on many of the "bread and butter" issues, while allowing different nations, and different groups within nations, to develop distinctive cultures and lifestyles.

At times, it seems that we need a new ideology that can unite all mankind. There is a paradox here, however. If a nation or a group of nations believe so strongly that they already have the ideology for the world, then they may be tempted to declare war on other nations to convert them to that ideology, rather than seeking coexistence in a context of interdependence.

It must be realized that the leaders of any nation—no matter how responsive they are to local problems—will continually be concerned with responding to national interests. As a result, the citizens of one nation may well be concerned that a network will be used to exploit their resources, rather than to provide them with mutual aid. If, for example, the United States were to develop a global resource-sharing network, the leaders of an African nation might well be forgiven for refusing the gift of the million-dollar computer they need to get on the network. This would be because of fear that the network would be used to increase the flow of resources to the United States, rather than to aid the developing nation. If, as one hopes, the United States genuinely believes that it must help other nations to develop, there still remains a major political problem of convincing the leaders of other nations that this is truly part of United States foreign policy.

Even if the United States is sincere in its claims about the use of the network, the technocrats of the developing nation would want to make sure that the network had safety features which could be called into action should American policy change. Thus, when we speak trustingly of how beneficial computers can be in helping to solve global problems, we must never forget the difference in finding out what is best for all, and ensuring that some small fanatical group does not seek power to force the adoption of a policy that enriches them at considerable cost to other segments of the world population.

On the one hand, we may expect that as resources get scarce a country with such resources might wish to classify information about them. On the other hand, a country might abuse information it would obtain from others over the network, seeking to be the first to observe a trend and extract short-range advantages. Perhaps the only consoling statement that one can make here is that such problems have always been with us, and that if intelligence-gathering (spying!) is done in the open, with all nations relatively likely to have eventual access to the information gathered, stability is perhaps easier to achieve than it is at present. While increasing shortages will encourage a tendency toward cutthroat tactics, we can observe that a properly designed network will decrease the likelihood of a sufficiently bad imbalance in distribution for these tactics to become tempting to national leaders.

Just as with the rights of individuals to privacy with respect to data banks (Section 4.3), so must there be legitimate security grounds for privacy on the planning networks, whether national or international. Each node will want private files to maintain options and to preserve local data bases from external interference. We will thus need international treaties on data access to ensure that minimal standards of interregional cooperation are met, while other treaties will protect privacy as a safeguard against the imposition of conformity. The question of what data and procedures shall be available raises the paradox that requiring the "free flow of information" can restrict freedom. For one thing, the requirement that all decisions be available for general scrutiny can be a costly drain on scarce resources. For another, the dissemination of all information required for decision-making can, as we have seen, infringe individual and regional privacy.

Perhaps the most damning criticism of proposals like the international planning networks that would constitute our "Brain for

Planet Earth" is that we have viewed many of the world's problems as if they were purely informational. We know, however, from our dealings with other people, let alone international politics, that it is often difficult for people to lay their differences before the arbitration of sweet reason—"ideologies are not easily permeable to information." It is no small challenge to determine to what extent networks can span political systems as diverse as those of the United States and China. Perhaps the evolution of air traffic agreements, and of policies for fiscal exchange, will provide basic networks from which fuller forms of cooperation can evolve. There is a very real challenge to continually carry on a comparative study of different political systems, to determine what elements of planning can be interchanged between the different "world views." It is clear that the planners at any one node can only proceed if they have a realistic (even if simplified) model of the power structures and motivation of other nations. While a nation will have many planning centers involved in regional and global networks, it will also require planning centers to handle national security needs. It would be naive to ignore the threat of war at this time in human history. However, by opening up paths of communication even by opposing nations, we can increase the mutual understanding between those nations. One proposal, for example, suggests that computer conferencing be set up between nations with a view to coming up with models of the decision-making structures in the two nations. To start, each nation would make models of the other's power structure. Then the other nation would respond with corrections. In this way, the planners in each nation would have a better idea of the motivation of the other nation, and so might be less likely to start a war. In such modeling of political motivations, it will be vitally important to distinguish what a nation *says* its goals are from the *motivations* that actually determine the government's actions.

From Regional Simulations to Global Networks

To provide a more concrete example of the establishment of international planning networks, let us reexamine the work of Mesarović and Pestel in their study, "Mankind at the Turning Point." We saw, in Section 3.3, that they responded to "The Limits to Growth" study by stressing that we had to divide the world into at least 10 interacting regions if we were to have a sufficiently clear view of global interactions. Without this view, we can only despair as we see the limits to growth being reached. With this view, however, we can see ways in which transfer of capital between nations can yield increases in standards of the underdeveloped world with little decrease in the standards of the developed world. In the years since that study was made Mesarović and Pestel have been spreading their world simulation techniques to be used for the development of "local" models with finer detail. We briefly examine the models that have been built in Iran, West Germany, and Latin America. The key to each of these models is a process of **subregionalization** and **disaggregation**—in other words, breaking the regions in the vicinity of the host country into smaller regions so that the impact on that nation can be more carefully assessed.

The Iranian model is part of Iran's sixth development plan, and is part of the Plan and Budget Organization's efforts to relate local problems to international order. For example, they have developed scenarios to assess the impact of food resources on the world economy. They study questions such as whether Iran can or should move to self-sufficiency in its food resources; they assess the extent to which they should be producing meat from their grain rather than using grain as a human food stuff; and they try to assess the balance between devoting resources to agriculture and using it to build up Iran's industrial base. They look at the extent to which crop patterns should be based on self-sufficiency or on profit through trade, and they look at both domestic and international food availability to assess the probability of famines.

We mentioned above the problems that sudden rises in oil prices have caused in the last few years. One of the goals of the Iranian model is to look at the impact of different oil prices on Iranian development. While oil is an easy source of foreign exchange—which is the catalyst of development—Iranian planners realize that if they raise prices unduly, they will stimulate the development of alternate energy sources—such as solar power—and thus decrease the market for their oil.

The Iranians are also developing cooperative bonds with a modeling effort in Egypt, which will allow a dialog on common objectives in the Middle East. Perhaps we can see here the germ of a network in which each nation will have a model that is most detailed for its own needs, but that has enough information for a linkage with the models developed elsewhere. From the viewpoint of world peace, one must ask to what extent one can expect the network growing in the Middle East to link only those nations which hold to Islam—Iran and the Arab countries. It would be encouraging if one could see a way for Israel to be linked to such a network as a step toward stabilization in the

Middle East, but it is perhaps more realistic to expect that the mutual distrust will prevent the linkage.

Another regional model is being developed for the Ministry for Science and Research in Technology in West Germany to address such pressing problems as unemployment, inflation, and dwindling resources. For West Germany, there is a large stake in the export of capital goods. For this reason, the trade model has been greatly expanded with a detailed 19-sector model of the Germany economy. This model not only includes the flow of money, goods, and services, but also includes such technological factors as material and energy flows, and the properties of a labor pool described by educational status. This detailed model of West Germany is coupled with a somewhat less detailed model of the European economic community, and with a rather sketchy model—much at the level of the "Turning Point" study—of the rest of the world.

The Latin American Regional Project divides Latin America into seven subregions: Argentina, Brazil, the Andean Pact countries, Venezuela, Central America, the Caribbean, and Mexico. It has special submodels for petroleum and energy, copper, aluminum, and food. The need for breaking Latin America down into subregions, and for developing models of this kind, can be seen by the fact that Venezuela is oil rich while many other Latin American countries are oil poor. Latin Americans are thus especially sensitive to the impact of changes in oil prices on the economies of underdeveloped, oil-poor nations; and the need to invest in alternate energy sources. Latin America is at present a deficit area for food, and the discussion of new agricultural methods is coupled with an analysis of the economic problems of balance of payments for countries which must import both food and energy.

The Latin American model also includes a model of population that relates food needs, birth rate, and the increasing migration from the countryside to the cities. One of the greatest concerns of the Latin American planners is that increasing population not only puts demands on food resources, but also raises grave problems of unemployment. Their preliminary data gathering has shown that industrialization appears to be proceeding at a very uneven pace. This industrialization is important, however, not only to make Latin America less reliant on imports and to strengthen the balance of payments, but also to create the new jobs required for an increasing population.

The reader will recall from our discussion of world simulation in Section 3.3, and our comparison of world models with weather-forecasting, that the predictions made by such models are at the moment unreliable unless there is a wealth of accurate data available, and predictions are made locally and for a short amount of time. One of the dangers of the establishment of regional models of the kind we have just been discussing is that government officials for whom computers are still mysterious will confuse the ability of these systems to generate numbers with validity. There is something tremendously impressive about being able to sit at a computer console and pose questions about energy and employment trends over the next 50 years for a number of different scenarios. In fact this is so impressive, that I have heard a high government official from France claim that a couple of days of this sort of experience had shown him the validity of such models! For the time being, it will be very important to carry out a careful analysis of the assumptions that went in to any prediction of the model that will be relied on in any major decision-making. In other words, the need for **model validation** must always be uppermost in the minds of the planners.

There are many other problems associated with the impressive responsiveness of the Mesarović–Pestel systems. A number of the governments that are putting money into the development of these planning tools seem to be unaware of the fact that there are many other approaches that are definitely superior for certain applications. As we mentioned in Section 3.3, there are techniques of optimal **control,** which allow one to compute patterns of action which will lead to desired results, rather than carrying out long, tedious patterns of trial and error with one scenario after another being plugged into the computer until the system responds in a desirable way. Much other research is being done in system theory and mathematical economics that already contributes to the planning process in many countries. Yet no effort seems to be made by Mesarović and Pestel to incorporate these methods into their own work. While this did not matter when they were preparing the single study "Mankind at the Turning Point," it does become a cause for grave concern when their techniques are being used more and more in national planning.

Another problem with this approach is that little attention has been paid to the fact—which we have stressed again and again—that there is such a thing as having too much data. The need is to look continually for new scientific principles that will systematize planning, focusing on a few relevant pieces of data—rather than trying to project trends on every piece of data that can be measured.

Be that as it may, the development of techniques that many different nations can use in projecting food energy and population levels and industrial development into the future provide a firm basis for the type of planning networks we have discussed. Given that these planning centers must use a wider range of techniques from system theory and mathematical economics and that they must find more efficient ways to organize their data bases and cut them back to basic variables, there still remains the question of how the various nodes could communicate.

A key observation is that each region will want to examine in far more detail the activity within the country, in its close neighbors, in its trading partners, and in its likely enemies, than it will want in modeling the rest of the world. When a nation needs to make projections based on the values that are not included in its own model, it can use the network to obtain those values from the other nodes. However, a value which is only approximated at the regional level at one node may get more and more out of line with the actual value being established elsewhere. What we need for this is an "active data base" which can draw the attention of planners to discrepancies between actual and predicted values, between local and regional projections. The point of such an *alerting system*—as should be clear from our earlier discussion—is not simply to provide local planners with more accurate data, but also to make them aware that their model is not as accurate as they think it is. Thus the discrepancy serves as a cue for model updating, and perhaps a reassessment of the assumptions that the planners have been making.

We have seen that the planning styles of regions with different ideologies may differ greatly. Thus one node may discover that the reason for the discrepancy between its projections and the actual trends elsewhere is a completely different emphasis in priorities between the two nations. This ties back to our earlier comments on the need for a continual process of value and ideology modeling of one nation by another.

Another reason why communication between nodes is crucial is to ensure that countries do not simultaneously and independently decide to develop factories that produce the same product without ensuring that the total capacity of these factories will not greatly exceed the world demand for their product.

In time we can expect certain nations to be closely tied together in their planning process—as is already beginning to happen in the European Common Market, the eastern European nations, and in Latin America. We can thus expect patterns of tight linkage between groups that share common interests in a relatively defined geographical area, with looser linkages between these different regions. This is in strong contrast to the somewhat unnatural lumping of nations into regions that we criticized in the original Mesarović–Pestel model in Section 3.3.

We stress that it would be a mistake to use the electronic speed of the computer to make all decisions as quickly as possible. In the previous section, for example, we said that "push-button democracy" was a mistake because it would have legislation passed into law before its implication had been considered in full detail. Thus we must find the right "time constants" for decision-making, seeing which problems can in fact be disposed of in a day or two of routine decision-making; and which problems have such far-reaching implications that years of careful international discussion are required before they should be put into effect.

We have repeatedly stressed the risk of war brought about by the fiercely different ideologies of different nations. Unfortunately, the drive of the superpowers to extend and stabilize their spheres of influence have denied many small nations the chance to try out their own system of government. The United States' boycott of Castro's Cuba is one example of a large nation's intolerance to social experimentation within its sphere of influence. The Russian invasion of Czechoslovakia in 1968 was not only tragic for what it did to the Czechs as individuals, but also for the fact that it crushed an "experiment" from which the Russians could have learned. This "experiment" combined socialist ideas with various approaches to democratic *two-party* decision-making which were not part of the Soviet system. I would like to think that the international networks of the kind we have discussed would encourage experiments, with nations sharing "objective" information as to how well a Marxist analysis might fit in certain data, and how well a capitalist scheme could solve certain labor problems.

However, let us return to the analysis of power which, as we saw in Section 7.2, places certain limitations on the extent of democracy. If detailed economic and resource-sharing networks had been in place back in 1968, but with the Soviet Union still holding the world view that it had at that time, it is probable that the network would not have served to help the Czechs. Rather, it would have given the Russians earlier warning of the changes taking place in Czechoslovakia, and so would have hastened repression rather than avoided it.

We see again a need for the "maximal autonomy" of certain aspects of network function that we discussed earlier in the section. In any case, whether with or without the use of networks designed with appropriate safeguards, it would be worthwhile if the United Nations—instead of reviling each other for adopting different social systems—would instead applaud diversity and cooperate to set up objective studies of the success of different organization in tackling different problems.

A final example: The Rand Corporation was the "think tank" that played a vital role in American involvement in the Viet Nam war. Scientists at the Rand Corporation used computers to try to answer the question "How do we fight the North Vietnamese?" However, the question of "Should we be fighting the North Vietnamese?" was hardly considered at all. The central question of any study of "Computers and the Cybernetic Society"—whether considering the use of computers by a government, a credit card agency, or in the home—is *not* simply—"Given a narrowly stated problem, how well and how efficiently is the computer being used to solve it?"—But—"Is the right problem being solved? What is the *real* problem? Are people doing the right things? Should the computer be used at all?"

Suggestions for Further Reading

R. H. Kupperman and S. C. Goldman: Towards a Viable International System: Crisis Management and Computer Conferencing, in "Views from the International Conference on Computer Communications 74" (N. Macon, ed.), pp. 71–80.
A discussion is presented of the use of computer conferencing and modeling to reduce crises—whether triggered by freak weather reducing food supplies to famine level, terrorists threatening to blow up a city, or foreign leaders poised at the brink of war. The need to understand the value systems and viewpoints of others is stressed.

S. Beer: "Designing Freedom: The CBC Massey Lectures 1973." CBC Publ., Toronto, 1974.
A look is taken, by an English management specialist, at the use of cybernetics to build more responsive structures of government.

R. N. Gardner: "In Pursuit of World Order: U.S. Foreign Policy and International Organizations." Praeger, New York, 1966.
Stock is taken of the mechanisms of international cooperation afforded by the United Nations and other organizations, and the ways in which they can be strengthened is examined.

J. Frankel: "Contemporary International Theory and the Behavior of States." Oxford University Press, London and New York, 1973.

R. J. Lieber: "Theory and World Politics." Winthrop, 1972.
These two books discuss the ways in which a variety of theoretical concepts, including those from cybernetics, may be applied to the study of international relations.

M. Mesarović and E. Pestel: "Mankind at the Turning Point," E. P. Dutton/ Readers Digest Press, New York, 1974.

John Clark and Sam Cole: "Global Simulation Models." Wiley, London, 1975. A report of one global simulation project, and a perspective on a number of such simulations.

Summary

We have stressed that global planning networks are inevitable, and that the challenge is to decrease areas of conflict and misunderstanding and to increase cooperation. This will require a basic commitment toward world order in addition to national interest.

We saw that our grand aims for international cooperation to share resources and prevent war must be replaced by realistic subgoals. We must look for many different networks handling specialized problems in international cooperation, rather than a single grand scheme of world government and universal peace. We saw that the planners in any one nation will need to protect certain information in their national interest. However, they must also seek to understand better the ideology and decision making processes of planners in other nations to reduce the risk of reaching a level of misunderstanding that could escalate into war.

Finally, we have analyzed the way in which simulation techniques can be used to relate a detailed model of a nation's economy to simpler models of activity in other nations, and looked at the advances in simulation techniques and data base management required to link these local planning nodes.

Glossary

Principle of maximal autonomy: The *principle of maximal autonomy* says that the purpose of a planning network is to provide tools for local planning, rather than primarily to provide centralized control of the planning at different nodes.

Separatism: *Separatism* is the advocacy of breaking up a country into several smaller states. *Devolution* is the process whereby regions of a country move toward increased self-government. These are both political processes.

Disaggregation: In modeling a complex system, we study a number of subsystems. *Disaggregation* breaks these systems into smaller systems—for the purpose of more accurate simulation. *Subregionalization* is disaggregation as applied to world models—replacing regions of the simulation by several smaller ones.

Model validation: Checking the predictions of a model against the actual changes of the original over time is called *model validation*. An analysis of differences can be used to modify the model to get one that more accurately predicts important activities of the original.

Control: *Control* is achieved by choosing the inputs to a system to make the state or output change in some desired way, or at least close to it.

Exercises

1. Draw a system diagram of the kind shown in Fig. 3 of Section 3.3 which includes the following nodes and interconnections:

(a)   Rising world population implies dwindling resources (per capita).

(b)   Several countries (show U.S., China, U.S.S.R.) have several resources each (draw three: food, energy, hardware technology; show population as a negative link to food and energy per capita).

(c)   Two of these countries (U.S. and U.S.S.R.) have highly developed industry (hardware); one is very agricultural (food).

(d)   Each nation has an "ideological fervor" state variable which, when high in *both* of two connected countries (and all three are interconnected here), increases a "war level" variable for both.

(e)   Increasing polarization leads to increasing war level.

(f)   Threat of nuclear war (raised war level) is "grim" but increases technology level (hardware). (Guns versus butter!)

(g)   Technology rise yields energy rise (nuclear power, etc.).

(h)   Energy rise yields hardware rise (more oil and gas available means more cars, etc.).

(i)   As energy increases, so does food (fertilizer plants, mechanical harvesting and agrobusiness).

(j)   Total energy supply is limited (fossil and nuclear fuels) so an increase in energy level of any country effectively decreases it (when competitive) in another.

(k)   A source of unpredictable perturbations provides random inputs to each food and ideology level. (One example in the first case is the influence of weather.)

(l)   More food yields more people (assuming food storage is limited and none is allowed to spoil—ignore transfer to third world countries in exchange for ideological influence and raw materials).

(m)   War increase gives population decrease (to be blunt).

These 13 propositions translate into a network of 22 nodes (six each—hardware, energy, food, population, ideology, and war—for U.S., China, U.S.S.R.; three (one per pair) for ideological polarization; and one noise node: "no noise is good news") and 48 links (three each: $H \Rightarrow E$, $E \Rightarrow H$, $E \Rightarrow F$, $F \Rightarrow P$, $P \Rightarrow F$, $W \Rightarrow H$, $W \rightarrow F$, $W \Rightarrow P$, $N \Rightarrow F$, $N \Rightarrow I$; 6 each: $I \rightarrow$ ideopolar, ideopolar $\rightarrow W$, $E \Rightarrow E$).

Although it would take a computer to explore the dynamics of this model fully, write a page of ideas you get by looking at this diagram.

2.   The world-modeling technique of disaggregation chops nations into sectors of the national economy. The Leontieff model in economics uses a similar technique. Each nation is divided into, say, 100 industries, and the effective cash flow between each of the 4950 pairs of industries (see Exercise 6, Section 7.1) is measured. This requires asking questions of the data base such as: "What percentage of the nation's glass production goes into the automobile industry?" A computer manipulation of this information allows predictions of the impact of changes by any industry on any other, or of resource dependence, or of inflationary leverage. Explain, briefly, why we cannot directly combine the Leontieff and Mesarović/Pestel methods by considering the size of a model with 100 industries in each of 100 international regions, any two of which might have some interaction. What does this mean for planning?

3.   The "energy crisis" hurt the U.S. and U.S.S.R. slightly and China not at all, but Europe and Japan were severely hit by industrial and economic setbacks. Support or challenge the following theory: "The energy crisis was totally bogus. It was a fake engineered by the U.S., Russia, and the oil nations to prevent Europe and Japan from becoming equally strong superpowers."

4.   More than a third of the world's uranium reserves are in Africa. Based on this section's discussion of resource competition, energy needs, and the origins of war, support or challenge the following theory: "Recent wars in Africa are actually the initial battles of a major war for nuclear energy resources."

5.   Suppose the entire world tried to copy the American style of life. This would include, worldwide, over one billion automobiles. At one ton each, this requires one billion tons of steel. Compare this with any figures you can find on current steel production. Similarly, compare the one billion gallons per day of gasoline consumption with current resources or production. Complete one of these calculations, or a similar one (half-an-hour in the library will do it), and present the result, and your conclusion of its significance to world planning, as a one page report.

6.   Plutonium is the active ingredient in A-bombs. Enough is unaccounted for in processing each year to make a dozen undetected warheads. Thus the likelihood that a radical, terrorist, or paramilitary organization possesses such a secret weapon increases daily. In a paragraph, why does this encourage the construction of a global planning network, at least a special-purpose network of limited purpose?

7.   *Library project:*   (a) What do these UN organizations—WHO, WMO, FAO—really do? (b) What type of disputes are adjudicated by the World Court? Note that it only settles technical grievances involving two countries, each of which has agreed to abide by World Court decisions. (c) How do your findings relate to the design of a Brain for Planet Earth? Write a ½ page answer to each question.

8.   In several major corporations, all information on personnel, resources, policy, sales, etc. is stored in a data base. The higher one's position in the organizational hierarchy, the greater one's access to the data base. "Those at the bottom have no access," and the president has total access. Why do you think this is done? Should access to the Brain for Planet Earth be distributed this way? Explain.

9. Look up "symbiosis" in your dictionary. What would it mean for people to live in symbiosis with machines?

8

Down and
Up from
Machine Language

This chapter is designed just for those readers who wish to obtain more insight into the circuitry that computers use to execute a program, and who wish to understand a program to the detailed level of machine-language instructions, in which we must specify where all data and instructions are stored in memory.

SECTION 8.1. HOW HARDWARE WORKS

This section looks at the registers in primary memory and in the central processing unit required for executing machine-language instructions. We then examine nine such instructions. We explore the hardware activity required to fetch an instruction from memory, and give a detailed analysis of the execution of two of the nine instructions. The required background is provided by Section 1.1, and the discussion of primary memory and the central processing unit in Section 1.2.

SECTION 8.2. PROGRAMMING AND COMPILING

To obtain a feeling for machine-language programming, we see how to write a program for adding together 100 numbers. Then, to obtain more insight into how to write a compiler to translate from high-level to machine language, we outline how such a compiler would translate a high-level program for adding the numbers. The first part of the section requires Section 8.1 as background; the second part also requires the discussion of translators in Section 2.1.

8.1. HOW HARDWARE WORKS

Instructions and Data in Memory

Warning to the Reader: This section makes *very* heavy use of concepts from Sections 1.1 and 1.2. Before proceeding further, it is wise to reread those sections, unless the material contained there is fresh in your mind. Many of the important definitions are repeated in the glossary of the present section to help you review the necessary concepts.

Machine language uses instructions that the hardware of the computer is wired up to execute directly. We shall study a very basic computer, with (recall the concepts from Section 1.2) a **central processing unit** (CPU) and **primary memory,** but with no **secondary memory.** In this chapter, then, we shall write "memory" as short for "primary memory," since secondary memory will not concern us. To further simplify matters, we assume that the necessary program and data are already in memory, and see how the CPU can follow a machine-language program to process the data and place the results in memory. We will thus ignore input and output devices.

As we saw in Section 1.1, there are two main types of instruction. A **test** tells the computer to test whether or not some specified condition is met. An **operation** tells the computer how to change some information. The study of how the CPU **executes** the two kinds of instructions—test and operate—should be enough to give you the general idea of all machine-language processing.

We must now look in more detail at the structure of the memory and of the CPU. The important point about memory is that it is divided into locations, and each **location** has its own **address.** For example, in the payroll program of Section 1.2, we stored specific data on an employee in specific locations—with his name coded at address 1, his department coded in the 2nd location, and so on. Recall, too, that a **word** is the information stored in a single memory location. A word may be the code for a number or an instruction. In either case, it is stored in the machine by the state of some number of two-state devices.

The CPU has a special register called the **accumulator** which it uses to hold data and results on which it is working. Suppose, for example, that we want to program a computer to add two numbers, which are stored in locations 17 and 20, and to place the result in location 19. Consider what happens if we start (after loading data, or previous calculations) with the number 219 in the accumulator, 100 in location 17, 200 in location 19, and 300 in location 20. Recalling our notation that $\langle X \rangle$ stands for "the contents of the location with address X" we set this out as

$$\langle ACC \rangle = 219$$
$$\langle 17 \rangle = 100$$
$$\langle 19 \rangle = 200$$
$$\langle 20 \rangle = 300$$

The job of the CPU is to add 100 and 300 (the contents of locations 17 and 20) and place 400 (the total) in location 19. It is wired to do this in three steps, with each step specified by a machine-language instruction as shown in Table I.

In a high-level language we might have written

$$A := B + C$$

which means make the *new* value of A equal to the sum of the *old* values of B and C. We have seen that this single instruction gets replaced by three machine-language instructions, and that we cannot use names like A, B, and C but must use explicit addresses—with $\langle 19 \rangle$ for A, $\langle 17 \rangle$ for B, and $\langle 20 \rangle$ for C.

TABLE I

Instruction	Description of CPU activity	State of the registers at the end of the step
LDA 17	*Loads Accumulator:* Places a copy of the number in location 17 (the first of the numbers to be added together) in the accumulator. It thus destroys the old contents of the accumulator, but does not change $\langle 17 \rangle$, the contents of location 17.	$\langle ACC \rangle = 100 = \langle 17 \rangle$ $\langle 17 \rangle = 100$ $\langle 19 \rangle = 200$ $\langle 20 \rangle = 300$
ADD 20	*Adds* to the accumulator the number in location 20 (the second of the numbers to be added together). The accumulator now contains the sum. Again, it is only the accumulator that changes contents.	$\langle ACC \rangle = 400 = 100 + 300$ $\langle 17 \rangle = 100$ $\langle 19 \rangle = 200$ $\langle 20 \rangle = 300$
STO 19	*Stores* the contents of the accumulator (the sum of the two numbers) in location 19, as was required. This time, it is location 19 where the only change occurs.	$\langle ACC \rangle = 400$ $\langle 17 \rangle = 100$ $\langle 19 \rangle = 400 = \langle ACC \rangle$ $\langle 20 \rangle = 300$

Look more carefully at the three machine-language instructions that we have just used. They are made of two parts—an *instruction type* followed by an *address.* Many machines are wired to handle these single-address instructions, and these are the only kind that we study in this chapter. It should be clear, though, that similar ideas apply to machines with several addresses—for example, a three-address machine might have a single instruction ADD 17 20 19 (add the contents of locations 17 and 20 and put the result in location 19).

Later in this section we shall look at the hardware in the CPU that lets it:

(1)   pull an instruction out of memory;
(2)   find out its instruction type to tell it what circuitry to use (a testing device for a test; adding circuitry for addition, and so on); and
(3)   find out the address in memory that it must go to in storing the result or finding the next instruction.

Remember, instructions as well as data are stored in memory. For this reason, the CPU must also keep a register—called the **instruction counter**—that tells it where to go for its next instruction. It also has a register called the **instruction register,** which holds the current instruction while the CPU is decoding its instruction type, and while the CPU is using the address in the instruction to guide its use of memory.

How are both instructions and data stored in memory? Recall our discussion of **binary coding** from Section 1.2. Each location in memory is a string of 2-state devices. For definiteness, let us assume that our computer is a **12-bit machine.** This means that each word (whether coding an instruction or data) stored in a memory location will be a string of 12 0s and 1s like:

010111010010

There are $10^{12} = 4096$ different 12-bit strings, and so we could, for example, use a single word to code any number from 0 to 4095, as long as we assign a different string (a different binary code) to each number. (Of course, this does not give much precision, and most large computers have much larger words. We choose 12 here because it is an easy number with which to work—it is easy to look at a string of 12 0s and 1s.)

In many applications, we need negative as well as positive numbers. In that case, we let the first bit stand for the sign of the number. We use a 0 for $+$ and a 1 for $-$. With 12 bits, zero is coded by both 000000000000 and 100000000000 since $+0 = -0$. With 12 bits, and the first bit used for the sign, we can store numbers from -2047 to 2047 in binary code, since we have 11 bits after the sign, and $2047 = 2^{11} - 1$

But if every 12-bit string codes a number, how do we code instructions? We can let the same string be a code for both a number and an instruction. This is because *the CPU only treats the word in a location as an instruction if its address is in the instruction counter.* Here, then, is how to code instructions. Suppose that the machine language has 15 different instruction types. Remember that $2^4 = 16$. Thus we can code each different instruction type by a different 4-bit string. Earlier, we met 3 instruction types: LDA (Load Accumulator), ADD (Add to the contents of the Accumulator), and STO (store the accumulator's contents). We could code LDA as 0001, ADD as 0010, STO as 0011, and so on. This leaves 8 bits for the address portion of the instruction. Since $2^8 = 256$, we see that a 12-bit machine with single-address instructions and 2-bits for the instruction type can handle only 256 locations in its memory. Since many computers today have *millions* of locations in memory, you can see that their word size must be considerably larger than 12 bits.

Anyway, if we can use binary code for the instruction type and the address in the instructions for our 12-bit machine, then each instruction can be stored with a single location of memory—with four bits for the instruction type, and 8 bits for the address referred to in the instructions. For example,

$$\text{LDA 21} \quad \text{is coded as} \quad 000100010101$$

where 0001 codes LDA, and (recall Section 1.2) 00010101 is the 8-bit binary code for 21. Similarly,

$$\text{LDA 23} \quad \text{is coded as} \quad 000100010111$$
$$\text{STO 23} \quad \text{is coded as} \quad 001100010111$$

To summarize: any word in memory—whether an instruction or piece of data—is coded as a string of 0s and 1s. In a little while, we shall see how the computer "knows" when to treat a word as data, and when to treat a word as an instruction. For now, note that if the word is *not* an instruction, we decode the whole string of 0s and 1s as a number or other piece of data. However, if the word is an instruction, we break it into an **instruction field** followed by an **address field.** The string of bits in the address field is decoded to give the address to be used in executing the instruction.

For example, in our 12-bit example, we use instructions with a 4-bit instruction field and an 8-bit address field. We code ADD as

0010, while 00011011 is the 8-bit binary code for 27. Thus the instruction ADD 27 is coded as

$$\underbrace{00100}_{\substack{\text{instruction}\\\text{field}}}\underbrace{0011011}_{\substack{\text{address}\\\text{field}}}$$

Note, then, that the instruction counter contains only an address. Thus it is the same length as the address field. In our 12-bit example, it would hold 8-bit words, while the instruction register and the accumulator would hold full 12-bit words.

Strictly speaking, in machine language all instructions and data are in binary code. If we wanted to run the machine-language program, it is the binary code that we would have to punch on the cards to be read into the computer. However, it is so hard to remember these codes without making mistakes that we shall always use the easy-to-remember abbreviations like LDA 21 and STO 23 in this book.

Of course, we are actually writing in a programming language when we write LDA 21, and so on. It is close to machine language, but different from it—we call it **assembly language.** We might say that assembly language is a "not-very-high-level" language. If you want the computer to accept a deck in assembly language—saving you the trouble of working out the binary code for each instruction—you need a **compiler.** It is called an **assembler.** This ASSEMBLY LANGUAGE → MACHINE LANGUAGE compiler not only lets you use easy-to-remember abbreviations for instruction types, but lets you use names instead of addresses for locations.

An Instruction Set

In this subsection, we list a set of machine-language instructions (although we write them in the easy-to-remember form, not in binary code). Then, in the next two subsections, we shall see how circuitry in the CPU can execute them.

Each instruction is comprised of an *instruction field* followed by an *address field:* a 3-letter code for an instruction type, followed by X, which can be filled in with the address of any location in memory. In some cases, X is a "dummy" address—for example, a halting instruction does not involve any address, and so the CPU ignores X in the instruction.

We first list three instructions for moving data in and out of the accumulator:

CLA X: Clear Accumulator (X is a dummy address)

Before   After

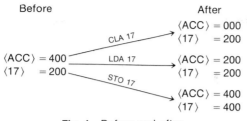

Fig. 1   Before and after.

When the CPU follows this instruction, it *clears* the accumulator by setting its contents to (the binary code for) zero.

   LDA X: Load Accumulator with ⟨X⟩, the contents of X
When the CPU follows this instruction, it copies the contents of location X into the accumulator. Location X is left unchanged.

   STO X: Store ⟨ACC⟩ in X
When the CPU follows this instruction, it copies the contents of the accumulator into location X. The accumulator is left unchanged.

   We can see these in action in Fig. 1. Here we take X = 17, and look at the effect of the three instructions on location 17 and the accumulator.
   We next list two instructions for number crunching (see Fig. 2).

   ADD X: Add ⟨X⟩ to the Accumulator
The CPU adds the number coded in location X to the number coded in the accumulator. The accumulator then contains the (binary code for) the sum of the two numbers, while location X is left unchanged.

   SUB X: Subtract ⟨X⟩ from the Accumulator
The CPU subtracts the number coded in location X from the number coded in the accumulator. The difference is left in the accumulator, and the number in location X is left unchanged.

Before   After

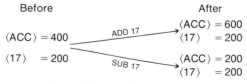

Fig. 2   More before and after.

Recall the := notation from our Section 1.1 discussion of the digital wristwatch. A := B means the *new* value of A is obtained by the expression B. We then have that the effect of ADD X is ⟨ACC⟩ := ⟨ACC⟩ + ⟨X⟩ (the *new* contents of the accumulator equals the sum of the *old* contents of the accumulator and the contents of location X). By the same token, the effect of SUB X is ⟨ACC⟩ := ⟨ACC⟩ − ⟨X⟩.

A machine can have similar instructions for multiplication, division, and other arithmetic operations; but we shall not need them here.

Here is the easiest instruction:

HLT X: Halt (X is a dummy variable)
When the CPU comes to this instruction it halts, and does not go on to look for any more instructions. It will not start again until a user or computer operator types in an instruction to get it going again.

Next we treat the instruction that is hardest to follow the first time. Suppose we wanted the computer to add together the numbers stored in locations 00, 01, . . . , through 99. We could use the 100 instructions, ADD 00, ADD 01, . . . , ADD 99. But this is too inefficient—we need a **loop** (recall the robot example from Section 1.1). We need an instruction ADD N where we can change N. Instead we use

ADA Y: Add what is Addressed by Y
This means the same thing as ADD ⟨Y⟩. The CPU does *not* add the contents of Y to the accumulator. Instead, it adds the contents of the location whose *address* is in Y.

We then store the parameter N at address Y, updating N by adding 1 to ⟨Y⟩ each time around the loop.

Figure 3 shows that if ⟨18⟩ = 17, then ADA 18 has the same effect as ADD 17—and a different effect from ADD 18. As an exercise in the ⟨ ⟩ notation, note that—after applying ADA Y—the new contents of the accumulator may be written ⟨ACC⟩ := ⟨ACC⟩ + ⟨⟨Y⟩⟩. Using again the := notation, this reads: "the *new* contents of the accumulator equal the sum of the *old* contents of the accumulator together with ⟨⟨Y⟩⟩." Now ⟨⟨Y⟩⟩ is the contents ⟨Y⟩—in other words, the contents of the location whose *address* is in Y. In our Fig. 3 example, ⟨18⟩ = 17 and so ⟨⟨18⟩⟩ = ⟨17⟩ = 200; thus ADA 18 does indeed add 200 to the accumulator.

After executing an instruction, the CPU usually goes on to the

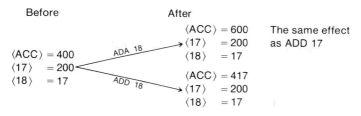

Fig. 3 Adding with indirect (ADA) and direct (ADD) addressing.

instruction stored in the next location in memory. For example, after getting an instruction from location 211, the CPU would normally go to location 212 for the next instruction. Only a test can change the order.

Let us look, then, at the basic test instructions in the machine language:

JMP X: Jump to X on zero

If the contents of the accumulator are zero, the next instruction to be executed is in location X. Otherwise, go on to the next instruction stored immediately after JMP X in the memory.

JUP X: Jump to X on nonzero

Go to the instruction after JMP X in memory if ⟨ACC⟩ *is* zero; otherwise, next execute the instruction stored in location X.

For example, if the CPU takes the instruction from location 99 and finds that it is JMP 107, then its next instruction will be in location 100 unless ⟨ACC⟩ = 0—in which case its next instruction will be in location 107. (Look at Fig. 4, recalling that it is the instruction counter that tells the CPU where to find the instruction it is to execute.)

We now look in more detail at the hardware involved in carrying out these machine-language instructions.

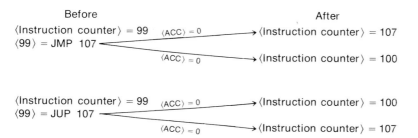

Fig. 4 Before and after the execution of the instruction stored at address 99. The job of a jump instruction is to set the instruction counter to the address of the next instruction to be executed.

Getting Information In and Out of Memory

In the previous section we studied a number of machine-language instructions. In each case, the CPU had to **fetch** the instruction from memory, and then **execute** the instruction. Further, the execution of an instruction often involved the transfer of information in or out of memory. It is thus time to look in some detail at how these transfers take place.

In Fig. 5, we see the memory of the computer, divided into locations, with the locations at addresses 0, 1, 2, . . . , 26, 27, . . . drawn in. There are two other registers shown in the figure. The **memory buffer register** can hold one word of information—either the word (data or instruction) that the CPU is retrieving from memory, or the word that the CPU is going to store in memory. The **memory address register** holds the address of the location that the word is coming from or going to, in the memory. The **address decoder** has circuitry that

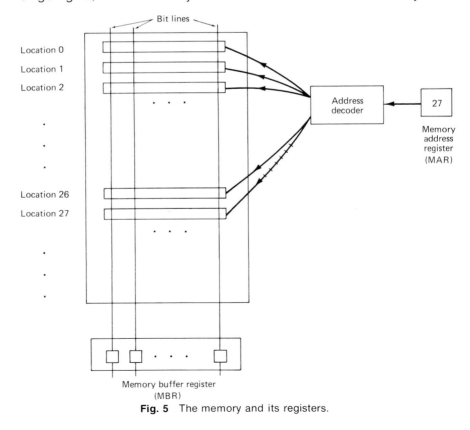

Fig. 5 The memory and its registers.

ensures that only the location whose address is in the memory address register will share its information with the memory buffer register. The **bit lines** provide the wires along which each bit of information can be shared between memory locations and the memory buffer register.

Let us see how this works on a specific example, LDA 27, in which we wish to read out the contents of location 27 of the memory. To start with, then, the number 27 must be placed in the memory address register. The address decoder then activates the location—in this case number 27—whose address sits in the memory address register. The CPU then issues a **read** command, the bit lines are activated, and they send a copy of the contents of the active word—in this case, the word in location 27—down to the memory buffer register (MBR, for short), which is primed to receive them. Next, the CPU must get the information from the MBR to the accumulator. Thus the computer control makes the MBR the **transmitter** and the accumulator the **receiver.** We shall say more about this transmission process later in the section, but first let us just look at how the circuitry in Fig. 5 can be used to *store* information in memory.

We see how to execute the machine-language instruction STO 26—store the contents of the accumulator in location 26. This time the computer control works as follows:

1.   Transfer the data from the accumulator to the MBR.
2.   Place 26 in the memory address register (MAR, for short). This causes the address decoder to activate location 26 of the store.
3.   Issue a **write** command, which causes a transfer of the contents of the MBR (which—thanks to Step 1—equals the contents of the accumulator) into the activated location (which is 26, thanks to Step 2).

Just for practice, we put these three steps in the := notation, using $\langle X \rangle$ to mean "the contents of X," and using the abbreviations ACC for accumulator, MAR for memory address register, and MBR for memory buffer register.

1. $\langle MBR \rangle := \langle ACC \rangle$
Replace the contents of the memory buffer register by the contents of the accumulator (but do not change the contents of the accumulator)

2. $\langle MAR \rangle := 27$
Set up address 27 in the memory address register (thus automatically "activating" location 27 via the address decoder)

3. $\langle \langle MAR \rangle \rangle := \langle MBR \rangle$

⟨⟨MAR⟩⟩ is the contents of ⟨MAR⟩—the contents of the location whose *address* is *contained* in MAR. Thanks to Step 2 ⟨MAR⟩ = 27, and so this instruction says ⟨27⟩ := ⟨MBR⟩. This says replace the contents of location 27 by the contents of the memory buffer register, which equals ⟨ACC⟩ by Step 1.

Combining the effects of these three replacements, we have

$$⟨27⟩ = ⟨ACC⟩$$

which is the desired information transfer for STO 27. We also have two **side-effects**

$$⟨MBR⟩ = ⟨ACC⟩ \quad and \quad ⟨MAR⟩ = 27$$

which change the contents of registers even though we did not specify those changes as part of the effect of the machine-language instruction STO 27.

We have now seen the basic mechanisms for moving data back and forth between the accumulator and some location in memory. Recall, however, that the CPU is involved in another important information transfer: moving an instruction from memory to the CPU's *instruction register.* This register is where CPU analyzes the instruction type, and gets the address contained in the instruction. We saw that the address of the current instruction was contained in the *instruction counter.* Later on, we shall examine how the instruction counter is updated to give the right address for the next instruction. We shall also see how the CPU uses the information in the instruction register. For now let us just look at the information transfers involved in getting an instruction into the instruction register.

The address of the instruction is in the instruction *counter,* so the CPU sends this address to the MAR to activate the correct memory location

$$⟨MAR⟩ := ⟨INSTRUCTION COUNTER⟩$$

The CPU next sends a *read* instruction, which transfers the instruction—because its address is in the MAR—to the MBR

$$⟨MBR⟩ = instruction$$

Finally, the CPU transmits the contents of the MBR to the instruction *register*

$$⟨INSTRUCTION REGISTER⟩ := ⟨MBR⟩$$

as a result of which the instruction register holds the instruction, at last,

⟨INSTRUCTION REGISTER⟩ = instruction

Again and again in its work, the computer must *move informa-tion* from one place to another. We have just seen the transfers involved in moving data in and out of memory, and in moving instructions from memory to the instruction register. We shall see further transfers when we analyze how the CPU executes an instruction. *Communication is at the heart of computation.*

Much of the CPU's work is involved in activating one place in the computer as the *transmitter* and one as *receiver.* The contents of the transmitter are then sent over all the output lines radiating from it (Fig. 6), but this information is ignored by all places except the receiver, which changes to store the transmitted message. The contents of all other places (including the transmitter) are unchanged.

The meaning of a piece of information *to the computer* is given by the place it is stored at a given time. If it is in the instruction register, it *is* an instruction *to the computer;* if it is placed in the accumulator during an ADD operation, it *is* a number *to the computer.* In just the same way, the meaning of a piece of paper bearing the information

Age: 26 years
Height: 1.8 meters
Weight: 56 kilograms

will depend on the file in which a bureaucrat places it. If it is misplaced in John Smith's file instead of Rosalie Dubois' file, then henceforth these *are* the age, height, and weight of John Smith *to the bureaucracy.*

So in the computer, a word need have no tag on it—the interpretation of the word will depend on where it is stored. Much of the cost

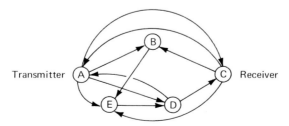

Fig. 6 If A is designated transmitter, and C a receiver, then a transfer command has the effect C := A.

and complexity of computers thus goes into ensuring that information is in the right place at the right time. The major limitation on the speed of computers is the speed of light! Light travels 186,000 miles per second. At first glance it seems absurd that such an immense speed could set any limits on communication in a device that can fit into a cabinet. Recall, however, that some computers execute a billion operations a second. Thus in the time it takes to execute a single instruction, light travels

$$\frac{186{,}000 \text{ miles}}{10^9} \doteq \frac{2 \times 10^5 \text{ miles}}{10^9} \doteq \frac{2 \times 10^5 \times (5 \times 10^3 \text{ feet})}{10^9} = 1 \text{ foot}$$

If we designed a computer to carry out a complete instruction before starting the next, and it executed a billion operations a second, the distance from the store to the control circuitry would have to be less than 4 inches. This is because at least three transfers are involved in executing the instruction:

Total
path length   Send address of instruction to memory address register
of 1 foot   Transfer instruction from store to instruction register
               Retrieve data from store or put answer back in store

A 4-inch cube is, however, too small to hold the circuitry of a really powerful computer—even with the latest advances in micro-miniaturization—and so computer designers are now developing more and more techniques to let parts of consecutive instructions be executed at the same time.

Science-fiction freaks may note that if we build a "space-warp" to defeat the speed of light (do not expect it to happen!), the first application may be to computer design rather than to interstellar travel.

How the Computer Follows a Program

We have seen that information transfer is at the heart of the computer. We now see how the computer can follow a *sequence* of instructions *without human intervention.* We have repeatedly stressed that electronic speed is so valuable precisely because, once we have loaded a program into the computer, the machine can chase through the loops, processing a mass of data, without further work on our part.

Let us briefly recall the circuitry we have so far given our computer:

A **memory** equipped with **MAR** (memory address register); and
                              MBR (memory buffer register).

A **CPU** equipped with   **ACC** (accumulator);
                           IR (instruction register); and
                           IC (instruction counter).

We mentioned that the instruction register was the place the CPU puts an instruction to dissect it; and that the instruction counter keeps track of where the instruction came from in memory (without this the general rule "go to the *next* instruction" would not mean anything).

Consider, now, a computer that has

ADD	37	in location 109

JMP	114	in location 110

We will not keep drawing boxes around the parts of the instruction. We do it this time to remind you that each instruction can be divided into an *instruction field* followed by an *address field*.

In what follows, we will not need to worry about binary codes. All we need to know is that when an instruction is in the instruction register, there is a definite part of the register—the instruction field—whose contents the CPU can decode to find the instruction type; and that the rest of the register—the address field—contains code for the address specified as part of the instruction.

Given the above two instructions, the CPUs job is as follows:

(1) Execute instruction 109
Add $\langle 37 \rangle$ to the number already in the accumulator:

$$\langle ACC \rangle := \langle 37 \rangle + \langle ACC \rangle$$

(2) Execute instruction 110
Test $\langle ACC \rangle$. If it is 0, the next instruction is in location 114; if not, it is in location 111, the next location after 110.

The execution of an instruction involves two parts: the **FETCH cycle** gets the instruction into the instruction register; the **EXECUTE cycle** carries out the instruction. At the end of the execute cycle, the address of the *next* instruction must be in the instruction counter. This ensures that, when the CPU goes back to the FETCH cycle, it will fetch the right instruction. Let us follow these two cycles for the two instructions: $\langle 109 \rangle$ = ADD 37, and then $\langle 110 \rangle$ = JMP 114.

The FETCH Cycle for $\langle 109 \rangle$ = ADD 37:
We start with the situation in Fig. 7, with the address 109 already in the instruction counter. Before the computer can execute the instruc-

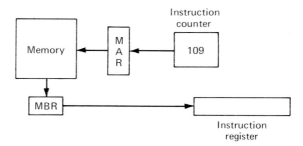

Fig. 7 The computer's task is to load the instruction register with the instruction stored in location 109—the instruction referred to by the instruction counter.

tion in location 109, it must place it in the instruction register:

    (i)   ⟨MAR⟩ := ⟨instruction counter⟩
This tells the memory which word is required.

    (ii) Read: ⟨MBR⟩ := ⟨⟨MAR⟩⟩
The word whose address is in the MAR is transferred into the memory buffer register. In this case ⟨MAR⟩ = 109, and so ⟨MBR⟩ = ⟨109⟩ and the MBR now contains the desired instruction.

    (iii) ⟨instruction register⟩ =: ⟨MBR⟩
The contents of the MBR—the instruction from location 109—are transferred to the instruction register.

Thus it takes the computer three steps to get the new instruction into the instruction register. Note that these three steps are instructions *below* the level of machine language: we call them *microinstructions.* The execution of a **microprogram**—a sequence of micro-instructions—does not involve retrieval of the instructions from memory in the hardware we study here. Rather, the CPU has a special circuit wired into it for carrying out the FETCH cycle. It also has a special circuit for each machine-language instruction—like ADD, JMP or LDA—which lets it execute the EXECUTE cycle for that in-struction type. In the same way, the update programs of the digital wristwatch of Section 1.1 were wired into the watch's special purpose circuitry. A computer becomes general-purpose when there is a memory separate from CPU that can store different programs, so that the choice of program determines which part of the CPU circuitry will be used at any time.

    The FETCH cycle involves one more piece of bookkeeping. The computer has now put the new instruction in the instruction register. It thus no longer needs the address of that instruction, and updates the content of the instruction register to 110, the address of the next instruction:

   (iv)   ⟨instruction counter⟩ := ⟨instruction counter⟩ + 1.

Thus if the computer goes through a FETCH, starting from the situation in Fig. 7, with the instruction ADD 37 in location 109 of its memory, then at the end of the FETCH it will be in the situation shown in Fig. 8.

In summary, the FETCH cycle requires four microinstructions:

   (i)   ⟨MAR⟩ := ⟨instruction counter⟩
   (ii)   ⟨MBR⟩ := ⟨⟨MAR⟩⟩
   (iii) ⟨instruction register⟩ := ⟨MBR⟩
   (iv)   ⟨instruction counter⟩ := ⟨instruction counter⟩ + 1

The EXECUTE Cycle for ADD 37:

Now that the instruction ⟨109⟩ = ADD 37 is in the instruction register, the computer must execute it. This EXECUTE phase proceeds in several steps. The first step is always the same—to decode the instruction field to determine which microinstructions must be followed. In this case, the ADD code causes the control to activate circuitry for executing the ADD microprogram.

The ADD circuitry includes a special circuit called the **adder** which is so designed that if we feed two numbers into it, one after the other, it will compute their sum. Thus the ADD microprogram has the following stages:

   ADD (i):   ⟨adder⟩ := ⟨ACC⟩

The contents of the accumulator are transferred to the adder. At the same time, the adder is set up to *add* the next number it receives.

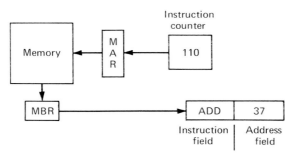

Fig. 8   The computer's task is to execute the instruction in the instruction register, adding 37 to the contents of the accumulator.

Now if 37 is in the AIC (short for Address field of the Instruction Counter) we want to make ⟨37⟩—the contents of location 37—the next input to the adder. The computer does this as follows:

ADD (ii):   ⟨MAR⟩ := ⟨AIC⟩
Set 37 up in the memory address register.

ADD (iii):   Read: ⟨MBR⟩ := ⟨⟨MAR⟩⟩
Places ⟨37⟩ in the memory buffer register.

ADD (iv):   Transfer ⟨MBR⟩ to adder
Since ADD (i) primed the adder to add on its next input, this transfer will trigger an addition. Thus the overall effect is ⟨adder⟩ := ⟨adder⟩ + ⟨MBR⟩. We replace the adder's contents by the old contents added to the MBR's contents, but by ADD(i) and ADD(iii) this means we end up with ⟨adder⟩ := ⟨ACC⟩ + ⟨37⟩.

Finally, we must put this result back in the accumulator:

ADD (v): ⟨ACC⟩ := ⟨adder⟩

Control is then transferred back to the FETCH cycle. With this, the addition is completed and the sum is stored in the accumulator.

We have now seen how the computer can carry out the instruction ⟨109⟩ = ADD 37 using built-in circuitry. The overall processing scheme for *all* instruction types is shown in Fig. 9. The computer *fetches* the instruction from the store; *tests* the instruction field of the instruction register to jump to a microprogram which executes the instruction; then—except for HLT—transfers control to the FETCH cycle, to start the process all over again.

At the end of the ADD 37 execution, we have

⟨instruction counter⟩ = 110
and   ⟨110⟩ = JMP 114
⟨instruction register⟩ = ADD 37

as in Fig. 8. Let us now see how the computer executes its next instruction. First, it goes to the FETCH cycle.

The FETCH Cycle for ⟨110⟩ = JMP 114:

The CPU does just what it did in the previous example, but fetches a different instruction since the instruction counter now contains 110 instead of 109.

(i)   ⟨MAR⟩ := ⟨instruction counter⟩
Load 110 into the memory address register.

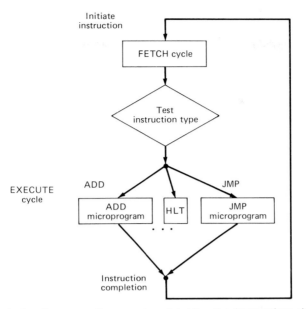

Fig. 9 Instruction execution requires *fetching* the instruction; decoding the instruction type; then activating the appropriate CPU circuitry. Only a HALT instruction fails to send the CPU back to the FETCH cycle, to start processing the next instruction.

(ii) $\langle MBR \rangle := \langle \langle MAR \rangle \rangle = \langle 110 \rangle$
Transfer $\langle 110 \rangle$ = JMP 114—the desired instruction—into the memory buffer register.

(iii) $\langle$Instruction register$\rangle := \langle MBR \rangle$ = JMP 114
The instruction JMP 114 is now in the instruction register, ready for execution.

(iv) $\langle$Instruction counter$\rangle := \langle$instruction counter$\rangle + 1 = 111$
The machine is now set up to look for its next instruction—after completing the EXECUTE cycle—in location 111.

The reader may sense that something is wrong. The interpretation of JMP 114 is "If $\langle ACC \rangle$ = 0, take the next instruction from location 114; otherwise go on to the next location." However, the computer has already set up 111, the address of the next location, in the instruction counter. Well, that really works out quite well. It says that the JMP microprogram should use special circuitry—we call it TEST—to see if $\langle ACC \rangle$ is zero or not. If TEST finds that $\langle ACC \rangle$ = 0, it should load 114 into the instruction counter; otherwise, it should

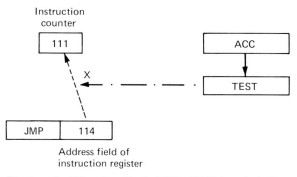

Fig. 10 The transfer X is only activated if the TEST box finds the contents of the accumulator to be zero.

leave the instruction counter's contents as 111. We have the situation shown in Fig. 10.

The EXECUTE Cycle for JMP 114:
Test the instruction field of the instruction register, which now contains JMP 114. Since the instruction type is JMP, the CPU transfers control to the JMP microprogram which has the following steps:

JMP (i):   ⟨test⟩ := ⟨ACC⟩
Transfer the contents of the accumulator to TEST to check whether they are 0.

JMP (ii):   TEST
If TEST contains 0, go on to JMP (iii); otherwise, ⟨ACC⟩ ≠ 0, and there is nothing more to be done, and control is transferred back to the FETCH cycle, which will then fetch the next instruction from location 111.

JMP (iii):   ⟨instruction counter⟩ := ⟨AIC⟩
If a jump is necessary—the test revealed that ⟨ACC⟩ = 0—then the next instruction is to have the address in the address field of the instruction. That is, ⟨AIC⟩, which in this case is 114, is to be placed in the instruction counter. Control is then transferred back to the FETCH cycle, which will then fetch the next instruction from location 114.

In this way, following the alternation of FETCH and EXECUTE cycles shown in Fig. 9, the computer proceeds from instruction to instruction automatically, consulting the instruction counter at each stage to find the address of the next instruction; fetching the instruction; adding 1 to the address in the instruction counter (which will need further modification only if a jump is required); and then decoding the instruction and executing it. It then returns to the FETCH cycle to start the whole process all over again. At the heart of all this are the information transfers which ensure that the right information is in the right place at the right time through every state of the FETCH and EXECUTE cycles of the execution of every instruction.

With this, we see how—once a program and data are loaded into the memory of a computer—it can execute the entire program without human intervention. Actually to see the detailed circuitry required to carry out the information transfers or to implement the microprograms for different instruction types requires detailed study beyond the scope of this book. Hopefully, we have broken the FETCH and EXECUTE cycles down into such small steps that it is clear that each step is simple enough to be carried out by electronic circuitry.

Suggestions for Further Reading

C. C. Foster: *Computer Architecture,* Van Nostrand-Reinhold, Princeton, New Jersey, 1970.
  The section on coordinate addressed storage (pp. 58–65) gives a good account of a primary memory structure of the type we have discussed, while Chapter 5 gives a description of the fetch and execute cycles for a fuller set of instructions than that we have given here.
W. H. Ware: The Ultimate Computer, *IEEE Spectrum,* March 1972, pp. 84–91.
  An attempt is made to project the ultimate speeds and capacities of computers, and the computing problems that could use them.

Summary

We have examined **machine-language** instructions that transfer information (CLA, LDA, STO), do arithmetic (ADD, SUB, ADA), stop the machine (HLT), and handle jumps (JMP, JUP).

We stressed that communication is at the heart of computation. Much of the computer's time is spent moving information from one place to another. When a word is decoded as data or an instruction will depend on where it is and when it is there.

We saw that the memory required a **memory address register** and a **memory buffer register** to get words in and out of the locations in which they are stored. We saw that the **central processing unit** (CPU) needed an **accumulator** to hold data on which it was working, an **instruction counter** to keep track of which instruction it was executing, and an **instruction register** to hold the current instruction.

The CPU took two steps to carry out the instruction. In the **FETCH** cycle it fetched the instruction from memory and placed it in the instruction register. In the **EXECUTE** cycle, it decoded the instruction type, and used this to activate appropriate circuitry. For example, ADD required circuitry for adding numbers together, while JMP required circuitry for testing whether or not the contents of the accumulator were zero.

Glossary

Machine language: The instructions that the hardware of the computer is wired to execute directly comprise the *machine language.*

Execution: A computer *executes* an instruction when it carries it out. We say a computer executes a program when it operates according to the instructions of that program.

Loop: A *loop* is a sequence of instructions that the computer must follow again and again in doing its job.

Operation: An instruction is an *operation* if it tells the computer how to change some information.

Test: An instruction is a *test* if it tells the computer to test whether or not some specified condition is met—such as whether or not some number equals zero. The outcome of the test determines which instruction the computer will go to next.

Jump: The instructions of a program are usually written one after another in a list. After it has executed an instruction, the computer usually goes to the next instruction in the list. If this is not the case, we say that a *jump* has occurred.

Memory: The *memory* of a computer comprises a *primary memory* to and from which the CPU can very quickly move information; and a *secondary memory,* made up of devices like magnetic tape units and magnetic disk units, which are larger and cheaper than primary memory, but also much slower.

Location: The primary memory of a computer is divided into *locations* which can each hold an instruction or piece of data. Each location can be referred to by a distinct number, called its *address.* If every location in memory is built with some number n of two-state devices, it is called an *n-bit machine.* A *word* is the information stored in a single memory location. Thus the words in an n-bit machine are strings of n 0s and 1s.

Memory address register: The *memory address register (MAR)* is used to get at information stored in a computer's *memory.* This register holds the address of the *location* in memory at which a word is to be stored (or from which it is to be retrieved). The *address decoder* activates the location in memory whose address is in the MAR. The *memory buffer register (MBR)* holds this word before it is stored (or after it is retrieved). In a *read* operation, the contents of the activated location are copied into the MBR; in a *write* operation, the reverse transfer takes place.

Central processing unit: The *CPU* is the part of the computer that retrieves and carries out the instructions in a program: obeying operation instructions, carrying out tests, and controlling input and output devices in response to input and output instructions.

Bit: A *bit* is a piece of information representing one of two possible choices, such as 0 or 1. For example, the pattern of ups and downs of four light switches would be a 4-bit pattern. We say information is in *binary form* when it is coded as a string of *bits* such as the string 0111010110 of 0s and 1s. By contrast, our usual *decimal numbers* are made up of strings of *digits,* each of which represents one of the 10 possible choices 0,1,2,3,4,5,6,7,8,9. Coding is the process of transforming information fron one form to another. Each way of representing information is called a *code.* An example of coding is transforming a decimal number into *binary code*—a string of 0s and 1s.

Accumulator: An *accumulator* is a special register in which the computer can store partial results while they are being computed on; or which it can use as a "way station" for data that it is moving from one part of the machine to another.

Instruction counter: This register holds the address of the next *instruction* the computer is to execute (and so must be updated as soon as the computer executes that instruction).

Instruction register: This *register* holds an *instruction* while the computer analyzes it to determine what type the instruction is, and what address is to be used in executing it.

Instruction field: When an instruction is stored as a word in computer memory, the word is usually divided into two parts: the *instruction field* is decoded by the computer to tell what type (e.g., an ADD or a JUMP) the instruction is; the *address field* is decoded to give the address to be used in executing the instruction.

Compiler: A *compiler* is a computer program that enables a computer to take a program written in a high-level language and translate it into a complete program—designed to process data to get the same results—in another language. If this second language is the computer's machine language, then the compiled program can be run on the computer with any set of data.

Assembly language: An *assembly language* is a "not-very-high-level" language. It is almost the same as machine language, except that the instructions are not written in binary code. We can use easy-to-remember abbreviations for the instruction type, and names instead of location numbers for the addresses. An *assembler* is an assembly language → machine language compiler.

Side-effect: A *side-effect* is any "unintended result," an effect of running a program—like placing partial results in various locations of the store—that was not part of the program specification.

Fetch cycle: Before executing an instruction, the computer must first fetch the instruction from store and place it in the instruction register—this is the *fetch cycle.* It then decodes the instruction, gets any data it needs from the

store, executes the instruction, possibly changing some further registers—
this is the *execute cycle.*

Exercises

1. Suppose we build a computer whose components (connected to each
other by radio, cable, or laser) are scattered about the surface of our planet.
Memory, for instance, is in Africa, while the CPU is in America. Suppose that
the longest connecting link used in executing a typical instruction is 18,600
miles. (a) How many operations per second could this computer operate?
Why? (b) A global-scale computer has its speed limited by communication
lag time. How, then, is it reasonable to link together computers on several
continents, for a "world brain" or in a special-purpose network?

2. Define the FETCH and EXECUTE cycle for the following instruction

JMA 3

which has the interpretation "If $\langle ACC \rangle = 0$, go to the *next* instruction; if
$\langle ACC \rangle = 0$ go three instructions beyond that for the next one to be executed."

3. Explain how instructions similar to ADA could be used to operate with a
large memory (a million locations) without lengthening the address field of
the machine language.

4. Programming a computer is like moving furniture. In the case of furniture
(a) you can only move one heavy piece at a time, (b) you must put the item on
a dolly to move it, (c) you can't put two things in the same place. In a computer, (a) you can only change one number at a time, (b) you must have the
number in the accumulator (or some other register) to deal with it quickly, (c)
you can only have one value in a given location.

Suppose I very sensibly decide to move my refrigerator from the bedroom to the kitchen, and my stereo from the kitchen to the bedroom. Each
room is too small to contain both, but there is room in the hall to leave one
while I move the other. Each is so heavy I need the dolly to move it. Step by
step, how can I make this shift?

5. Often, in a program, it becomes necessary to exchange the values in two
locations, so that each location ends up with what the other started with.
Write a seven-step machine language program to exchange the values stored
initially in locations 1976 and 1984, using location 2001 "if you get your hands
full." Use only the LDA, STO, and HLT instructions.

6. Initially the four variables W,X,Y,Z have these values: $W = 1$, $X = 2$, $Y = 3$,
$Z = 4$. What are their values after the following sequence of operations is
performed?

$$W := X, \quad X := Y, \quad Y := Y + Z,$$
$$Z := W \times X, \quad W := W/2, \quad X := X + X + W$$

7. The accompanying table is a "picture" of a piece of core before a certain computer program is run.

Address	Value	Address	Value
725	733	731	734
726	0	732	727
727	729	733	25
728	735	734	732
729	727	735	731
730	730		

Using the notation in the text, where $\langle X \rangle$ means the value stored in the location whose address is X, what are the values of the following expressions?
 (1) $\langle 726 \rangle$ (2) $\langle 733 \rangle$ (3) $\langle 725 \rangle$ (4) $\langle \langle 725 \rangle \rangle$ (5) $\langle \langle 727 \rangle \rangle$
 (6) $\langle 728 \rangle$ (7) $\langle \langle 728 \rangle \rangle$ (8) $\langle \langle \langle 728 \rangle \rangle \rangle$ (9) $\langle \langle \langle \langle 728 \rangle \rangle \rangle \rangle$
 (10) $\langle \langle \langle \langle \langle \langle \langle \langle \langle 730 \rangle \rangle \rangle \rangle \rangle \rangle \rangle \rangle \rangle$

8. What kind of additional instructions must be added to a computer with secondary memory? (*Hints:* Consider what buttons are seen on a tape recorder, what new paths of information are now available.)

9. How is the accumulator different from other registers?

10. The LOAD instruction takes a value from a location in memory and transfers it to the accumulator. But this "transfer" leaves the value in the original location unchanged. What has really been accomplished, and why?

8.2. PROGRAMMING AND COMPILING

In the previous section, we introduced a number of types of machine-language instruction, and saw that the CPU needs *special circuitry* to execute each type of machine-language instruction. In the present section, we give an example of machine-language programming. We then outline the behavior of a program which acts as a HIGH-LEVEL LANGUAGE → MACHINE LANGUAGE compiler. We see that the compiler needs *special subroutines* to compile each type of high-level instruction into machine language.

Adding 100 Numbers

Suppose that a computer has 100 numbers stored in locations 000, 001, . . . , through 099 of its memory, and must add them together and store the result in location 101. It is clear how to proceed—set the accumulator to 0, and then simply add on each

TABLE I

Instructions	Comments
CLA 000	Set ⟨ACC⟩ to zero (the address 000 is a dummy)
ADD 000 ⎤	
ADD 001 ⎥	
ADD 002 ⎬	Add in the numbers one-by-one, updating the total in the accumu-
• ⎥	lator until, with the execution of ADD 099, the last number has
• ⎥	been added on
• ⎥	
ADD 098 ⎥	
ADD 099 ⎦	
STO 101	Store the result in location 101
HLT	Halt, the job is done

number until the total is in the accumulator. Finally, store the result in location 101. The machine-language program shown in Table 1 will do the job.

We know from our discussion of the robot in Section 1.1 that this is a bad way to solve the problem. Instead of writing out 100 ADD instructions, we should simply use a loop to add on one number at a time, and test to see when we have used up all the numbers. The general strategy is shown in Fig. 1.

Clearly we need a location in memory to store SUM, the current total of the numbers added together so far. We must also set aside a

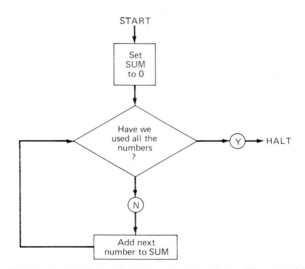

Fig. 1 Strategy for adding together a list of numbers. We start with 0, and keep adding numbers until we have used them all up.

location to hold a **counter** to keep track of the location from which we are adding the number. Let X be the value of the counter. Then X also tells us how many times we have been around the loop. Recalling the $:=$ notation, we can write out the basic loop operation as

$$\text{SUM} := \text{SUM} + \langle X \rangle$$
$$X := X + 1$$

The first instruction says that the new value of the SUM is obtained by adding the old value to the contents of X, just as it should be. The second one says "the *new* value of X is 1 greater than the *old* value of X"—in other words, it says go on to the next location to obtain your next number.

For example, suppose that we have just added the contents of locations 000, 001, and 002, and that the sum is 27. Suppose, too, that location 003 contains the number 11. Then we have

$$X = 003$$
$$\text{SUM} = 27 = \langle 000 \rangle + \langle 001 \rangle + \langle 002 \rangle$$
$$\langle 003 \rangle = 11$$

(where $=$ is the *ordinary* equal sign).

The high-level instruction $\text{SUM} := \text{SUM} + \langle X \rangle$ yields

$$X = 003 \quad \text{no change}$$
$$\text{SUM} = 27 + \langle X \rangle = 27 + \langle 003 \rangle = 38$$
$$\langle 003 \rangle = 11 \quad \text{no change}$$

After this, $\text{SUM} = 38 = \langle 000 \rangle + \langle 001 \rangle + \langle 002 \rangle + \langle 003 \rangle$ as required.

Then the high-level instruction $X := X + 1$ changes this to

$$X = 004 \quad X \text{ is the only change}$$
$$\text{SUM} = 38$$
$$\langle 003 \rangle = 11$$

and we are ready for the test.

What happens, then, to the test "Have we used all the numbers yet? We want to keep adding numbers through $\langle 99 \rangle$, but we do not want to add in $\langle 100 \rangle$. Thus the test is simply

$$\text{Does } X = 100?$$

Using this notation, the flow diagram of Fig. 1 becomes the flow diagram of Fig. 2. We now translate this into machine-language form. A good rule is that whenever you have a **variable** in the flow diagram—

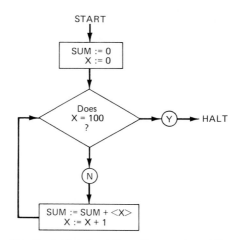

Fig. 2   A high-level flow diagram for adding.

in this case we have SUM and X—we must reserve a location to store their *current value.* We also need a location to store the values of the **constants** we will use—the numbers that are fixed as part of the program, rather than being specified by the input, or changing for different data. In this case, there are three numbers mentioned in the flow diagram—they are 0, 100, and 1—and so we store three constants. We thus need five locations, and we might as well take the first five that were not used in storing the numbers:

⟨100⟩ = X
⟨101⟩ = SUM
⟨102⟩ = 0
⟨103⟩ = 100
⟨104⟩ = 1

We have now "used up" 105 memory locations. With this choice of locations, SUM : = 0 requires us to set ⟨101⟩ to 0, and we do this in two machine language steps:

> CLA 000   places zero in the accumulator; and
> STO 101   stores this number in location 101.

To execute X : = 0, we can simply store ⟨ACC⟩ = 0 in location 100. This takes 1 step:

> STO 100   stores the number 0 in location 100.

After three machine-language steps have been taken, we have

$$\text{SUM, which is } \langle 101 \rangle = 0$$
$$\text{X, which is } \langle 100 \rangle = 0$$

So far, we have not mentioned where the instructions are stored in memory; but with the test portion of the flow diagram, we *must* know *where* the instructions are, so that we can tell the computer *where to go* for the next instruction. Before we translate "Does X = 100?" into machine language, let us specify that the first three instructions of our machine-language program are stored in the first three locations still unused in the machine:

$\langle 105 \rangle = \text{CLA } 000$
$\langle 106 \rangle = \text{STO } 101$
$\langle 107 \rangle = \text{STO } 100$

As we have said before, when the CPU has completed an instruction, it will automatically go on to the next location for its next instruction, unless a jump tells it to do otherwise. Hence, once the CPU starts on CLA 000 from location 105, it will automatically go on to execute STO 101 from 106, then $\langle 107 \rangle = \text{STO } 100$. It will then look for its next instruction in location 108.

If X = 100, the test in Fig. 2 sends the CPU to the HALT instruction. If X $\neq$ 100, then the CPU must next go to the machine-language instruction for SUM := SUM + X. Suppose, then, that the HALT instruction is stored at location M and the instructions for SUM := SUM + X start at location N (we will figure out what M and N are, later). How do we write the test? The idea is:

If X = 100, the next instruction is at M—go to the HALT instruction.

If X $\neq$ 100, the next instruction is at N—keep computing.

The usual test instruction is

JMP Z   If the contents of the accumulator are zero, go next to the instruction stored at location Z; otherwise go on to the next instruction.

To use this to test if X = 100, we instead test if X $-$ 100 = 0. This requires us to load X into the accumulator, subtract 100, and test to see if the result is 0. If it is 0, we must jump to M. If X = 100, we must go on to N:

LDA 100 $\langle \text{ACC} \rangle := X$ (Put X = $\langle 100 \rangle$ in the accumulator)

SUB 103 $\langle ACC \rangle := \langle ACC \rangle - \langle 103 \rangle$
                     $= X - 100$ (Subtract 100 =
                          $\langle 103 \rangle$ from $X = \langle ACC \rangle$)
JMP M   Go to M (i.e., HALT) if $X - 100 = 0$
                 Go to the next instruction if $X \neq 100$

We now specify that these instructions are stored in the next three unused locations:

$\langle 108 \rangle$ = LDA 100
$\langle 109 \rangle$ = SUB 103
$\langle 110 \rangle$ = JMP M

The next instruction after the jump—the first instruction of the SUM := SUM + $\langle X \rangle$; $X := X + 1$ subroutine—must thus be stored in location 111. In other words, N = 111.
    For SUM := SUM + $\langle X \rangle$ we might use the "obvious" subroutine:

LDA 101 $\langle ACC \rangle := \langle 101 \rangle = SUM$
ADD $\langle 100 \rangle$ $\langle ACC \rangle := \langle ACC \rangle + \langle\langle 100 \rangle\rangle$
                     $= SUM + \langle X \rangle$
STO 101   SUM := $\langle 101 \rangle := \langle ACC \rangle = SUM + \langle X \rangle$

The catch, of course, is that instruction ADD $\langle 100 \rangle$. ADD 100 adds *the number stored at location* 100 to the accumulator; but we want to add the number stored *at the address that is stored in location* 100! It was for just this reason that we use the instruction ADA 100, which does the job of ADD $\langle 100 \rangle$ without spoiling our usual format of having a numerical address in the second half of a machine language instruction. The SUM := SUM + $\langle X \rangle$ routine can now be stored in the next three locations in the form:

$\langle 111 \rangle$ = LDA 101
$\langle 112 \rangle$ = ADA 100
$\langle 113 \rangle$ = STO 101

    The subroutine for $X := X + 1$ is easy: we need just three machine-language instructions, which we store in the next three locations of memory:

$\langle 114 \rangle$ = LDA 100 $\langle ACC \rangle := \langle 100 \rangle = X$
$\langle 115 \rangle$ = ADD 104 $\langle ACC \rangle := \langle ACC \rangle + \langle 104 \rangle$
                                     $= X + 1$
$\langle 116 \rangle$ = STO 100 $\langle 100 \rangle := \langle ACC \rangle = X + 1.$

    When it has completed this subroutine, the machine must return to instruction 108 to repeat the test. We can do this in two steps as follows:

$\langle 117 \rangle$ = CLA 000
$\langle 118 \rangle$ = JMP 108   Since the accumulator has just been set to zero,
                                 this is an *unconditional jump* to location 108
                                 for the next instruction.

With this, all that remains is the halt instruction, which we store in
location 119:

$\langle 119 \rangle$ = HLT

so that we must change M to 119 in the instruction JMP M stored at
location 110.

   Now we can write out the full machine-language program. The
italicized phrases are **comments** that help us understand the program; the other lines show what data or instructions are to be loaded
into specified locations of the machine if it is to do its job.

> *This program will add up 100 numbers if they are
> placed in locations 000 through 099 of the com-
> puter prior to program execution. Location 100 will
> contain the address X of the term to be added;
> while location 101 will contain the current value of
> the SUM. Locations 102 through 104 contain the
> constants:*

102	0
103	100
104	1

> *Initially, SUM and X are set to 0*

105	CLA 000
106	STO 101
107	STO 100

> *At each iteration we test to see if X has reached 100.
> If it has, the machine is to halt. (To make the pro-
> gram easy to read, we have put the halt instruction
> in this block, instead of later. The left hand column
> ensures that each instruction will be stored in the
> right place.)*

108	LDA 100
109	SUB 103
110	JMP 119
119	HLT

If not, add the number in location X to the SUM;

111	LDA 101
112	ADA 100
113	STO 101

We then increment X by 1,

114	LDA 100
115	ADD 104
116	STO 100

After which we return to the test:

117	CLA 000
118	JMP 108

A good rule of programming is: *full and clear comments not only make the program easier to read; they also reduce the chance of making errors in writing the program.*

Compiling

In Section 2.1 we studied **compilers**. We suggested that it was easy to specify for each instruction in a high-level language a subroutine in machine language that would do the same job. We also suggested that extra problems were raised when we had to keep track of the relationship between the different instructions of a high-level program.

In the previous subsection, we saw how to write a machine-language program that could add together a list of numbers. We did this by providing a high-level flow diagram (Fig. 2) and then translating this into a machine-language program. However, this "translation" was something we did "by hand." Our task in this subsection is to spell out step-by-step how a compiler would carry out such a translation. Although the steps will be specified in English, they will be specified in such detail that you should get a feel for the fact that they could be spelled out in a computer program. This will give you a feel for what would be involved in writing the program for a real compiler.

A compiler usually works with a program written in a high-level language, rather than with a flow diagram. (*Warning:* An interesting thing is going to happen. Our "compiler" will produce a machine-language program that does the same job as our high-level program—adding together 100 numbers. However, it will *not* be the same machine-language program as that we wrote "by hand" in the previous subsection.) So, let us write a high-level program which does the job.

```
            NUMBER A (0 TO 99)
            SUM : = 0
            DO 1 X = 0 TO 99
         1  SUM : = SUM + A(X)
            HALT
```

The first line tells the computer that it will be dealing with 100 numbers, and that in the program we will refer to the numbers as A(0), A(1), A(2) and so on up to A(98) and A(99). The second line sets the SUM to its initial value of 0. The third line tells the computer to DO the instruction with the **label** 1 one hundred times, as X goes from 0, 1, 2 on up to 98 and 99 in that order. The fourth line, labeled 1, just adds the latest number into the sum.

Thus the DO instruction contains both the X : = X + 1 instruction of Fig. 2 (DO the instruction labelled 1 again and again, increasing X by 1 each time); and the TEST of Fig. 2 (keep DOing SUM : = SUM + A(X) until you have done it for X = 99).

The last line is a HALT instruction. When the machine has finished the **DO-loop,** it has added all 100 numbers together. So, when it moves on to the next instruction, it is time to stop.

Let us now suggest how a compiler might examine the above five-line program and translate it into a machine-language program that does the same job. The compiler makes two passes:

Stage 1: It reads through the whole program to find what data, variables and constants are involved. It then reserves the necessary storage space in memory, and prepares a table showing what is to be stored in each location.

Stage 2: It reads through the whole program, translating the instructions. When it translates an instruction, it uses the table it prepared in Stage 1 to fill in the address fields of the machine language instructions that it uses.

Here then are these two stages for our number-adding program.

Stage 1: Reserving Storage. The compiler looks at each line of the high-level program, using an appropriate subroutine to reserve storage. At each step it adds to a table of location assignments, and deletes addresses from a table of free space. Here, then, is how it processes each of the five instructions to allocate storage.

(i) NUMBER A (0 to 99)

Tells it to set aside 100 locations. It chooses locations 0 through 99 and specifies that A(k) will be stored in location k of memory. Thus, A(0) is to be stored in location 0, A(29) is to be stored in location 29, and so on.

(ii)   SUM := 0

Tells it to set aside one location in memory for SUM—it takes the first which is free, namely location 100—and one for the constant 0, namely location 101.

(iii)   DO 1 X = 0 TO 99

Tells it that it needs a location for the counter X, a location for the constant 100 (because we exit from the loop *after* using X = 99)—and also for the increment 1 by which X must be updated each time round the loop. It sets aside locations 102, 103, and 104, respectively.

(iv)   SUM := SUM + A(N)

Requires no new locations for variables and constants.

(v)   HALT

Requires no new locations for variables and constants.

Thus, at the completion of Stage 1, the compiler has prepared the accompanying table and all locations from 105 on are still free.

Name	Location
A(k)	k
	(for k = 0 –99)
SUM	100
0	101
X	102
100	103
1	104

In describing Stage 2, we shall use {C} to indicate the location assigned to C in Stage 1. Thus {A(k)} = k, {SUM} = 100, and so on.

Stage 2: Translating the Instructions.   The compiler looks at each line and uses an appropriate subroutine, consulting the assignment table to specify addresses.

(i)   NUMBER A (0 TO 99)

This does not yield any instructions.   [If we were including instructions for reading A(0) through A(99) into the computer, the compiler would need to take the assignment of A(k) to location k into account translating them. The computer also needs instructions to load the constants—0 goes into location 101, 100 goes into location 103—but this may well be done by loading with the instructions.]

   (ii)   SUM := 0

The compiler has a subroutine which translates any instruction of the form

$$B := C$$

where C is a single variable or constant into the form

   LDA   {C}   Load into the accumulator the contents
                         of the location corresponding to C in the
                         assignment table.
   STO   {B}   Store the contents of the accumulator in
                         the location corresponding to B in the
                         assignment table.

   In the present case, the assignment table has {SUM} = 100 and {0} = 101. The compiler then withdraws locations 105 and 106 from free space and adds

                         105   LDA 010
                         106   STO 100

to the compiled program.

   (iii)   DO 1 X = 0 TO 99

Whenever the compiler sees

                         DO LABEL X = B TO C

for some LABEL it proceeds as follows:
   (a)   The compiler initializes X to value B. However, X := B is
            handled by the subroutine used in step (ii). In this example
            B is 0, and we have   {X}   = 102 and   {0} = 101; So we
            obtain the code

                         107   LDA 101
                         108   STO 102

            and locations 107 and 108 are removed from the free list.
            [Note: A programmer will immediately notice that

                              LDA 101
                              STO 100
                              LDA 101
                              STO 102

has the same effect as

$$\text{LDA 101}$$
$$\text{STO 100}$$
$$\text{STO 102}$$

It may not be worth building into the compiler any subroutines to check this sort of thing.]

(b) The compiler must translate the LABELed instruction—we save that for step (iv). Note, however, that its first machine-language instruction will go in location 109. The compiler must then add the instruction to update X, which in high-level language, takes the form $X := X + 1$. Recall that the compiler set aside location 104 to store this increment, which is 1. The compiler then calls the subroutine which tells it that wherever it sees

$$B := C + D$$

with C and D either variables or constants, it must use the machine language sequence

$$\text{LDA} \quad \{C\}$$
$$\text{ADD} \quad \{D\}$$
$$\text{STO} \quad \{B\}$$

Thus, in the present case, it translates $X := X + 1$ into

N	LDA 102
N + 1	ADD 104
N + 2	STO 102

Note that it has to use symbolic addresses N, N + 1, and N + 2 at this stage. Until it translates the LABELed instruction, it does not know how many locations it will need for it.

(c) The compiler has a subroutine which tells it that when it compiles DO LABEL X = B TO C, it places the test for "$X = C + 1$?" after the compilation of the LABELed instruction. This subroutine also specifies that if the location M has been set aside for the first machine-language instruction of that compilation, the test "$X = C + 1$?" yields the three machine-language instructions

$$\text{LDA X}$$
$$\text{SUB} \quad \{C + 1\}$$
$$\text{JUP M}$$

where JUP jumps on *nonzero* accumulator contents. In other words, go back to M to repeat the DO loop *unless* X = C + 1. If X = C + 1, you can go on to the next machine-language instruction; which is the first instruction outside the loop.

In this case, the test is "X = 100?" and M = 109 (from (b)). The compiler then yields

$$N + 3 \quad \text{LDA } 102$$
$$N + 4 \quad \text{SUB } 103$$
$$N + 5 \quad \text{JUP } 109$$

(iv)   We have already seen how to handle B := C + D. The compiler first translates SUM := SUM + A(X) by

LDA 100
ADD X
STO 100

using the fact that A(X) is stored in location X. It then translates this to

109   LDA 100
110   ADA 102
111   STO 100

using the fact that X is stored in location 102, to replace ADD X by ADA 102. Recall that in step (b), we had to use N as a symbolic address for the first machine-language instruction for X := X + 1. However, the compiler is instructed to make N the first location following the locations taken up by the translation of the LABELED instruction. At this stage, then, the compiler can set N = 112.

(v)   HALT then compiles as HLT 000. Since the compiler used up the locations through N + 5 = 117 in step (c), it places HLT 000 in location 118:

118   HLT 000

Thus the compiler completes its task by printing out its location table (which includes specification of the contents) together with the machine language program

105   LDA 101
106   STO 100
107   LDA 101
108   STO 102
109   LDA 100
110   ADA 102

```
111  STO 100
112  LDA 102
113  ADD 104
114  STO 102
115  LDA 102
116  SUB 103
117  JUP 109
118  HLT 000
```

Let us just check this program by seeing that it adds the first three of our 100 numbers correctly. Suppose that $A(0) = 2$, $A(1) = 4$, and $A(2) = 8$. Suppose that we start with $X = 10$ and $SUM = 19$ and $\langle ACC \rangle = 29$. We start, then, with

$$\langle ACC \rangle = 29$$
$$\langle 0 \rangle = A(0) = 2$$
$$\langle 1 \rangle = A(1) = 4$$
$$\langle 2 \rangle = A(2) = 8$$
$$\cdot$$
$$\cdot$$
$$\cdot$$
$$\langle 100 \rangle = SUM = 19$$
$$\langle 101 \rangle = 0$$
$$\langle 102 \rangle = X = 10$$
$$\langle 103 \rangle = 100$$
$$\langle 104 \rangle = 1$$

We trace the effects of our program on the register holding SUM and X and on the accumulator, as shown in Table II.

Finally, we check the addition of the last two terms of the list. Suppose, then, that we have just executed STO 100, placing

$$SUM = A(0) + A(1) + A(2) + \cdots + A(96) + A(97) = 1694$$

in location 100; that $X = 97$ is in location 100, and that 1694 is also in the accumulator. Suppose, also, that

$$\langle 98 \rangle = A(98) = 11$$
$$\langle 99 \rangle = A(99) = 19$$

Then the trace continues as shown in Table III.

TABLE II

Instruction	Contents of registers after instruction execution		
	⟨ACC⟩	SUM = ⟨100⟩	X = ⟨102⟩
	29	19	10
LDA 101	0	19	10
STO 100	0	0	10
LDA 101	0	0	10
STO 102	0	0	0
LDA 100	0	0	0
ADA 102	2	0	0
STO 100	2	2	0
LDA 102	0	2	0
ADD 104	1	2	0
STO 102	1	2	1
LDA 102	1	2	1
SUB 103	−99	2	1
JUP 109	−99	2	1
LDA 100	2	2	1
ADA 102	6	2	1
STO 100	6	6	1
LDA 102	1	6	1
ADD 104	2	6	1
STO 102	2	6	2
LDA 102	2	6	2
SUB 103	−98	6	2
JUP 109	−98	6	2
LDA 100	6	6	2
ADA 102	14	6	2
STO 100	14	14	2

$$14 = 2 + 6 + 8$$
$$= A(0) + A(1) + A(2)$$

is now stored in location 100

With this, we complete our quick look at machine language, the hardware that implements it, and the compilers that bring high-level programs down to a level of detail which a computer can execute. May it whet the appetite of you who have read this far to learn more about the workings of those amazing computers at the same time as you ponder their implications for the cybernetic society.

TABLE III

Instruction	Contents of registers after instruction execution		
	$\langle ACC \rangle$	SUM = $\langle 100 \rangle$	X = $\langle 102 \rangle$
STO 100	1694	1694	97
LDA 102	97	1694	97
ADD 104	98	1694	97
STO 102	98	1694	98
LDA 102	98	1694	98
SUB 103	−2	1694	98
JUP 109	−2	1694	98
LDA 100	1694	1694	98
ADA 102	1705	1694	98
STO 100	1705	1705	98
LDA 102	98	1705	98
ADD 102	99	1705	98
STO 102	99	1705	99
LDA 102	99	1705	99
SUB 103	−1	1705	99
JUP 109	−1	1705	99
LDA 100	1705	1705	99
ADA 102	1724	1705	99
STO 100	1724	1724	99
LDA 102	99	1724	99
ADD 104	100	1724	99
STO 102	100	1724	100
LDA 102	100	1724	100
SUB 103	0	1724	100
JUP 109	0	1724	100
HLT 000	0	1724	100

At long last, the JUP instruction has found $\langle ACC \rangle = 0$, and sends the computer on to the next instruction, HLT 000. The machine stops, and 1724, the sum of all 100 numbers, is in the SUM-Register, 100.

Suggestions for Further Reading

With this section, you have passed the stage at which there are any introductory references. To go any further, you have to make a serious commitment to computer science. With a year of programming both in high-level language and in assembly language, and college algebra to about the junior level, you will be ready to study the design of compilers. One useful book is:

D. Gries: "Compiler Construction for Digital Computers." Wiley, New York, 1971.

Summary

After writing a **machine-language** program, we studied how such a program could be automatically prepared by a **compiler** using a high-level program as input. We saw that a compiler would have to make two passes through the high-level program to translate it: the first pass sets aside the necessary storage locations; the second translates each instruction, using the specified locations to fill in addresses. The compiler requires a complex subroutine for each instruction type of the high-level language—just as the CPU requires a special circuit to execute each instruction type of the machine language itself.

Glossary

Compiler: A *compiler* is a computer program that enables a computer to take a program written in a high-level language and translate it into a complete program—designed to process data to obtain the same results—in another language.

Counter: A *counter* is a place in which a computer stores a number which keeps track of the number of times some process has been repeated, e.g., keeping a count of how many times a loop has been traversed, or how many numbers in a list have been added together, or . . . .

Constant: A *constant* in a computer program is a piece of data which is specified as part of the program, and does *not* change during the computation. A *variable* is a piece of data—such as the value of a counter—that *can* change during the computation.

Comments: When we write a program, we often write notes to remind us of what different parts of the program make the computer do. These notes are called *comments.* The complete package of comments together with the program in human-readable form is called *documentation.*

Label: A *label* is a number or other name we can give to an instruction to tell us where it occurs in a program. We label those instructions of a program that are the targets of jumps, or are specified in other lines of a program in some other way.

DO-loop: This is a loop in a high-level language which is of the form DO LABEL X = B TO C followed by several instructions, the last of which is labeled LABEL. These several instructions are to be repeated again and again starting with X = B and increasing the value of the variable X by one each time, until the instructions are executed for the last time when X = C.

Exercises

1. The accompanying table shows what is in core when the operator types START 103. Flowchart the program that starts at location 103. What value is in location 101 when the program halts? With any possible set of numbers in 001–099, what would this program do? Why? [*Hint:* Write X= $\langle 100 \rangle$, Y= $\langle 101 \rangle$.].

Address	Value	Address	Value
001	7	103	LDA 102
002	396	104	STO 100
003	15	105	CLA
004	0	106	ADA 100
005	82	107	JMP 113
006	69	108	STO 101
. . .	. . .	109	LDA 100
101	1	111	STO 100
102	1	112	JMP 105
		113	HLT

2. What would happen if the instruction register "jammed" and never changed during the execution of a program?

3. What are three advantages and three disadvantages of writing in machine language rather than a higher level language like TURTLE or FORTRAN which is automatically translated (by an Interpreter or Compiler program) into machine language?

4. The "hand-compiled" program we came up with to add 100 numbers together seems fairly complicated to someone who is new to computer programming—writing 18 instructions of a complicated program may not seem much better (even if more challenging) then writing out the 103 instructions of the loop-free program we started with. However, while it is a *lot more* work to write out a loop-free program to add 1000 numbers, it takes *no more* work to write out the program with loops. Write out the 18 instruction program to add 1000 numbers. [*Hint:* Do not put the instructions where you are storing numbers. Do write full comments for your program.]

5. In our program we used the instruction

ADA X   which yields $\langle ACC \rangle := \langle ACC \rangle + \langle \langle X \rangle \rangle$

Early stored program computers did not have this instruction (that is, they could only use direct addressing in which the address to be used had to be written out as part of the instruction). A clever way out was to pretend that

ADD X

was a number, add 1 to it, and get

ADD X + 1.

Rewrite the hand-compiled program using this technique.

6. The program to add 100 numbers sets a counter to 0, tests, and increments the counter to see if it is equal to 99. Rewrite the program starting the counter at −1.

7. At the start of a program, variables have the following values: A = 0, B = 1, C = 3, D = 5. What are their values after the following operation sequence is executed?

$$A := B, \quad B := C, \quad C := D, \quad D := A,$$
$$A := A + B, \quad B := A + B,$$
$$C := C + D, \quad D := C + D$$

Name Index

Subject Index

An entry of the form G461 following an item indicates that the definition of the item may be found in the glossary on page 461.

E
F
G   2
H   3
I   4
J   5